# Social Trends 27

## 1997 Edition

Editor: JENNY CHURCH

Associate Editor: CAROL SUMMERFIELD

Production team: PHIL BROWNE
CHRIS COUSINS
STEPHEN DREWELL
MARTIN HARGREAVES
TIM HARRIS
AYSHA MALIK
PETE NEWMAN
ASPA PALAMIDAS
TONY SYMMONDS
PETER WHITE
ALYSON WHITMARSH
STEVE WHYMAN

Graphic design: MICHELLE FRANCO

London:    The Stationery Office

# Contents

# Contents

## 3 Education and Training

# Contents

Labour Market 4

Social Trends 27, © Crown copyright 1997

# Contents

7
Health

8
Social Protection

# Contents

## Crime and Justice 9

Housing
10

# Contents

## Environment 11

# Contents

Transport 12

Lifestyles 13

# Contents

# Introduction

*Social Trends* draws together statistics from a wide range of government departments and other organisations to paint a broad picture of British society today, and how it has been changing. The 13 chapters each focus on a different social policy area, described in tables, charts and explanatory text. *Social Trends* is aimed at a very wide audience: policy makers in the public and private sectors; market service providers; lawyers; people in local government; journalists and other commentators; academics and students; schools; and the general public.

The editorial team always welcomes readers' views on how *Social Trends* could be improved. Please write to the Editor at the address shown below with any comments or suggestions you have.

### Article

This year *Social Trends* contains an article entitled 'Projections: a look into the future' which examines official projections such as those of the population, the labour market, households and marital status. It looks at the social picture produced by the projections as well as the reasons for producing them and the assumptions which lie behind them.

### New material and sources

To preserve topicality, over half of the 348 tables and charts in the chapters of *Social Trends 27* are new compared with the previous edition.

In all chapters, the source of the data is given below each table and chart, and where this is a major survey, the name of the survey is also given. At the end of each chapter a list of references directing readers to other published sources of data (both government and non government) and a list of contact telephone numbers are given, including the contact number of the chapter author. Those using *Social Trends* as a first point of reference should find this particularly useful. Regional and other sub-national breakdowns of some of the information in *Social Trends* may be found in the ONS's publication *Regional Trends* published by The Stationery Office.

### Availability on electronic media

The data contained in the tables and charts in *Social Trends 27* are available on diskette. This is available free of charge to all customers with a standing order for *Social Trends*. Please contact the ONS Sales Desk on 0171 533 5678 for more details.

The first 25 editions of *Social Trends* are available on CD-ROM and a separate *Social Trends 26* CD-ROM is also available. Please contact the ONS Sales Desk for details.

For the first time later this year, excerpts from *Social Trends 27* will be available on the Internet. The ONS can be reached at http://www.emap.co.uk.ons

### Contributors

The Editor and Associate Editor wish to thank all their colleagues in the Government Statistical Service and contributors in other organisations without whose help this publication would not be possible. Thanks also go to the ONS Graphic Design Unit.

### Appendix

The Appendix gives definitions and general background information, particularly on administrative and legal structures and frameworks. Anyone seeking to understand the tables and charts in detail will find it helpful to read the corresponding entries in the Appendix in addition to the footnotes relevant to each table and chart. A full index to this edition can be found starting on page 243.

Social and Regional Statistics
The Office for National Statistics
B2/10
1 Drummond Gate
London
SW1V 2QQ

# Projections: a look into the future

**Tim Harris**

*Office for National Statistics*

*Social Trends* records how aspects of life in Britain have changed over past years. The ageing of the population, the increased propensity for women to work, the fall in fertility and the rise in divorce have all contributed to the picture of British society today. But what trends will be shown in *Social Trends* in 20 years time? Projections help us to look into the future. This article looks at the social picture produced by projections for the next century as well as the reasons for producing them and the assumptions which lie behind them.

Many different organisations and individuals, both within and outside government, use projections for a variety of purposes. One of the main uses is estimating future demand for services and allocating resources. For example, the number of people in particular age groups will have implications for the type and quantity of health services which are needed in an area. As well as being used by central and local government, projections are also used by businesses. Changes in the age structure of the population will have many implications for those in the retail sector where, for example, an ageing population will have different patterns of food and drink consumption. Those interested in recruiting graduates may be particularly interested in projections of the number of young people in higher education. The number of households, their size and where they are will be important for planners, environmentalists, the construction industry and, increasingly, for the community at large.

Government departments make projections across a range of topics. These include seeking to estimate the future size and structure of the population, people's participation in education and the labour force and the numbers and types of households. Strictly, projections are simply the outcome of a given set of assumptions and not necessarily a forecast of future events. Indeed a 'scenario' or 'what if' projection may sometimes be made to illustrate the consequences of a particular, but not necessarily the most likely, set of assumptions. In practice the main official projections discussed in this article are based on assumptions set at the most appropriate level. These are based on the available statistical evidence at the time. However, it is inevitable that users of projections will treat them as if they were forecasts of the most likely course of future events. Official projections ensure that the many users of projections can work on consistent assumptions.

Although the assumptions used are judged the best which can be made at the time, it is almost certain that the way things actually turn out in the future will be different to a greater or lesser extent. Uncertainty increases with the degree of detail of the projections, for example narrow age groups and small areas, and also with distance into the future. To help users take account of the consequences of future experience being different from the assumptions which have been used, alternative projections using different sets of assumptions are sometimes made; these are called variant projections and are discussed later in this article.

Projections are produced for different time periods according to particular needs. For some purposes, for example pensions, a long lead time is involved so projections are required far into the future. For shorter term policies projections may not be needed beyond three or four years hence. The projections presented here are therefore not on a common time frame.

## National population projections

The best known and most widely used projections are those relating to the population of countries. National population projections show how the numbers of males and females at each age in the United Kingdom, and its constituent countries, are likely to change in the future. The Government Actuary's Department has been responsible for their production since 1954, in consultation with the Registrars General for England and Wales, Scotland and Northern Ireland. As well as being useful in themselves, they underpin many other types of projections used in the social and economic policy fields.

The most recent projections show the population of the United Kingdom increasing from 58.4 million in 1994 to 61.2 million in 2023 (**Chart A.1**). After this, deaths are projected to exceed births which together with an assumed zero net flow of migrants, leads to the population slowly decreasing. The rapid increase in deaths around this time is due to the large cohorts born in the post Second World War baby boom reaching elderly ages. More details are shown in Table 1.3 in the Population chapter.

The projections for the constituent countries of the United Kingdom show that the population numbers peak in different years in each country. The population of Scotland is projected to start falling by the end of the century. In Wales the population is projected to continue rising until 2014 when the natural decrease outweighs the small net gain through migration. The projected population of England rises until 2024 while that of Northern Ireland is still increasing in the year 2030. Projections for the separate countries are shown in Table 1.2 in the Population chapter.

Although the total population is expected to rise slowly and then decline, bigger changes are seen in the age structure of the population. The numbers in different age groups will increase and decrease at different rates. The combination of low fertility and people living longer leads to a continuation in the trend of an ageing population, with particularly large rises in the numbers of very elderly people.

# A.1

## Population: by age

**United Kingdom**

Millions

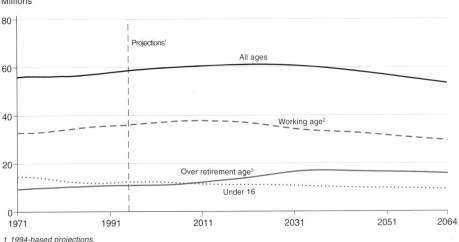

1 1994-based projections.
2 Males aged 16 to 64, females aged 16 to 59.
3 Males aged 65 and over, females aged 60 and over.
**Source: Office for National Statistics; Government Actuary's Department; General Register Office (Scotland); General Register Office (Northern Ireland)**

The number of children aged under 16 is expected to start declining from around the year 2000 so that by 2034 there will be 15 per cent fewer than in the mid-1990s. The working age population (based on the current state retirement ages) is projected to grow gradually until 2011 and then decline. In contrast the number of people aged over the current state retirement ages is projected to increase by more than half up to 2034. The number of people aged 75 and over is likely to rise even more sharply: from 4.0 million in 1994 to 6.8 million in 2034.

One method of measuring the changing age structure of the population is to calculate dependency ratios which compare the number of people aged under 16, or over state retirement ages, with the population of working age. This ratio gives an indication of the relative number of people to be supported economically by the working age population. These projected dependency ratios played a part in the Government's decision to equalise the state retirement age at 65 for both men and women by 2020.

**Table A.2** shows dependency ratios which take into account the planned change in retirement age for women. The overall dependency ratio is expected to rise from 64 dependents for every 100 people of working age in 1994 to 68 per 100 in 2031. However, this overall dependency ratio hides the differences between the ratios for children and the retired population. With fewer children being born, the child dependency ratio is expected to fall. Conversely, the

elderly dependency ratio is projected to rise from 29 per 100 to 39 per 100 in the first 30 years of the next century.

A wide range of assumptions are inherent in any projection. In the case of population projections the starting point is an estimate of the current or base year population. The latest set of population projections are the 1994-based projections, so called because their starting point is the 1994 mid-year population estimates. To move this forward it is necessary to estimate both the number of people joining and leaving in a future period. If no one joined or left, the projected population, one year later, would be the same size but each person would be one year older. However, people are constantly joining and leaving the population. People join by being born or immigrating and people leave by dying or emigrating. Assumptions on fertility, mortality, immigration and emigration are therefore required for the calculation of population projections.

Projections for these factors take account of recent experience. For example, in the case of fertility there has been a trend to delay the starting of a family, and for women to have fewer children on average. By observing such trends, assumptions are made about future fertility patterns which are then applied to the projected number of women in the relevant age groups to generate a projected number of births. This process also requires projections of immigration and emigration by age and gender in order to project the number of women of childbearing age.

**Projected dependency ratios[1]**

| United Kingdom | | | Ratios[1] |
|---|---|---|---|
| | Child dependency | Elderly dependency | Overall dependency |
| 1994 | 34 | 30 | 64 |
| 2001 | 33 | 29 | 62 |
| 2011 | 30 | 31 | 60 |
| 2021 | 28 | 30 | 58 |
| 2031 | 29 | 39 | 68 |
| 2041 | 28 | 43 | 72 |
| 2051 | 28 | 43 | 71 |
| 2061 | 29 | 44 | 73 |

1 1994-based projections. Number of children and people over retirement age to every 100 people of working age. The ratios take account of the change in state pension age for women from 60 years to 65 years between 2010 and 2020.
*Source: Government Actuary's Department*

Key fertility assumptions underpinning the population projections are summarised in Table A.3 by the average number of children per woman and the average age at motherhood. The 1994-based projections assume that, for women born in, or after, 1975, the average age at which they have children will rise to 28.4 years and the number of children per woman will decline to 1.8 and stabilise at that level. This compares with an average completed family size of 2.2 children for women born in 1945. An increase is also projected in the proportion of women who do not have children.

The ratio of boys to girls at birth combined with the effect of mortality at young ages means that women need to have approximately 2.1 children to replace themselves in number. In the absence of net migration, this is the level of fertility required to maintain a stable population. The generations born after 1950 are therefore all projected to reproduce below this replacement level although the momentum of past demographic trends is such that population decline is not projected for another 30 years.

In the twentieth century Britain has seen a continuation of the fall in death rates that began in the nineteenth century. The 1994-based population projections assume that overall death rates will continue to fall, but at a gradually reducing rate. However, for some young adult age groups it is assumed that rates will continue to rise for a few further years before starting to decline. Falling death rates are reflected in the increase in the expectation of life at birth. Chart 7.1 in the Health chapter shows that between 1996 and 2031 life expectancy at birth is expected to increase from 74 to 78 years for males and from 79 to 83 years for females.

The other factor in population projections is the effect of migration. Information on migration is derived mainly from the International Passenger Survey. A migrant into the United Kingdom is defined as someone who has lived abroad for the previous year or more and who intends to stay in this country for a year or more.

Past trends and future projections of net migration are shown in Chart 1.16 in the Population chapter. In the medium term the projections assume an inflow of nearly 300 thousand people each year and an outflow of nearly 250 thousand people. The resulting net inflow of 50 thousand migrants each year is then assumed to fall to zero by 2019 and then remain at this level. People

# A.3

Average completed family size and age at motherhood: by year of birth of mother

| United Kingdom | | | Numbers |
|---|---|---|---|
| | Assumed average completed family size | Average family size by end 1994 | Average age at motherhood (years) |
| **Women born in:** | | | |
| 1945 | 2.22 | 2.22 | 26.0 |
| 1950 | 2.09 | 2.09 | 26.4 |
| 1955 | 2.03 | 2.00 | 27.1 |
| 1960 | 1.96 | 1.75 | 27.7 |
| 1965 | 1.85 | 1.18 | 28.1 |
| 1970 | 1.83 | 0.57 | 28.2 |
| 1975 | 1.80 | 0.15 | 28.4 |
| 1980 | 1.80 | - | 28.4 |
| 1985 | 1.80 | . | 28.4 |
| 1990 | 1.80 | . | 28.4 |

*Source: Government Actuary's Department*

entering the United Kingdom tend to have a slightly younger age distribution than those leaving. Therefore the latest projections assume a net gain of young adults, which effectively boosts the number of births as they soon enter the main childbearing years.

So far this article has looked at the 'principal' population projections. In addition, the Government Actuary's Department also prepares projections based on alternative assumptions of future fertility, mortality and migration. The usual practice in the United Kingdom is to illustrate the uncertainty of each component of population change separately. So, fertility variants, for example, assume different levels of fertility from the principal projection but leave the mortality and migration assumptions unchanged. However, users may need to consider for themselves the effects of particular combinations of assumptions. For example, the largest population size would arise from high fertility, high migration and low mortality while the oldest age structure would result from low fertility, low migration and low mortality.

Another way of looking at uncertainty is to look at past projections and see how well they mirror what actually happened. This reveals that, historically, the greatest uncertainty has been in projections of the very young and the very old. Recent projections have tended to overestimate future births but, looking further back, projections made after the Second World War failed to anticipate the baby boom of the 1960s. Projections have also tended to be too pessimistic about the prospects for future mortality improvement, leading to underestimates of the future population in older age groups.

National population projections are used for decision making in their own right, such as in the decision to equalise state retirement ages for men and women. However they are also important as a major input into many other types of projections. The remaining sections of this article examine some of these.

## Sub-national population projections

Sub-national population projections for England are prepared by the Office for National Statistics for local authority areas and district health authority areas; the latest set are the 1993-based projections. These are particularly important as it is at the local level that many planning decisions are taken, for example whether, or where, to build a new school or hospital. The sub-national projections provide a consistent framework for those planning the provision of local services. They are also used by planners outside government, such as in estimating future demand for gas or telephone services.

The populations of the non-metropolitan counties and Greater London are projected to increase by 4.0 per cent and 3.4 per cent respectively between 1993 and 2001. In contrast, the populations of the metropolitan counties are projected to remain fairly stable. Greater London is projected to have the largest increase in the number of children aged under 16, while in the Northern region this age group decreases by 3.2 per cent. East Anglia has the largest projected increase in both the working age population and those over retirement age.

For these sub-national projections, the Office for National Statistics uses methodology which combines local fertility and mortality differentials, averaged over three years, with internal migration assumptions. The migration assumptions used are derived primarily from moves of doctors' patients recorded in the National Health Service Central Register, as well as from the 1991 Census and the International Passenger Survey. For small areas, net migration often has a larger effect than natural change (births and deaths) on population change. As the information available about migration is less reliable than that about births and deaths, the sub-national population projections are subject to greater uncertainty than those for the national population. It should be noted that, unlike many locally produced projections, the Office for National Statistics sub-national projections are controlled to add up to the national population projections produced by the Government Actuary's Department.

## Educational participation and the labour force

The Department for Education and Employment (DfEE) is responsible for producing projections of educational participation in England. They are used to help plan Government expenditure on education. In combination with other assumptions, such as future pupil/teacher ratios and the ageing of the teaching workforce, they are used to produce targets of the number of teachers which need to be trained. Projections of participation in further and higher education are also an important input into projections of the labour force. Information up to 1998/99 from the latest set of projections is used to provide information for the Government's Public Expenditure Survey.

Pupil projections are largely determined by the underlying population projections. As education is compulsory between the ages of 5 and 15, the number of pupils in this age group in schools tends to be marginally smaller than the comparable number in the general population. Pupils aged under 5 and those aged 16 and over are also included in the projections. In all three age groups the projections classify pupils by type of school. This classification is essential since most expenditure planning is related to the number of pupils in the maintained sector. As education is not compulsory for those aged 16 and over, the most significant influence on the extent of participation among 16 and 17 year olds is GCSE attainment at the age of 15. Other factors include past education participation rates, education and training initiatives and socio-economic factors such as parental background and the labour market.

The proportion of 16 to 18 year olds who are full-time or sandwich students in schools, sixth form colleges or in other further education in England is projected to rise up to 1998/99 but not as rapidly as during the first half of the 1990s. Most of the rise is expected to come from higher proportions attending sixth form colleges or other

## A.4

Participation in Government-supported education and training[1]: by age

| England | | | | | Percentages |
|---|---|---|---|---|---|
| | 1990/91 | 1992/93 | 1994/95 | 1996/97[2] | 1998/99[2] |
| **Age** | | | | | |
| 16 | 77 | 80 | 81 | 83 | 84 |
| 17 | 65 | 70 | 72 | 73 | 76 |
| 18 | 40 | 49 | 52 | 55 | 58 |

1 Percentage of people in each age group participating in Government-supported education and training.
2 1995-based projections.
**Source: Department for Education and Employment**

colleges of further education rather than schools. Table A.4 shows participation in Government-supported education and training in England. This shows that, in 1998/99, three fifths of 18 year olds are projected to participate in this type of education or training compared with only two fifths in 1990/91.

The number of higher education students has also been growing rapidly over the past few years. In the four years to 1994/95 the number of full-time and part-time students in England rose by 40 per cent to 1.3 million. Projections for the following four years indicate that numbers will continue to rise but at a slower rate so that by 1998/99 there will be 1.4 million of these students.

Economic activity rates measure the percentage of the population which is in the labour force (that is either working or looking for work). Projections of economic activity rates in Great Britain are modelled by the DfEE and agreed by the Office for National Statistics. They reflect economic, demographic and social factors that influence activity rates. These include levels of unemployment, past trends in economic activity rates and numbers of dependent children for women.

Projections of full-time student numbers are important in the calculation of projections of the labour force because, while some students work or look for work, a much higher proportion of non-students do so. Labour force projections are produced by the Office for National Statistics in consultation with the DfEE. Projections of economic activity rates are produced for different age groups for both men and women, with separate rates produced for students in younger age groups.

Economic activity rates[1]: by gender

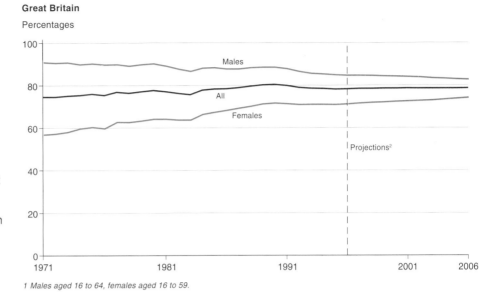

**Great Britain**
Percentages

1 Males aged 16 to 64, females aged 16 to 59.
2 1994-based projections.
**Source: Office for National Statistics**

Economic cycles are known to affect the size of the labour force. High levels of unemployment are linked with lower rates of economic activity. Official projections of the labour force make the neutral assumption that unemployment will remain at the current level because the Government does not forecast either unemployment or employment.

The overall economic activity rates for men aged 16 to 64 and women aged 16 to 59 (the working age population) are shown in Chart A.5. Past data show that there has been a sharp rise in the proportion of women working or looking for work in the last couple of decades while there has been a slight decline for men. Economic activity rates for men of working age are projected to fall slightly between 1995 and 2006 - by 2 percentage points to 83 per cent. Those for women are projected to rise by 3 percentage points to 74 per cent in the same period.

The projected changes in economic activity rates vary between different age and gender groups. For men aged 25 to 54, the declining trend in economic activity rates since the 1970s is expected to stabilise between 1995 and 2006. In contrast, rates for 55 to 59 year old men are expected to continue to show decreases: from 74 per cent in 1995 to 69 per cent in 2006. Economic activity rates for women aged 25 to 54 are projected to increase by 2006. The largest increases are indicated for 25 to 34 year old women for whom economic activity rates are expected to rise by 10 percentage points, to 81 per cent in 2006. Rates for women aged 35 to 44 are expected to increase relatively little because women tend to have children at an older age than previously and to participate less in the labour force when they have dependent children. Economic activity rates for both men and women aged 16 to 24 are projected to decline as an increasing proportion of this age group studies full time.

Projections of the size of the labour force are calculated by applying the various economic activity rates for age and gender groups (including the separate projections for students aged 16 to 24) to the number of people in each of these groups obtained from population projections. Changes in the labour force can therefore result either from the changing size and age structure of the projected population or from changes in the projected economic activity rates.

The projected size of the labour force is shown in Table 4.3 in the Employment chapter. In 1996 it stood at 27.8 million and it is projected to grow by 1.4 million by 2006. Women account for 1 million of this rise. In 2006 women are projected to make up 45 per cent of the total labour force.

The labour force in 2006 will be older on average than in 1996: the projected rise of 1.8 million people aged 35 to 54 and 0.8 million aged 55 and over contrasts with the fall of 1.2 million people aged under 35. Although projections of men and women show similar trends, the decline among young women is generally smaller than for young men, whereas the rises for older women is larger than for older men. Changes in the age structure of the population are the main factor in this ageing of the workforce.

The Office for National Statistics' labour force projections do not cover the types of work that may be available in the future. However, projections by Business Strategies Limited do give information on employment by industry and occupation. Although these are not government projections they are funded by the DfEE. These show total employment growing by 3.5 per cent between 1996 and 2001 with an extra 0.9

# A.6

**Changes in employment[1]: by occupation, 1996 to 2006**

**United Kingdom**
Thousands

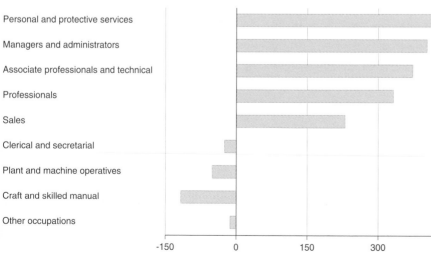

1 1996-based projections.
**Source: Business Strategies Limited**

million jobs in the UK economy. This growth in total employment is projected to continue, growing by a further 2.7 per cent between 2001 and 2006. However the number of full-time employees is not projected to change significantly between 1996 and 2006 while the number of part-time employees is projected to grow by over a tenth and self-employment by almost a quarter.

This same source shows the numbers of managers and administrators, professional and associate professional and technical occupations growing rapidly over the period 1996 to 2006 (Chart A.6). The number of managers and administrators is projected to grow by almost 10 per cent and professional employment by 14 per cent.

**Legal marital status[1]**

| England & Wales | | | | Percentages |
|---|---|---|---|---|
| | 1992 | 2000[1] | 2010[1] | 2020[1] |
| **Males** | | | | |
| Single | 31 | 32 | 34 | 35 |
| Married | 59 | 56 | 52 | 50 |
| Widowed | 3 | 3 | 3 | 4 |
| Divorced | 7 | 9 | 11 | 12 |
| | | | | |
| All males (=100%)(thousands) | 19,753 | 20,423 | 21,584 | 22,313 |
| **Females** | | | | |
| Single | 23 | 23 | 24 | 25 |
| Married | 56 | 54 | 51 | 48 |
| Widowed | 14 | 14 | 13 | 14 |
| Divorced | 7 | 10 | 12 | 14 |
| | | | | |
| All females (=100%)(thousands) | 21,116 | 21,439 | 22,252 | 22,843 |

*1 People aged 16 and over. 1992-based projections.*
***Source: Government Actuary's Department***

## Marital status and households

In addition to population numbers, the Government Actuary's Department also produces projections by marital status. In view of the rapid changes which have taken place over the last 30 years in patterns of family formation and dissolution, these are inevitably subject to uncertainty.

The latest legal marital status projections for England and Wales, which are 1992-based, are summarised in Table A.7. The proportion of the adult population that is married is projected to fall from 57 per cent in 1992 to 49 per cent by 2020. The proportion that is single (that is never married) is expected to grow a little, while the proportion that is divorced is projected to almost double from 7 per cent during the three decades to 2020.

These 1992-based marital status projections were the first to be extended to include projections of the number of people

cohabiting. The projections for each legal marital status group are split between those who are cohabiting and those who are not. Information on past trends in cohabitation comes mainly from the General Household Survey and this indicated that for most of the 1980s the proportions cohabiting gradually increased. However, the latest data used for these projections suggested that the increases were levelling off. The projections therefore assume that the proportions cohabiting in each legal marital status group will remain approximately constant in the future. Despite this assumption, the number of cohabiting couples is projected to rise from 1.3 million in 1992 to 1.7 million in 2020. This is mainly due to the changes in the proportions in each legal marital status group, particularly the rises expected in the proportions of single and divorced people.

The marital status and other population projections discussed above are important inputs into projections of the number of households which are produced for England and Wales by the Department of the Environment. Projections of the number of households in Scotland are produced by the Scottish Office. The latest projections for England are the 1992-based projections. These use the household definition from the 1991 Census which is one person living alone or a group of people who share common housekeeping - that is sharing at least one meal a day or a living room. Under this definition, two or more households may share one dwelling and therefore the number of dwellings needed to house the population does not need to equal the projected number of households. The number of dwellings which are currently vacant will also be a factor in the number of new dwellings which will be needed.

The number of households is projected to grow at a faster rate than the population in the next 20 years. This is due to an expected decrease in the average size of households, brought about by the projected rise in households containing only one person. In the two decades from 1996, the number of households in England is projected to grow by an average of around 170 thousand each year which is slightly slower than the projections for the first half of the 1990s. The pattern of household composition is also projected to change (Table A.8). The proportion of households where the head is one of a married couple has declined from seven in ten households in 1971 to only around half of households in the first half of the 1990s. This is projected to fall further so that by 2016 married couple households will account for only four in ten households.

The increase in single person households is projected to be the most notable change; by 2016, 36 per cent of all households will consist of a single person living alone. Much of this is due to an increase in the number of men aged under 65 who live alone. The projected growth in elderly people, who often live alone, also contributes to the rise in single person households (see Table 2.4 in the Households and Families chapter).

The overall projected growth in the number of households is made up of changes in four components: the adult population living in

# A.8

Households: by type of household

England     Percentages

| | Married couple[1] | Cohabiting couple[1] | Lone parent | Other multi-person | One person | All households (=100%) (thousands) |
|---|---|---|---|---|---|---|
| **Estimates** | | | | | | |
| 1971 | 71 | 1 | 2 | 7 | 18 | 15,942 |
| 1981 | 64 | 3 | 4 | 7 | 23 | 17,306 |
| 1991 | 55 | 6 | 5 | 7 | 27 | 19,215 |
| **Projections[2]** | | | | | | |
| 1996 | 51 | 7 | 6 | 7 | 29 | 20,177 |
| 2001 | 49 | 7 | 6 | 8 | 31 | 21,046 |
| 2006 | 46 | 7 | 6 | 8 | 33 | 21,897 |
| 2011 | 44 | 7 | 6 | 9 | 35 | 22,769 |
| 2016 | 42 | 7 | 5 | 9 | 36 | 23,598 |

1 With or without children.
2 1992-based projections.

**Source: Department of the Environment**

private households; the age structure of the population; marital status; and the likelihood that people in particular age, gender and marital status groups will be the head of a household. More than two thirds of the projected growth in households in England between 1991 and 2016 is due to the projected increase in population and its changing age structure.

The marital status projections and household projections indicate the changes which are likely in the way people live together. With people wanting greater independence and more people living longer, often alone, the number of single person households increases. The number of lone parent households is also likely to increase and, as women are likely to have fewer children in the future, the number of households containing no children is also likely to increase.

## Other projections

The projections discussed in this article are used extensively in the decision making process of government. Several uses within policy areas have been noted, such as the use of population projections in pension policy formation. Taken together the projections also have much wider uses. For example, the increasing numbers of people and households will lead to an increase in the number of dwellings needed which in turn implies increasing pressure on the use of land. These projections thereby feed into the Department of the Environment's projections of the amount of land in urban uses **(Chart A.9)** and policies on balancing

the demand for land for new housing, industry and retailing with the desire to protect the countryside.

Other projections are considered in this edition of *Social Trends*: the Health chapter contains projections of the number of AIDS cases, the Crime and Justice chapter examines projections of the prison population while the Transport chapter looks at projections of road traffic.

## Conclusion

Whether the projections discussed in this article will correspond with future trends is impossible to say. If future trends change in unforeseen ways or the effects of policies change behaviour then reality may turn out to be very different from the picture painted by the projections. However, it is fairly safe to conclude that the United Kingdom will have an ageing population and that the total population size will start to decline sometime in the first half of the next century. The proportion of women working or looking for work will continue to rise while higher proportions of young people will continue in education after the age of 16. Pressure on land will increase as the trend towards living alone causes increases in the number of households which will mean more dwellings are needed.

Only time will tell if these projections will become reality. A glance back at this article sometime in the next century alongside the *Social Trends* of the day will allow an assessment of the extent to which these projections were realised.

### Area of land in urban uses

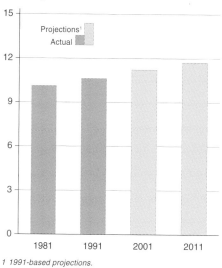

**England**

Percentages

1 1991-based projections.

***Source: Department of the Environment***

## References and further reading

The following list contains selected publications relevant to this article. Those published by The Stationery Office are available from the addresses shown on the inside back cover of *Social Trends*.

*Accuracy and uncertainty of the national population projections for the United Kingdom*; Shaw C, Population Trends No 77, The Stationery Office, 1994

*British labour force projections: 1996-2006*; Ellison R, Melville D and Gutman R, Labour Market Trends May 1996, Office for National Statistics, 1996

*National population projections: 1994-based*; ONS series PP2, The Stationery Office, 1996

*Population projections, Scotland (1994-based), by administrative area*; GRO(S), 1997

*Projections of households in England to 2016*; Department of the Environment, The Stationery Office, 1995

*Urbanization in England: projections 1991-2016*; Department of the Environment, The Stationery Office, 1996

*1993-based sub-national population projections*; The Stationery Office, 1995

*1994-based population projections for Wales*; Welsh Office, 1997

## Contacts

Telephone contact points for further information relating to this article:

| | |
|---|---|
| **Office for National Statistics** | |
| Article author | 0171 533 5782 |
| Labour force | 0171 533 6131 |
| Sub-national population | 0171 533 5148 |
| **Department for Education and Employment** | |
| Educational participation | 0171 925 5427 |
| Employment | 0114 259 3080 |
| **Department of the Environment** | |
| Households | 0171 890 3265 |
| Urbanization | 0171 890 5536 |
| **General Register Office (Scotland)** | 0131 314 4298 |
| **Government Actuary's Department** | 0171 211 2622 |

# Chapter 1 Population

**Population structure and change**

The population of the United Kingdom was 58.6 million in 1995; an increase of 11 per cent since 1961. (Table 1.2)

The number of people living in resort and retirement areas in Great Britain increased by 14 per cent between 1971 and 1995. (Page 30)

Around 3.3 million people in Great Britain belonged to an ethnic minority group in Spring 1996 - just under 6 per cent of the population. (Table 1.8)

**Births and deaths**

Jack and Jessica were the most common first names given to baby boys and girls in England and Wales in 1995 while, in Scotland, Ryan and Lauren were the most common (Page 32)

There were 732 thousand live births and 642 thousand deaths in the United Kingdom in 1995 (Chart 1.12)

**Migration**

The North West had the largest net loss of people due to internal migration in 1995 while the South West had the largest net gain. (Table 1.14)

There were 44 thousand applications for asylum (excluding dependants) in 1995, over half of which were made by people from Africa. (Table 1.18)

**World population**

The world's population reached 5.8 billion in mid-1996 and is projected to reach 8.3 billion by 2025. (Table 1.20)

## 1.1

**Dependent population: by age**

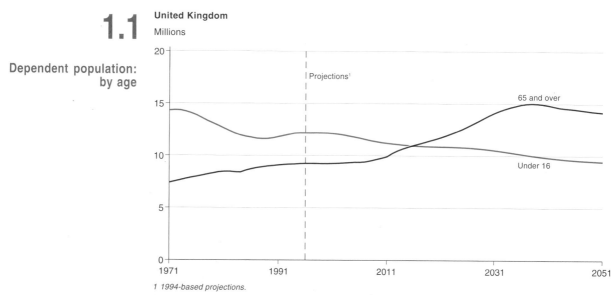

**United Kingdom**

Millions

1 1994-based projections.

*Source: Office for National Statistics; Government Actuary's Department; General Register Office (Scotland); General Register Office (Northern Ireland)*

# 1.2

## Population[1] of the United Kingdom

Thousands

| | 1961 | 1971 | 1981 | 1991 | 1995 | 2011 | 2031 |
|---|---|---|---|---|---|---|---|
| England | 43,561 | 46,412 | 46,821 | 48,208 | 48,903 | 50,757 | 51,150 |
| Wales | 2,635 | 2,740 | 2,813 | 2,891 | 2,917 | 2,955 | 2,886 |
| Scotland | 5,184 | 5,236 | 5,180 | 5,107 | 5,137 | 5,083 | 4,934 |
| Northern Ireland | 1,427 | 1,540 | 1,538 | 1,601 | 1,649 | 1,699 | 1,750 |
| United Kingdom | 52,807 | 55,928 | 56,352 | 57,808 | 58,606 | 60,493 | 60,720 |

1 Data are mid-year estimates for 1961 to 1995 and 1994-based projections for 2011 and 2031. See Appendix, Part 1: Population estimates and projections.

**Source: Office for National Statistics; Government Actuary's Department; General Register Office (Scotland); General Register Office (Northern Ireland)**

# 1.3

## Population change[1]

**United Kingdom**                              Thousands

| | Population at start of period | Average annual change | | | | Overall annual change |
|---|---|---|---|---|---|---|
| | | Live births | Deaths | Net natural change | Net migration and other | |
| **Census enumerated** | | | | | | |
| 1901-1911 | 38,237 | 1,091 | 624 | 467 | -82 | 385 |
| 1911-1921 | 42,082 | 975 | 689 | 286 | -92 | 194 |
| 1921-1931 | 44,027 | 824 | 555 | 268 | -67 | 201 |
| 1931-1951 | 46,038 | 785 | 598 | 188 | 25 | 213 |
| **Mid-year estimates** | | | | | | |
| 1951-1961 | 50,287 | 839 | 593 | 246 | 6 | 252 |
| 1961-1971 | 52,807 | 963 | 639 | 324 | -12 | 312 |
| 1971-1981 | 55,928 | 736 | 666 | 69 | -27 | 42 |
| 1981-1991 | 56,352 | 757 | 655 | 103 | 43 | 146 |
| 1991-1995 | 57,808 | 765 | 639 | 125 | 74 | 199 |
| **Mid-year projections[2]** | | | | | | |
| 1995-2001 | 58,606 | 722 | 640 | 83 | 61 | 143 |
| 2001-2011 | 59,472 | 679 | 626 | 54 | 49 | 102 |
| 2011-2021 | 60,493 | 678 | 629 | 50 | 14 | 64 |
| 2021-2031 | 61,130 | 644 | 685 | -41 | 0 | -41 |

1 See Appendix, Part 1: Population estimates and projections.
2 1994-based projections.

**Source: Office for National Statistics; Government Actuary's Department; General Register Office (Scotland); General Register Office (Northern Ireland)**

Information on the size and structure of the population is vital in understanding many other aspects of society such as the labour market and household composition; it also affects the demand for the provision of various services including health care, social security benefits and education.

## Population structure and change

The population of the United Kingdom continues to grow and is projected to peak at 61.2 million in 2023. In 1995 the population of the United Kingdom was 58.6 million people, an increase of 11 per cent since 1961 (Table 1.2). However, there have been wide variations in the rate of increase between the constituent countries. Over this period Northern Ireland experienced the greatest percentage growth, with the population increasing by around 16 per cent. In contrast, the population of Scotland was almost 1 per cent lower in 1995 than in 1961, although it has increased slightly in each of the last seven years. Both Wales and Scotland are projected to have lower populations in 2031 than in 1995. The population projections used throughout this chapter are based on assumptions using past trends as a guide, and are not forecasts of what will actually happen. The projections article, starting on page 15, provides more information on how projections are made.

The first decade of this century was a period of fast population growth in the United Kingdom, averaging around 385 thousand people each year, due to a high number of births (Table 1.3). The 'baby boom' period during the 1960s again led to the overall annual increase exceeding 300 thousand per year. However, during the 1970s a lower number of births, a slight increase in deaths and higher outward migration led to the smallest overall population increase this century of only 42 thousand each year on average. Although it has risen during the 1980s and early 1990s, the rate of annual population growth is projected to decrease again over the next 25 years, and between 2021 and 2031 the population is expected to fall. This is due to a fall in the number of births and an increase in the number of deaths.

The age structure of the population reflects the variation in the past annual number of births, together with increased longevity and changes arising from migration. The age distributions for males and females in the United Kingdom in 1995 are illustrated as population pyramids in Chart 1.4. The bulge in the pyramid for people in their late forties is a consequence of the 'baby boom' which followed the Second World War. A second peak among people around the age of 30 is caused by the high birth rates of the 1960s. Overall there were more females than males in the United Kingdom in 1995 and the ratio of women to men increases with age since, on average, women live longer than men. In general there are more boys born each year than girls and males outnumber females at every age until they reach their mid-forties, when the numbers become similar. As they then get older, women increasingly outnumber men until, for those aged 85 and over, there are three women to every man. In 1991 there were around 4.4 thousand centenarians, people aged 100 and over, in England and Wales; nearly nine in ten were female.

The United Kingdom has an ageing population profile, in common with most of Western Europe. In 1961, 4 per cent of people in the United Kingdom were aged 75 and over; by 1995 this had risen to 7 per cent while around 16 per cent of the population were aged 65 and over (Table 1.5). In recent years the rate of increase in

# 1.4

## Population: by gender and age, 1995

**United Kingdom**

Thousands

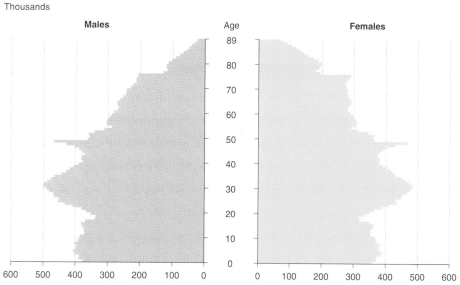

Source: Office for National Statistics; General Register Office (Scotland); General Register Office (Northern Ireland)

# 1.5

## Population[1]: by age and gender

**United Kingdom**

Percentages

|  | Under 16 | 16-34 | 35-54 | 55-64 | 65-74 | 75 and over | All ages (=100%) (millions) |
|---|---|---|---|---|---|---|---|
| **Mid-year estimates** | | | | | | | |
| 1961 | 25 | 24 | 27 | 12 | 8 | 4 | 52.8 |
| 1971 | 25 | 26 | 24 | 12 | 9 | 5 | 55.9 |
| 1981 | 22 | 29 | 23 | 11 | 9 | 6 | 56.4 |
| 1991 | 20 | 29 | 25 | 10 | 9 | 7 | 57.8 |
| 1995 | 21 | 27 | 26 | 10 | 9 | 7 | 58.6 |
| Males | 22 | 29 | 27 | 10 | 8 | 5 | 28.7 |
| Females | 20 | 26 | 26 | 10 | 9 | 9 | 29.9 |
| **Mid-year projections[2]** | | | | | | | |
| 2001 | 20 | 25 | 29 | 10 | 8 | 7 | 59.5 |
| 2011 | 18 | 24 | 29 | 12 | 9 | 7 | 60.5 |
| 2021 | 18 | 23 | 26 | 14 | 11 | 8 | 61.1 |
| 2031 | 17 | 22 | 25 | 13 | 13 | 11 | 60.7 |
| Males | 18 | 22 | 26 | 13 | 12 | 9 | 30.1 |
| Females | 17 | 21 | 24 | 13 | 13 | 12 | 30.6 |

1 See Appendix, Part 1: Population estimates and projections.
2 1994-based projections.

Source: Office for National Statistics; Government Actuary's Department; General Register Office (Scotland); General Register Office (Northern Ireland)

# 1.6

## Population: by type of area, 1971 and 1995

| Great Britain | | Millions |
|---|---|---|
| | 1971 | 1995 |
| Prospering areas | 11.0 | 12.6 |
| Mining and industrial areas | 13.0 | 12.1 |
| Urban centres | 11.2 | 11.6 |
| Rural areas | 8.9 | 10.4 |
| Maturer areas | 6.3 | 6.6 |
| Inner London | 4.1 | 3.6 |
| All areas | 54.4 | 57.0 |

*Source: Office for National Statistics; General Register Office (Scotland)*

# 1.7

## Change in population aged 65 and over: by area[1], 1994 to 2011[2]

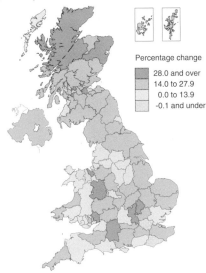

Percentage change

- 28.0 and over
- 14.0 to 27.9
- 0.0 to 13.9
- -0.1 and under

*1 Counties for England, unitary authorities for Wales and Scotland.*
*2 1992-based projections for Scotland; 1993-based projections for England; 1994-based projections for Wales and Northern Ireland.*
*Source: Office for National Statistics; Government Actuary's Department; Welsh Office; General Register Office (Scotland); General Register Office (Northern Ireland)*

the number of elderly people has slowed: from an annual growth rate of 1.5 per cent in the 1970s to only 0.4 per cent in the first half of the 1990s. However, in 2007, as people born in the post-Second World War 'baby boom' reach their sixties, the rate will rapidly increase. In contrast, the proportion of children aged under 16 in the United Kingdom fell from a quarter in 1961 to a fifth in 1995. This trend is assumed to continue to at least 2031. Major factors that have led to the growth in the elderly population and decline in the number of children are increasing longevity, which is discussed in The nation's health section of the Health chapter, and a fall in the birth rate. Further information on births and deaths is given later in this chapter.

People over retirement age, combined with the population under working age, form the dependent population: a crude measure of the number of people supported economically by those of working age. **Chart 1.1** at the beginning of the chapter shows the steady decline in the number of children under 16 between 1972 and the late 1980s. After increasing slowly during the first half of the 1990s this number is projected to fall again, by around a fifth, between 1996 and 2051. In 2016, for the first time, those aged 65 and over are projected to exceed those aged under 16.

Around a fifth of the population of Great Britain lived in rural areas in 1995 (**Table 1.6**). These include places like the Highlands and Islands of Scotland, the remoter parts of England and Wales and towns in rural areas such as Leominster. Overall the population of rural areas grew by 17 per cent between 1971 and 1995, faster than that of urban centres. In contrast, the population living in mining and industrial areas fell by 7 per cent

over the period; these include former coalfields in Wales and Durham, coastal industrial towns and the cities of Glasgow and Dundee. Manufacturing areas, such as Pennine towns and areas with a large ethnic minority population, have also seen a slight decline in population over this period.

The number of people living in resort and retirement areas, which are sub-categorised within Maturer areas, increased by 14 per cent to 2.5 million between 1971 and 1995, reflecting the general ageing of the population. Coastal retirement areas, such as Christchurch, have the largest proportion of elderly people. In contrast, areas with new towns such as Milton Keynes tend to have low proportions of elderly people. **Chart 1.7** illustrates the projected change in the population aged 65 and over in different parts of the United Kingdom between 1994 and 2011, assuming that past migration patterns will continue. The largest increases over this period, of around two fifths, are projected to occur in East Dumbartonshire, West Lothian and Bedfordshire. In contrast, the City of Glasgow, together with the Greater London boroughs of Barking and Dagenham, and Hammersmith and Fulham, are expected to see a decrease of more than a fifth in the number of elderly people. Overall Greater London is projected to have a reduction of nearly 5 per cent in the elderly population between 1994 and 2011.

People from ethnic minority groups are less likely than White people to live in affluent areas. For example, more than 60 per cent of Pakistani/Bangladeshi households lived in council estates and low income areas in 1994-95 compared with 19 per cent of White households. Information on the ethnicity of the population is collected by the Labour

**1.8**

Force Survey (LFS). In Spring 1996 the LFS estimated that around 3.3 million people in Great Britain belonged to an ethnic minority group - just under 6 per cent of the population. The Indian group formed the largest ethnic minority group; at 877 thousand people they amounted to 27 per cent of the ethnic minority population (Table 1.8). The ethnic minority population has a much younger age structure than the White population, reflecting past immigration and fertility patterns. About a third of the ethnic minority population was aged under 16 in Spring 1996 compared with around a fifth of the White population. The Pakistani and Bangladeshi groups have particularly young age structures - around three quarters were under the age of 35, with two fifths under 16. Much of the recent growth in Britain's ethnic minority population has been through children born in this country; just over half were born in the United Kingdom. The proportion decreases with age so that nine in ten ethnic minority children under the age of 16 were born in this country, whereas about nine in ten ethnic minority people aged 35 and over were born abroad.

The LFS can also provide a breakdown of the economically active population of working age by social class, a classification based on occupational status. Considerable differences exist in the social class structure of men and women in Great Britain. In Spring 1996 men were four times more likely than women to be in the professional group (Chart 1.9). However, women were three times more likely than men to be in the skilled non-manual group; 36 per cent of women were in this group. This reflects the predominance of women in certain occupations such as clerical and secretarial work.

**Population: by ethnic group and age, Spring 1996**

Great Britain — Percentages

| | Under 16 | 16-34 | 35-54 | 55 and over | All ages (=100%) (thousands) |
|---|---|---|---|---|---|
| White | 20 | 27 | 27 | 26 | 52,942 |
| Black Caribbean | 23 | 36 | 24 | 17 | 477 |
| Black African | 28 | 43 | 23 | 6 | 281 |
| Other Black | 49 | 38 | 12 | .. | 117 |
| Indian | 27 | 32 | 29 | 12 | 877 |
| Pakistani | 40 | 33 | 19 | 8 | 579 |
| Bangladeshi | 40 | 35 | 17 | 8 | 183 |
| Chinese | 16 | 40 | 30 | 15 | 126 |
| Other Asian | 27 | 31 | 36 | 6 | 161 |
| Other ethnic minorities[1] | 51 | 30 | 15 | 5 | 506 |
| All ethnic groups[2] | 21 | 27 | 27 | 25 | 56,267 |

1 Includes those of mixed origin.
2 Includes ethnic group not stated.

*Source: Labour Force Survey, Office for National Statistics*

**1.9**

**Population[1]: by gender and social class[2], Spring 1996**

Great Britain

Percentages

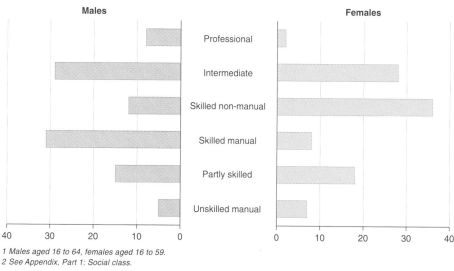

1 Males aged 16 to 64, females aged 16 to 59.
2 See Appendix, Part 1: Social class.

*Source: Labour Force Survey, Office for National Statistics*

# 1.10

### Total period fertility rate[1]

**United Kingdom**
Children per woman

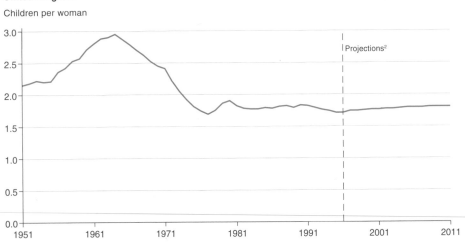

1 The average number of children who would be born per woman if women experienced the age-specific fertility rates of the reference years throughout their child-bearing lifespan.
2 1994-based projections.

*Source: Office for National Statistics; Government Actuary's Department; General Register Office (Scotland); General Register Office (Northern Ireland)*

# 1.11

### Most popular first names, 1971 and 1995

**England & Wales**

|  | 1971 | Rank in 1995 | Rank in 1995 | 1971 |
|---|---|---|---|---|
| **Males** | | | | |
| 1st | Paul | 67 | Jack | 344 |
| 2nd | Mark | 52 | Daniel | 33 |
| 3rd | David | 30 | Thomas | 45 |
| 4th | Andrew | 26 | James | 14 |
| 5th | Jason | 62 | Joshua | 260 |
| **Females** | | | | |
| 1st | Sarah | 17 | Jessica | 159 |
| 2nd | Joanne | 151 | Lauren | 300 |
| 3rd | Lisa | 90 | Rebecca | 27 |
| 4th | Sharon | 557 | Sophie | 106 |
| 5th | Nicola | 74 | Charlotte | 67 |

*Source: Office for National Statistics*

## Births and deaths

The total period fertility rate (TPFR) measures the average number of children that would be born to each woman if age-specific birth rates in the reference period persisted throughout her child-bearing life. It is a more reliable measure of current fertility than crude birth rates because it is not affected by changes in the age structure of the female population. However, trends in the TPFR are affected by changes in the ages at which women have children. In the United Kingdom the TPFR peaked at 2.95 in 1964 and then fell by over 40 per cent to a low point of 1.69 in 1977 (Chart 1.10). This is thought to have been influenced by more women receiving higher education, an increase in female participation in the workforce and greater control over fertility due to the introduction of the contraceptive pill. After a slight rise between 1977 and 1980, the TPFR remained fairly stable until 1990, since when slight falls each year have led to a rate of 1.71 children per woman in 1995, well below the rate of 2.1 which is associated with long-term population replacement. However, the TPFR is projected to increase very gradually, and the long-term assumption is that it will be 1.8 from the year 2008. Further information on fertility is also given in the Family building section of the Households and Families chapter.

Babies' names are constantly changing in popularity. In 1995 Jack and Jessica were the most common first names given to baby boys and girls in England and Wales (Table 1.11). However, neither of these names were within the top 100 most popular names in 1971. Out of the five most popular names for each gender chosen in 1971 only David, Andrew and Sarah were in the top 50 in 1995. In Scotland, Lauren was the most common girl's name given to babies registered in 1995, followed by Rebecca and Emma. For baby boys, Ryan was the most common name followed by Andrew and Daniel. During the mid-1930s, John and Margaret were among the most popular names for baby boys and girls in England, Wales and Scotland.

In the early part of this century it was very common for there to be over a million births each year but since 1922 births have only reached this level twice - during the post-Second World War 'baby boom' in 1947 and again in 1964 (Chart 1.12). Throughout the 1980s the number of live births each year

# 1.12

remained at around 750 thousand, rising at the end of the decade to reach almost 800 thousand in 1990. However since then the number of births has declined slowly each year and this trend is assumed to continue in the future. In 1995 there were 732 thousand births and 642 thousand deaths in the United Kingdom. Deaths have only exceeded births once this century - in 1976. Projections from the Government Actuary's Department suggest that deaths are likely to exceed births again from the year 2024.

Generally, death rates in all age groups are higher for men than for women (Table 1.13). The crude death rate, which takes no account of the age structure of the population, fell from 17.1 per thousand at the start of the century to 10.9 in 1995. The male death rate was 12.6 per thousand in 1961, compared with 11.4 for females. Conversely, by the 1990s the death rate for females exceeded that for males. Generally, death rates increase sharply between those in the 65 to 74 age group and those aged 75 and over, and similarly fall sharply between those aged under one and children aged between 1 and 15 years old. Of the age bands shown in Table 1.13 the largest projected proportionate reduction in the death rate between 1995 and 2011 is for males aged under one - from around seven to three deaths per thousand. The different age structures of the male and female population explain the apparent anomaly of male death rates at different ages exceeding those for women while the total death rate for men is lower than that for women. Information on causes of death is given in the Health chapter.

**Births and deaths**

**United Kingdom**

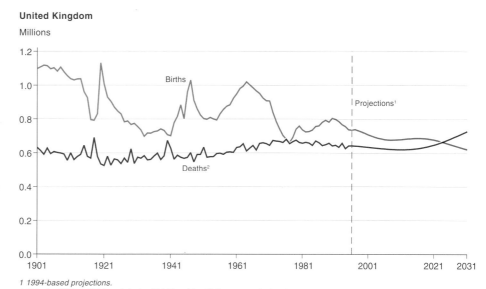

1 1994-based projections.
2 Data for 1901 to 1921 exclude the Irish Republic which was constitutionally a part of the United Kingdom during this period.
*Source: Office for National Statistics; Government Actuary's Department; General Register Office (Scotland); General Register Office (Northern Ireland)*

# 1.13

**Deaths: by gender and age**

**United Kingdom**

Rates

| | Death rates per 1,000 in each age group | | | | | | | All ages | All deaths (thousands) |
|---|---|---|---|---|---|---|---|---|---|
| | Under 1[1] | 1-15 | 16-34 | 35-54 | 55-64 | 65-74 | 75 and over | | |
| **Males** | | | | | | | | | |
| 1961 | 26.3 | 0.6 | 1.1 | 5.0 | 22.4 | 54.8 | 142.5 | 12.6 | 322 |
| 1971 | 20.2 | 0.5 | 1.0 | 4.8 | 20.4 | 51.1 | 131.4 | 12.1 | 329 |
| 1981 | 12.7 | 0.4 | 0.9 | 4.0 | 18.1 | 46.4 | 122.2 | 12.0 | 329 |
| 1991 | 8.3 | 0.3 | 0.9 | 3.1 | 14.2 | 38.7 | 110.6 | 11.1 | 314 |
| 1995 | 6.9 | 0.2 | 0.9 | 2.9 | 12.6 | 36.5 | 110.4 | 10.8 | 309 |
| 2001[2] | 4.7 | 0.2 | 0.8 | 2.6 | 10.9 | 32.7 | 105.6 | 10.4 | 306 |
| 2011[2] | 3.1 | 0.2 | 0.7 | 2.3 | 9.7 | 27.5 | 99.5 | 10.3 | 308 |
| **Females** | | | | | | | | | |
| 1961 | 18.2 | 0.4 | 0.6 | 3.2 | 11.0 | 31.6 | 110.4 | 11.4 | 310 |
| 1971 | 15.5 | 0.4 | 0.5 | 3.1 | 10.3 | 26.6 | 96.6 | 11.0 | 317 |
| 1981 | 9.5 | 0.3 | 0.4 | 2.5 | 9.8 | 24.7 | 90.2 | 11.4 | 329 |
| 1991 | 6.3 | 0.2 | 0.4 | 1.9 | 8.4 | 22.3 | 83.9 | 11.2 | 332 |
| 1995 | 5.4 | 0.2 | 0.4 | 1.9 | 7.5 | 21.7 | 85.4 | 11.1 | 333 |
| 2001[2] | 4.0 | 0.2 | 0.4 | 1.6 | 6.5 | 19.6 | 85.2 | 10.9 | 328 |
| 2011[2] | 2.7 | 0.1 | 0.3 | 1.4 | 5.7 | 16.0 | 82.5 | 10.2 | 312 |

1 Rate per 1,000 live births.
2 1994-based projections.

*Source: Office for National Statistics; Government Actuary's Department; General Register Office (Scotland); General Register Office (Northern Ireland)*

# 1.14

Inter-regional migration[1] within the United Kingdom, 1995

Thousands

| | | Region of origin | | | | | | | | | | | |
|---|---|---|---|---|---|---|---|---|---|---|---|---|---|
| | United Kingdom | North | York-shire & Humber-side | East Mid-lands | East Anglia | South East | South West | West Mid-lands | North West | England | Wales | Scot-land | North-ern Ireland |
| **Region of destination** | | | | | | | | | | | | | |
| United Kingdom | . | 54 | 98 | 92 | 53 | 258 | 108 | 98 | 111 | 108 | 53 | 52 | 12 |
| North | 47 | . | 9 | 4 | 2 | 11 | 3 | 3 | 8 | 40 | 1 | 5 | 1 |
| Yorkshire & Humberside | 91 | 11 | . | 15 | 4 | 23 | 6 | 7 | 17 | 82 | 3 | 5 | 1 |
| East Midlands | 101 | 4 | 18 | . | 8 | 32 | 7 | 14 | 11 | 94 | 3 | 4 | 1 |
| East Anglia | 62 | 2 | 5 | 7 | . | 32 | 4 | 3 | 4 | 57 | 2 | 2 | - |
| South East | 251 | 14 | 26 | 30 | 26 | . | 56 | 30 | 31 | 213 | 16 | 18 | 4 |
| South West | 132 | 3 | 7 | 8 | 4 | 68 | . | 16 | 10 | 117 | 10 | 5 | 1 |
| West Midlands | 90 | 3 | 8 | 12 | 3 | 28 | 12 | . | 12 | 78 | 8 | 3 | 1 |
| North West | 98 | 9 | 17 | 9 | 3 | 26 | 8 | 12 | . | 82 | 8 | 6 | 1 |
| England | 108 | 47 | 89 | 85 | 49 | 220 | 95 | 86 | 92 | . | 51 | 48 | 9 |
| Wales | 55 | 1 | 3 | 3 | 1 | 16 | 8 | 9 | 10 | 53 | . | 2 | - |
| Scotland | 49 | 5 | 5 | 3 | 2 | 16 | 4 | 3 | 7 | 44 | 2 | . | 3 |
| Northern Ireland | 14 | 1 | 1 | 1 | - | 5 | 1 | 1 | 2 | 11 | - | 2 | . |

1 Data are based on patient movements recorded by the National Health Service Central Registers at Southport and Edinburgh and the Central Services Agency in Belfast.

**Source: Office for National Statistics; General Register Office (Scotland); Central Services Agency, Northern Ireland**

# 1.15

Net inter-regional migration changes between 1981 and 1991: by age in 1981

Numbers

| | Age in 1981 | | | | | | | |
|---|---|---|---|---|---|---|---|---|
| | 0-15 | 16-24 | 25-34 | 35-54 | 55-64 | 65-74 | 75 and over | All ages[1] |
| North | -232 | -250 | -61 | 27 | 52 | 15 | -5 | -454 |
| Yorkshire & Humberside | -80 | -134 | -54 | -27 | 34 | 0 | -2 | -263 |
| East Midlands | 35 | 128 | 169 | 206 | 109 | 56 | 19 | 722 |
| East Anglia | 164 | 189 | 197 | 275 | 220 | 39 | 9 | 1,093 |
| South East | 344 | 544 | -649 | -1,363 | -944 | -222 | -46 | -2,336 |
| South West | 447 | 246 | 487 | 876 | 480 | 112 | 14 | 2,662 |
| West Midlands | -295 | -248 | -74 | -101 | -41 | 8 | 6 | -745 |
| North West | -350 | -426 | -128 | -161 | -82 | -42 | -1 | -1,190 |
| Wales | -36 | -44 | 110 | 264 | 173 | 35 | 6 | 508 |

1 Excluding those whose age was unknown.

**Source: Longitudinal Study, Office for National Statistics**

## Migration

In addition to births and deaths, changes in regional populations of the United Kingdom are caused by international migration and by people moving house within the country. Migration within the United Kingdom, which is shown in Table 1.14, is estimated by using information on registrations with General Practitioners. In 1995 Scotland experienced a small outward migration while Wales and Northern Ireland had small inward gains. England experienced no net change due to migration during 1995, although there were large gains and losses at a regional level. The biggest fall occurred in the North West region where 111 thousand people moved from there to other regions in the United Kingdom and 98 thousand moved into the region; a net loss of 13 thousand people. On the other hand, the South West region had the largest net gain of 24 thousand people. Since 1971 more people have migrated from northern to southern areas - to the South West, South East, East Anglia and East Midlands regions - than from south to north. This net flow reached a peak of around 70 thousand in 1986. However, during the following years the net gain to the south decreased rapidly until, in 1989, there was a small net flow to the north of the United Kingdom. Since 1992 there have again been net increases in the number of people moving from north to south.

There is a strong link between age and residential mobility. Information from the 1991 Census shows that mobility rates are highest for young adults. Data from the Longitudinal Study, which show net changes in regional population between 1981 and 1991, for people of different ages in 1981, are given in Table 1.15. In England and Wales the South East saw the largest net increase in those aged under 25 at the start of the period, of just under 0.9 thousand, while having the biggest net loss of around 1.2 thousand people aged 55 and over.

Since the beginning of this century the pattern of people entering and leaving the United Kingdom has changed. There was an average net loss of around 80 thousand people per year in the first 30 years of the century (Chart 1.16). However, in the 1930s there was an overall net inflow of people, mainly refugees from other European countries, into the United Kingdom. After a period of net outflow during the 1960s and 1970s, the direction of the trend reversed and since 1980 more people have entered the country than have left it. Net migration into the country, of 50 thousand people per year, is projected to continue over the next

### Net international migration[1]

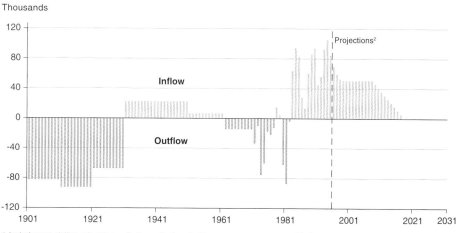

**United Kingdom**

Thousands

1 Includes net civilian migration and other adjustments. Ten year averages are used before 1931 and between 1951 and 1971. A twenty year average is used between 1931 and 1950. Data prior to 1971 are for calendar years, data after 1971 are mid-year estimates and projections.
2 1994-based projections.

*Source: Office for National Statistics; Government Actuary's Department; General Register Office (Scotland); General Register Office (Northern Ireland)*

12 years. Migration is then assumed to decline to zero by 2018. According to information from the International Passenger Survey, the South East region accounted for around half the number of people both entering and leaving the United Kingdom between 1984 and 1993. Greater London alone was stated as the destination of a third of all arrivals during this period.

The number of people accepted for settlement in the United Kingdom fell from a peak of over 90 thousand in 1972 to a low of 46 thousand in 1987. During the 1990s the number of acceptances has remained relatively stable. In 1995 there were around 55 thousand acceptances for settlement, over a third of which were from wives (Table 1.17). Acceptances on the basis of marriage accounted for nearly 60 per cent of the total in 1995. Nearly half of all those accepted for settlement were from Asia while around a fifth were from Africa. The number of acceptances from Africa has almost trebled since 1986.

### Acceptances for settlement: by category of acceptance

| United Kingdom | | | Percentages |
| --- | --- | --- | --- |
| | 1981 | 1991 | 1995 |
| Wives | 28 | 35 | 36 |
| Husbands | 11 | 22 | 23 |
| Children | 24 | 17 | 16 |
| Four years' employment | 12 | 6 | 8 |
| Refugees | 6 | 1 | 1 |
| Other | 19 | 19 | 16 |
| All categories (=100%)(thousands) | 59.1 | 53.9 | 55.5 |

*Source: Home Office*

# 1.18

Asylum applications (excluding dependants) and decisions[1]: by main geographical area of origin, 1995

**United Kingdom**   Thousands

| | Europe and Americas | Africa | Middle East | Rest of Asia | Other[2] | All areas |
|---|---|---|---|---|---|---|
| **Applications received** | 8.4 | 22.5 | 2.3 | 10.7 | - | 44.0 |
| | | | | | | |
| **Decisions[1] taken** | | | | | | |
| Recognised as a refugee and granted asylum | 0.4 | 0.1 | 0.8 | 0.1 | 0.0 | 1.3 |
| Not recognised as a refugee but granted exceptional leave | 0.8 | 2.5 | 0.2 | 0.9 | 0.0 | 4.4 |
| Refused asylum and exceptional leave | 3.0 | 8.9 | 0.6 | 5.3 | 0.0 | 17.7 |
| **Applications withdrawn** | 0.8 | 0.9 | 0.1 | 0.7 | - | 2.6 |
| **Applications outstanding at end of year** | 16.9 | 35.2 | 3.3 | 14.1 | 0.1 | 69.6 |

1 Excludes South East Asia Refugees. Information is for initial determination decisions, excluding the outcome of appeals or other subsequent decisions. Decisions figures do not necessarily relate to applications made in 1995. See Appendix Part 1: Asylum.
2 Includes nationality not known.
**Source: Home Office**

# 1.19

World urbanisation[1], 1995

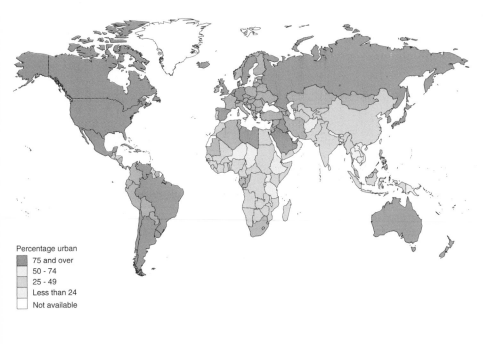

Percentage urban
- 75 and over
- 50 - 74
- 25 - 49
- Less than 24
- Not available

1 The proportion of the population living in urban areas.
**Source: United Nations**

In 1995 there were around 44 thousand applications for asylum in the United Kingdom (Table 1.18), a third more than in 1994. Over half of the applicants in 1995 came from Africa. More applicants were from Nigeria (13 per cent) than any other country, followed by Somalia at 8 per cent. The majority of principal applicants were relatively young: over 78 per cent were under 35 years old. Of the 1.3 thousand applicants recognised as refugees and granted asylum in 1995, nearly 80 per cent were nationals from three countries: Iraq (44 per cent), the former Yugoslavia (22 per cent) and Iran (13 per cent).

## World population

The urban population is growing faster than the world population as a whole. The United Nations estimates that within ten years just over half the world population, 3.3 billion people of the projected 6.6 billion total, will be living in cities (Chart 1.19). In 1994 there were over 280 cities or city systems with populations over 1 million, nearly three and a half times as many as in 1950. All the new cities with populations of over a million since 1950, and 11 out of the 15 most populated cities, are in developing countries.

In mid-1996 the world population was estimated at 5.8 billion and this is projected to increase by more than two fifths to reach 8.3 billion in 2025 (Table 1.20). Although fertility rates have fallen worldwide and are projected to continue to fall, the world population is continuing to increase by more than 86 million people a year. Over the past 20 years the infant mortality rate for the world as a whole has fallen; between 1970 and 1975 there were, on average, 93 deaths per thousand live births each year, compared with 64 per thousand between 1990 and 1995.

  Social Trends 27, © Crown copyright 1997

# 1.20

## World population indicators

| | Population (millions) | | 1995-2000 | | | | | |
|---|---|---|---|---|---|---|---|---|
| | | | Growth rate (percen-tages) | Population per hectare of arable land | Infant mortality[1] | Total period fertility rate[2] | Life expectancy | |
| | 1996 | 2025 | | | | | Males | Females |
| Europe | 727.7 | 718.2 | 0.1 | .. | 12 | 1.6 | 69 | 77 |
| European Union | | | | | | | | |
| Austria | 8.0 | 8.3 | 0.4 | 10 | 6 | 1.6 | 74 | 80 |
| Belgium | 10.1 | 10.4 | 0.3 | .. | 6 | 1.7 | 74 | 81 |
| Denmark | 5.2 | 5.1 | 0.1 | 8 | 7 | 1.7 | 73 | 79 |
| Finland | 5.1 | 5.4 | 0.4 | 14 | 5 | 1.9 | 73 | 80 |
| France | 58.2 | 61.2 | 0.4 | 8 | 7 | 1.7 | 74 | 81 |
| Germany | 81.8 | 76.4 | - | 14 | 6 | 1.3 | 74 | 80 |
| Greece | 10.5 | 9.9 | 0.2 | 23 | 9 | 1.4 | 76 | 81 |
| Irish Republic | 3.6 | 3.9 | 0.3 | 8 | 7 | 2.1 | 73 | 79 |
| Italy | 57.2 | 52.3 | - | 19 | 7 | 1.3 | 75 | 81 |
| Luxembourg | 0.4 | 0.4 | 1.4 | .. | 6 | 1.7 | 73 | 80 |
| Netherlands | 15.6 | 16.3 | 0.6 | 26 | 6 | 1.6 | 75 | 81 |
| Portugal | 9.8 | 9.7 | - | 39 | 9 | 1.6 | 72 | 79 |
| Spain | 39.7 | 37.6 | 0.1 | 12 | 7 | 1.2 | 75 | 81 |
| Sweden | 8.8 | 9.8 | 0.4 | 10 | 5 | 2.1 | 76 | 82 |
| United Kingdom | 58.4 | 61.5 | 0.3 | 6 | 6 | 1.8 | 74 | 79 |
| Northern & Southern Europe | | | | | | | | |
| Albania | 3.5 | 4.7 | 1.0 | 142 | 26 | 2.7 | 70 | 76 |
| Bosnia & Herzegovina | 3.5 | 4.5 | 4.5 | .. | 13 | 1.6 | 70 | 76 |
| Croatia | 4.5 | 4.2 | -0.3 | .. | 9 | 1.6 | 68 | 76 |
| Estonia | 1.5 | 1.4 | -0.5 | .. | 16 | 1.6 | 64 | 75 |
| Latvia | 2.5 | 2.3 | -0.7 | .. | 14 | 1.6 | 63 | 75 |
| Lithuania | 3.7 | 3.8 | - | .. | 13 | 1.8 | 65 | 76 |
| Macedonia | 2.2 | 2.6 | 0.8 | .. | 24 | 2.0 | 70 | 76 |
| Norway | 4.4 | 4.7 | 0.4 | 22 | 7 | 2.0 | 74 | 81 |
| Slovenia | 1.9 | 1.8 | - | .. | 7 | 1.5 | 69 | 78 |
| Switzerland | 7.3 | 7.8 | 0.8 | 11 | 6 | 1.7 | 75 | 82 |
| Yugoslavia (former) | 10.9 | 11.5 | -0.3 | 31 | 18 | 2.0 | 70 | 75 |
| Eastern Europe | 308.2 | 299.4 | -0.1 | .. | 17 | 1.6 | 64 | 74 |
| North America | 295.7 | 369.6 | 0.9 | .. | 7 | 2.1 | 74 | 80 |
| Canada | 29.8 | 38.3 | 1.0 | 1 | 6 | 1.9 | 75 | 81 |
| United States | 265.8 | 331.2 | 0.9 | 1 | 7 | 2.1 | 73 | 80 |
| Africa | 748.1 | 1,495.8 | 2.7 | .. | 85 | 5.3 | 53 | 56 |
| Asia | 3,513.2 | 4,960.0 | 1.5 | .. | 57 | 2.9 | 65 | 68 |
| Of which: China | 1,234.3 | 1,526.1 | 1.0 | 155 | 38 | 2.0 | 68 | 72 |
| Latin America and Caribbean | 490.4 | 709.8 | 1.7 | .. | 41 | 2.8 | 67 | 72 |
| Oceania | 29.0 | 41.0 | 1.4 | .. | 24 | 2.5 | 71 | 76 |
| Of which: Australia | 18.3 | 24.7 | 1.2 | - | 6 | 1.9 | 75 | 81 |
| New Zealand | 3.6 | 4.4 | 1.0 | 2 | 8 | 2.1 | 73 | 79 |
| World | 5,804.1 | 8,294.3 | 1.5 | .. | 57 | 3.0 | 64 | 68 |
| More developed[3] | 1,170.7 | 1,238.4 | 0.3 | .. | 9 | 1.7 | 71 | 79 |
| Less developed[3] | 4,633.4 | 7,055.9 | 1.8 | .. | 63 | 3.3 | 62 | 65 |

1 Per thousand live births.
2 The average number of children who would be born per woman if women experienced the age-specific fertility rates of the reference years throughout their child-bearing span.
3 More developed: Europe, North America, Australia, New Zealand and Japan. Less developed: Africa, Latin America, Asia (excluding Japan) and Melanesia, Micronesia and Polynesia.

**Source: United Nations**

## References and further reading

The following list contains selected publications relevant to **Chapter 1: Population**. Those published by The Stationery Office are available from the addresses shown on the inside back cover of *Social Trends*.

*Annual report of the Registrar General for Northern Ireland*, The Stationery Office

*Annual Report of the Registrar General for Scotland*, General Register Office (Scotland)

*Asylum Statistics - United Kingdom*, Home Office

*Birth Statistics (Series FM1)*, The Stationery Office

*Control of Immigration: Statistics - United Kingdom*, Home Office

*First Names*, The Stationery Office

*General Household Survey*, The Stationery Office

*International Migration Statistics (Series MN)*, The Stationery Office

*Key Population and Vital Statistics (Series VS/PP1)*, The Stationery Office

*Labour Force Survey*, The Stationery Office

*Mortality Statistics for England and Wales (Series DH1, 2, 3, 4, 5, 6)*, The Stationery Office

*National Population Projections (Series PP2)*, The Stationery Office

*Persons Granted British Citizenship - United Kingdom*, Home Office

*Population Estimates, Scotland*, The Stationery Office

*Population Projections for the Counties and District Health Authorities of Wales*, Welsh Office

*Population Projections, Scotland (for Standard Areas)*, General Register Office (Scotland)

*Population Trends*, The Stationery Office

*Regional Trends*, The Stationery Office

*Social Focus on Women*, The Stationery Office

*Social Focus on Ethnic Minorities*, The Stationery Office

*Subnational Population Projections - England (Series PP3)*, The Stationery Office

*The State of the World Population*, UNFPA

## Contacts

Telephone contact points for further information relating to
**Chapter 1: Population**

**Office for National Statistics**

| | |
|---|---|
| Chapter author | 0171 533 5779 |
| Labour Force Survey | 0171 533 6180 |
| Other inquiries | 0171 533 6262 |
| **General Register Office (Northern Ireland)** | 01232 252031 |
| **General Register Office for Scotland** | 0131 314 4254 |
| **Government Actuary's Department** | 0171 211 2622 |
| **Home Office** | 0181 760 8631 |
| **United Nations** | 0171 630 1981 |

# Chapter 2 Households and Families

**Households**

The average size of households in Great Britain has almost halved since the beginning of this century to 2.4 people per household in 1995-96. (Table 2.2)

**Families**

Over half of men aged between 20 and 24 in England still lived with their parents in 1995-96 compared with just over a third of women of the same age. (Table 2.8)

Lone parents headed 23 per cent of all families with dependent children in Great Britain in 1994, nearly three times the proportion in 1971. (Chart 2.9)

**Cohabitation**

The proportion of non-married women aged between 18 and 49 who were cohabiting in Great Britain has doubled since 1981, to 25 per cent in 1995-96. (Chart 2.12)

**Marriage and divorce**

In 1994 there were 208 thousand first marriages in the United Kingdom which was around two fifths fewer than in 1971. (Chart 2.14)

The United Kingdom had the highest divorce rate in the European Union in 1994. (Chart 2.15)

**Family building**

In England and Wales less than 12 per cent of women born in 1944 were childless at age 35 compared with 20 per cent of those born in 1954. (Chart 2.21)

There were over 6 thousand adoption orders in England and Wales in 1994, compared with 21 thousand in 1971. (Chart 2.27)

## 2.1

**Births outside marriage as a percentage of all live births**

**England & Wales**

Percentages

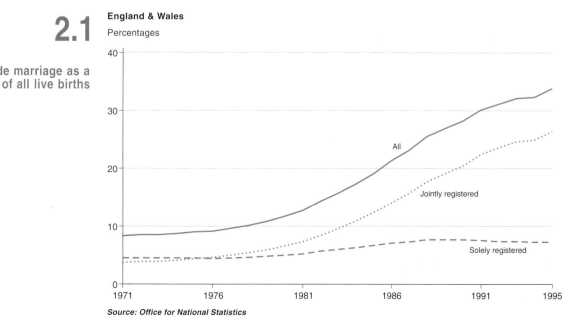

*Source: Office for National Statistics*

# 2.2

## Households[1]: by size

| Great Britain | | | | | Percentages |
|---|---|---|---|---|---|
| | 1961 | 1971 | 1981 | 1991 | 1995-96 |
| One person | 14 | 18 | 22 | 27 | 28 |
| Two people | 30 | 32 | 32 | 34 | 35 |
| Three people | 23 | 19 | 17 | 16 | 16 |
| Four people | 18 | 17 | 18 | 16 | 15 |
| Five people | 9 | 8 | 7 | 5 | 5 |
| Six or more people | 7 | 6 | 4 | 2 | 2 |
| All households | | | | | |
| (=100%)(millions) | 16.3 | 18.6 | 20.2 | 22.4 | 23.5 |
| Average household | | | | | |
| size (number of people) | 3.1 | 2.9 | 2.7 | 2.5 | 2.4 |

1 See Appendix, Part 2: Households.
*Source: Census and General Household Survey, Office for National Statistics; Department of the Environment*

# 2.3

## Households[1]: by type of household and family

| Great Britain | | | | | Percentages |
|---|---|---|---|---|---|
| | 1961 | 1971 | 1981 | 1991 | 1995-96 |
| **One person** | | | | | |
| Under pensionable age | 4 | 6 | 8 | 11 | 13 |
| Over pensionable age | 7 | 12 | 14 | 16 | 15 |
| **Two or more unrelated adults** | 5 | 4 | 5 | 3 | 2 |
| **One family** | | | | | |
| Married couple[2] | | | | | |
| No children | 26 | 27 | 26 | 28 | 29 |
| 1-2 dependent children[3] | 30 | 26 | 25 | 20 | 19 |
| 3 or more dependent children[3] | 8 | 9 | 6 | 5 | 4 |
| Non-dependent children only | 10 | 8 | 8 | 8 | 6 |
| Lone parent[2] | | | | | |
| Dependent children[3] | 2 | 3 | 5 | 6 | 7 |
| Non-dependent children only | 4 | 4 | 4 | 4 | 3 |
| **Two or more families** | 3 | 1 | 1 | 1 | 1 |
| **All households** | | | | | |
| (=100%)(millions) | 16.3 | 18.6 | 20.2 | 22.4 | 23.5 |

1 See Appendix, Part 2: Households and Families.
2 Other individuals who were not family members may also be included.
3 Households may also include non-dependent children.
*Source: Census and General Household Survey, Office for National Statistics; Department of the Environment*

The structure and characteristics of the households and families in which people live affect not only the individuals concerned, but also help us to achieve a wider understanding of society.

## Households

The average size of households in Great Britain has almost halved since the beginning of this century to 2.4 people per household in 1995-96 (Table 2.2). This has been the result of the increase in the number of households exceeding the growth in the population. There were over 7 million more households in Great Britain in 1995-96 than in 1961. The size of household with the largest percentage increase has been one person households: over a quarter of households comprised just one person living alone in 1995-96. The Continuous Household Survey provides information on households in Northern Ireland. Data from this source show that although the average household size is larger than in Great Britain, at 2.8 people, the trend of an increasing number of households and decreasing average household size has been similar over recent years.

The proportion of 'traditional' households, comprising a couple family with dependent children, has been falling. In 1961, 38 per cent of all households in Great Britain were of this type but by 1995-96 this proportion had decreased to only 24 per cent (Table 2.3). Indeed, in 1991 households comprising a couple family with no children outnumbered those comprising a couple family with dependent children. In Northern Ireland, a higher proportion of households are made up of 'traditional' families than in Great Britain: 29 per cent comprised a couple family with dependent children in 1995-96. Multi-family households formed 3

## 2.4

per cent of all households in Great Britain in 1961 but this declined to less than 1 per cent in 1995-96. Part of this decline has been attributed to the increased housing stock and part to lone parent families in particular increasingly becoming one family households. However, the incidence of multi-family households, which often consist of extended families, is more common amongst some ethnic minority groups. In 1991 nearly one in ten of both Indian and Pakistani/Bangladeshi households contained two or more families compared with only 1 in 100 of households from the White or Black ethnic groups. Both Indian and Pakistani/Bangladeshi households also had around twice the proportion of households consisting of a couple with children than the White or Black groups.

Women aged 60 and over formed the largest proportion of people living alone in England and Wales in 1996 (Table 2.4). However, this proportion has remained fairly stable over the last 25 years or so. In recent years, the largest increase in people living alone has been among men under the age of 65 - the proportion of all households which were of this type was over two and a half times higher in 1996 than in 1971. This reflects the decline in marriage and the rise in separation and divorce. It is projected that this group will continue to increase and will overtake women aged 60 and over within about 10 years to form the largest proportion of one person households.

Whereas Table 2.4 showed that over one in four households in Great Britain in 1995-96 comprised a person living alone, Table 2.5 is based on people; it shows that just over one in ten people live alone. Most people live in households headed by a couple. In 1995-96 three quarters of people lived in such households. The situation in Northern Ireland is broadly the same with a similar

proportion of people living in households headed by a couple. The number of people in private households in Great Britain increased by just under 3 million between 1971 and 1995-96.

**One person households as a percentage of all households: by gender and whether under or over pensionable age**

| England & Wales | | | | | | Percentages |
|---|---|---|---|---|---|---|
| | 1971 | 1981 | 1991 | 1996[1] | 2006[1] | 2016[1] |
| **Males** | | | | | | |
| Under 65 | 3 | 5 | 7 | 9 | 12 | 13 |
| 65 and over | 2 | 3 | 3 | 3 | 4 | 4 |
| **Females** | | | | | | |
| Under 60 | 3 | 3 | 4 | 5 | 6 | 6 |
| 60 and over | 10 | 12 | 12 | 11 | 11 | 12 |
| **All one person households** | 18 | 23 | 27 | 29 | 33 | 36 |

1 1992-based projections.
*Source: Department of the Environment*

## 2.5

**People in households and communal establishments: by type of household and family in which they live[1]**

| Great Britain | | | | | Percentages |
|---|---|---|---|---|---|
| | 1961 | 1971 | 1981 | 1991 | 1995-96 |
| **One family households** | | | | | |
| Living alone | 4 | 6 | 8 | 11 | 12 |
| Married couple | | | | | |
| No children | 18 | 19 | 20 | 23 | 25 |
| Dependent children[2] | 52 | 52 | 47 | 41 | 40 |
| Non-dependent children only | 12 | 10 | 10 | 11 | 9 |
| Lone parent | 3 | 4 | 6 | 10 | 11 |
| **Other households** | 12 | 9 | 9 | 4 | 4 |
| **All people in private households** | | | | | |
| (=100%)(millions) | .. | 53.4 | 53.9 | 55.4 | 56.3 |
| **People not in private** | | | | | |
| **households** (millions) | .. | 0.9 | 0.8 | 0.8 | 0.7 |
| **Total population** (millions) | 51.4 | 54.4 | 54.8 | 56.2 | 57.0 |

1 See Appendix, Part 2: Households and Families.
2 Households may also include non-dependent children.
*Source: Census and General Household Survey, Office for National Statistics*

## 2.6

Adults' experience of household change: by type of household, 1993 to 1994

**Great Britain**                                                                                             Percentages

| | Single, no children | | | Couple, no children | | Couple or single with children | |
| --- | --- | --- | --- | --- | --- | --- | --- |
| | Living with parents | Aged under 45 | Aged 45 and over | Aged under 45 | Aged 45 and over | Dependent children[1] | Non-dependent children only |
| No change | 73 | 67 | 95 | 77 | 95 | 85 | 75 |
| Separation from partner | . | . | . | 6 | - | 2 | 1 |
| Death of partner | . | . | . | 0 | 2 | - | 1 |
| Departure of children | . | . | . | . | . | 4 | 19 |
| Separation from parent | 15 | . | . | - | - | - | - |
| Birth of child | 1 | - | 0 | 12 | 0 | 6 | 0 |
| Other separations | 8 | 18 | 3 | 4 | 1 | - | - |
| Other joins | 3 | 15 | 3 | 1 | 2 | 2 | 4 |
| All changes | 100 | 100 | 100 | 100 | 100 | 100 | 100 |

1 Households may also contain non-dependent children.

**Source: British Household Panel Survey, ESRC Research Centre on Micro-social Change**

## 2.7

People in households[1]: by gender, age and family type, Spring 1996

**United Kingdom**                                                                                             Percentages

| | | Couple | | Lone parent | | |
| --- | --- | --- | --- | --- | --- | --- |
| | One person | No children | With children | Dependent children[2] | Non-dependent children only | All people (=100%) (millions) |
| **Males** | | | | | | |
| Under 16 | 0 | . | 78 | 22 | . | 6.2 |
| 16-24 | 15 | 7 | 64 | 8 | 7 | 3.3 |
| 25-34 | 21 | 22 | 51 | 1 | 5 | 4.7 |
| 35-44 | 14 | 12 | 69 | 2 | 3 | 4.0 |
| 45-54 | 12 | 27 | 57 | 1 | 3 | 3.7 |
| 55-64 | 16 | 57 | 25 | .. | 2 | 2.8 |
| 65-74 | 21 | 68 | 9 | .. | 2 | 2.3 |
| 75 and over | 34 | 59 | 4 | .. | 3 | 1.4 |
| **Females** | | | | | | |
| Under 16 | 0 | . | 78 | 22 | . | 5.9 |
| 16-24 | 14 | 11 | 55 | 14 | 5 | 3.2 |
| 25-34 | 12 | 20 | 51 | 15 | 2 | 4.6 |
| 35-44 | 7 | 11 | 67 | 13 | 2 | 4.0 |
| 45-54 | 11 | 32 | 47 | 4 | 5 | 3.8 |
| 55-64 | 21 | 58 | 15 | 1 | 5 | 2.9 |
| 65-74 | 40 | 50 | 5 | .. | 4 | 2.7 |
| 75 and over | 68 | 25 | 1 | .. | 5 | 2.4 |

1 See Appendix, Part 2: Households and Families.
2 Families may also include non-dependent children.

**Source: Labour Force Survey, Office for National Statistics**

The membership of households changes over time. For example, people who are living alone may move into cohabitation or marry and thus become members of couple households, or one member of an elderly couple household may die leaving their spouse to live alone. Results from the British Household Panel Survey (BHPS) show that adults aged under 45 were much more likely than those aged 45 and over to have experienced household change between 1993 and 1994 (Table 2.6). For a couple aged under 45 with no children at the start of the period, the most common reason for household change was the birth of a child. For those households containing only non-dependent children, the most common cause of change was the departure of children. Single people aged under 45, not living with their parents, have quite high levels of other joins and separations due to being particularly likely to move into and out of households containing unrelated sharers. Also, any new partnerships formed by those

## 2.8

in this group are included in other joins. The BHPS estimates that overall, around 15 per cent of all households in Great Britain change their composition each year.

## Families

A family is defined as a married or cohabiting couple, with or without their never-married children who have no children of their own, or a lone parent with such children. People living alone are not normally considered to form a family.

The stage at which people are in their life-cycle has an effect on the sort of household in which they live. Children usually live with either both or one of their parents. As they become young adults, they may move on either to live alone or form a couple household firstly without, and then with, children. Their children may then eventually move on leaving a couple household with no children once more and this may then become a one person household when one of the partners (usually the man) dies. Couple households may also be changed by divorce or separation. The tendency for women to marry men older than themselves and then outlive them means that around two thirds of women aged 75 and over lived alone in Spring 1996 (Table 2.7). Among people in the 25 to 34 age group men are more likely than women to live alone: one in five men lived alone compared with only one in eight women.

Not all young adults move away from the parental home: many people in their twenties still live with their parents. This is much more likely to occur among men than women. In 1995-96 over half of men aged 20

to 24 in England lived with their parents compared with just over a third of women of the same age (Table 2.8). In Northern Ireland the proportion of adults still living with their parents is higher than in England. For example, among 20 to 24 year olds, 77 per cent of men and 53 per cent of women lived with their parents. The Survey of English Housing also asked people at what age they first became responsible for their own accommodation, which is a good proxy for the age at which they left the parental home. The proportions of men that had become responsible for their own accommodation by age 25 or 30 were highest among those who were born between 1945 and 1954 and declined for those born after 1954.

There has been a substantial growth in lone parent families over the last 25 years. Lone parents headed almost 23 per cent of all families with dependent children in Great Britain in 1994, which was nearly three times the proportion in 1971 (Chart 2.9). There was a gradual increase up to the mid 1980s after which there was a more rapid rise. A large part of the increase up to the mid 1980s was due to divorce, whilst after 1986 single lone mothers grew at a faster rate as the proportion of live births outside marriage accelerated. Most lone parent families are headed by a lone mother. In 1995-96 nearly two fifths of lone mothers were single and a slightly smaller proportion were divorced. An analysis of the BHPS found that in the early 1990s, on average, around 15 per cent of lone mothers per year ceased to be lone parents, usually as a result of forming a new partnership. The study concluded that, if such a departure rate was maintained over time, half of all lone mothers would have a duration of lone parenthood of around four years or less.

**Adults living with their parents: by age**

| England | | | Percentages |
|---|---|---|---|
| | 1977-78 | 1991 | 1995-96 |
| **Males** | | | |
| 20-24 | 52 | 50 | 54 |
| 25-29 | 19 | 19 | 24 |
| 30-34 | 9 | 9 | 11 |
| **Females** | | | |
| 20-24 | 31 | 32 | 36 |
| 25-29 | 9 | 9 | 11 |
| 30-34 | 3 | 5 | 5 |

*Source: National Dwelling and Household Survey and Survey of English Housing, Department of the Environment; Labour Force Survey, Office for National Statistics*

## 2.9

**Families headed by lone parents as a percentage[1] of all families with dependent children**

**Great Britain**
Percentages

*1 Three year moving average used (apart from 1994).*
*Source: General Household Survey, Office for National Statistics*

# 2.10

**Percentage of dependent children[1] living in different family types**

| Great Britain | | | | | Percentages |
| --- | --- | --- | --- | --- | --- |
| | 1972 | 1981 | 1986 | 1991-92 | 1995-96 |
| **Couple with** | | | | | |
| 1 child | 16 | 18 | 18 | 17 | 16 |
| 2 children | 35 | 41 | 41 | 37 | 38 |
| 3 or more children | 41 | 29 | 28 | 28 | 26 |
| **Lone mother with** | | | | | |
| 1 child | 2 | 3 | 4 | 5 | 5 |
| 2 children | 2 | 4 | 5 | 7 | 7 |
| 3 or more children | 2 | 3 | 3 | 6 | 6 |
| **Lone father with** | | | | | |
| 1 child | - | 1 | 1 | - | 1 |
| 2 or more children | 1 | 1 | 1 | 1 | 1 |
| **All dependent children** | 100 | 100 | 100 | 100 | 100 |

1 See Appendix, Part 2: Families.
*Source: General Household Survey, Office for National Statistics*

# 2.11

**Contact with relatives[1], 1995**

| Great Britain | | | | Percentages |
| --- | --- | --- | --- | --- |
| | Mother | Father | Brother/sister | Children |
| At least once a week | 48 | 39 | 28 | 58 |
| At least once a month | 21 | 19 | 21 | 16 |
| Less often/never | 30 | 38 | 49 | 20 |
| Not answered | 2 | 3 | 2 | 6 |
| All | 100 | 100 | 100 | 100 |

1 Respondents were asked how often they saw or visited each living relative who did not live in their household.
*Source: British Social Attitudes Survey, Social & Community Planning Research*

In 1995 the British Social Attitudes Survey (BSAS), carried out by Social & Community Planning Research, asked people about their attitudes to unmarried mothers. Thirty two per cent agreed with the statement that 'unmarried mothers who find it hard to cope have only themselves to blame', whilst 26 per cent agreed that 'unmarried mothers get too little sympathy from society'.

In spite of the growth in single parent families, most dependent children live in a family with two parents: four fifths of children in Great Britain lived in such families in 1995-96. However, this proportion has fallen since 1972 when over nine tenths of children lived in a couple family (Table 2.10). The proportion of children in couple families with three or more children declined during the 1970s but has remained relatively stable since the early 1980s. In 1995-96 just over a quarter of dependent children lived in a family with three or more children. In Northern Ireland, a higher proportion of children live in these larger families - 38 per cent did so in 1995-96.

Some children live in step-families. In 1991 there were around half a million step families containing dependent stepchildren in Great Britain with around 1 million dependent children, both stepchildren and natural children, living in such families. There were more than three times as many stepfathers as stepmothers, due to the tendency for children to stay with their mother rather than their father following divorce or separation. Families containing stepchildren tend to be larger than families with natural children only. In married couple step-families there were on average 2.3 dependent children compared with only 1.9 in married couple families with only natural children.

As family members grow up, they usually move away to establish their own households. In 1995 the BSAS asked respondents how often they saw or visited relatives who did not live in the same household. Many people saw their mother, father or children at least once a week (Table 2.11). However, three in ten saw their mothers less than once a month and nearly four in ten saw their fathers less than once a month. Contacts with brothers and sisters were less frequent than those with parents or offspring: around half of people saw their brothers and sisters less than once a month.

The survey also asked questions on family attitudes. The majority of respondents thought that it was important to keep in touch with other relatives, even if they did not have much in common with them. People also thought that, once children had flown the nest, they should still be able to turn to their parents for help. The survey concluded that the family is still the dominant source of support and care for most people. There has been a drop in contact with relatives over the last decade (from a very high base) alongside a small increase in people's reliance on friends for support. There is also an association between strong family centred attitudes and age. Those in older age groups were more likely to think it important to keep in touch with the wider family.

## Cohabitation

One of the main changes in family life over the last decade or so has been the fall in the proportion of people living in married couples and the increase in cohabitation. The proportion of all non-married women aged 18 to 49 who were cohabiting in Great Britain has doubled since 1981, to 25 per cent in 1995-96 (Chart 2.12). Among this group, women in their late twenties and men in their late twenties and thirties were the most likely to cohabit - over a third were doing so. Those whose marriage had ended in divorce were the most likely to cohabit although cohabiting was more common among divorced men than divorced women. Out of all women aged 16 to 59, 9 per cent were cohabiting, more than double the proportion in 1986-87. Those without dependent children were slightly more likely to be cohabiting than those with dependent children.

An analysis of BHPS data suggests that on average half of cohabitations last around two years or less. The main reason for a period of cohabitation ending is that the partners marry (Table 2.13). Of those women entering cohabitation each year, the majority are single.

The BHPS also asked respondents in 1994 if they thought that 'living together outside marriage was always wrong'. It found that those people in older age groups were more likely than those in younger groups to think that cohabitation was wrong. Forty per cent of men born before 1930 thought that it was

# 2.12

## Percentage of women[1] cohabiting

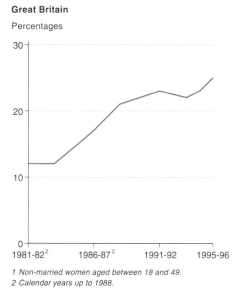

**Great Britain**

Percentages

*1 Non-married women aged between 18 and 49.*
*2 Calendar years up to 1988.*

**Source: General Household Survey, Office for National Statistics**

# 2.13

## Women leaving and entering cohabitation[1] each year, 1991-1994

| **Great Britain** | Percentages |
|---|---|
| | 1991-1994 |
| **Women leaving cohabitation[2]** | |
| Marry partner | 16 |
| Partnership dissolves | |
|   Never married | 9 |
|   Widowed, divorced or separated | 4 |
| All women leaving cohabitation | 28 |
| **Women entering cohabitation[3]** | |
| Single | 14 |
| Divorced | 5 |
| Separated | 4 |
| Widowed | 1 |
| All women entering cohabitation | 23 |

*1 Those who changed cohabiting partners were not treated as leaving or entering.*
*2 As a percentage of all women cohabiting at the start of the period.*
*3 Previous marital status. As a percentage of all women cohabiting at the end of the period.*

**Source: British Household Panel Survey, ESRC Research Centre on Micro-social Change**

# 2.14

### Marriages and divorces

**United Kingdom**
Thousands

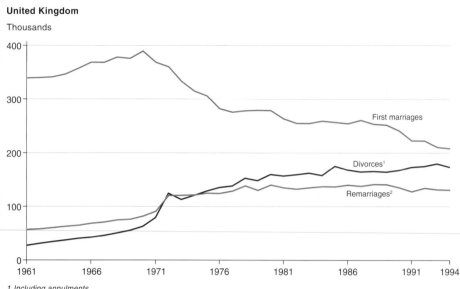

1 Including annulments.
2 For one or both partners.

**Source: Office for National Statistics; General Register Office (Scotland); General Register Office (Northern Ireland)**

# 2.15

### Marriage and divorce rates: EU comparison, 1994

Rates per 1,000 population

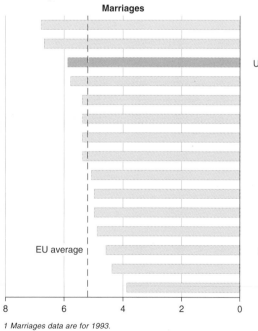

1 Marriages data are for 1993.
2 Divorce is not permitted.

**Source: Eurostat**

wrong compared with only seven per cent of those born between the years 1960 and 1978. A slightly lower proportion of women thought that living together outside marriage was wrong.

The 1994 BSAS also asked people about their attitudes to cohabitation. Nearly two thirds of respondents agreed that it was alright for people to live together without intending to get married. A slightly lower proportion (58 per cent) thought that it was a good idea for couples intending to marry to live together first.

## Marriage and divorce

The number of first marriages in the United Kingdom has decreased substantially since the late 1960s (Chart 2.14). In 1994 there were 208 thousand first marriages, which was around two fifths fewer than in 1971. In total there were 338 thousand marriages in 1994, around 3 thousand fewer than in the previous year. Remarriages accounted for over a third of this total. In contrast, the number of divorces has more than doubled over the same period, although in 1994 there were slightly fewer divorces than the previous year. The *Divorce Reform Act 1969*, which came into force in 1971 introduced a new ground for divorce, that of irretrievable breakdown. This contributed to the increase in both divorces and remarriages in the early 1970s.

In common with the United Kingdom, most European Union (EU) countries have seen a decline in their marriage rates since 1981. A notable exception to this has been Denmark

# 2.16

where the marriage rate has actually risen. In 1994, Sweden had the lowest marriage rate in the EU while Denmark had the highest (Chart 2.15). The United Kingdom had the highest divorce rate, followed by Finland. Much of the variations that exist are due to by religious, social, cultural and legal differences between the countries.

There has been a slight shift away from religious marriage ceremonies to civil ones over the past decade. In 1981 just over half of all marriage ceremonies were religious whilst in 1993 just over half were civil ceremonies (Table 2.16). There is a striking difference between the types of ceremonies for first and subsequent marriages. In 1993 nearly two thirds of first marriages had religious ceremonies but for second or subsequent marriages the proportion was less than a fifth. Saturday was the most common day for weddings to take place - over two thirds of all marriages in England and Wales took place on Saturdays in 1994. However, in 1979 over three quarters of marriages took place on Saturdays. Civil marriages were seven times more likely than religious marriages to take place during the week, with Friday being the most common weekday in 1994. There was a small peak of weddings on St Valentine's Day, particularly amongst couples where both the partners were remarrying after divorce. The summer months are generally the most favoured time to get married and January the least popular month for a wedding.

Differences exist between the EU countries in the ages at which people get married for the first time. In 1994 the country with the youngest newly-weds was Portugal while

**Marriages: by type of ceremony, 1981 and 1993**

| Great Britain | | | | | | Percentages |
|---|---|---|---|---|---|---|
| | First marriages[1] | | Remarriages[1] | | All marriages[2] | |
| | 1981 | 1993 | 1981 | 1993 | 1981 | 1993 |
| Religious ceremonies | 69 | 65 | 17 | 19 | 52 | 49 |
| Civil ceremonies | 31 | 35 | 83 | 81 | 48 | 51 |
| All ceremonies (=100%)(thousands) | 254.7 | 203.2 | 60.7 | 57.6 | 388.2 | 332.6 |

1 For both partners.
2 Includes remarriages for one or both partners.
**Source: Office for National Statistics; General Register Office (Scotland)**

# 2.17

Denmark had the oldest (Table 2.17). Traditionally, women marry men older than themselves. The greatest difference in the average ages of people getting married for the first time was four years in Greece while the Irish Republic had the least difference in age between partners. The average age for people getting married for the first time in the EU has been increasing since the mid 1970s - in 1993 it was 28.5 for men and 26.1 for women, compared with 25.7 and 23.0 respectively in 1975.

In the United Kingdom, around 6 per cent of women marrying for the first time in 1993 were under the age of 20 compared with only 2 per cent of men. On the other hand, 23 per cent of men were aged over 30 when they first married, compared with just 14 per cent of women. Around two thirds of first marriages involved brides and grooms who were both in their twenties.

**Average age at first marriage: EU comparison, 1994**

| | | Years |
|---|---|---|
| | Males | Females |
| Denmark | 31.3 | 28.9 |
| Sweden | 30.8 | 28.5 |
| Greece | 29.6 | 25.6 |
| Netherlands | 29.3 | 27.0 |
| Italy[1] | 29.1 | 26.1 |
| Germany | 28.9 | 26.3 |
| Irish Republic[2] | 28.8 | 27.0 |
| France | 28.7 | 26.7 |
| Finland | 28.6 | 26.7 |
| Luxembourg | 28.4 | 26.3 |
| Austria | 28.4 | 25.8 |
| Spain[1] | 28.3 | 26.2 |
| United Kingdom[1] | 28.0 | 25.8 |
| Belgium | 27.1 | 25.2 |
| Portugal | 26.6 | 24.6 |

1 Data are for 1993.
2 Data are for 1992.
**Source: Eurostat**

# 2.18

## Divorce: by gender and age

| England & Wales | | | | | Rates per 1,000 married population |
|---|---|---|---|---|---|
| | 1961 | 1971 | 1981 | 1991 | 1995 |
| **Males** | | | | | |
| 16-24 | 1.4 | 5.0 | 17.7 | 25.9 | 17.1 |
| 25-29 | 3.9 | 12.5 | 27.6 | 32.9 | 26.6 |
| 30-34 | 4.1 | 11.8 | 22.8 | 28.5 | 27.9 |
| 35-44 | 3.1 | 7.9 | 17.0 | 20.1 | 20.4 |
| 45 and over | 1.1 | 3.1 | 4.8 | 5.6 | 6.2 |
| All aged 16 and over | 2.1 | 5.9 | 11.9 | 13.6 | 13.2 |
| **Females** | | | | | |
| 16-24 | 2.4 | 7.5 | 22.3 | 27.7 | 19.9 |
| 25-29 | 4.5 | 13.0 | 26.7 | 31.3 | 27.7 |
| 30-34 | 3.8 | 10.5 | 20.2 | 25.1 | 25.9 |
| 35-44 | 2.7 | 6.7 | 14.9 | 17.2 | 18.1 |
| 45 and over | 0.9 | 2.8 | 3.9 | 4.5 | 5.0 |
| All aged 16 and over | 2.1 | 5.9 | 11.9 | 13.4 | 13.1 |

*Source: Office for National Statistics*

# 2.19

## Women remarrying[1]: by year, and length, of separation, 1993-1995[2]

**Great Britain**
Percentages

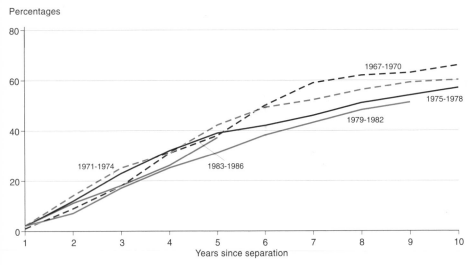

1 Percentage of women aged 16 to 59 who were under 35 when their first marriage ended in separation who had remarried.
2 Combined years: 1993-94, 1994-95.
**Source: General Household Survey, Office for National Statistics**

Recent data suggest that the trend in increasing divorce rates could have levelled out and this seems especially so for the younger age groups. In England and Wales, although divorce rates are highest among men aged 30 to 34 and women aged 25 to 29 (Table 2.18), reflecting the age differences at marriage, for both groups the rates have fallen since 1991.

Almost three quarters of decrees are granted to wives. The most common reason for women to be granted divorce is unreasonable behaviour; for men it is adultery. Reasons for divorce vary with age. For younger women, unreasonable behaviour is by far the most common fact proven for them to be granted a divorce. This remains the most common reason for women of all ages, as women get older, they are increasingly likely to divorce on grounds of adultery or after two years' separation. However, the proportion granted for these two grounds falls for women in their forties and fifties as separation after five years becomes more common. In 1993 8 per cent of divorces in the United Kingdom were of marriages that had lasted under three years. Nearly 30 per cent of divorces occurred in marriages that were between their fifth and ninth years.

In recent years, the number of divorces involving couples with children aged under 16 has risen. When people were interviewed in the 1994 BSAS, over half thought a married couple should not have to stay together if they didn't get along, even if there were children in the family. Also, over 90 per cent of respondents disagreed with the statement that it was better to have a bad marriage than no marriage at all.

Marriage is, however, not yet a dead institution - most people who separate do eventually remarry. For example, among women aged 16 to 59 who were under 35 when their first marriage ended in separation between 1967 and 1970, two thirds had remarried within ten years of their separation (Chart 2.19). The likelihood of remarriage after separation appears to be decreasing: around half of women who separated between 1967 and 1970 had remarried within six years, but only two fifths of those separated twelve years later had remarried within the same period. Men are even more likely than women to remarry following separation.

### Family building

Chart 1.10 in the Population chapter showed that overall fertility rates in the United Kingdom declined between 1964 and 1977. Although there was a slight increase after 1977, since the 1980s the rate has been fairly stable. However, the changes in fertility rates have been different for women of different ages (Chart 2.20). In general, rates for older women have increased since the early 1980s whilst those for younger women have declined. Women aged 25 to 29 are still the most likely to give birth, but since 1992 those in the 30 to 34 group have been more likely to give birth than those aged 20 to 24. There has recently been an increase in fertility rates for women in their forties, although births to these women still represent only a tiny proportion of all births.

Over the past decade there has been a rise in the rate of multiple births, from 10.1 per thousand maternities in 1984 to 13.2 in

1994. An increase in the use of fertility treatments is thought to be a reason for the rise in the rate of multiple births. Older women are more likely to experience multiple births. For women in their late thirties, multiple births accounted for around 20 in every thousand maternities in England and Wales in 1994, compared with less than seven in every thousand maternities for women aged under 20.

Whilst most women do eventually have children, there is a growing proportion of women who never have a child. In England and Wales less than 12 per cent of women born in 1944 were childless at age 35 compared with 20 per cent of those born in 1954 (Chart 2.21).

Fertility rates: by age

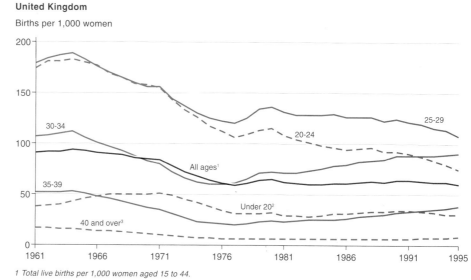

**United Kingdom**

Births per 1,000 women

1 Total live births per 1,000 women aged 15 to 44.
2 Live births to women aged under 20 per 1,000 women aged 15 to 19.
3 Live births to women aged over 40 per 1,000 women aged 40 to 44.
**Source: Office for National Statistics; General Register Office (Scotland); General Register Office (Northern Ireland)**

## 2.21

Women remaining childless: by age and birth cohort, 1994

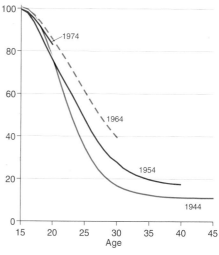

**England & Wales**

Percentages

**Source: Office for National Statistics**

# 2.22

### Percentage of live births outside marriage: by area, 1995

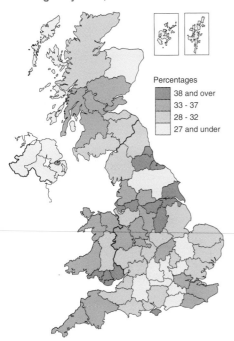

Percentages

- 38 and over
- 33 - 37
- 28 - 32
- 27 and under

*Source: Office for National Statistics; General Register Office (Scotland); General Register Office (Northern Ireland)*

Women are also delaying having children until later on in life. Whereas only 16 per cent of those born in 1944 were childless at age 30, over 38 per cent of those born in 1964 had no children at this age. This is partly due to women delaying having children and partly to not having children at all. The average age of a mother at the birth of her first child (inside or outside marriage) increased from 24.6 in 1981 to 26.5 in 1994.

Chart 2.1, at the beginning of this chapter, shows that out of all live births in England and Wales in 1995, over a third were outside marriage. This was four times the proportion in 1971. The rise in this proportion was particularly steep in the 1980s but may have slowed in more recent years. Despite the increase in births outside of marriage, there

is evidence to suggest that the majority of such births now occur within a stable relationship. Around four fifths were jointly registered by both parents in 1995. Of these, four fifths of the parents of were living together at the same address.

There are regional variations in the proportion of live births that are outside marriage. Merseyside had the highest proportion at 47 per cent of all live births in 1995 whilst the Southern Board of Northern Ireland had the lowest at 15 per cent (Chart 2.22). Indeed, with the exception of Belfast, the proportions were very low throughout Northern Ireland.

There were 802 thousand conceptions leading to either maternity or legal abortion in England and Wales in 1994, 50 thousand more than in 1981 but 33 thousand fewer than in 1971 (Table 2.23). In 1994, 81 per cent of these conceptions resulted in a maternity compared with 88 per cent in 1971. The proportion of conceptions within marriage has fallen from over three quarters in 1971 to around half in 1994.

The Longitudinal Study carried out by the Office for National Statistics links the results of the decennial censuses and event registration records for about 1 per cent of the population of England and Wales. It takes as its starting point a sample of records from the 1971 Census of England and Wales - all people born on one of four dates in any year. It showed that half of women in England and Wales who were unmarried at their first birth were married by the time their second child was born. For

# 2.23

### Conceptions: by marital status and outcome

| England & Wales | | | | | Percentages |
|---|---|---|---|---|---|
| | 1971 | 1981 | 1991 | 1993 | 1994 |
| **Inside marriage** | | | | | |
| Maternities | 72.6 | 65.9 | 51.9 | 51.2 | 50.1 |
| Legal abortions[1] | 5.2 | 5.6 | 4.4 | 4.3 | 4.3 |
| **Outside marriage** | | | | | |
| Maternities inside marriage | 8.1 | 5.5 | 3.7 | 3.5 | 3.3 |
| Maternities outside marriage[2] | | | | | |
| Joint registration | 3.5 | 6.8 | 18.9 | 20.2 | 21.2 |
| Sole registration | 4.1 | 4.8 | 6.0 | 6.0 | 6.0 |
| Legal abortions[1] | 6.7 | 11.4 | 15.0 | 14.9 | 15.2 |
| **All conceptions** (=100%)(thousands) | 835 | 752 | 854 | 819 | 802 |

1 Legal terminations under the 1967 Abortion Act.
2 Births outside marriage can be registered by one parent only, usually the mother, (sole registrations) or by both parents (joint registrations).

*Source: Office for National Statistics*

# 2.24

those who jointly registered a first birth outside of marriage, 44 per cent also jointly registered their second birth.

The proportion of teenage girls becoming pregnant fell during the 1970s but started to increase during the 1980s. Since reaching 65 per thousand women aged 13 to 19 in 1991, the teenage conception rate has decreased to 59 per thousand in England and Wales in 1994 (Table 2.24). Conception rates for girls under 16 fell from 9.3 per thousand girls aged 13 to 15 in 1991 to 8.3 per thousand in 1994. The Health of the Nation target for England is 4.8 per thousand girls aged 13 to 15 by the year 2000. In 1995 there was a total of 42 thousand live births to teenage girls in England and Wales compared with a total of 83 thousand in 1971.

The likelihood that a conception will lead to an abortion decreases as the age of the woman increases until around the age of 30 from when the likelihood starts to increase again (Chart 2.25). In 1994 over 50 per cent of conceptions led to abortions for those women aged under 16 and those aged 44 and over. Whereas for women in their late twenties and early thirties this was around 13 per cent. In 1993 a higher proportion of conceptions to women aged 17 to 31 ended in an abortion than ten years earlier but for those aged over 31 the proportion was lower. Most abortions are carried out in the very early stages of pregnancy. In England and Wales nearly nine in ten were carried out before 13 weeks gestation in 1993 while less than 2 per cent were carried out at 20 or more weeks gestation.

**Teenage conceptions: by age**

| England & Wales | | | | Rates per 1,000 women | |
|---|---|---|---|---|---|
| | 1971 | 1981 | 1991 | 1993 | 1994 |
| **Age at conception** | | | | | |
| Under 14[1] | 1.0 | 1.1 | 1.3 | 1.2 | 1.3 |
| 14 | 5.3 | 4.6 | 6.6 | 5.9 | 6.1 |
| 15 | 20.5 | 15.8 | 19.8 | 18.1 | 17.8 |
| All aged under 16[1] | 8.8 | 7.3 | 9.3 | 8.1 | 8.3 |
| 16 | 54.1 | 37.7 | 43.4 | 39.6 | 40.3 |
| 17 | 83.6 | 56.8 | 65.3 | 60.7 | 61.0 |
| 18 | 111.7 | 76.2 | 84.3 | 77.8 | 78.1 |
| 19 | 130.9 | 94.0 | 95.6 | 89.1 | 88.3 |
| All aged under 20[1] | 81.5 | 57.1 | 65.1 | 59.6 | 58.6 |

*1 Rates for girls aged under 14, under 16 and under 20 are based on the population of girls aged 13, 13 to 15, and 15 to 19 respectively.*
**Source: Office for National Statistics**

# 2.25

Conceptions leading to abortion[1]: by age of woman at conception, 1994

**England & Wales**
Percentages

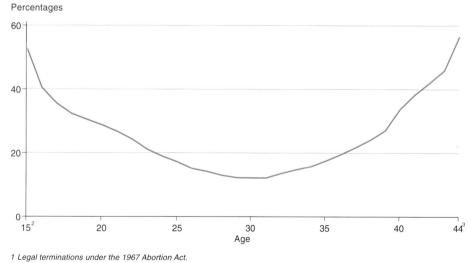

*1 Legal terminations under the 1967 Abortion Act.*
*2 Women aged under 16.*
*3 Women aged 44 and over.*
**Source: Office for National Statistics**

# 2.26

Abortions[1]: by marital status and age

| Great Britain | | | | | Percentages |
|---|---|---|---|---|---|
| | 1971 | 1981 | 1986 | 1991 | 1995 |
| **Single women** | | | | | |
| Under 16 | 4 | 4 | 4 | 3 | 3 |
| 16-19 | 36 | 39 | 34 | 27 | 23 |
| 20-34 | 56 | 55 | 60 | 67 | 69 |
| 35-44 | 2 | 2 | 2 | 3 | 4 |
| 45 and over | - | - | - | - | - |
| | | | | | |
| All abortions[2] (=100%)(thousands) | 63.4 | 96.4 | 115.2 | 127.6 | 116.3 |
| **Married women** | | | | | |
| 16-19 | 1 | 2 | 2 | 1 | 1 |
| 20-34 | 64 | 67 | 67 | 70 | 67 |
| 35-44 | 32 | 30 | 31 | 28 | 31 |
| 45 and over | 1 | 1 | 1 | 1 | 1 |
| | | | | | |
| All abortions[2] (=100%)(thousands) | 58.6 | 55.5 | 47.2 | 42.0 | 36.3 |
| **All women[3]** | | | | | |
| Under 16 | 2 | 2 | 3 | 2 | 2 |
| 16-19 | 18 | 23 | 22 | 19 | 16 |
| 20-34 | 61 | 61 | 63 | 68 | 69 |
| 35-44 | 17 | 13 | 12 | 11 | 12 |
| 45 and over | 1 | - | - | - | - |
| | | | | | |
| All abortions[2] (=100%)(thousands) | 133.1 | 171.5 | 181.9 | 190.6 | 173.6 |

1 Legal terminations under the 1967 Abortion Act.
2 Includes age not known.
3 Includes women who are widowed, divorced, separated or whose marital status is not known.

**Source: Office for National Statistics; National Health Service in Scotland**

Single women who conceive are much more likely to have an abortion than married women. The number of abortions in Great Britain to single women doubled between 1971 and 1991, but the number fell to 116 thousand in 1995 (Table 2.26). There were fewer abortions to married women in 1995 than in 1971. Women aged between 20 and 34 account for over two thirds of all abortions. Whilst the 35 to 44 age group was the next most common group to have an abortion for married women, it was the 16 to 19 age group that was the second most common group for single women. In response to a question asked in a survey carried out by MORI in August 1996, over eight out of ten respondents agreed that it was important for women to have the right to choose whether or not to continue with their pregnancy, but over half agreed that it was wrong for a women to have an abortion for purely social and not medical reasons.

The increase in abortions and lone parenthood has contributed to a fall in the number of children available for adoption. In the mid 1970s, adoption orders decreased quite sharply and there has been a general, but more gentle, decline since (Chart 2.27). There were over 6 thousand adoption orders in England and Wales in 1994. Children born outside marriage have always formed the majority of children adopted since 1971. However, the difference in the numbers of children born inside and outside marriage who were adopted was much less in 1994 than in 1971. There has also been a gradual trend towards the adoption of older children. In 1981 a quarter of all children adopted were under one year old, compared with only 6 per cent in 1994 when two thirds of all children adopted were aged five or over.

Another contributory factor to the fall in the number of children available for adoption has been the increase in the use of contraception. In order to prevent unwanted conceptions, 73 per cent of women aged 16 to 49 in Great Britain used some form of contraception in 1995-96 (Table 2.28). The pill was the most common form of contraception used, although slightly less so than in 1976. The proportions using some form of surgical contraception almost doubled between 1976 and 1995-96.

There were differences in the types of contraception used by women of different ages: younger women tend to use the pill while older women tend to use surgical methods. Around 45 per cent of women in their forties in Great Britain had been sterilised or had partners who had been sterilised. Sterilisation was also common among women who had had children and particularly those who already had as many children as they wanted.

Of those women who were not using any method of contraception, around half had no partner or were abstaining from sex and a quarter were either pregnant or said that they wanted to be. Only just over half of women aged 16 to 49 in Northern Ireland used some form of contraception and again the pill was the most common form of contraception used. The General Household Survey in 1993-94 also asked women if they had used emergency contraception. Just under one in ten single women said that they had done so in the two years prior to interview; the proportion for married women who had used emergency contraception was half that of single women.

Adoption orders

**England & Wales**
Thousands

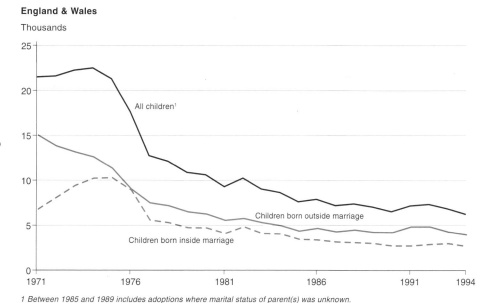

1 Between 1985 and 1989 includes adoptions where marital status of parent(s) was unknown.
**Source: Office for National Statistics**

Contraception[1]: by method used

| Great Britain | | Percentages |
|---|---|---|
| | 1976 | 1995-96 |
| **Non-surgical** | | |
| Pill | 29 | 25 |
| Male condom | 14 | 18 |
| IUD | 6 | 4 |
| Withdrawal | 5 | 3 |
| Cap | 2 | 1 |
| Safe period | 1 | 1 |
| Injection | .. | 1 |
| Spermicides | .. | - |
| **Surgical** | | |
| Female sterilisation | 7 | 12 |
| Male sterilisation | 6 | 11 |
| **At least one method** | 68 | 73 |

1 By women aged 16 to 49.
**Source: General Household Survey, Office for National Statistics**

## References and further reading

The following list contains selected publications relevant to **Chapter 2: Households and Families**. Those published by The Stationery Office are available from the addresses shown on the inside back cover of *Social Trends*.

*1991 Census Communal Establishments, Great Britain*, The Stationery Office

*Annual Report of the Registrar General for Northern Ireland*, The Stationery Office

*Annual Report of the Registrar General for Scotland*, General Register Office for Scotland

*Birth Statistics (Series FM1)*, The Stationery Office

*British Social Attitudes*, Dartmouth Publishing

*Changing Households: The British Household Panel Survey*, ESRC Research Centre on Micro-social Change

*General Household Survey*, The Stationery Office

*Housing in England 1994-95*, The Stationery Office

*Key Population and Vital Statistics (Series VS/PP1)*, The Stationery Office

*Marriage and Divorce Statistics (Series FM2)*, The Stationery Office

*Population Trends*, The Stationery Office

*Projections of Households in England to 2016*, The Stationery Office

*Regional Trends*, The Stationery Office

*Social Focus on Children*, The Stationery Office

*Social Focus on Ethnic Minorities*, The Stationery Office

*Social Focus on Women*, The Stationery Office

## Contacts

Telephone contact points for further information relating to
**Chapter 2: Households and Families**

| | |
|---|---|
| **Office for National Statistics** | |
| Chapter author | 0171 533 5778 |
| General Household Survey | 0171 533 5444 |
| Labour Force Survey | 0171 533 6180 |
| **Department of the Environment** | 0171 890 3303 |
| **General Register Office for Scotland** | 0131 314 4243 |
| **General Register Office (Northern Ireland)** | 01232 252031 |
| **National Health Service in Scotland** | 0131 551 8899 |
| **Northern Ireland Statistics and Research Agency** | |
| Census Office | 01232 526942 |
| Department of Finance and Personnel | 01232 252653 |
| **ESRC Research Centre on Micro-social Change** | 01206 872957 |
| **Eurostat** | 00 352 4335 2251 |
| **Social & Community Planning Research** | 0171 250 1866 extn 369 |

# Chapter 3 Education and Training

**Educational attainment**

Half of girls in their last year of compulsory schooling in England and Wales gained five or more GCSEs at or above grade C compared with two fifths of boys in 1994/95. (Chart 3.1)

Over 60 per cent of those who left full-time education by the age of 16 in Great Britain had low numeracy scores at the age of 37 compared with only 12 per cent of those who left at age 21 and over. (Table 3.3)

**School pupils and staffing**

Only 3 per cent of pupils in maintained primary schools attended a grant-maintained school in England in January 1996 compared with over 19 per cent of secondary pupils. (Chart 3.9)

More than four out of five nursery and primary school teachers were female in 1994/95. Women made up only half of head or deputy head teachers in primary schools. (Page 60)

**School curricula**

Virtually all pupils participate in physical education: 55 per cent of secondary school pupils in England spent over two hours a week in PE lessons in 1994. (Chart 3.12)

**Post-compulsory education**

In 1994/95 there were around twice as many enrolments by men for undergraduate courses in the United Kingdom compared with 1970/71 and just over four times as many enrolments by women. (Table 3.16)

**Adult education and training**

Well over 1 million adults in England and Wales were enrolled on courses at adult education centres in 1994/95. (Table 3.20)

People with higher qualifications are more likely to participate in job-related training than those with lower qualifications: 23 per cent of economically active people with higher educational qualifications trained in a four week period in Spring 1996. (Table 3.22)

## 3.1

**Examination results[1]:
by gender**

**England & Wales**

Percentages

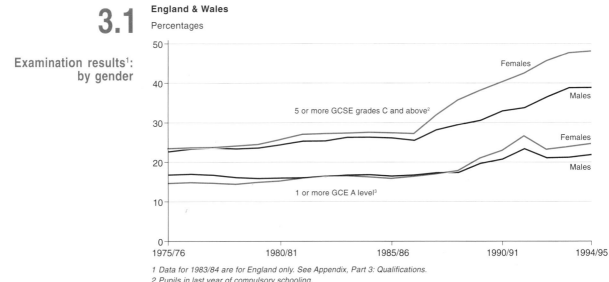

1 Data for 1983/84 are for England only. See Appendix, Part 3: Qualifications.
2 Pupils in last year of compulsory schooling.
3 Or equivalent.

**Source: Department for Education and Employment; Welsh Office**

The education and training which young people receive and the qualifications and skills which they acquire can have an important influence on their chances of leading successful working lives. However, education and training are not just important for young people: 'lifetime learning' is now essential for everyone.

## Educational attainment

School pupils in England and Wales are formally assessed at three key stages before GCSE level - at 7 (Key Stage 1), 11 (Key Stage 2) and 14 years old (Key Stage 3). The assessments at all three key stages cover the core subjects of English, mathematics and science (and Welsh in Welsh-speaking schools in Wales) with the intention of informing teachers and parents about the progress of individual pupils and to give a measure of performance of

schools. There are two forms of assessment: tests and teacher assessment. Pupils' attainment is shown as a level on the National Curriculum scale. A typical 7 year old is expected to achieve level two, a typical 11 year old level four and a typical 14 year old levels five to six. Among 7 year olds, girls outperformed boys in all areas of assessment in 1995 (Table 3.2). For 11 and 14 year olds, girls outperformed boys in English teacher assessments and tests, and mathematics teacher assessments.

There has been a general increase in examination attainment in the last 20 or so years. In England and Wales males were more likely than females to gain at least one GCE A level in 1975/76 (Chart 3.1). However, females have since caught up with and passed males, so that in 1994/95, 25 per cent of females gained at least one GCE A level compared with 22 per cent of males. At GCSE level 39 per cent of boys, in the last year of compulsory schooling, gained five or more GCSEs at or above grade C, compared with 48 per cent of girls in 1994/95. As the proportion of those gaining good examination results has increased, so the proportion of those who leave school with no formal qualifications has decreased. In 1975/76, 20 per cent of males and 18 per cent of females left school with no qualifications while in 1994/95 just 9 per cent of boys and 7 per cent of girls, in the last year of compulsory schooling, had no graded results.

Many people now choose to do National Vocational Qualifications (NVQs) rather than traditional A levels, enabling them to get qualified to the Foundation Target levels (see Appendix, Part 3: Foundation Targets). Foundation Target 1 stipulates that, by the year 2000, at least 85 per cent of those aged 19 to 21 should reach NVQ level 2 (equivalent to an Intermediate General

# 3.2

**Pupils reaching or exceeding expected standards[1]: by gender and age, 1995**

**England & Wales**                                                              Percentages

|  | Teacher assessment | | Tests | |
| --- | --- | --- | --- | --- |
|  | Boys | Girls | Boys | Girls |
| **7 year olds[2]** | | | | |
| English | 76 | 85 | . | . |
| Mathematics | 76 | 80 | 77 | 81 |
| Science | 83 | 85 | . | . |
| **11 year olds[3]** | | | | |
| English | 50 | 64 | 41 | 56 |
| Mathematics | 53 | 57 | 45 | 46 |
| Science | 64 | 65 | 71 | 69 |
| **14 year olds[4]** | | | | |
| English | 53 | 72 | 45 | 64 |
| Mathematics | 59 | 63 | 57 | 58 |
| Science | 59 | 61 | 57 | 54 |

1 See Appendix, Part 3: The National Curriculum: assessments and tests.
2 Percentage of pupils achieving level 2 or above at Key Stage 1.
3 Percentage of pupils achieving level 4 or above at Key Stage 2.
4 Percentage of pupils achieving level 5 or above at Key Stage 3.
**Source: Department for Education and Employment; Welsh Office**

# 3.3

National Vocational Qualification (GNVQ) or five GCSEs at grade C or above). Foundation Target 3 states that 60 per cent of 21 to 23 year olds should reach NVQ level 3 (equivalent to an Advanced GNVQ or two GCE A levels). Steady progress is being made towards reaching the NVQ level 3 target but progress towards the NVQ level 2 target has slowed.

At the other end of the attainment scale to those who meet or exceed the foundation learning targets are those who have difficulty with basic skills. In 1995 the National Child Development Study collected information on the basic skills levels of 37 year olds. This is a longitudinal study of 10 per cent of all people born in Great Britain in a single week in 1958, with data collected at birth, 7, 11, 16, 23, 33 and 37 years. It showed that in general, the earlier someone had left full-time education, the more likely they were to have problems with basic skills (Table 3.3). For example, over 60 per cent of those who left full-time education by the age of 16 had low numeracy scores compared with only 12 per cent of those who left at the age of 21 and over. Women tended to have lower numeracy levels than men, but there was not much difference between the genders for literacy. Overall, far fewer had low literacy scores than low numeracy scores.

## School pupils and staffing

Demographic factors are the main determinant of the number of children aged between 5 and 16 in schools. Parents can choose whether or not their child should attend school before the age of 5 and pupils can choose whether to stay at school beyond the age of 16. The results of these demographic and decision making factors can be seen in Table 3.4 which gives an

**Literacy and numeracy standards of 37 year olds: by age on leaving full-time education, 1995**

| Great Britain | | | | Percentages |
|---|---|---|---|---|
| | Low literacy[1] | High literacy[2] | Low numeracy[1] | High numeracy[2] |
| **Age on leaving full-time education** | | | | |
| Under 16 | 22 | 78 | 67 | 33 |
| 16 | 25 | 75 | 59 | 41 |
| 17-18 | 10 | 90 | 36 | 64 |
| 19-20 | 6 | 94 | 25 | 75 |
| 21 and over | 0 | 100 | 12 | 88 |
| All 37 year olds | 18 | 82 | 47 | 53 |

1 People generally not able to demonstrate skills above The Basic Skills Agency's foundation standard.
2 People generally able to demonstrate skills above The Basic Skills Agency's foundation standard.

*Source: City University, from the National Child Development Study*

# 3.4

**School pupils[1]: by type of school[2]**

| United Kingdom | | | | | Thousands |
|---|---|---|---|---|---|
| | 1970/71 | 1980/81 | 1990/91 | 1994/95 | 1995/96[3] |
| **Public sector schools[4]** | | | | | |
| Nursery[5] | 50 | 89 | 105 | 85 | 84 |
| Primary[5] | 5,902 | 5,171 | 4,955 | 5,255 | 5,335 |
| Secondary | | | | | |
| Modern | 1,164 | 233 | 94 | 90 | 79 |
| Grammar | 673 | 149 | 156 | 184 | 182 |
| Comprehensive[6] | 1,313 | 3,730 | 2,844 | 3,093 | 3,130 |
| Other secondary | 403 | 434 | 300 | 289 | 280 |
| All public sector schools | 9,507 | 9,806 | 8,433 | 8,996 | 9,096 |
| **Non-maintained schools[4]** | | | | | |
| Pupils aged 10 and under | 238 | .. | 266 | 262 | 268 |
| Pupils aged 11 and over | 383 | .. | 347 | 338 | 335 |
| All non-maintained schools | 621 | 619 | 613 | 600 | 603 |
| **Special schools[7]** | 103 | 148 | 114 | 116 | 114 |
| **All schools** | 10,230 | 10,572 | 9,180 | 9,714 | 9,813 |

1 Headcounts.
2 See Appendix, Part 3: Main categories of educational establishments and Stages of education.
3 Data for Wales are for 1994/95.
4 Excludes special schools.
5 Nursery classes within primary schools are included in primary schools except for Scotland in 1990/91 when they are included in nursery schools.
6 Excludes sixth form colleges from 1980/81 for England and from 1994/95 for Wales.
7 Includes maintained and non-maintained sectors.

*Source: Department for Education and Employment; Welsh Office; The Scottish Office Education and Industry Department; Department of Education, Northern Ireland*

# 3.5

**Children under five[1] in schools as a percentage of all children aged three and four**

**United Kingdom**

Percentages

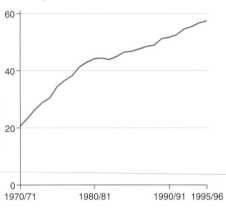

*1 Pupils aged 3 and 4 at 31 December each year.*

*Source: Department for Education and Employment; Welsh Office; The Scottish Office Education and Industry Department; Department of Education, Northern Ireland*

# 3.6

**Class sizes[1] in public sector schools: by type of school**

England · Percentages

| | 1980/81 | 1985/86 | 1990/91 | 1994/95 | 1995/96 |
|---|---|---|---|---|---|
| **Primary schools** | | | | | |
| 1-10 pupils | 1.5 | 1.0 | 0.5 | 0.4 | 0.4 |
| 11-20 pupils | 10.0 | 9.2 | 6.7 | 4.8 | 4.5 |
| 21-30 pupils | 58.9 | 63.7 | 67.3 | 65.3 | 63.3 |
| 31 or more pupils | 29.6 | 26.1 | 25.5 | 29.6 | 31.7 |
| | | | | | |
| Number of classes (thousands) | 155 | 133 | 136 | 144 | 145 |
| Average number in class | 25 | 26 | 26 | 27 | 27 |
| **Secondary schools[2]** | | | | | |
| 1-10 pupils | 3.8 | 4.1 | 3.6 | 2.9 | 2.8 |
| 11-20 pupils | 25.6 | 27.2 | 28.1 | 21.7 | 21.0 |
| 21-30 pupils | 57.7 | 58.7 | 62.0 | 68.0 | 67.7 |
| 31 or more pupils | 13.0 | 10.0 | 6.3 | 7.3 | 8.5 |
| | | | | | |
| Number of classes (thousands) | 170 | 150 | 124 | 127 | 128 |
| Average number in class | 21 | 20 | 20 | 22 | 22 |

*1 Related to one selected period in each public sector school on the day of the count in January. One teacher classes only. See Appendix, Part 3: Pupil/teacher ratios.*
*2 Excludes sixth form colleges.*

*Source: Department for Education and Employment*

overview of the schools sector. Between 1970/71 and 1990/91, the number of pupils attending state nursery schools more than doubled, although the numbers have declined since then. There has been an shift over the last quarter of a century in the types of school that pupils attend after primary school. In 1995/96, 85 per cent of pupils in state secondary schools attended comprehensive schools, compared with 37 per cent in 1970/71. Between 1970/71 and 1995/96 the numbers in non-maintained schools declined slightly. The *Education Act 1981* and the *Education Act 1993* placed a qualified duty on local education authorities in England and Wales to ensure that children with Special Educational Needs (SEN) should have their needs met wherever possible in mainstream schools. In

Scotland, educational authorities are also encouraged to integrate children with SEN into mainstream schools wherever possible. This has resulted in a drop in the number of pupils attending special schools. The number of pupils with statements of SEN in public sector schools, other than special or hospital schools, more than doubled between 1989/90 and 1994/95.

In 1970/71 around 20 per cent of three and four year olds in the United Kingdom attended schools. By 1995/96 this had risen to over 57 per cent (Chart 3.5). Much of this increase has been due to children attending part time. The Government has introduced a new scheme to secure, over time, universal nursery education for four year olds. Parents of every four year old will be entitled to vouchers worth £1,100 for three terms of nursery education. They will be able to use their vouchers at any provider in either the state, private or voluntary sector which is registered to take part in the scheme. The scheme has been in operation in four pilot areas - Kensington and Chelsea, Wandsworth, Westminster and Norfolk - since April 1996. It will be implemented across England and Wales from April 1997.

There is some dispute about the educational significance of average class size and pupil/teacher ratios but these are widely regarded by parents as key indicators of the quality of education. Overall, the average size of primary and secondary school classes remained quite stable between 1980/81 and 1995/96 (Table 3.6). However, while in primary schools the proportion of pupils in classes with 31 or more pupils has remained quite steady, there has been a move away from smaller classes. Secondary school classes are usually smaller than primary school ones due to the increased subject specialisation of pupils. In 1994/95 the pupil/ teacher ratio for public sector schools was around twice that for non-maintained schools at 19 and 10 pupils per teacher respectively.

The Youth Lifestyles Survey, carried out by the Home Office between November 1992 and January 1993, asked secondary school pupils aged 14 and over in England and Wales what they thought of school. Nearly three quarters of respondents said that they liked it either a little or a lot (Chart 3.7). The survey also asked what pupils expected to do once they left school - over seven in ten thought that they would stay in some form of education, while one in seven thought that they would get a job straight away. Only 1 per cent of respondents expected to join a Youth Training Scheme. The survey discovered that pupils had an inflated opinion of their own school work, with over nine in ten saying that their work was average or better than average; 45 per cent said that their work was above or well above average.

In 1995 the British Social Attitudes Survey, carried out by Social and Community Planning Research, asked adults what they thought about changes in aspects of state secondary schools over the last ten years. Just under two fifths of respondents thought that school leavers were better qualified than ten years previously, compared with just under three in ten who thought they were less qualified; two fifths thought that teachers were better paid than ten years previously. On a less positive note, around three quarters thought that classroom behaviour was worse in 1995 than in 1985 and nearly 40 per cent thought that the standard of teaching had got worse over the same period.

Another way in which schools' performance is measured is in the amount of absence taken by pupils. Unauthorised absence is a problem for both schools and the wider community. It can lead to poor performance at school and disadvantage in later life. For all schools, the average amount of time missed due to unauthorised absence remained stable between 1993/94 and 1995/96. Special schools have the highest average number of both authorised and unauthorised half days missed per absent pupil (Table 3.8). Unauthorised absence is defined as absence without permission from a teacher or other authorised representative of the school. This includes all unexplained or unjustified absences from school.

In recent years there have been considerable changes in the administrative and financial structures of schools. Public sector schools are allowed to apply for grant-maintained status, if this has been approved by a ballot of parents at the school

**Pupils' attitudes towards school[1], 1994-1995[2]**

**England & Wales**
Percentages

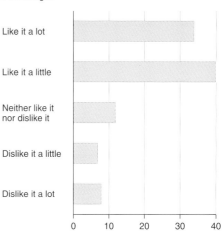

1 Pupils aged 14 and over in secondary school.
2 November 1994 to January 1995.
*Source: Youth Lifestyles Survey, Home Office*

# 3.8

**Absence from school: by type of school, 1995/96**

England

| | Authorised absence | | Unauthorised absence | |
|---|---|---|---|---|
| | Average number of half days missed per absent pupil | Percentage of half days missed by all pupils | Average number of half days missed per absent pupil | Percentage of half days missed by all pupils |
| Maintained primary | 20 | 6.0 | 10 | 0.5 |
| Maintained secondary | 28 | 8.4 | 21 | 1.0 |
| Special schools | 30 | 8.8 | 27 | 2.7 |
| City technology colleges | 22 | 6.6 | 6 | 0.2 |
| Independent schools | 13 | 3.8 | 8 | 0.1 |
| All schools | 23 | 6.9 | 15 | 0.7 |

*Source: Department for Education and Employment*

# 3.9

**Percentage of pupils in public sector schools with grant-maintained status[1]**

**England**

Percentages

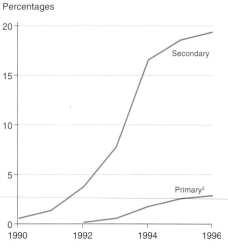

1 At January each year. Excludes sixth form colleges.
2 Data prior to 1992 are negligible.

**Source: Department for Education and Employment**

in question. When a school gets grant-maintained status, its governing body takes complete responsibility for management and is directly accountable to parents, leaving the local education authority with only a very limited role to play in the school's affairs. In January 1996, while only 3 per cent of primary school pupils attended a public sector grant-maintained school in England, over 19 per cent of secondary pupils did so **(Chart 3.9)**. The total number of primary schools in England which had grant-maintained status in 1995/96 was 448, and there were 642 grant-maintained secondary schools. In Wales in 1995/96, less than half of 1 per cent of primary schools and 5 per cent of secondary schools had grant-maintained status.

More than four out of five nursery and primary teachers in the United Kingdom in 1994/95 were female, with over half of these being aged between 35 and 49 **(Table 3.10)**. In secondary schools there is a much more

even gender balance. Women made up around half of heads or deputy heads in primary schools and less than a third of such grades in secondary schools. On average, in 1992/93 female nursery and primary school teachers earned nearly £3,000 per year less than their male counterparts. In nursery and primary schools in England and Wales, there were slightly more female teachers in 1994/95 than in 1980/81; however there were around a quarter fewer male teachers. For secondary school teachers, there were around 30 per cent fewer men in 1994/95 than in 1980/81 and 12 per cent fewer women. Overall there were 62 thousand fewer teachers in 1994/95 than in 1980/81.

## School curricula

The National Curriculum applies to primary and secondary schools in England and Wales. Its introduction has been phased over the period since 1989 and will not be completed until the late 1990s. In England, the following subjects are included: English, mathematics, science, design technology, information technology, physical education, modern languages, geography, history, art and music. However, modern languages are not required in primary schools and the last four subjects are not required after the third year of secondary schooling. In Wales, Welsh is now compulsory in primary schools and will be in all secondary schools from 1999. In addition, statutory requirements for some subjects are different in secondary schools in Wales.

Unlike England and Wales, there is no national curriculum in Scotland. Pupils aged 5 to 14 study a broad curriculum based on national guidelines which set out the aims of study, the ground to be covered, the way pupils should be assessed and the reports

# 3.10

**Full-time teachers: by type of school, gender and age, 1994/95**

**United Kingdom**      Thousands

|  | Nursery and primary | | Secondary | |
|---|---|---|---|---|
|  | Males | Females | Males | Females |
| Under 25 | 0.8 | 8.9 | 2.1 | 4.5 |
| 25-29 | 3.0 | 23.2 | 8.1 | 13.8 |
| 30-34 | 3.5 | 15.4 | 10.2 | 13.1 |
| 35-39 | 4.2 | 19.4 | 15.4 | 17.0 |
| 40-44 | 8.0 | 36.8 | 25.3 | 23.4 |
| 45-49 | 9.1 | 37.8 | 27.0 | 22.0 |
| 50-54 | 4.6 | 21.3 | 13.9 | 12.6 |
| 55-59 | 1.8 | 10.8 | 6.1 | 5.5 |
| 60 and over | 0.5 | 2.1 | 1.4 | 1.0 |
| All ages | 35.6 | 175.7 | 109.5 | 113.0 |

**Source: Department for Education and Employment; Welsh Office; The Scottish Office Education and Industry Department; Department of Education, Northern Ireland**

parents should receive. Those aged 14 and over take courses leading to awards in the Scottish Certificate of Education at Standard grade and Higher grade and/or SCOTVEC modules. They can also take the Certificate of Sixth Year Studies in their final year.

Little information is available on the time school pupils spend on the various subjects covered by the National Curriculum. The main source of information on the subjects they study is the GCSE records. This shows the wide variety of subjects available for pupils to choose to study at GCSE level and some of the most common are shown in Table 3.11. In 1994/95 the greatest number of attempts in Great Britain was in mathematics, followed by English. While the three traditional science subjects (biology, chemistry and physics) all had very high proportions of attempts leading to a good pass (grade C or above), the majority of science GCSE attempts were in the science single or double awards - there were 585 thousand attempts in these compared with a total of 186 thousand attempts in the traditional science subjects.

Overall, a similar number of boys and girls attempted a GCSE in 1994/95, although there were differences between the genders in the subjects that they attempted. Craft, design and technology was attempted by nearly three times as many boys as girls and home economics was attempted by nearly seven times as many girls as boys. For the majority of subjects girls were more likely than boys to achieve a grade C or above. The pattern was much the same for A levels, although there was a smaller difference between the genders in those achieving grades A to C. The most commonly attempted GCE A level in England and Wales was social studies followed by mathematics and English literature.

GCSE[1] attempts and achievements[2]: by gender and selected subject, 1994/95

**Great Britain**

| | Number of attempts (thousands) | | | Achieving grades C and above (percentages) | | |
|---|---|---|---|---|---|---|
| | Males | Females | All | Males | Females | All |
| Science double award | 239.4 | 237.7 | 477.1 | 49 | 50 | 50 |
| Science single award | 52.7 | 54.9 | 107.6 | 38 | 44 | 41 |
| Biological science | 31.2 | 32.4 | 63.6 | 81 | 78 | 79 |
| Chemistry | 36.5 | 26.2 | 62.7 | 85 | 86 | 86 |
| Physics | 39.5 | 20.1 | 59.5 | 87 | 88 | 87 |
| Other science | 14.8 | 9.6 | 24.4 | 34 | 33 | 34 |
| Mathematics | 336.8 | 333.0 | 669.8 | 45 | 44 | 44 |
| Design and technology[3] | 147.6 | 152.9 | 300.5 | 33 | 49 | 41 |
| Business studies | 50.7 | 55.0 | 105.6 | 45 | 54 | 50 |
| Craft, design and technology | 56.8 | 21.4 | 78.2 | 42 | 54 | 45 |
| Computer studies | 22.2 | 14.2 | 36.3 | 51 | 56 | 53 |
| Information systems[3] | 21.9 | 12.2 | 34.0 | 45 | 51 | 47 |
| Geography | 173.1 | 131.3 | 304.4 | 48 | 54 | 51 |
| History | 125.8 | 133.9 | 259.7 | 50 | 57 | 54 |
| Art and design | 111.8 | 111.1 | 222.9 | 47 | 65 | 56 |
| Religious studies | 39.1 | 60.1 | 99.2 | 47 | 59 | 54 |
| Home economics | 7.5 | 51.2 | 58.7 | 20 | 42 | 39 |
| Economics | 8.2 | 4.0 | 12.2 | 57 | 58 | 57 |
| English | 330.0 | 320.4 | 650.4 | 48 | 65 | 56 |
| English literature | 223.1 | 243.3 | 466.4 | 55 | 69 | 62 |
| Modern languages | | | | | | |
| French | 186.7 | 211.7 | 398.4 | 41 | 55 | 48 |
| German | 71.0 | 80.5 | 151.4 | 46 | 61 | 54 |
| Spanish | 15.3 | 22.9 | 38.2 | 44 | 59 | 53 |
| Other languages | 16.3 | 21.3 | 37.7 | 60 | 71 | 66 |
| Physical education | 56.8 | 29.3 | 86.0 | 47 | 46 | 47 |
| Drama | 29.1 | 45.3 | 74.4 | 60 | 74 | 69 |
| Any subject | 384.9 | 378.9 | 763.7 | 69 | 77 | 73 |

1 SCE (S grade) in Scotland.
2 By pupils of all ages in all schools. Only the attempt achieving the highest grade is counted, although some double counting may occur if a student attempts more than one subject within a category.
3 Data are for England only.

**Source: Department for Education and Employment; Welsh Office; The Scottish Office Education and Industry Department**

# 3.12

Average time spent in PE lessons per week by primary and secondary school pupils, 1994

**England**

Percentages

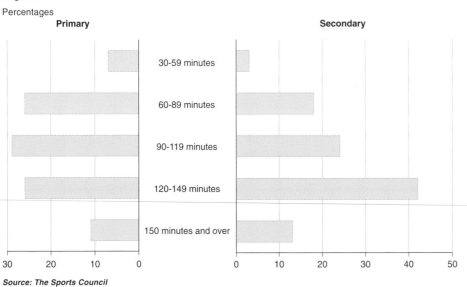

Source: The Sports Council

# 3.13

Time spent using computer software in secondary schools[1]: by year group and type of software, 1994

**England** Percentages

| | Year group | | | | | | | | |
|---|---|---|---|---|---|---|---|---|---|
| | 5 | 6 | 7 | 8 | 9 | 10 | 11 | 12 | 13 |
| Word processing | 46 | 30 | 34 | 32 | 29 | 33 | 39 | 32 | 36 |
| Data handling | 11 | 16 | 14 | 16 | 18 | 19 | 16 | 20 | 17 |
| Desk top publishing | 7 | 6 | 8 | 9 | 10 | 9 | 9 | 9 | 9 |
| Computer-aided drafting or design | 7 | 17 | 11 | 11 | 9 | 10 | 9 | 8 | 8 |
| Computer-aided musical composition | 5 | 2 | 3 | 4 | 4 | 5 | 6 | 5 | 6 |
| Simulation (eg business games) | 2 | 5 | 4 | 4 | 5 | 5 | 3 | 4 | 4 |
| Control or measurement of physical processes | 5 | 4 | 4 | 4 | 5 | 4 | 3 | 4 | 4 |
| Practice exercises and puzzles | 12 | 16 | 16 | 13 | 10 | 6 | 5 | 3 | 4 |
| Programming | 2 | 2 | 2 | 2 | 1 | 1 | 1 | 3 | 3 |
| Other software | 3 | 2 | 4 | 5 | 7 | 8 | 9 | 11 | 10 |
| All computer software | 100 | 100 | 100 | 100 | 100 | 100 | 100 | 100 | 100 |

1 Including middle deemed secondary schools.

Source: 1994 Survey of IT in Schools, Department for Education and Employment

Physical education (PE) plays an important part in the National Curriculum. The Young People and Sport in England Survey was carried out in 1994 by the Sports Council and found that 55 per cent of secondary pupils spent over two hours a week in PE lessons (**Chart 3.12**). Virtually all pupils participate in PE and 18 per cent of those in secondary years 10 and 11 were studying it at GCSE level. For primary schools, gym was the most frequent type of PE activity undertaken at least ten times in lessons, followed by swimming, while in secondary schools the most frequent activity was athletics, followed by hockey.

As might be expected, boys and girls participated to a different extent in some sporting activities: for example, among primary pupils, 35 per cent of boys participated in football at least ten times in lessons compared with only 8 per cent of girls. The differences are even greater in secondary schools, where netball was the top-ranked sport for girls, with 43 per cent of girls participating compared with only 2 per cent of boys.

Most pupils (around nine in ten) said that they enjoyed sport in school lessons although boys tended to enjoy sport more than girls. Also, enjoyment of sport tended to decrease as the age of pupils increased. The health and fitness message was well known to children, with over nine in ten agreeing that it was important to keep fit. Girls were more likely than boys to mind about certain aspects of sport, such as going outside for sport in bad weather or getting hot, sweaty or dirty. Those enjoyed most in lessons were those which had the highest participation rates outside lessons. Participation in sports by pupils in their leisure time is looked at in Chart 13.21 in the Lifestyles chapter.

# 3.14

The National Curriculum also attaches importance to the use of computers in schools. In secondary schools, word processing was the most common form of use in England in 1994, with 39 per cent of pupils' time using computers being spent for this purpose in year 11 (Table 3.13). The ratio of pupils to computers has been falling in recent years. In primary schools in 1993/94, there were 18 pupils per computer compared with 107 in 1984/85. Secondary schools had an even lower ratio with ten pupils per computer in 1993/94 compared with 60 in 1984/85. In 1994 there were ten computers per primary school and 85 per secondary school on average. In primary schools, 44 per cent of computers were over five years old in 1993/94 whilst 37 per cent were over five years old in secondary schools. The main source of funding for computer equipment in schools is through the annual Grants for Education Support and Training (GEST). It is, however, open to schools to take advantage of other sources of funding, such as those offered by supermarket schemes or other Government or privately funded initiatives.

Many schools form links with businesses in their area, both to help prepare pupils for the world of work and to provide advice, equipment and other such help. In England in 1994/95, 58 per cent of primary schools and 92 per cent of secondary schools had links or contacts with local businesses, additional to those contacts made through work experience schemes. For primary schools, the most common forms of practical help from local businesses were donations of cash and equipment, each reported by 19 per cent of schools (Table 3.14). For secondary schools, technical advice was the most common form of practical help, with just over half of schools reporting that they had received this. Other kinds of link activity

besides practical help included visits to business premises by pupils and talks in schools by the business community.

Another way in which local businesses help schools is by allowing work experience placements at their premises. Almost all secondary schools were involved in such placements and two thirds of secondary schools reported that work experience had contributed to assessed GCSE course work.

## Post-compulsory education

The main choices that people can make after reaching the minimum school leaving age of 16 are to remain in education, go into training or seek employment. In recent years there has been a strong trend towards remaining in full-time education. Around three quarters of those aged between 16 and 18 in England were in education and training at the end of 1995 (Table 3.15). While the proportion of 16 year olds in

**Percentage of schools with links with local businesses, 1994/95**

| England | | Percentages |
|---|---|---|
| | Primary | Secondary |
| Technical advice | 14 | 52 |
| Donations of cash | 19 | 47 |
| Donations of equipment | 19 | 44 |
| Staff development | 8 | 38 |
| Provision of specialist equipment | 9 | 28 |
| Management training | 3 | 14 |
| Other kinds of links | 15 | 33 |
| Any kind of link | 58 | 92 |

*Source: Department for Education and Employment*

# 3.15

**Young people in education and training: by gender and age[1]**

| England | | | | | | Percentages |
|---|---|---|---|---|---|---|
| | 1990 | 1991 | 1992 | 1993 | 1994 | 1995 |
| **Males** | | | | | | |
| 16 | 82 | 85 | 85 | 87 | 88 | 85 |
| 17 | 76 | 76 | 77 | 78 | 77 | 78 |
| 18 | 50 | 54 | 60 | 60 | 62 | 60 |
| All males aged 16-18 | 68 | 71 | 73 | 75 | 76 | 75 |
| **Females** | | | | | | |
| 16 | 84 | 88 | 89 | 90 | 90 | 88 |
| 17 | 68 | 74 | 77 | 80 | 79 | 80 |
| 18 | 42 | 44 | 51 | 57 | 56 | 59 |
| All females aged 16-18 | 64 | 68 | 72 | 75 | 75 | 76 |

1 Age at end of August. Data are at end of each year.
*Source: Department for Education and Employment*

# 3.16

Enrolments[1] in further and higher education: by type of course and gender

**United Kingdom**                                                                                                      Thousands

| | Males | | | | Females | | | |
|---|---|---|---|---|---|---|---|---|
| | 1970/71 | 1980/81 | 1990/91 | 1994/95 | 1970/71 | 1980/81 | 1990/91 | 1994/95 |
| **Further education** | | | | | | | | |
|     - Full time | 116 | 154 | 219 | 375 | 95 | 196 | 261 | 393 |
|     - Part time | 891 | 697 | 768 | 735 | 630 | 624 | 986 | 1104 |
| **Higher education** | | | | | | | | |
| Undergraduate - Full time | 241 | 277 | 345 | 513 | 173 | 196 | 319 | 511 |
|     - Part time | 127 | 176 | 193 | 210 | 19 | 71 | 148 | 273 |
| Postgraduate - Full time | 33 | 41 | 50 | 74 | 10 | 21 | 34 | 56 |
|     - Part time | 15 | 32 | 50 | 92 | 3 | 13 | 36 | 84 |

1 Home and overseas students. Excludes adult education centres. Includes Open University for higher education and for 1980/81.

*Source: Department for Education and Employment; Welsh Office; The Scottish Office Education and Industry Department; Department of Education, Northern Ireland*

# 3.17

Enrolments on further education courses leading to a qualification: by type of course and gender, 1994/95

**United Kingdom**                                                              Thousands

| | Full time | | Part time | |
|---|---|---|---|---|
| | Males | Females | Males | Females |
| **NVQs[1]** | | | | |
|   Level 1 | 13.9 | 6.9 | 40.7 | 26.0 |
|   Level 2 | 25.7 | 34.4 | 62.4 | 54.1 |
|   Level 3 | 10.0 | 12.7 | 35.0 | 27.8 |
| **GNVQs[1]** | | | | |
|   Foundation | 2.2 | 3.4 | 0.3 | 0.9 |
|   Intermediate | 22.4 | 22.3 | 1.8 | 2.3 |
|   Advanced | 34.6 | 39.0 | 3.4 | 3.6 |
| Other vocational qualifications[2] | 139.8 | 139.5 | 256.2 | 371.1 |
| GCE A level/AS exam[3] | 76.3 | 91.0 | 50.2 | 76.7 |
| GCSE[4] | 13.1 | 11.8 | 50.7 | 88.8 |
| All courses leading to specified qualifications | 338.0 | 361.0 | 500.8 | 651.3 |
| All courses leading to unspecified qualifications | 30.3 | 27.2 | 222.1 | 430.4 |
| All further education courses | 368.3 | 388.3 | 723.0 | 1,081.7 |

1 GNVQ/NVQ split is not available for Northern Ireland. Data are included in Other vocational qualifications.
2 Includes GSVQs and SVQs in Scotland and GNVQs/NVQs in Northern Ireland.
3 Includes SCE Higher grades.
4 Includes SCE Standard grades.

*Source: Department for Education and Employment; Welsh Office; The Scottish Office Education and Industry Department; Department of Education, Northern Ireland*

education and training increased only slightly between the end of 1990 and 1995, the proportion of 18 year olds increased more, especially for females.

At the start of the 1990s there was rapid growth in enrolments in further and higher education. Between 1990/91 and 1994/95 the number of students enrolled in full-time higher education in the United Kingdom increased by 55 per cent and the numbers in full-time further education by 60 per cent (Table 3.16). For undergraduate courses, in 1994/95 there were around twice as many enrolments by men than in 1970/71 and just over four times as many enrolments by women. Indeed, in 1994/95 more women enrolled on undergraduate courses than men. The increase in enrolments on postgraduate courses by women has been even sharper with an increase of over ten times between 1970/71 and 1994/95.

# 3.18

Many people choose to enrol on further education courses to improve their qualification levels. In 1994/95 over 2.5 million people enrolled on full or part-time further education courses leading to a qualification in the United Kingdom (Table 3.17). Part-time courses had many more enrolments than full-time courses and women were more likely than men to enrol, especially for part-time courses. Of the courses that lead to a specified qualification, vocational qualifications were the most popular and those enrolled on a GNVQ or A level course were more likely to be studying full time than part time. A higher proportion of full-time courses led to a specified qualification than part-time ones, with 92 per cent of enrolments on full-time courses leading to a specified qualification compared with 64 per cent of part-time course enrolments. Of those who enrolled on further education courses in 1994/95, there were over twice as many aged over 19 than aged between 16 and 18.

In the United Kingdom, 'human sciences' was the most common subject category for first degree awards in 1992 and this was true for most of the other countries shown in Table 3.18. Information from the OECD also suggests that, in general, across almost all countries, a higher proportion of men than women graduate in science, engineering, and law and business whilst the opposite is true for the medical sciences and human sciences. Nearly 30 per cent of degrees awarded in 1992 in the United Kingdom were in subjects that were classified as science-based, the third highest in the

European Union (EU) after the former Federal Republic of Germany and Belgium. The proportion of mathematics and computing degrees awarded in the United Kingdom was the highest in the EU. The United Kingdom also has the highest proportion of science graduates amongst its labour force aged between 25 and 34 compared with other EU countries.

Around two fifths of graduates entered permanent UK employment in 1994, the proportion, although rising slightly in the most recent year, has dropped by a fifth

**First degree awards: by subject, international comparison, 1992**

Percentages

|  | Medical science | Natural and physical science | Engineering and architecture | Law and business | Human sciences | All subjects |
|---|---|---|---|---|---|---|
| Belgium | 12.8 | 12.1 | 23.9 | 29.3 | 21.9 | 100 |
| Denmark | 14.2 | 8.2 | 16.6 | 20.0 | 40.9 | 100 |
| Germany[1] | 11.7 | 17.6 | 22.2 | 24.7 | 23.7 | 100 |
| Greece | 10.5 | 16.8 | 13.7 | 12.4 | 46.6 | 100 |
| Irish Republic | 5.8 | 19.2 | 12.4 | 16.8 | 45.8 | 100 |
| Italy | 25.1 | 12.2 | 11.4 | 27.1 | 22.8 | 100 |
| Netherlands | 15.6 | 9.7 | 16.0 | 20.5 | 38.1 | 100 |
| Spain | 13.4 | 10.4 | 9.7 | 25.3 | 41.2 | 100 |
| Sweden | 17.1 | 12.0 | 16.6 | 23.4 | 31.0 | 100 |
| United Kingdom | 6.8 | 17.1 | 15.2 | 21.8 | 39.1 | 100 |
| Australia | 11.5 | 14.9 | 7.3 | 24.7 | 41.5 | 100 |
| Canada | 6.7 | 12.0 | 7.0 | 22.6 | 51.7 | 100 |
| Japan | 5.3 | 7.3 | 21.6 | 39.4 | 26.3 | 100 |
| New Zealand | 6.2 | 11.7 | 5.1 | 23.4 | 51.6 | 100 |
| United States | 7.1 | 10.3 | 8.1 | 27.3 | 47.3 | 100 |

1 Former Federal Republic.

*Source: OECD*

# 3.19

## Destination of first degree graduates

| United Kingdom | | | | Percentages |
|---|---|---|---|---|
| | Year of graduation | | | |
| | 1986[1] | 1991 | 1993 | 1994 |
| UK employment | | | | |
| Permanent | 50 | 39 | 39 | 41 |
| Temporary | 3 | 5 | 6 | 6 |
| Overseas employment[2] | 2 | 3 | 2 | 2 |
| Further education or training | 19 | 20 | 21 | 19 |
| Believed unemployed | 7 | 10 | 10 | 8 |
| Other destinations[3] | 6 | 10 | 10 | 10 |
| Unknown | 14 | 13 | 12 | 14 |
| All first degree graduates (=100%)(thousands) | 112.4 | 135.9 | 165.0 | 189.3 |

1 Data are for Great Britain only.
2 Home students only.
3 Includes overseas graduates leaving the United Kingdom and graduates not available for employment.
**Source: Department for Education and Employment**

since 1986, while temporary employment has become more common (**Table 3.19**). Around one in five graduates went on to further education or training in 1994, a proportion which has changed little since 1986. A slightly higher proportion of women graduates than men entered employment in 1994 and women were also marginally more likely to stay in education or training after their first degree.

Not all those people who begin their first degree manage to complete it. The proportion of those 'dropping out' has fluctuated at around 16 per cent for the last decade or so though with some increase evident over the period. In 1994 the British Social Attitudes Survey asked people how important they thought it was that universities should aim to develop certain qualities in their students. Nearly half of respondents thought that it was essential that people leaving university should be able to speak and write clearly. Other skills regarded as essential or very important included skills and knowledge which would help those leaving university to get a good job (88 per cent) and knowledge that would equip them for life in general (81 per cent).

## Adult education and training

There is a wide variety of day and evening courses on which adults can enrol - academic, vocational and leisure. Around 1.1 million adults in England and Wales were enrolled on courses in adult education centres in 1994/95 (**Table 3.20**). The many general courses that are available to adults cover subject areas as diverse as holiday French, yoga, machine knitting, motor maintenance, pre-retirement courses and British Sign Language. Enrolment rates are generally higher for women than men and are highest in the South East. In 1994 the lowest enrolment rate for both men and women was in Yorkshire and Humberside. Other opportunities for adults to further their academic education include the Open

# 3.20

## Enrolments on adult education centre courses: by type of course, gender and age, 1994/95

| England & Wales | | | | | | | Thousands |
|---|---|---|---|---|---|---|---|
| | Academic | | Vocational | | Other[1] | | |
| | Males | Females | Males | Females | Males | Females | All enrolments |
| 16-18 | 2.9 | 4.9 | 1.3 | 4.8 | 15.4 | 22.4 | 51.7 |
| 19 and over | 17.6 | 44.5 | 31.0 | 97.9 | 231.9 | 641.4 | 1,064.3 |
| All aged 16 and over | 20.5 | 49.4 | 32.3 | 102.7 | 247.3 | 663.8 | 1,116.0 |

1 Includes those on Basic Education and General Courses (that is, languages, physical education/sport/fitness, practical craft/ skills, role education, other adult education). See Appendix, Part 3: Adult education.
**Source: Department for Education and Employment; Welsh Office**

# 3.21

University degree courses, for which people can study mainly at home, and further education college courses.

Adults may improve their basic literacy and numeracy skills by enrolling on a basic skills course. The Basic Skills Agency provides information on the number of students who receive basic skills tuition. The numbers increased steadily between 1986/87 and 1994/95 in England and Wales (Table 3.21). However, it must be noted that the figure for 1994/95 is not comparable with previous years due to a change in the method of measurement - as footnoted in Table 3.21.

People can improve their job performance, or, if they are unemployed, improve their chances of getting a job, by undertaking job-related training. In Spring 1996 around 3.8 million economically active people in the United Kingdom said that they had received job-related training in the last four weeks, an increase of 130 thousand on the previous year. Females were slightly more likely than males to receive job-related training although this difference was small compared with the differences in receipt of such training by educational level (Table 3.22). Also those with high levels of qualifications were much more likely to receive job-related training than those with low or no qualifications. Those in the younger age groups were more likely than those in the older ones to receive job-related training. Youth Training is looked at in more detail later in this section.

The incidence of job-related training also varies by region. Yorkshire and Humberside and the Northern region had the largest proportions of their economically active population receiving job-related training in

**Students receiving adult literacy and numeracy tuition**

| England & Wales | | | | | Thousands |
|---|---|---|---|---|---|
| | 1986 | 1988 | 1990 | 1991 | 1994/95[1] |
| Literacy | 57 | 58 | 59 | 63 | 98 |
| Numeracy | 17 | 18 | 20 | 21 | 37 |
| Both | 34 | 35 | 41 | 43 | 73 |
| All students receiving adult literacy and numeracy tuition | 108 | 111 | 120 | 128 | 208 |

1 Data are not comparable with earlier years. 1994/95 represents all students receiving tuition at any time in the year: previous years are counts of students at first week in November.
*Source: The Basic Skills Agency*

Spring 1996 while Northern Ireland and the East Midlands had the lowest. The length of job-related training varied widely but much was of fairly short duration, lasting less than one week, or was ongoing with no definite time limit.

Among employees, off-the-job training is the most common form of job-related training and around 9 per cent of employees received only this sort of training in the

# 3.22

**Economically active[1] people receiving job-related training[2]: by gender and highest qualification held, Spring 1996**

| United Kingdom | | | Percentages |
|---|---|---|---|
| | Males | Females | All |
| Degree or equivalent | 21.7 | 25.1 | 22.9 |
| Higher education below degree level | 20.4 | 25.5 | 23.0 |
| GCE A Level or equivalent | 11.2 | 16.6 | 12.8 |
| GCSE grade C and above or equivalent | 14.5 | 14.5 | 14.5 |
| Other qualification | 8.9 | 10.7 | 9.7 |
| No qualification | 3.8 | 4.3 | 4.0 |
| All qualification levels | 12.4 | 14.7 | 13.4 |

1 Includes employees, self employed, unpaid family workers, those on government employment and training programmes and the ILO unemployed.
2 Data are for people of working age (males aged 16 to 64 and females aged 16 to 59) receiving job-related training, on or off-the-job, in the four weeks prior to interview.
*Source: Department for Education and Employment, from the Labour Force Survey*

# 3.23

Employees[1] receiving job-related training[2]: by occupation and method of training, Spring 1996

**United Kingdom**                                                                                          Percentages

| | On-the-job training only | Off-the-job training only | Both on and off-the-job training | All methods of training |
|---|---|---|---|---|
| Professional | 5.8 | 14.9 | 3.7 | 24.4 |
| Associate professional and technical | 5.0 | 13.8 | 5.3 | 24.2 |
| Managers and administrators | 3.7 | 10.2 | 2.6 | 16.4 |
| Personal and protective service | 4.8 | 8.2 | 2.9 | 15.9 |
| Sales | 3.6 | 8.8 | 1.5 | 13.9 |
| Clerical and secretarial | 3.9 | 8.0 | 1.8 | 13.7 |
| Craft and related | 3.3 | 4.7 | 2.5 | 10.4 |
| Plant and machine operatives | 2.3 | 2.8 | 0.8 | 5.9 |
| Other occupations/no answer | 1.9 | 3.9 | 0.7 | 6.5 |
| All occupations | 3.9 | 8.5 | 2.4 | 14.8 |

1 Employees are those in employment excluding the self-employed, unpaid family workers and those on government schemes.
2 Data are for people of working age (males aged 16 to 64 and females aged 16 to 59) receiving job-related training in the four weeks prior to interview.

**Source: Department for Education and Employment, from the Labour Force Survey**

# 3.24

Destination of Youth Training leavers[1], 1994-95

**England & Wales**

Percentages

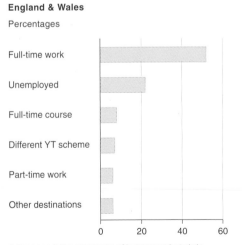

1 Based on follow-up surveys of leavers conducted six months after leaving. Figures are for those for whom leaving certificates were returned. Includes leavers from Youth Training and from Youth Credits.

**Source: Department for Education and Employment**

United Kingdom in Spring 1996 (Table 3.23). The amount and type of job-related training varies in different occupations. Those in professional occupations were the most likely to receive training, with almost a quarter doing so, closely followed by associate professional and technical occupations. Plant and machine operatives were the least likely of the occupations shown to receive any form of training. When employees undertook off-the-job training, the most common location was at an educational institution. The second most common location was at the employer's premises. These two types of location together accounted for over two thirds of such training.

For young people who do not wish to stay in full-time education after the minimum school leaving age, one option available is to go on a Youth Training course. In 1994-95 there were 304 thousand starts on Youth Training, which was over 13 thousand more than the previous year.

As well as gaining experience in a certain vocation, participants can gain qualifications. In 1994-95 nearly two thirds of those who completed their Youth Training course gained a full qualification. Males were more likely than females to have been on a Youth Training course, although the disparity has been narrowing recently.

In 1994-95 over half of those who left Youth Training went into full-time work (Chart 3.24). This was an increase of 4 percentage points on the previous year. However, this is still lower than five years previously when nearly two thirds of leavers went into full-time employment. Just over a fifth of leavers in 1994-95 became unemployed.

A more traditional form of training young people for the workplace is through apprenticeships. The Labour Force Survey found that there were 183 thousand apprentices in the United Kingdom which in Spring 1996 was a little over half the number ten years previously. The construction and manufacturing industrial sectors together accounted for 42 per cent of apprentices.

## Spending on education

Total government expenditure on education was 62 per cent higher in real terms in the United Kingdom in 1994-95 than in 1970-71, although its share of Gross Domestic Product was the same as in 1970-71 (Table 3.25). The increase in spending can be partly explained by the increase in student numbers over the same period. For schools, secondary school pupils are more expensive to educate than primary school pupils due to the increased specialisation and smaller classes. In 1994-95 average public spending per state nursery and primary school pupil in the United Kingdom was £1,770 while that for a secondary school pupil was £2,430. Funding per student in further and higher education was even greater.

The standard student maintenance grant, paid to those staying in education after the age of 18, has decreased in real terms since the late 1980s. In 1990/91 a loans scheme was introduced so that students could top up their grant, giving a higher total income in real terms. The cash value of the grant itself was frozen at its 1990/91 level until 1994/95, since when it has been reduced by about 10 per cent each year. This, together with increases in the size of the loan is intended to bring grants and loans into broad parity during 1996/97.

The proportion of students taking out loans increased from 28 per cent in the first year of the scheme to 55 per cent in 1994/95 (Table 3.26). However, in real terms, the amount borrowed increased by over six and a half times as much in the same period. Some 1.7 million loans to a value of £1.3 billion have been taken out between the beginning of the scheme and the end of the 1994/95 academic year. At the end of the 1994-95 financial year, the amount repaid (loan and interest) to the funding departments was £46 million. Those who take out loans start to repay them in the April after their course ends, unless they qualify for deferral due to low income.

Other sources of income for students include Access Funds and Career Development Loans. Access Funds are administered by the educational institutions and provide discretionary support for individual cases of hardship. Career Development Loans are administered by banks and are aimed at those who would otherwise not have reasonable or adequate access to the funds required.

**Government expenditure on education in real terms[1]: by type**

| United Kingdom | | | | £ million at 1994-95 prices[1] |
|---|---|---|---|---|
| | 1970-71 | 1980-81 | 1990-91 | 1994-95 |
| Schools | | | | |
| Nursery and Primary | 5,169 | 6,495 | 7,908 | 9,611 |
| Secondary | 5,983 | 8,394 | 8,838 | 9,439 |
| Special | 478 | 993 | 1,343 | 1,488 |
| Higher, further and continuing education[2] | 5,642 | 6,729 | 7,934 | 9,314 |
| Other education expenditure | 766 | 1,112 | 1,584 | 1,026 |
| Total | 18,038 | 23,724 | 27,607 | 30,877 |
| Related education expenditure | 2,951 | 3,243 | 2,854 | 3,627 |
| VAT incurred on above expenditure | 729 | 400 | 572 | 639 |
| Total expenditure | 21,718 | 27,366 | 31,033 | 35,144 |
| Total expenditure as a percentage of GDP | 5.2 | 5.5 | 4.8 | 5.2 |

1 Adjusted to 1994-95 prices using the GDP market prices deflator.
2 Includes universities. In April 1989 fees for polytechnics and colleges transferred to the former Polytechnics and Colleges Funding Council.
*Source: Department for Education and Employment; Welsh Office; Scottish Office Education and Industry Department; Department of Education, Northern Ireland*

## 3.26

**Take-up of student loans: by gender**

**United Kingdom**

| | 1990/91 | 1991/92 | 1992/93 | 1993/94 | 1994/95 |
|---|---|---|---|---|---|
| **Students taking out loans** (percentages)[1] | | | | | |
| Males | 33 | 41 | 46 | 51 | 59 |
| Females | 23 | 31 | 36 | 42 | 51 |
| All students | 28 | 36 | 41 | 47 | 55 |
| **Total amount borrowed** (£ million at September 1995 prices)[2] | | | | | |
| Males | 50.0 | 91.2 | 138.3 | 183.3 | 297.1 |
| Females | 33.6 | 66.1 | 107.8 | 149.9 | 258.4 |
| All students | 83.5 | 157.3 | 246.2 | 333.2 | 555.5 |

1 Percentage of eligible students taking up loans. See Appendix, Part 3: Student grants and loans.
2 Adjusted to September 1995 prices using the retail prices index.
*Source: Department for Education and Employment; Student Loans Company*

## References and further reading

The following list contains selected publications relevant to **Chapter 3: Education and Training**. Those published by The Stationery Office are available from the addresses shown on the inside back cover of *Social Trends*.

*Achievement for All,* HM Inspectors of Schools, Scotland

*Annual Report of Her Majesty's Chief Inspector of Schools*, The Stationery Office

*Annual Survey of Trends in Education*, National Foundation for Educational Research

*Basic Skills of Young Adults,* Basic Skills Agency

*Department for Education and Office for Standards in Education Departmental Report: The Government's Expenditure Plans*, The Stationery Office

*Difficulties with Basic Skills*, Basic Skills Agency

*Education at a Glance*, OECD

*Education Statistics for the United Kingdom*, The Stationery Office

*Examination Results in Scottish Schools,* HM Inspectors of Schools, Scotland

*Higher Education Statistics for the United Kingdom*, The Stationery Office

*Scottish Education Statistics,* The Stationery Office

*Social Focus on Children*, The Stationery Office

*Social Focus on Women,* The Stationery Office

*Standards and Quality in Education (Report of Her Majesty's Chief Inspector of Schools),* The Stationery Office

*Statistical Bulletins*, from: Department for Education and Employment, The Scottish Office Education and Industry Department; Department of Education, Northern Ireland

*Statistics of Education* (5 volumes), The Stationery Office

*Statistics of Education and Training in Wales*, Welsh Office

*Taught Time: an interim report*, OFSTED

*Results of the 1995 National Curriculum assessments of 7 year olds in England,* Department for Education and Employment

*Results of the 1995 National Curriculum assessments of 11 year olds in England,* Department for Education and Employment

*Results of the 1995 National Curriculum assessments of 14 year olds in England,* Department for Education and Employment

## Contacts

Telephone contact points for further information relating to

**Chapter 3: Education**

| | |
|---|---|
| **Chapter author** | 0171 533 5778 |
| **Department for Education and Employment** | 01325 392658 |
| **Department of Education, Northern Ireland** | 01247 279677 |
| **The Scottish Office Education and Industry Department** | 0131 244 0313 |
| **Welsh Office** | 01222 825060 |
| **Basic Skills Agency** | 0171 405 4017 |
| **Social & Community Planning Research** | 0171 250 1866 extn 369 |

# Chapter 4 Labour Market

**Economic activity**  There were almost 28 million people in the labour force in Great Britain in Spring 1996, more than in Spring 1995 but less than the all time peak in 1990. (Table 4.3)

**Type of employment**  Only 8 per cent of male employees worked part time in the United Kingdom in Spring 1996 compared with 45 per cent of female employees. (Table 4.7)

Women are more likely than men to work for a woman: only 10 per cent of male workers in Great Britain had a female boss in 1994-1995 while this was the case for 50 per cent of female workers. (Page 77)

**Time at work**  Full-time male managers and administrators worked 48.4 hours, on average, compared with 41.8 for those in clerical and secretarial occupations in Spring 1996. (Page 79)

The United Kingdom has a higher proportion of people working from home than any other EU country. Three in ten male employees and one in four female employees in this country worked from home at least sometimes in 1995. (Page 80)

**Industrial relations and trade unions**  Union membership is now concentrated in a small number of very large unions: seven unions accounted for three fifths of UK union members in 1994. (Page 82)

**Unemployment**  Unemployment rates are highest among young people. A fifth of economically active 16 to 19 year old men were unemployed in the United Kingdom in Spring 1996. However the lengths of their spells of unemployment are generally relatively short. (Table 4.23 and Table 4.26)

People with no qualifications had an unemployment rate more than three times higher than for those educated above A level standard in Winter 1995-96. (Table 4.28)

## 4.1

**Economic activity rates[1]: by gender and age, 1971 to 1996**

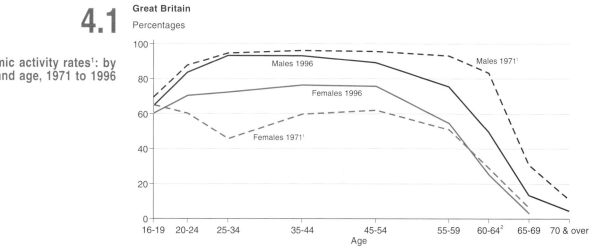

**Great Britain**

Percentages

1 The percentage of the population that is in the labour force. The definition of the labour force differs between the 1971 and 1996 data: the former Great Britain civilian labour force definition of unemployment has been used to produce the 1971 data while, for the 1996 data the ILO definition has been used and members of the armed forces included.
2 Includes females aged 70 and over.

**Source: Census and Labour Force Survey, Office for National Statistics**

## Glossary of terms

**Employees (Labour Force Survey measure)** - a measure, obtained from household surveys, of persons aged 16 and over who regard themselves as paid employees. People with two or more jobs are counted only once.

**Self-employed** - a measure obtained from household surveys, of persons aged 16 and over who regard themselves as self-employed, ie who in their main employment work on their own account, whether or not they have employees.

**Government employment and training programmes** - a measure, obtained from household surveys, of those who said they were participants on Youth Training, Employment Training, Employment Action or Community Industry or a programme organised by a TEC/LEC.

**Labour force in employment** - a measure, obtained from household surveys and censuses, of employees, self-employed persons, participants in government employment and training programmes, and persons doing unpaid family work.

**Workforce in employment** - a measure of employees in employment (from employer survey based measures), self-employed persons, all HM forces and participants in government employment and training programmes.

**Claimant unemployed** - a measure, known as the claimant count, and derived from administrative sources, which counts as unemployed those who are claiming unemployment related benefits at Employment Service local offices (formerly Unemployment Benefit Offices).

**ILO unemployed** - an International Labour Organisation (ILO) recommended measure, used in household surveys such as the Labour Force Survey, which counts as unemployed those aged 16 and over who are without a job, are available to start work in the next two weeks, who have been seeking a job in the last four weeks or are waiting to start a job already obtained.

**Workforce** - the **workforce in employment** plus the **claimant unemployed**.

**Economically active** - the **labour force in employment** plus the **ILO unemployed**.

**Claimant unemployment rate** - the percentage of the **workforce** who are **claimant unemployed**.

**ILO unemployment rate** - the percentage of the **economically active** who are **ILO unemployed**.

**The economically inactive** - people who are neither part of the labour force in employment nor ILO unemployed. For example, all people under 16, those looking after a home or retired, or those permanently unable to work.

**The population of working age** - males aged 16 to 64 years and females aged 16 to 59 years.

**Economic activity rate** - the percentage of the population in a given age group which is in the labour force.

Some of these terms are covered in more detail in the Appendix, Part 4.

# 4.2

After finishing their initial education, most people become members of the country's labour force for a good deal of the rest of their lives. The composition of the labour force and type of work that people do has undergone fundamental changes in recent years. For example, more and more women have entered paid employment, particularly part-time work, and returned to work after having their children.

## Economic activity

The number of people of working age, which is shown in Table 4.2, gives a broad indication of the potential number of economically active people in the country. However, not everyone of working age is either working or looking for work - some may be sick while others will be students or chose not to work in order to look after their family or home. On the other hand there are people above state pension age in the labour force: over three quarters of a million in Great Britain in Spring 1996.

Throughout the last quarter of a century the number of people of working age has been increasing and this is projected to continue for at least another 10 to 15 years. The composition of the population of working age at any point in time is a reflection of demographic factors in earlier years, mainly the birth rate. The peak of births in the post Second World War baby boom and again around 1964, and the intervening trough in the 1950s, dominate the age profile. The increase in the population of working age in the first half of the 1990s was slower than in the late 1970s and early 1980s because the birth rate was particularly low between 1973 and 1979. However this decline in the number of newcomers to the working age population will be reversed in future due to

the number of births increasing again in in the 1980s. Even so there will be a major change in the age composition by 2006, with older age groups accounting for an increasing proportion. Further information on the birth rate and other demographic factors is given in the Population chapter.

There are different patterns in the economic activity of men and women. In Spring 1996, 71 per cent of women of working age in the United Kingdom were economically active compared with 85 per cent of men. Men are also far more likely to be self-employed than women: around three times more men than women were self-employed. Conversely more than five times as many women as men were part-time employees.

**Population of working age[1]: by gender and employment status, Spring 1996**

| United Kingdom | | | Millions |
|---|---|---|---|
| | Males | Females | All |
| **Economically active** | | | |
| In employment | | | |
|   Full-time employees | 10.8 | 5.9 | 16.7 |
|   Part-time employees | 0.8 | 4.5 | 5.3 |
| All employees | 11.6 | 10.4 | 22.0 |
| Full-time self-employed | 2.2 | 0.4 | 2.6 |
| Part-time self-employed | 0.2 | 0.4 | 0.5 |
| All self-employed | 2.4 | 0.7 | 3.1 |
| Others in employment[2] | 0.2 | 0.2 | 0.4 |
| All in employment | 14.2 | 11.3 | 25.4 |
| ILO unemployed | 1.5 | 0.8 | 2.3 |
| All economically active | 15.7 | 12.0 | 27.8 |
| **Economically inactive** | 2.9 | 4.9 | 7.8 |
| **Population of working age** | 18.6 | 17.0 | 35.5 |

1 Males aged 16 to 64, females aged 16 to 59.
2 Those on government employment and training programmes and unpaid family workers.
*Source: Labour Force Survey, Office for National Statistics*

# 4.3

## Labour force[1]: by gender and age

| Great Britain | | | | | | | Millions |
|---|---|---|---|---|---|---|---|
| | 16-24 | 25-44 | 45-54 | 55-59 | 60-64 | 65 and over | All aged 16 and over |
| **Males** | | | | | | | |
| 1971 | 2.9 | 6.3 | 3.1 | 1.5 | 1.2 | 0.5 | 15.6 |
| 1981 | 3.1 | 7.0 | 2.9 | 1.4 | 0.9 | 0.3 | 15.7 |
| 1991 | 3.0 | 7.9 | 2.9 | 1.1 | 0.7 | 0.3 | 16.0 |
| 1996 | 2.4 | 7.9 | 3.3 | 1.1 | 0.6 | 0.3 | 15.6 |
| 2001 | 2.3 | 8.1 | 3.4 | 1.2 | 0.7 | 0.3 | 15.9 |
| 2006 | 2.4 | 7.8 | 3.4 | 1.3 | 0.7 | 0.3 | 16.0 |
| **Females** | | | | | | | |
| 1971 | 2.2 | 3.4 | 2.1 | 0.9 | 0.5 | 0.3 | 9.4 |
| 1981 | 2.6 | 4.4 | 2.1 | 0.9 | 0.4 | 0.2 | 10.6 |
| 1991 | 2.5 | 6.0 | 2.3 | 0.8 | 0.3 | 0.2 | 12.1 |
| 1996 | 2.0 | 6.2 | 2.8 | 0.8 | 0.3 | 0.2 | 12.3 |
| 2001 | 2.0 | 6.3 | 3.0 | 0.9 | 0.4 | 0.1 | 12.8 |
| 2006 | 2.1 | 6.3 | 3.1 | 1.1 | 0.5 | 0.2 | 13.3 |

1 The former Great Britain civilian labour force definition of unemployment has been used to produce the estimates for 1971 and 1981; in later years the ILO definition has been used and members of the armed forces excluded. Data for 2001 and 2006 are Spring 1995-based projections.

*Source: Census and Labour Force Survey, Office for National Statistics*

# 4.4

## Reasons for economic inactivity[1]: by gender, Autumn 1995

| United Kingdom | | | Percentages |
|---|---|---|---|
| | Males | Females | All of working age |
| Student | 30 | 15 | 20 |
| Looking after family or home | | | |
| One or more children | | | |
| under school age | 1 | 28 | 19 |
| One or more other children | 2 | 15 | 10 |
| Dependent adult relative | 3 | 5 | 4 |
| Other reasons | 0 | 8 | 5 |
| All looking after family or home | 7 | 55 | 39 |
| Temporarily sick or injured | 4 | 2 | 3 |
| Long-term sick or disabled | 49 | 19 | 29 |
| Discouraged worker | 4 | 4 | 4 |
| Other reasons | 6 | 5 | 5 |
| All reasons | 100 | 100 | 100 |

1 Males aged 16 to 64, females aged 16 to 59. Excludes those who have not yet started looking for work or those who did not state their reason for inactivity.

*Source: Labour Force Survey, Office for National Statistics*

The total number of economically active people form the labour force. In Spring 1995 there were 27.7 million people in the labour force in Great Britain, almost 2 per cent less than the all time peak of 28.2 million in Spring 1990. However, the number had increased again by Spring 1996 and the labour force is expected to rise steadily to 29.3 million by 2006 **(Table 4.3)**. Due to a change in definition there is a slight discontinuity between the data for 1971 and 1981 and those for 1991 onwards shown in Table 4.3. The effect of this is to slightly overstate the increase for men and slightly understate the increase for women. One of the most fundamental changes in the British labour market this century has been the increasing participation of women, particularly the extent to which they have taken up part-time work. In 1971 women made up 38 per cent of the labour force compared with 44 per cent in 1996.

This different picture for men and women is also evident in the economic activity rates shown in **Chart 4.1** at the beginning of this chapter. This measures the percentage of the population who are in the labour force. Although men are still more likely than women to be economically active at all ages, the gap has closed in the last 25 years. The decline in the economic activity rates for 16 to 19 year olds is partly a reflection of the number of young people staying on in full-time education. However, more and more students are taking part-time work or holiday jobs. In Spring 1996 nearly 40 per cent of 16 to 19 year olds in full-time education in Great Britain were also in employment. The strong upward trend in the participation of women aged 25 to 54 can be explained by the tendency for women to give birth at an older age (see the Households and Families chapter) and then to return to the labour force more quickly.

# 4.5

The high level of unemployment in the early 1980s may have discouraged people from entering or remaining in the labour market and is thought to have been a factor in explaining the declining economic activity rates of men. In addition older workers may have been encouraged to leave the labour force in the 1980s by the introduction of early retirement initiatives, such as the job release scheme. However the longer term trend towards early retirement seems to have abated recently.

These people who retire early are included in the 7.6 million people of working age who were economically inactive in the United Kingdom in Autumn 1995. Most of these people, more than two thirds of both men and women, did not want a job. However, women have very different reasons from men for being economically inactive. Just over half of economically inactive women were looking after their homes or a member of their family, usually their children (Table 4.4). Among men the most common reason for economic inactivity was being long term sick or disabled. Discouraged workers, that is people who said that they were not seeking work as they thought that no jobs were available, accounted for only a small proportion of both men and women, at 4 per cent.

The economic status of people of working age who lived as a couple in the United Kingdom in Spring 1996 is shown in Table 4.5. In nearly a third of these working age couples both partners were working full time while in almost as many couples the head of the family was working full time and their partner was working part time. If the head of the family was unemployed then their partner was far less likely to be in work than if the head was employed.

## Economic activity status of couples of working age[1], Spring 1996

**United Kingdom**                                                                 Percentages

| | Head of family | | | | |
| | Working full time | Working part time | Unemployed[2] | Inactive | All |
|---|---|---|---|---|---|
| **Partner** | | | | | |
| Working full time | 31.7 | 1.0 | 0.8 | 2.1 | 35.6 |
| Working part time | 30.2 | 1.2 | 0.9 | 2.3 | 34.7 |
| Unemployed[2] | 2.1 | 0.1 | 0.7 | 0.2 | 3.1 |
| Inactive | 16.0 | 1.1 | 3.0 | 6.5 | 26.6 |
| All | 79.9 | 3.4 | 5.5 | 11.2 | 100.0 |

1 Males aged 16 to 64 and females aged 16 to 59.
2 Based on the ILO definition. See Appendix, Part 4: Unemployment - ILO definition.
**Source: Labour Force Survey, Office for National Statistics**

Whether a women is economically active or not depends to some extent on the number and ages of her children. Women with a child under school age are the least likely to be in paid work (Table 4.6). As the age of the youngest child increases, women are increasingly likely to be in work, and in particular more likely to be in full-time employment.

# 4.6

## Economic activity status of women[1]: by age of youngest dependent child, Spring 1996

**United Kingdom**                                                                 Percentages

| | Age of youngest dependent child | | | No dependent children | All women aged 16-59 |
| | 0-4 | 5-10 | 11-15 | | |
|---|---|---|---|---|---|
| Working full time | 17 | 22 | 34 | 47 | 37 |
| Working part time | 31 | 43 | 41 | 24 | 29 |
| Unemployed[2] | 5 | 5 | 4 | 4 | 5 |
| Inactive | 46 | 30 | 21 | 25 | 29 |
| All women[1] (=100%) | | | | | |
| (millions) | 3.1 | 2.2 | 1.5 | 10.2 | 17.0 |

1 Aged 16 to 59.
2 Based on the ILO definition. See Appendix, Part 4: Unemployment - ILO definition.
**Source: Labour Force Survey, Office for National Statistics**

# 4.7

**Percentage of employees working part time: by gender and age, Spring 1996**

| United Kingdom | | | Percentages |
|---|---|---|---|
| | Males | Females | All |
| 16-19 | | | |
| In FTE[1] | 97 | 99 | 98 |
| Not in FTE[1] | 12 | 26 | 19 |
| All aged 16-19 | 51 | 65 | 58 |
| 20-24 | 11 | 23 | 17 |
| 25-44 | 3 | 42 | 21 |
| 45-54 | 3 | 47 | 25 |
| 55-59 | 7 | 54 | 30 |
| 60-64 | 16 | 71 | 38 |
| 65 and over | 73 | 84 | 78 |
| All aged 16 and over | 8 | 45 | 25 |

1 Full-time education.

*Source: Labour Force Survey, Office for National Statistics*

# 4.8

**Employees[1]: by gender and occupation, 1991 and 1996**

| United Kingdom | | | | Percentages |
|---|---|---|---|---|
| | Males | | Females | |
| | 1991 | 1996 | 1991 | 1996 |
| Professional | 10 | 12 | 8 | 10 |
| Managers and administrators | 16 | 19 | 8 | 10 |
| Associate professional and technical | 8 | 8 | 10 | 10 |
| Clerical and secretarial | 8 | 8 | 29 | 26 |
| Personal and protective services | 7 | 8 | 14 | 16 |
| Sales | 6 | 6 | 12 | 12 |
| Craft and related | 21 | 17 | 4 | 3 |
| Plant and machine operatives | 15 | 15 | 5 | 4 |
| Other occupations | 8 | 8 | 11 | 9 |
| All employees | 100 | 100 | 100 | 100 |

1 At Spring each year. Excludes those who did not state their occupation.

*Source: Labour Force Survey, Office for National Statistics*

The 1994 British Social Attitudes Survey, carried out by Social and Community Planning Research, asked women about their attitudes to working mothers. In answer to the question 'should a woman work outside the home when her children are under school age', 55 per cent said that she should not while 28 per cent said that she should work part time only; 5 per cent said that she should work full time.

The Family and Working Lives Survey (FWLS) was commissioned by the Department for Education and Employment (DfEE), the Employment Service, the Department of Social Security, the Department of the Environment and the Home Office. The main fieldwork took place in Great Britain between July 1994 and February 1995. The survey asked partner respondents with children in the household whether the presence of children affected their working arrangements. Around two thirds of women and only a sixth of men said that it did. In general female partners said that their hours and type of work had been affected and 10 per cent specifically mentioned missing out on promotion. Although there were also some constraints on male partners, like taking the children to school or not working away from home, the impact of having children was small compared with the impact on the female partners.

## Type of employment

The type of work which people do varies widely. Over the past decade part-time working has become more common for both men and women. Between 1986 and 1996 the number of women in part-time employment in the United Kingdom increased by 18 per cent to 5.3 million; among men the number almost doubled, but to only 1.2 million. Women are far more likely than men to be part-time employees: 45 per cent of female employees, but only 8 per cent of male employees, were working part time in Spring 1996 (Table 4.7). Among both men and women, it is the youngest and the oldest employees who are most likely to be in part-time work. The high rate among the young is due to the number of students who take part-time jobs to supplement their income.

Part-time working is more common in certain industries. For example, 44 per cent of employees in distribution, and 34 per cent in public administration, worked part time in Spring 1996 compared with only 4 per cent of employees in the energy and water supply industries.

Most people who have a part-time job do not want to work full time and this is particularly true of women. Eight in ten women and nearly four in ten men in the United Kingdom

# 4.9

who had a part-time job in Spring 1996 said that they did not want a full-time job; this rises to over nine in ten among women with a partner. Just over a third of both men and single women who had a part-time job had one because they were a student or still at school.

Certain occupations are considered to be traditionally done by women. Results from the FWLS for Great Britain indicate that 44 per cent of working women worked mainly with other women while 51 per cent of all working men worked mainly with other men. The survey also found that only 10 per cent of men, but 50 per cent of women, have a female boss.

In Spring 1996 over a quarter of female employees in the United Kingdom worked in clerical and secretarial occupations compared with only a twelfth of male employees (Table 4.8). Of all those in employment, women outnumber men by four to one in the health and social work sector and by two to one in education, whereas men outnumber women by nine to one in the construction industry. Even within those industries in which women predominate they tend to be in the less senior posts.

Among the self-employed, women are under represented. According to estimates from the Labour Force Survey (LFS) there were 3.3 million self-employed people in the United Kingdom in Spring 1996, of whom three quarters were men. The number of self-employed people increased throughout the 1980s to peak at 3.6 million in 1990. It then fell during the recession, but has increased again since the recovery has got underway. Chart 4.9 illustrates those industries in which self-employment is more common by expressing the number of self-employed as a percentage of all in employment. Almost half of the people

**Self-employed as a percentage of all in employment: by industry, Spring 1996**

**United Kingdom**
Percentages

| | |
|---|---|
| Agriculture and fishing | |
| Construction | |
| Banking, finance and insurance | |
| Distribution, hotels and restaurants | |
| Transport and communication | |
| Public administration, education and health | |
| Manufacturing | |
| Other services | |

*Source: Labour Force Survey, Office for National Statistics*

working in agriculture and fishing and construction in Spring 1996 were self-employed compared with, at the other end of the scale, only 5 per cent of those in public administration, education and health and manufacturing.

The proportion of full-time employees who had been in their current job for less than a year is an indicator of job tenure and turnover, as shown in Chart 4.10. Throughout the period shown in the chart, job turnover in Great Britain has been higher among women than men, although the gap has narrowed over time. In 1996, 16 per cent of men and 17 per cent of women who were full-time employees had started their job in the previous 12 months. Turnover is very cyclical, being highest in times of job growth as more jobs are created and people are more likely to change jobs. However, the underlying trend in job turnover seems to have changed very little over the last ten years: average job tenure has fallen slightly for men, from 9.4 to 8.9 years, and increased slightly for women, from 6.5 to 7.1 years.

# 4.10

**Percentage of full-time employees who started their current job in the previous 12 months[1]**

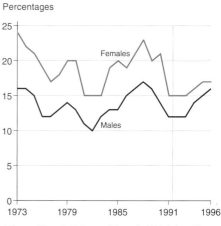

**Great Britain**
Percentages

1 General Household Survey data up to 1991; Labour Force Survey data from 1992 onwards.

*Source: General Household Survey and Labour Force Survey, Office for National Statistics*

# 4.11

## Percentage of employees with a temporary job: EU comparison[1], 1995

| | Males | Females | All |
|---|---|---|---|
| | | | Percentages |
| Spain | 33 | 38 | 35 |
| Finland | 13 | 19 | 16 |
| Sweden | 10 | 14 | 12 |
| France | 11 | 13 | 12 |
| Denmark | 11 | 13 | 12 |
| Netherlands | 9 | 14 | 11 |
| Germany | 10 | 11 | 10 |
| Irish Republic | 9 | 12 | 10 |
| Greece | 9 | 11 | 10 |
| Portugal | 9 | 11 | 10 |
| Italy | 6 | 9 | 7 |
| United Kingdom | 6 | 8 | 7 |
| Austria | 6 | 6 | 6 |
| Belgium | 4 | 7 | 5 |
| EU average | 11 | 12 | 11 |

1 Data for Luxembourg are not available.

*Source: Labour Force Survey, Eurostat*

# 4.12

## People with a second job[1]: by gender

**United Kingdom**

Thousands

1 At Spring each year.

*Source: Labour Force Survey, Office for National Statistics*

Research commissioned by the DfEE, indicates that the UK labour market is not only characterised by long tenure but also by a high level of turnover. This apparent contradiction can be explained by the fact that most of the people who leave jobs have been in them for a short period and most are young. The DfEE sponsored research found that the under 30s accounted for 60 per cent of people starting new jobs and 50 per cent of the flow onto the claimant unemployment count. So while people may have several jobs in a lifetime, most of these are in their first years in the labour market.

Although more than nine in ten employees are in permanent jobs, both businesses and individuals are increasingly considering, and using, alternatives to full-time permanent employment. For employers, flexibility aids competitiveness by adjusting the amount of labour used more quickly. At the same time many employees choose to work on a part-time or temporary basis to balance work with other commitments, such as their family. Research carried out in mid-1995 on behalf of the DfEE found that the two main reasons for employing temporary workers are to match staffing levels to peaks in demand and as a short term cover while staff are away on holiday or on sick leave.

Overall 1.5 million people, 7 per cent of employees, in the United Kingdom had a temporary job in 1995. This proportion is low compared with most other countries in the European Union (EU) - only in Austria and Belgium was it lower (Table 4.11). The highest rate occurred in Spain which, at 35 per cent, was more than double that of the next highest country, Finland. Around two fifths of temporary workers in the United Kingdom said that they had a temporary job because they could not find a permanent job, much the same proportion as the average for the EU.

Some people take a second job to supplement their income. There were 1.3 million people in the United Kingdom with a second job in Spring 1996, more than double the number in 1983 which is the first year for which figures are available on a consistent basis (Chart 4.12). Although over this period the underlying trend has been upwards, dips occurred for men in both 1987 and 1992, and for women in 1992. The hours worked in second jobs tend to be low, at around nine hours a week. Around three fifths of people who have a second job are an employee in both of their jobs.

The FWLS asked people in Great Britain who had ever worked if they had ever turned down promotion when offered it. Out of those respondents who had worked, 14 per cent of men and 11 per cent of women had been offered a promotion and not taken it. Of these people, about a fifth of both men and women said that one of the reasons that they were not interested in promotion was because they did not want the responsibility the promotion would bring (Table 4.13) Fifteen per cent of men, but only 8 per cent of women, gave not wanting to move to a different area as one of their reasons. However, a far higher proportion of women than men said that they had turned down promotion because they were constrained

## 4.13

by not being able to work the hours necessary. Women were no more likely than men to think that they were unequal to the proposed task.

## Time at work

On average full-time employees in this country are working longer hours than they used to. The average number of hours that full-time male employees in the United Kingdom usually worked a week, including overtime but excluding meal breaks, increased from 44.5 hours in 1985 to 45.8 hours in Spring 1996. For women the average increased from 39.6 to 40.6 hours over the same period. Employees in the agriculture and fishing industries worked the longest average hours in Spring 1996, while those in the public administration, education and health sector tended to work the shortest hours (Table 4.14). In all industries men worked longer hours on average than women.

Hours worked also vary by occupation. The longest hours among male full-time employees were worked by managers and administrators, at 48.4 hours a week in Spring 1996. At the other end of the scale, men in clerical and secretarial occupations worked only 41.8 hours a week. The full-time self-employed work even longer hours on average than full-time employees. Full-time self-employed men worked nearly six hours more a week in Spring 1996 than their employee counterparts and self-employed women worked nearly eight hours more.

**Reasons for turning down promotion[1]: by gender, 1994-1995[2]**

**Great Britain**                                                          Percentages

|  | Males | Females | All people |
|---|---|---|---|
| Did not want the responsibility | 18 | 22 | 20 |
| Happy with the way things are | 16 | 14 | 15 |
| Don't want to move to a different area | 15 | 8 | 12 |
| I can't work the hours necessary | 2 | 14 | 7 |
| Would not have been paid any more | 9 | 5 | 7 |
| I don't think I'm up to it | 4 | 4 | 4 |
| My family wouldn't like it | 3 | 6 | 4 |
| Would have made no difference to my job | 2 | 2 | 2 |
| My main interests lie outside work | - | 2 | 1 |

1 Percentages are based on respondents who had refused promotion; they could give more than one reason.
2 Main fieldwork took place between July 1994 and February 1995.
**Source: Family and Working Lives Survey, Department for Education and Employment**

## 4.14

**Average hours[1] worked by full-time employees: by gender and industry, Spring 1996**

**United Kingdom**                                                    Hours per week

|  | Males | Females | All people |
|---|---|---|---|
| Agriculture and fishing | 49.5 | 41.9 | 48.1 |
| Transport and communication | 47.9 | 40.9 | 46.5 |
| Energy and water supply | 47.0 | 40.8 | 46.1 |
| Construction | 46.3 | 39.9 | 45.7 |
| Distribution, hotels and restaurants | 46.5 | 40.6 | 44.4 |
| Manufacturing | 45.3 | 40.7 | 44.2 |
| Banking, finance and insurance | 45.5 | 39.9 | 43.1 |
| Public administration, education and health | 44.6 | 40.9 | 42.5 |
| Other services | 45.5 | 41.7 | 43.9 |
| All industries | 45.8 | 40.6 | 44.0 |

1 Total usual hours including paid and unpaid overtime and excluding meal breaks.
**Source: Labour Force Survey, Office for National Statistics**

## 4.15

Employees with flexible working patterns: by gender, Spring 1996

**United Kingdom**                                                                          Percentages

|  | Males | Females | All employees |
|---|---|---|---|
| **Full-time employees** | | | |
| Flexible working hours | 8.6 | 13.2 | 10.2 |
| Annualised working hours | 3.7 | 4.2 | 3.9 |
| Four and a half day week | 2.7 | 2.4 | 2.6 |
| Term-time working | 1.0 | 4.7 | 2.3 |
| Nine day fortnight | 0.5 | 0.2 | 0.4 |
| Any flexible working pattern | 16.6 | 24.7 | 19.4 |
| **Part-time employees** | | | |
| Flexible working hours | 5.9 | 7.4 | 7.1 |
| Annualised working hours | 2.6 | 3.2 | 3.1 |
| Term-time working | 4.6 | 9.7 | 8.9 |
| Job sharing | .. | 2.4 | 2.2 |
| Any flexible working pattern | 14.2 | 22.9 | 21.5 |

*Source: Labour Force Survey, Office for National Statistics*

## 4.16

Percentage of employees who work on Saturdays and Sundays: EU comparison, 1995

Percentages

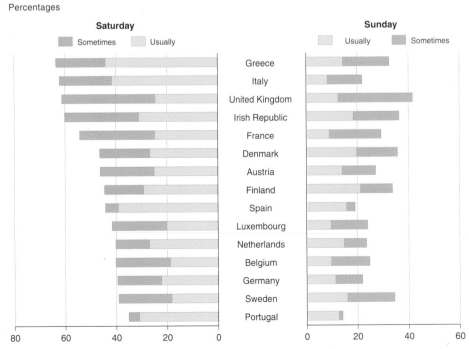

*Source: Labour Force Survey, Eurostat*

Although employees are usually expected to work a set number of hours each week, there is increasing use of flexible working patterns. Among full-time employees, around a sixth of men and a quarter of women worked some form of flexible working patterns in Spring 1996 (Table 4.15). The most common form was flexible hours working which was worked by 9 per cent of male, and 13 per cent of female, full-time employees. Overall the second most frequently used form was annualised working hours. This is where a set number of hours are worked over the course of a year. However, among women, term-time working was even more popular, presumably because it allows them to combine work and child care responsibilities once their children have started school.

Some people work so-called 'unsocial hours', such as at weekends, at night or on shift work. The proportion of employees in the United Kingdom who said that they worked at least sometimes on a Saturday in 1995 was 61 per cent compared with 41 per cent who said that they worked at least sometimes on a Sunday (Chart 4.16). These are among the highest rates in the EU: the United Kingdom is ranked third for Saturday working and has a higher rate than any other country for Sunday working. However, if the comparison is confined to those people who said that they 'usually' worked on a Saturday or on a Sunday then the United Kingdom's position drops to eleventh for Saturday working and tenth for Sunday working.

The Labour Force Surveys also collect information on home working. In 1995, 29 per cent of employed men in the United Kingdom, and 24 per cent of employed women, worked from home at least sometimes. These are higher rates than in any other country in the EU.

# 4.17

Annual paid holiday entitlement, Autumn 1995

**United Kingdom**                                                                                                          Percentages

| | | | | Days | | | | | |
|---|---|---|---|---|---|---|---|---|---|
| | 0 | 1-5 | 6-10 | 11-15 | 16-20 | 21-25 | 26-30 | 31 and over | All |
| **Males** | | | | | | | | | |
| Full-time permanent employees | 3 | - | 2 | 7 | 23 | 39 | 18 | 8 | 100 |
| Part-time permanent employees | 55 | 5 | 9 | 9 | 11 | 7 | 2 | .. | 100 |
| Full-time temporary employees | 42 | .. | 4 | 6 | 15 | 19 | 7 | 4 | 100 |
| Part-time temporary employees | 83 | .. | .. | .. | .. | .. | .. | .. | 100 |
| All employees | 8 | 1 | 3 | 7 | 22 | 36 | 16 | 7 | 100 |
| **Females** | | | | | | | | | |
| Full-time permanent employees | 3 | - | 2 | 7 | 23 | 39 | 15 | 11 | 100 |
| Part-time permanent employees | 27 | 4 | 10 | 14 | 18 | 16 | 5 | 5 | 100 |
| Full-time temporary employees | 41 | .. | .. | 6 | 14 | 18 | 7 | 10 | 100 |
| Part-time temporary employees | 71 | 3 | 3 | 5 | 5 | 3 | .. | 7 | 100 |
| All employees | 17 | 2 | 5 | 10 | 20 | 28 | 10 | 9 | 100 |

*Source: Labour Force Survey, Office for National Statistics*

The average number of days of paid holiday entitlement of full-time employees was just under five weeks in Spring 1996, at 23 days for men and 24 days for women. However, there are wide variations according to employment status. While a quarter of both male and female full-time employees received more than five weeks holiday a year and a tenth had more than six weeks, an eighth were entitled to three weeks or less (Table 4.17). As might be expected temporary employees have a far lower holiday entitlement than permanent employees. Indeed, two fifths of those who worked full time, and more than seven tenths of those who worked part time, had none at all. However, part-time permanent employees are also much less likely to have any paid holiday entitlement than those working full time.

As well as annual paid holidays, employees are entitled to time off work when they are ill. The amount of sickness absence among employees in the United Kingdom was roughly the same in 1996 as in 1986 (Table 4.18). In both years the percentage of women employees who had at least one day off work in the week before they were interviewed in the LFS was higher than that for men. The percentages also vary by age and are highest among those just under

# 4.18

Employees absent from work owing to sickness[1]: by gender and age, 1986 and 1996[2]

**United Kingdom**                                                                                                          Percentages

| | Males | | Females | |
|---|---|---|---|---|
| | 1986 | 1996 | 1986 | 1996 |
| 16-19 | 3.6 | 3.6 | 4.7 | 4.0 |
| 20-24 | 4.5 | 4.0 | 5.3 | 5.0 |
| 25-44 | 3.8 | 3.5 | 4.6 | 5.2 |
| 45-54 | 4.3 | 3.5 | 5.3 | 5.1 |
| Females 55-59/males 55-64 | 5.8 | 5.4 | 6.3 | 5.4 |
| Females 60 and over/males 65 and over | .. | .. | 3.7 | 3.9 |
| All aged 16 and over | 4.2 | 3.7 | 4.9 | 5.0 |

1 At Spring each year. At least one day away from work during the week before interview.
*Source: Labour Force Survey, Office for National Statistics*

## 4.19

Labour disputes[1]: working days lost

**United Kingdom**

Millions

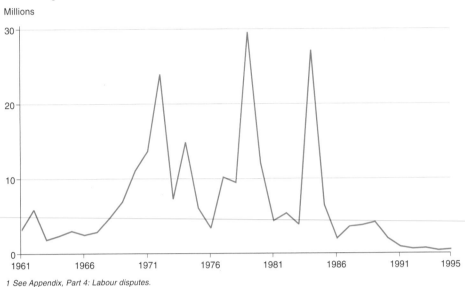

1 See Appendix, Part 4: Labour disputes.
**Source: Office for National Statistics**

just over half of the 29 million days lost, while another miners' strike in 1984 was responsible for over 80 per cent of the 27 million days lost in that year. The number of days which were lost through stoppages of work rose by almost half between 1994 and 1995, to 415 thousand. However, this is still a low figure historically. On average fewer days were lost each year in the first half of the 1990s than in any other decade this century and the 1994 figure was the lowest since records began in 1891. In 1995 disputes over pay continued to account for more stoppages than any other reason.

Linked to the fall in the number of days lost through stoppages of work may be the decrease in the level of trade union membership amongst the civilian workforce which is illustrated in **Chart 4.20**. The percentage of the civilian workforce in the United Kingdom who were members of a trade union has fallen from 53 per cent at its peak in 1980 to 32 per cent in 1994. The number of trade union members in the United Kingdom fell for the fifteenth consecutive year in 1994 to 8.3 million. This was the lowest number since 1945.

Although the number of members has only been falling since 1979, the number of unions has fallen steadily since 1920, to 243 at the end of 1994. This is partly a result of mergers of unions, as well as declining unionisation. For example, the largest union in the country, the Public Service Union (UNISON), was formed in 1993 as a result of the merger of the National and Local Government Officers' Association (NALGO), the National Union of Public Employees (NUPE) and the Confederation of Health Service Employees (COHSE). Union membership is now concentrated in a small number of very large unions. In 1994 just seven unions accounted for 59 per cent of union members.

## 4.20

Trade union membership[1] as a percentage of the civilian workforce in employment[2]

**United Kingdom**

Percentages

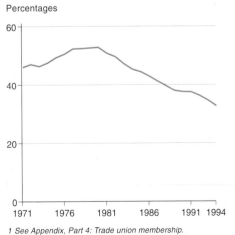

1 See Appendix, Part 4: Trade union membership.
2 Mid-year estimates up to 1977; end-year from 1978 onwards.
**Source: Office for National Statistics**

retirement age, particularly for men. It should be noted that the figures in Table 4.18 refer to Spring each year. Sickness absence does, of course, follow a seasonal pattern: Summer has the lowest sickness absence and Winter the highest. There is also some variation in sickness absence between people in different occupations. Those who are professionals, managers and administrators are the least likely to have reported sickness absence while plant and machine operatives are the most likely.

## Industrial relations and trade unions

The largest number of working days lost in one year in the United Kingdom was during the General Strike in 1926 when 160 million working days were lost - the coal industry alone accounted for 146 million of these days. More recently there were secondary peaks in 1972, 1979 and 1984 (Chart 4.19). In 1972 a miners' strike accounted for 45 per cent of the 24 million days lost and a strike by engineering workers in 1979 resulted in

## 4.21

Trade union membership varies widely by industry. People who are employed in the energy and water supply industries are almost six times as likely to be a member than those in the distribution, hotel and restaurant industries (Table 4.21). The public sector also has a high rate of unionisation, with nearly half of people working in public administration, education and health belonging to a union, although to some extent this is a reflection of low self-employment rates.

The fall in trade union membership has been much sharper amongst men than women. Between 1989 and 1995 the proportion of male employees who were a member of a trade union from 44 per cent to 35 per cent while among women there was only a slight decline. In addition the fall among manual employees has been sharper than among non-manual employees. In Autumn 1995 the rate of union membership was highest among those in the professional occupations: 36 per cent of men and, at 58 per cent, an even higher proportion of women were union members. The rate was lowest for those in the sales occupations, at around 10 per cent.

### Trade union membership[1]: by gender and industry, Autumn 1995

**United Kingdom**
Percentages

| | Males | Females | All |
|---|---|---|---|
| Energy and water supply | 56 | 36 | 52 |
| Public administration, education and health | 54 | 46 | 48 |
| Transport and communication | 45 | 27 | 41 |
| Manufacturing | 33 | 21 | 29 |
| Banking, finance and insurance | 17 | 19 | 18 |
| Construction | 15 | 10 | 15 |
| Distribution, hotels and restaurants | 8 | 10 | 9 |
| Other services | 22 | 13 | 18 |
| All industries | 28 | 27 | 27 |

1 Percentage of people in employment who were members of a trade union.
*Source: Labour Force Survey, Office for National Statistics*

is available quickly and it is particularly valuable for providing figures for small areas. The advantages of the ILO definition are that it is internationally comparable and is integrated with LFS measures of employment and economic activity. However, only quarterly estimates can be produced. A more detailed explanation of the two measures is given in the Appendix.

## Unemployment

This section looks at those people who are economically active, but unemployed. The measurement of unemployment has been a subject of debate for some time. In the United Kingdom two different measures are generally used: the claimant count and one based on the International Labour Organisation (ILO) definition. These measures are compared in Chart 4.22. The claimant count of the unemployed is produced monthly using administrative records of people claiming unemployment related benefits. This means that information

## 4.22

### Comparisons of alternative measures of unemployment[1]

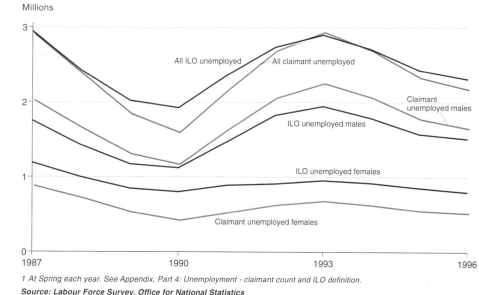

**United Kingdom**
Millions

1 At Spring each year. See Appendix, Part 4: Unemployment - claimant count and ILO definition.
*Source: Labour Force Survey, Office for National Statistics*

# 4.23

## Unemployment rates[1]: by gender and age

| United Kingdom | 1991 | 1992 | 1993 | 1994 | 1995 | Percentages 1996 |
|---|---|---|---|---|---|---|
| **Males** | | | | | | |
| 16-19 | 16.4 | 18.6 | 22.0 | 20.9 | 19.6 | 20.6 |
| 20-24 | 15.2 | 18.9 | 20.3 | 18.3 | 17.0 | 16.2 |
| 25-44 | 8.0 | 10.5 | 10.9 | 10.2 | 9.0 | 8.7 |
| 45-54 | 6.3 | 8.4 | 9.4 | 8.6 | 7.4 | 6.4 |
| 55-59 | 8.4 | 11.2 | 12.3 | 11.6 | 10.2 | 9.9 |
| 60-64 | 9.9 | 10.2 | 14.2 | 11.6 | 9.9 | 8.9 |
| 65 and over | 5.9 | 4.9 | 4.6 | 3.7 | .. | 4.1 |
| | | | | | | |
| All males aged 16 and over | 9.2 | 11.5 | 12.4 | 11.4 | 10.1 | 9.7 |
| **Females** | | | | | | |
| 16-19 | 12.7 | 13.6 | 15.9 | 16.0 | 14.8 | 14.6 |
| 20-24 | 10.1 | 10.2 | 11.8 | 10.7 | 10.6 | 8.9 |
| 25-44 | 7.1 | 7.3 | 7.3 | 7.0 | 6.7 | 6.3 |
| 45-54 | 4.6 | 5.0 | 5.0 | 5.0 | 4.5 | 4.1 |
| 55-59 | 5.5 | 4.5 | 6.0 | 6.5 | 4.7 | 4.2 |
| 60 and over | 4.4 | 3.1 | 3.9 | 2.9 | .. | .. |
| | | | | | | |
| All females aged 16 and over | 7.2 | 7.3 | 7.6 | 7.3 | 6.8 | 6.3 |

1 At Spring each year. Unemployment based on the ILO definition as a percentage of all economically active. See Appendix, Part 4: Unemployment - ILO definition.

**Source: Labour Force Survey, Office for National Statistics**

# 4.24

## Unemployment rates[1]: by age, EU comparison, 1995

Percentages

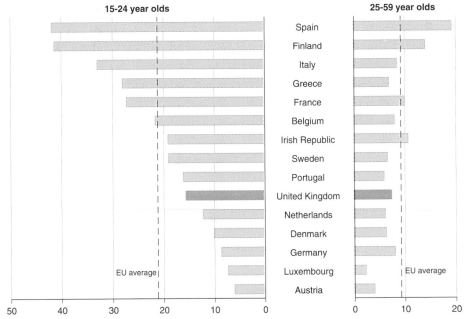

1 Unemployment based on the ILO definition as a percentage of all economically active. See Appendix, Part 4: Unemployment - ILO definition.

**Source: Labour Force Surveys, Eurostat**

Since some claimants do not fall within the ILO definition and some non claimants are included in the ILO unemployed, the two measures will not correspond exactly. Both measures do, however, follow a broadly similar trend which is linked to the economic cycle. Unemployment on both measures peaked in 1993 following the trough of the recession in 1992. Throughout the rest of this chapter it is the ILO measure of unemployment which has been used.

Unemployment rates are highest among young adults. In Spring 1996 a fifth of economically active 16 to 19 year old men, and a seventh of women of the same age, were unemployed (**Table 4.23**). However, this will include those in full-time further education who may only be seeking part-time jobs. About half of those aged 16 to 19 who were ILO unemployed were in full-time education. The rates for men are higher than those for women for all the age groups shown in the table and they also show a greater variability. In the year to Spring 1996 the unemployment rate fell for most age groups, with women aged 20 to 24 experiencing the biggest decrease. In contrast to the overall picture, the unemployment rate for 16 to 19 year old men increased slightly.

Comparisons with industrial competitors can give useful indicators of a country's performance. In 1995, while the unemployment rate in the United Kingdom was around 9 per cent, the EU average was 11 per cent. The highest rate of all the EU countries was in Spain at 23 per cent and the lowest was in Luxembourg at 3 per cent. Most EU countries, including the United Kingdom, experienced a fall in the rate of unemployment between 1994 and 1995; only in Italy, Greece and Portugal were there increases. **Chart 4.24** compares the unemployment rates for young and older

# 4.25

people in the countries of the EU. In all countries the unemployment rate in 1995 was higher for young people aged 15 to 24 than for people aged 25 to 59. Spain was the country with the highest unemployment rate for both these age groups. The unemployment rates in the United Kingdom were below the EU averages.

Unemployment rates also vary between the different areas of the United Kingdom with inner city areas and former industrial areas being particularly affected in recent years. Chart 4.25 shows unemployment rates in Spring 1996. Merseyside was the county with the highest unemployment rate, at 13 per cent. However, there are wide variations within counties. For example, Glasgow and Inner London have considerably higher unemployment rates, at 16 per cent and 15 per cent respectively, than their surrounding areas. Other counties which contain large

cities, such as Cleveland, Tyne and Wear and the West Midlands also have relatively high unemployment.

The lowest unemployment rates occur in the predominately rural counties, in particular in central and southern England. Oxfordshire had the lowest rate of all the counties in England and Wales in Spring 1996 at just 4 per cent. The counties of Northamptonshire, Berkshire and Surrey also had unemployment rates which were much lower than the average.

The duration of a spell of unemployment can vary for a number of reasons, such as skill factors and the type of work sought. Long term unemployment is defined as that which has lasted a year or more. Men are more likely to be long-term unemployed than women. Table 4.26 shows that nearly half of unemployed men in the United Kingdom had

**Unemployment rates[1]: by area, Spring 1996**

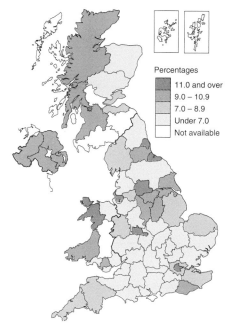

Percentages
- 11.0 and over
- 9.0 – 10.9
- 7.0 – 8.9
- Under 7.0
- Not available

1  Unemployment based on the ILO definition as a percentage of those economically active. See Appendix, Part 4: Unemployment - ILO definition.

**Source: Labour Force Survey, Office for National Statistics**

# 4.26

Duration of unemployment[1]: by gender and age, Spring 1996

**United Kingdom**                                                                                                                     Percentages

|  | Less than three months | Three months but less than six months | Six months but less than one year | One year but less than two years | Two years but less than three years | Three years or more | All durations |
|---|---|---|---|---|---|---|---|
| **Males** | | | | | | | |
| 16-19 | 39 | 21 | 22 | 12 | 5 | .. | 100 |
| 20-29 | 22 | 17 | 20 | 17 | 8 | 16 | 100 |
| 30-39 | 17 | 14 | 16 | 16 | 11 | 27 | 100 |
| 40-49 | 19 | 14 | 14 | 14 | 11 | 28 | 100 |
| 50-64 | 17 | 10 | 15 | 16 | 10 | 32 | 100 |
| | | | | | | | |
| All aged 16 and over[2] | 21 | 15 | 17 | 15 | 9 | 22 | 100 |
| **Females** | | | | | | | |
| 16-19 | 39 | 23 | 20 | 13 | .. | .. | 100 |
| 20-29 | 39 | 18 | 19 | 13 | 5 | 6 | 100 |
| 30-39 | 33 | 18 | 20 | 15 | 6 | 9 | 100 |
| 40-49 | 26 | 18 | 20 | 17 | 8 | 11 | 100 |
| 50-64 | 29 | 14 | 16 | 11 | .. | 20 | 100 |
| | | | | | | | |
| All aged 16 and over[2] | 34 | 18 | 19 | 14 | 6 | 8 | 100 |

1 Excludes those who did not state their duration. Unemployment is based on the ILO definition. See Appendix, Part 4: Unemployment - ILO definition.
2 Includes males aged 65 and over and females aged 60 and over who were unemployed.
**Source: Labour Force Survey, Office for National Statistics**

# 4.27

**People experiencing spells[1] of unemployment in their working life: by age, 1994-1995**

| Great Britain | | | | | Percentages |
|---|---|---|---|---|---|
| | None | One spell | Two spells | Three or more spells | All |
| 16-17 | 94 | 5 | 1 | 0 | 100 |
| 18-19 | 87 | 12 | 1 | - | 100 |
| 20-24 | 72 | 20 | 5 | 3 | 100 |
| 25-34 | 61 | 24 | 8 | 7 | 100 |
| 35-49 | 71 | 18 | 6 | 5 | 100 |
| 50-59 | 73 | 17 | 6 | 4 | 100 |
| 60-64 | 79 | 14 | 5 | 2 | 100 |
| 65 and over | 82 | 13 | 3 | 2 | 100 |
| All aged 16 and over | 72 | 18 | 6 | 4 | 100 |

1 Of one month or more.

*Source: Family and Working Lives Survey, Department for Education and Employment*

# 4.28

**Unemployment rates[1]: by highest qualification, Winter 1995-96**

| United Kingdom | | | Percentages |
|---|---|---|---|
| | Males | Females | All |
| Above A level[2] | 4.5 | 3.8 | 4.2 |
| GCE A level[3] | 8.0 | 5.7 | 7.3 |
| GCSE[3] | 10.6 | 6.2 | 8.1 |
| Other | 13.3 | 7.8 | 10.7 |
| None | 19.5 | 9.4 | 14.5 |
| All qualification levels | 10.0 | 6.4 | 8.4 |

1 People of working age. Males aged 16 to 64, females aged 16 to 59. Unemployment based on the ILO definition as a percentage of all economically active. See Appendix, Part 4: Unemployment - ILO definition.
2 Includes all nursing and teaching qualifications and degrees.
3 Or equivalent.

*Source: Labour Force Survey, Office for National Statistics*

been unemployed for a year or more in Spring 1996, compared with just over a quarter of women. The likelihood of long-term unemployment generally increases with age; nearly 60 per cent of unemployed men aged 50 to 64 were long-term unemployed compared with around 40 per cent of women.

The FWLS asked people in Great Britain about their experience of unemployment throughout their working lives. A spell of unemployment was defined as unemployment for a month or more as such significant spells of unemployment were felt to have a greater impact on a person's future labour market participation than shorter spells. Nearly three quarters of people had never had a significant spell of unemployment in their lives (Table 4.27). Of those who had experienced unemployment the majority had only had one spell. Having three or more spells of unemployment was relatively uncommon: only 4 per cent had recorded such experiences. People aged 25 to 34 were most likely to have had some

experience of unemployment and they were also the age group most likely to have experienced three or more spells of unemployment.

Qualifications can have a key impact on the likelihood of unemployment. People with no qualifications have an unemployment rate which is more than three times higher than for those educated above A level standard (Table 4.28). The difference is even more striking amongst males than females. Information on qualifications and training is contained in the Education and Training chapter.

There is a variety of means by which a person can find themselves a job. The main method which unemployed people used to try to obtain a job in Spring 1996 is shown in Table 4.29. People in non-manual groups were more likely to have used situations vacant columns than any other method. It was people in the manual groups who were the most likely to have visited a job centre.

Around a third of all vacancies in Great Britain are notified to Employment Service Jobcentres. In the year to September 1996, 221 thousand vacancies were notified, a fall of 7 thousand on the previous year. The region which experienced the greatest increase in vacancies over this period was Yorkshire and Humberside, where they rose by 4 per cent; the largest fall was recorded in the North West at 14 per cent.

Not all vacancies are filled easily. The Skill Needs in Britain Survey found that 38 per cent of firms experienced hard-to-fill vacancies in 1996. This is only slightly higher than the 1995 figure of 35 per cent which indicates a slow-down in recruitment

# 4.29

Main method of job search of the unemployed[1]: by socio-economic group, Spring 1996

**United Kingdom**                                                                                                                    Percentages

|  | Professionals and employers and managers | Intermediate non-manual | Junior non-manual | Skilled manual | Semi-skilled manual | Unskilled manual | All socio-economic groups |
|---|---|---|---|---|---|---|---|
| Visiting a job centre[2] | 14.3 | 12.2 | 25.2 | 32.3 | 35.4 | 39.6 | 29.0 |
| Studying situations vacant | 39.9 | 38.7 | 38.8 | 28.6 | 31.7 | 27.3 | 33.1 |
| Answering advertisements[3] | 12.7 | 16.7 | 12.1 | 8.2 | 7.5 | 7.6 | 9.6 |
| Personal contacts | 11.5 | 10.0 | 8.6 | 14.6 | 11.5 | 12.8 | 11.6 |
| Direct approach to firms/employers | 9.4 | 10.6 | 7.2 | 8.7 | 8.4 | 8.9 | 9.5 |
| Other methods[4] | 12.3 | 12.0 | 8.1 | 7.6 | 5.5 | .. | 7.1 |
| All methods | 100.0 | 100.0 | 100.0 | 100.0 | 100.0 | 100.0 | 100.0 |

1 Unemployment based on the ILO definition. See Appendix, Part 4: Unemployment - ILO definition. Excludes those who did not know or preferred not to state their job search methods and those temporarily not looking for work because they were either waiting to start a new job, temporarily sick or on holiday.
2 Includes Jobclubs, Jobcentres and Training/Employment Agency offices.
3 Includes notices outside factories or in shop windows.
4 Includes name on private agency books, advertising in newspapers/journals and awaiting job application results.
**Source: Labour Force Survey, Office for National Statistics**

difficulties. Hard-to-fill vacancies were most common in the associate professional and technical occupations, at 20 per cent.

The 1994 British Social Attitudes Survey found that job security was a major concern. Over a third of employees in Great Britain with a recognised trade union or staff association at their workplace said that the most important thing their trade union should try to do was to 'protect existing jobs'.

The general trend in redundancy rates has been downwards in the 1990s (Table 4.30). In Spring 1996 the redundancy rate for men was more than twice that for women: 13 per thousand employees compared with 6 per thousand. The highest redundancy rates occurred among people in the craft and related occupations and plant and machine operatives where 14 employees in every thousand were made redundant. Both these occupations have had high redundancy rates throughout the 1990s. People in the construction industry are more likely to have been affected by redundancy than those in

any other industry group, with a rate of 26 per thousand employees in Spring 1996. On the other hand employees in public administration, health and education experienced a redundancy rate of only 3 per thousand employees and were the least likely to have been made redundant.

# 4.30

Redundancy rates[1]: by occupation

**Great Britain**                                              Rate per 1,000 employees

|  | 1991 | 1992 | 1993 | 1994 | 1995 | 1996 |
|---|---|---|---|---|---|---|
| Managers and administrators | 13 | 12 | 8 | 10 | 10 | 8 |
| Professional | 8 | 6 | 6 | 5 | 5 | 7 |
| Associate professional and technical | 13 | 11 | 9 | 6 | 8 | 5 |
| Clerical and secretarial | 14 | 15 | 10 | 8 | 11 | 9 |
| Craft and related | 33 | 28 | 21 | 18 | 16 | 14 |
| Personal and protective services | 10 | 7 | 7 | 6 | 6 | 6 |
| Sales | 17 | 15 | 16 | 10 | 13 | 11 |
| Plant and machine operatives | 30 | 23 | 23 | 16 | 13 | 14 |
| Other occupations | 20 | 16 | 15 | 9 | 10 | 12 |
| All occupations | 18 | 15 | 12 | 10 | 10 | 9 |

1 At Spring each year. Redundancy in previous three months.
**Source: Labour Force Survey, Office for National Statistics**

## References and further reading

The following list contains selected publications relevant to **Chapter 4: Labour Market**. Those published by The Stationery Office are available from the addresses shown on the inside back cover of *Social Trends*.

*British Social Attitudes*, Dartmouth Publishing

*Living in Britain*, The Stationery Office

*How Exactly is Unemployment Measured?*, Office for National Statistics

*Labour Force Survey Quarterly Bulletin*, Office for National Statistics

*Labour Force Survey Historical Supplement*, The Stationery Office

*Labour Market Quarterly Report*, Office for National Statistics

*Labour Market Trends*, The Stationery Office

*Northern Ireland Labour Force Survey*, The Stationery Office

*Social Focus on Women*, The Stationery Office

*Statistics in Focus, Population and Social Indicators*, EUROSTAT

## Contacts

Telephone contact points for further information relating to

**Chapter 4: Labour Market**

| | |
|---|---|
| **Office for National Statistics** | |
| Chapter author | 0171 533 5780 |
| Claimant Count Unemployment Helpline | 0171 533 6104 |
| Labour Force Survey Helpline | 0171 533 6180 |
| **Department for Education and Employment** | |
| Family and Working Lives Survey | 0171 273 4879 |
| **Department of Economic Development (Northern Ireland)** | 01232 529550 |
| **Social & Community Planning Research** | 0171 250 1866 extn 369 |
| **Eurostat** | 00 352 4301 34567 |

# Chapter 5 Income and Wealth

**Household income and earnings**

Real household disposable income per head in the United Kingdom saw the highest year-on-year increase of the 1990s in 1995 at 2.2 per cent. (Chart 5.2)

Average gross weekly earnings in April 1996 were highest in Greater London at over £450 and lowest in Blaenau Gwent at £255. (Chart 5.6)

Almost a quarter of employees in Great Britain earned less than £4 an hour in Spring 1996. (Table 5.8)

**Income distribution**

The gap between high incomes and low incomes grew rapidly in the United Kingdom in the 1980s but has remained stable in the early 1990s. (Chart 5.1)

The proportion of people with incomes below half the average increased from 8 per cent in 1982 to just over 20 per cent between 1990 and 1992 since when it has fallen slightly. (Chart 5.18)

**Income dynamics**

At most, only 7 per cent of adults in Great Britain were among the poorest fifth throughout the period 1991 to 1994. (Page 100)

**Wealth**

Six in ten full-time male employees in Great Britain were members of an occupational pension scheme in 1995-96 while nearly three in ten had a personal pension. (Table 5.26)

**Income of the nation**

Luxembourg had the highest GDP per head in the European Union in 1995 and Greece the lowest; the United Kingdom was placed ninth at just below the EU average. (Chart 5.31)

## 5.1

**Real[1] household disposable income[2]**

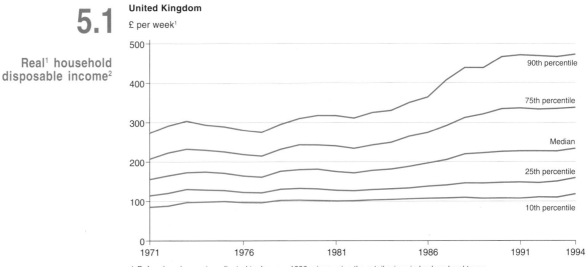

**United Kingdom**

£ per week[1]

1 Before housing costs, adjusted to January 1996 prices using the retail prices index less local taxes.
2 Equivalised disposable household income has been used for ranking the individuals. See Appendix, Part 5: Equivalisation scales.

*Source: Institute for Fiscal Studies*

# 5.2

### Real[1] household disposable income per head

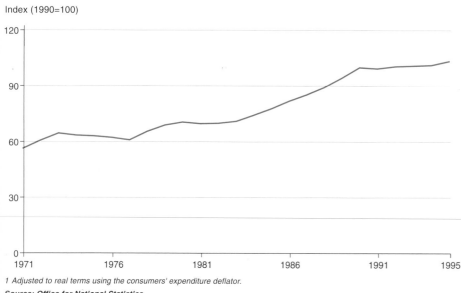

**United Kingdom**
Index (1990=100)

1 Adjusted to real terms using the consumers' expenditure deflator.
**Source: Office for National Statistics**

# 5.3

### Household income[1]

**United Kingdom**                                    Percentages

|  | 1971 | 1976 | 1981 | 1986 | 1991 | 1995 |
|---|---|---|---|---|---|---|
| **Source of income** | | | | | | |
| Wages and salaries[2] | 68 | 67 | 63 | 58 | 58 | 56 |
| Self-employment income[3] | 9 | 9 | 8 | 10 | 10 | 10 |
| Rent, dividends, interest | 6 | 6 | 7 | 8 | 9 | 7 |
| Private pensions, annuities, etc | 5 | 5 | 6 | 8 | 10 | 11 |
| Social security benefits | 10 | 11 | 13 | 13 | 11 | 13 |
| Other current transfers[4] | 2 | 2 | 2 | 3 | 2 | 3 |
| | | | | | | |
| Total household income | | | | | | |
| (=100%)(£ billion at 1995 prices[5]) | 314 | 365 | 398 | 472 | 573 | 599 |
| **Direct taxes etc as a percentage of** | | | | | | |
| **total household income** | | | | | | |
| Taxes on income | 14 | 17 | 14 | 14 | 14 | 13 |
| National insurance contributions[6] | 3 | 3 | 3 | 4 | 3 | 3 |
| Contributions to pension schemes | 1 | 2 | 2 | 2 | 2 | 1 |
| | | | | | | |
| Total household disposable income | | | | | | |
| (£ billion at 1995 prices[5]) | 256 | 284 | 320 | 379 | 467 | 493 |

1 See Appendix, Part 5: Household sector.
2 Includes Forces' pay and income in kind.
3 After deducting interest payments, depreciation and stock appreciation.
4 Mostly other government grants, but including transfers from abroad and non-profit making bodies.
5 Adjusted to 1995 prices using the consumers' expenditure deflator.
6 By employees and the self-employed.
**Source: Office for National Statistics**

Not only are income and wealth important measures of the standard of living of individuals and the country as a whole, they also directly influence the way that society is organised and its members behave.

## Household income and earnings

One of the most commonly used measures of living standards is disposable income: defined as the amount of money people have available to them to spend or invest. It is made up of income from all sources, less taxes on income, national insurance contributions and local taxes. The trend in household disposable income per head in the United Kingdom since 1971 is shown in **Chart 5.2**. This is expressed in real terms to allow meaningful comparisons from year to year by adjusting for the effect of inflation. It rose by nearly 80 per cent between 1971 and 1990 - equivalent to an average growth of 3.1 per cent a year. Since 1990 it has levelled off, although 1995 saw the highest year-on-year increase of this period at 2.2 per cent.

Households receive income from many sources; aggregate figures for the United Kingdom are summarised in **Table 5.3**. Wages and salaries account for more than half of all household income, although their share of income fell by 12 percentage points between 1971 and 1995. Over the same period income from private pensions and annuities doubled its share. This change is partly a result of the growing number of elderly people in the United Kingdom (see Table 1.5 in the Population chapter) and the increased likelihood of them having occupational pensions (see Table 5.5).

The figures in Chart 5.2 and Table 5.3 represent the aggregate income of the household sector in the United Kingdom as

# 5.4

defined in the national accounts (see Appendix, Part 5: Household sector). This covers the total income of all people living in households and institutions, and also income of private trusts. The following two tables, and some of the other charts and tables in this chapter, are based on sample surveys of individuals in households. The surveys collect information about households which enable household income to be analysed in more detail, for example by household type (Table 5.4). Couples with non-dependent children had the highest gross income in 1994-95, consisting mainly of earnings; these households contained more people of working age than other household types. Earnings represent at least three quarters of gross income for most households. The exceptions are retired and lone parent households who depend more on social security benefits.

Lone parents with dependent children received nearly half their income in the form of non-contributory cash benefits; these include income support and other benefits designed to supplement low incomes. Lone parent households earned three times as much when all children had become non-dependent. Retired households receive most of their income either from investment income, such as occupational and personal pensions, or from contributory cash benefits, such as the state retirement pension. Contributory benefits are based on the national insurance contributions made by the recipient when they were earning.

Table 5.5 measures changes over time in the pattern of gross income received by pensioners. They are defined here as single people over state pension age and couples where the husband is over state pension age, rather than the retired households included in Table 5.4. The proportion of income received from occupational pensions

## Sources of gross household income: by household type, 1994-95

United Kingdom
Percentages

| | Earned income[1] | Investment income[2] | Contributory cash benefits | Non-contributory cash benefits | Gross household income (=100%) (£ per week) |
|---|---|---|---|---|---|
| **Retired households[3]** | | | | | |
| Single person | - | 39 | 45 | 16 | 137 |
| Couple | 2 | 52 | 39 | 7 | 246 |
| Other | 16 | 37 | 32 | 15 | 301 |
| **Non-retired households** | | | | | |
| Single person | 80 | 8 | 4 | 9 | 266 |
| Lone parent | | | | | |
| Dependent children[4] | 37 | 12 | 1 | 49 | 203 |
| Non-dependent children only | 71 | 9 | 10 | 10 | 340 |
| Couple | | | | | |
| No children | 87 | 9 | 3 | 2 | 498 |
| Dependent children[4] | 88 | 4 | 1 | 7 | 537 |
| Non-dependent children only | 88 | 6 | 3 | 3 | 660 |
| Other | 76 | 9 | 5 | 11 | 503 |
| **All households** | 73 | 12 | 8 | 8 | 381 |

1 Including wages and salaries, self-employed income and income from 'fringe benefits'.
2 Including occupational pensions and annuities and other income.
3 Households where the combined income of retired members amounts to at least half the total gross income of the household.
4 Children aged under 16 and those aged 16 to 18 who are not married and receiving full-time non-advanced further education. This category includes households with a mixture of dependent and non-dependent children.
*Source: Family Expenditure Survey, Office for National Statistics*

# 5.5

## Gross income of pensioners[1]: by source

United Kingdom
Percentages

| | 1981 | 1990-1991 | 1992 | 1993 |
|---|---|---|---|---|
| Contributory benefits | 52 | 41 | 42 | 43 |
| Non-contributory benefits | 10 | 8 | 9 | 10 |
| Occupational pensions | 16 | 22 | 24 | 25 |
| Investments | 13 | 20 | 20 | 16 |
| Earnings | 9 | 7 | 6 | 6 |
| Other income | - | 1 | 1 | - |
| Gross income (=100%) (£ per week at July 1993 prices[2]) | 120.90 | 163.80 | 170.80 | 170.20 |

1 Single people above state pension age or couples where the husband is above state pension age.
2 Adjusted to July 1993 prices using the retail prices index less local taxes.
*Source: Department of Social Security*

# 5.6

## Average gross weekly earnings[1]: by area, April 1996

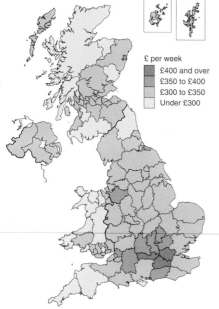

£ per week
- £400 and over
- £350 to £400
- £300 to £350
- Under £300

*1 Earnings include overtime for full-time employees on adult rates whose pay was not affected for the survey period by absence.*

**Source: New Earnings Survey, Office for National Statistics; Department of Economic Development, Northern Ireland**

has been increasing since 1981. The proportion received from investments increased in the 1980s but fell in the early 1990s, following a similar pattern to changes in interest rates. In 1993 pensioners who had retired in the last five years generally had higher gross incomes than those who had retired in earlier years, mainly due to higher incomes from earnings and occupational pensions. Investment income was also higher for recently retired pensioners.

For people with earnings from employment, the amount received varies according to where the employee works **(Chart 5.6)**. The main source of detailed earnings data is the New Earnings Survey, an annual survey of employers which collects information on full-time adult employees. In April 1996 the highest earners were concentrated in the South and South East, particularly Greater London where average gross weekly earnings were over £450. Elsewhere, the City of Aberdeen, Redcar and Cleveland and

Cheshire also had average earnings over £350. Employees in Blaenau Gwent had the lowest average weekly earnings at £255; likewise, earnings were below £300 for nearly half the unitary authorities in Wales. It is worth noting that it does not necessarily follow that employees in areas with low average earnings are being paid at a lower rate than employees in similar occupations elsewhere, since average earnings are also affected by the occupational and industrial structure of the labour market in each area.

There are large differences in earnings between different occupational groups in Great Britain. Of the occupations shown in **Chart 5.7**, medical practitioners earned the most in April 1996 at nearly four and a half times the rate of cleaners; this difference has increased since April 1981 when medical practitioners' earnings were three and a quarter times those of cleaners. The fall in real earnings of medical practitioners in April 1990 was due to part of their pay settlement for National Health Service (NHS) work not being paid until later in the year; the trend appears to return to its underlying level in 1992 since the full settlement for that year was paid in April. Real earnings of nurses and midwives working in the NHS grew at a faster rate than those of medical practitioners between 1981 and 1996, increasing by more than 50 per cent; the earnings of all nurses, including those working in the private sector, increased at an even faster rate. The rise in real earnings of nurses between 1988 and 1989 was largely due to the introduction of a new grading system which resulted in many nurses moving to higher paid grades.

Solicitors' earnings experienced the fastest growth of those occupations shown between 1981 and 1996, despite decreases in real terms between 1991 and 1995. In general, average earnings rose more rapidly for non-

# 5.7

## Real[1] gross earnings[2]: by selected occupation[3]

**Great Britain**

£ per week[1]

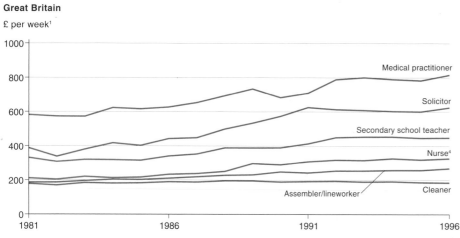

Medical practitioner

Solicitor

Secondary school teacher

Nurse[4]

Assembler/lineworker

Cleaner

*1 Adjusted to April 1996 prices using the retail prices index.*
*2 At April each year. Full-time employees on adult rates whose pay was not affected for the survey period by absence. Before 1983 average earnings are for men aged 21 and over and females aged 18 and over only.*
*3 The definitions of some of the occupations shown experienced minor changes when the Standard Occupational Classification was introduced in 1990. See Appendix, Part 5: Standard Occupational Classification.*
*4 National Health Service nurses and midwifery staff.*

**Source: New Earnings Survey, Office for National Statistics**

## 5.8

manual than manual occupations between 1981 and 1996, reaching £390 a week in April 1996 compared with £272 for manual workers.

The analysis in **Table 5.8** is based on the Labour Force Survey, a survey of households which includes part-time employees. It shows that average hourly earnings also vary widely for different industries, with employees in the banking, finance and insurance industries earning the most in Great Britain in Spring 1996 and those in agriculture and fishing earning the least. The earnings of those employees at the lower end of the earnings distribution are particularly relevant to discussions about a minimum wage. Overall, nearly 1 in 12 workers earns less than £3 an hour, while almost a quarter earn below £4 an hour. The industries with the highest proportion of low earners were agriculture and fishing, followed by distribution industries and other industries where more than one in three people work part time. More detailed analyses of part-time workers are given in the Labour Market chapter. The pattern of low earners does not vary greatly between the remaining industries other than for energy and water supply, where fewer than one in ten workers earns less than £5 an hour.

The majority of part-time employees are women (see Table 4.7 in the Labour Market chapter), but even among full-time employees women are more likely than men to be at the lower end of the earnings distribution **(Chart 5.9)**. More than half of women employed full time in the United Kingdom earned less than £250 a week in April 1996 compared with fewer than three in ten men. Conversely, only 5 per cent of women earned more than £500 a week compared with 15 per cent of men. The lower average earnings of women are due

**Gross hourly earnings[1]: by industry, Spring 1996**

Great Britain                                                         Percentages

|  | Earning below hourly rate of | | | Average earnings (£ per hour) |
|---|---|---|---|---|
|  | £3 | £4 | £5 |  |
| Banking, finance and insurance | 6 | 15 | 27 | 9.57 |
| Energy and water supply | - | 3 | 9 | 9.39 |
| Public administration, education and health | 5 | 17 | 29 | 8.08 |
| Transport and communication | 4 | 13 | 31 | 7.91 |
| Construction | 3 | 13 | 25 | 7.83 |
| Manufacturing | 4 | 15 | 31 | 7.66 |
| Distribution[2] | 18 | 47 | 66 | 5.10 |
| Agriculture and fishing | 23 | 44 | 68 | 4.91 |
| Other industries | 17 | 42 | 58 | 5.77 |
| All industries | 8 | 24 | 38 | 7.42 |

1 Both full and part-time employees, including overtime payments.
2 Includes retail, wholesale, repairs, hotels and restaurants.
**Source: Labour Force Survey, Office for National Statistics**

partly to the different patterns of occupations between men and women, and partly to the differences in status within those occupations.

## 5.9

**Average gross earnings[1]: by gender, April 1996**

**United Kingdom**
Percentages

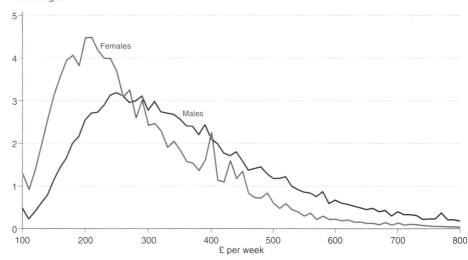

1 Full-time employees on adult rates whose pay was not affected for the survey period by absence.
**Source: New Earnings Survey, Office for National Statistics and Department of Economic Development, Northern Ireland**

# 5.10

### Relative earnings[1] of male and female partners[2], 1994-95

| Great Britain | Percentages |
|---|---|
| | 1994-95 |
| Man earns over £100 more | 54 |
| Man earns £50-£100 more | 11 |
| Earnings are equal[3] | 21 |
| Woman earns £50-£100 more | 4 |
| Woman earns over £100 more | 10 |
| All couples[2] | 100 |

1 Gross weekly earnings from employment or self - employment.
2 One man/one woman couples (with or without children) where both partners work full time.
3 Equal to within £50 per week.

**Source: Family Resources Survey, Department of Social Security**

Although the difference between male and female average earnings has decreased since 1986, in most couples the male partner earns more than the female. This is summarised in **Table 5.10** which concentrates on couples where both partners are working full time. This group represents nearly half of all couples of working age. The man earned at least £50 a week more than the woman in almost two thirds of these couples in 1994-95. More than five in ten couples, where the man earned at least £100 a week more than the woman, had dependent children; this compares with fewer than four in ten couples where the earnings were roughly equal.

Around 3.8 million people in the United Kingdom received self-employment income assessable to tax in 1994-95. This measure generally represents income earned in the previous financial year, after deductions for allowable losses and capital allowances (see Appendix, Part 5: Self-employment income assessable to tax). Self-employment income in the financial and business services industries was, at £18 thousand, 50 per cent higher than the average (**Chart 5.11**). However, there was little difference among the other industries which were around £10 or £11 thousand. More than 1 million self-employed people worked in the construction industry, which accounted for a quarter of all self- employment income, the same proportion as the financial industries and business services. The self-employed supplemented their earnings, with about a quarter of their total income assessable to tax coming from other sources over this period.

## Taxes

The Inland Revenue has estimated that there will be nearly 26 million income tax-payers in the tax year 1996-97, just over half the adult population of the United Kingdom, with a total income tax bill of over £70 billion (**Table 5.12**). There are three different rates of tax: lower, basic and higher. Income tax rates have been reduced since 1978-79, particularly for those with high incomes. The basic rate fell progressively from 33 per cent in April 1978 to 25 per cent in April 1988; the lower rate of 20 per cent was introduced in April 1992 and the basic rate was reduced once again to 24 per cent in April 1996. The higher tax rates, which were at a maximum of 83 per cent on earned income between 1974-75 and 1978-79, have been replaced by a single rate of 40 per cent. In 1996-97 nearly three quarters of taxpayers will have part of their income taxed at the basic rate, while fewer than one in ten will be taxed at

# 5.11

### Self-employment income assessable to tax[1]: by industry, 1994-95[2]

**United Kingdom**
£ thousand

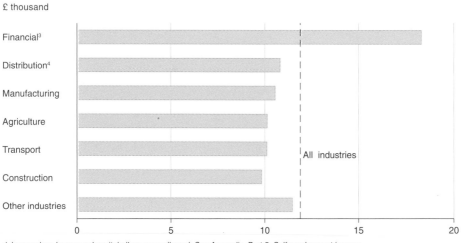

1 Income less losses and capital allowances allowed. See Appendix, Part 5: Self-employment income.
2 On average, income assessable to 1994-95 tax is that earned in 1993. See Appendix, Part 5: Self-employment income.
3 Includes business services and renting other than property.
4 Includes retail, wholesale, repairs, hotels and restaurants.

**Source: Inland Revenue**

# 5.12

the higher rate. The average taxpayer will pay 17 per cent of his or her income in income tax.

National Insurance Contributions (NICs) are paid by people earning over a certain amount (£61 a week in 1996-97). Most of this money goes into the National Insurance Fund from which contributory social security benefits are paid, while the rest goes to the National Health Service. The rates of NICs were simplified from five bands to two in 1989. Rates are calculated as a percentage of earnings and in 1996-97 will only be paid on the first £455 of weekly earnings. Employees entirely covered by the state pension scheme pay contributions of 2 per cent on the first £61 and 10 per cent on the balance. For those employees whose jobs have been contracted out of the earnings-related part of the state scheme, the rates are 2.0 per cent and 8.2 per cent respectively.

The data in Table 5.13 are not estimated from a survey of real households but are modelled based on assumptions about earnings and family circumstances. A single man on half average earnings will pay 14 per cent of his earnings in income tax in 1996-97, compared with only 11 per cent for a married man on the same earnings (with a non-earning wife). This gap closes as earnings increase. The average proportion of earnings paid in income tax is expected to fall between 1995-96 and 1996-97 because the 1995 Budget increased allowances and thresholds in real terms and reduced the basic rate of tax. The proportion of earnings paid in NICs by the men in Table 5.13 is not affected by marital status. However, those on average earnings in 1996-97 will pay a higher proportion than those on either half or twice average earnings.

## Income tax payable: by annual income[1], 1996-97[2]

United Kingdom

| | Number of taxpayers paying tax at | | | Total tax payable (£ million) | Average rate of tax payable (percent-ages) | Average amount of tax payable (£ per year) |
|---|---|---|---|---|---|---|
| | Lower rate (millions) | Basic rate (millions) | Excess over basic rate (millions) | | | |
| £3,765-£4,999 | 1.4 | . | . | 140 | 2 | 100 |
| £5,000-£7,499 | 4.0 | . | . | 1,390 | 6 | 350 |
| £7,500-£9,999 | 3.7 | 2.5 | . | 2,970 | 9 | 790 |
| £10,000-£14,999 | 6.1 | 5.8 | . | 9,500 | 13 | 1,560 |
| £15,000-£19,999 | 4.1 | 4.0 | . | 10,900 | 15 | 2,630 |
| £20,000-£29,999 | 4.1 | 4.0 | - | 16,800 | 17 | 4,090 |
| £30,000-£49,999 | 1.6 | 1.6 | 1.4 | 12,300 | 21 | 7,870 |
| £50,000-£99,999 | 0.5 | 0.5 | 0.5 | 9,060 | 28 | 18,700 |
| £100,000 and over | 0.1 | 0.1 | 0.1 | 9,700 | 35 | 66,000 |
| All incomes | 25.6 | 18.5 | 2.1 | 72,700 | 17 | 2,840 |

1 Total income of the individual for income tax purposes including earned and investment income. Figures relate to taxpayers only.
2 Based on projections from the 1994-95 Survey of Personal Incomes.
*Source: Inland Revenue*

# 5.13

## Percentage of earnings paid in income tax and national insurance contributions[1]: by marital status and level of earnings[2]

United Kingdom | | | | Percentages |

| | 1971-72 | 1981-82 | 1991-92 | 1996-97[3] |
|---|---|---|---|---|
| **Single man** | | | | |
| Half average earnings | | | | |
| Tax | 16 | 19 | 15 | 14 |
| NIC | 7 | 8 | 7 | 7 |
| Average earnings | | | | |
| Tax | 23 | 25 | 20 | 19 |
| NIC | 6 | 7 | 8 | 8 |
| Twice average earnings | | | | |
| Tax | 27 | 29 | 26 | 26 |
| NIC | 3 | 5 | 5 | 5 |
| **Married man[4]** | | | | |
| Half average earnings | | | | |
| Tax | 10 | 13 | 10 | 11 |
| NIC | 7 | 8 | 7 | 7 |
| Average earnings | | | | |
| Tax | 20 | 22 | 18 | 18 |
| NIC | 6 | 7 | 8 | 8 |
| Twice average earnings | | | | |
| Tax | 25 | 27 | 24 | 26 |
| NIC | 3 | 5 | 5 | 5 |

1 Employees' contributions. Assumes contributions at Class 1, contracted in, standard rate.
2 Average earnings for full-time male employees in all occupations working a full week on adult rates.
3 Based on projections from the 1994-95 Survey of Personal Incomes.
4 Assuming wife not in paid employment.
*Source: Inland Revenue*

# 5.14

**Direct taxes and social security contributions[1] as a percentage of personal income: G7 comparison, 1994**

Percentages

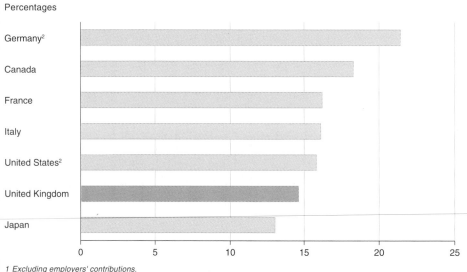

1 Excluding employers' contributions.
2 Data are for 1993.
**Source: OECD**

# 5.15

**Indirect taxes as a percentage of disposable income: by income grouping[1] of household, 1994-95**

**United Kingdom**
Percentages

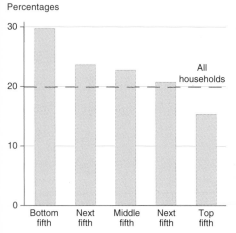

1 Equivalised disposable income has been used for ranking the households. See Appendix, Part 5: Equivalisation scales.
**Source: Office for National Statistics**

Direct taxes and social security contributions as a percentage of total personal income are compared in Chart 5.14 for the Group of Seven (G7) countries. These are the major industrialised countries and together they account for almost half of world Gross Domestic Product. Among these countries, deductions were highest for Germany at 21.4 per cent in 1993, the latest year for which this figure was available, while Japan had the lowest rate at 13.0 per cent in 1994. In 1985 deductions were highest for the United Kingdom at 16.3 per cent, but had fallen to 14.6 per cent of personal income in 1994 - the second lowest.

When making international comparisons it is necessary to make adjustments for definitions and coverages. This means that the United Kingdom figures used here are not strictly comparable with figures used elsewhere in this chapter. For example, council tax is classified as a direct tax here

but not in Table 5.3. A number of other factors should be taken into account when making these comparisons, particularly the differing balance between direct and indirect taxation. In 1994 the United Kingdom had the highest indirect taxes of the G7 countries when expressed as a proportion of total taxes and social security contributions, while Japan had the lowest. It should also be noted that there will be differences in government involvement in the provision of services and financial support (such as medical care and pensions) which are free or subsidised at the point of use.

As well as paying tax on their income and national insurance contributions, people in the United Kingdom also pay indirect taxes which include Value Added Tax (VAT), customs duties and Vehicle Excise Duty. In 1994-95 households paid one fifth of their disposable income in indirect taxes on average (Chart 5.15). The households in this chart have been divided into quintile groups according to the level of their equivalised disposable income, with each group representing one fifth of all households. Equivalisation takes into account the size and composition of the household in order to recognise differing demands on resources. For example, to achieve the same standard of living, a household of five would need a higher income than a single person (see Appendix, Part 5: Equivalisation scales).

The lower a household's disposable income, the higher the percentage paid in indirect taxes. However, the top fifth still pay the most in absolute terms (see Chart 5.17). Another way of comparing the burden of indirect taxation on a household is to express indirect taxes as a percentage of expenditure on goods and services, as households in the bottom fifth may have higher expenditure (on which most indirect taxes fall) than income. This is possible when households spend savings or loans. Indirect taxes paid by the bottom fifth represented 30 per cent of disposable income but only 22 per cent of expenditure, just one and a half percentage points above the average.

## Income distribution

Most government income is raised from households through direct and indirect taxes and social security contributions (see Table 5.29); much of its spending then benefits households. Some households will be taxed more than they benefit, while others will benefit more than they are taxed - this is the principle of redistribution of income. The tables and charts in this section generally present data by quintile groups of household income, using the same method to rank households as in Chart 5.15.

The average incomes of households in each quintile at each stage of the redistribution process are compared in Table 5.16. Households initially receive income from various non-government sources including employment, occupational pensions, investments and transfers from other households - this is called original income. Cash benefits from the state (for example, retirement pensions and income support) are added to original income to give gross income. This income is then reduced by income tax payments, NICs and local tax payments (such as council tax) to leave disposable income. The deduction of indirect tax payments, such as VAT, results in post-tax income. Households also benefit from government expenditure on services such as education and health; adding in

Redistribution of income through taxes and benefits[1], 1994-95

| United Kingdom | | | | | | £ per year |
|---|---|---|---|---|---|---|
| | Quintile group of households[2] | | | | | All house-holds |
| | Bottom fifth | Next fifth | Middle fifth | Next fifth | Top fifth | |
| **Average per household** | | | | | | |
| Wages and salaries | 1,180 | 3,830 | 10,230 | 17,820 | 28,250 | 12,260 |
| Imputed income from benefits in kind | 10 | 20 | 100 | 310 | 950 | 280 |
| Self-employment income | 260 | 510 | 1,050 | 1,550 | 6,160 | 1,910 |
| Occupational pensions, annuities | 280 | 780 | 1,300 | 1,520 | 2,220 | 1,220 |
| Investment income | 170 | 260 | 500 | 800 | 2,420 | 830 |
| Other income | 140 | 200 | 190 | 250 | 340 | 230 |
| **Total original income** | 2,040 | 5,600 | 13,380 | 22,250 | 40,330 | 16,720 |
| *plus* Benefits in cash | | | | | | |
| Contributory | 1,930 | 2,290 | 1,620 | 1,050 | 680 | 1,510 |
| Non-contributory | 2,730 | 2,180 | 1,540 | 900 | 490 | 1,570 |
| **Gross income** | 6,700 | 10,080 | 16,540 | 24,200 | 41,510 | 19,800 |
| *less* Income tax[3] and NIC[4] | 270 | 760 | 2,300 | 4,360 | 9,350 | 3,410 |
| *less* Local taxes[5] (gross) | 570 | 550 | 630 | 680 | 790 | 640 |
| **Disposable income** | 5,860 | 8,760 | 13,610 | 19,150 | 31,370 | 15,750 |
| *less* Indirect taxes | 1,740 | 2,070 | 3,090 | 3,960 | 4,810 | 3,130 |
| **Post-tax income** | 4,120 | 6,700 | 10,520 | 15,190 | 26,570 | 12,620 |
| *plus* Benefits in kind | | | | | | |
| Education | 1,600 | 1,250 | 1,390 | 1,200 | 670 | 1,220 |
| National Health Service | 1,790 | 1,720 | 1,660 | 1,460 | 1,270 | 1,580 |
| Housing subsidy | 80 | 80 | 40 | 20 | 10 | 50 |
| Travel subsidies | 50 | 60 | 60 | 90 | 130 | 80 |
| School meals and welfare milk | 80 | 20 | 10 | 10 | - | 30 |
| **Final income** | 7,720 | 9,840 | 13,690 | 17,970 | 28,640 | 15,570 |

1 See Appendix, Part 5: Redistribution of income.
2 Equivalised disposable income has been used for ranking the households. See Appendix, Part 5: Equivalisation scales.
3 After tax relief at source on mortgage interest and life assurance premiums.
4 Employees' national insurance contributions.
5 Gross council tax, rates and water charges. Rates in Northern Ireland.
**Source: Office for National Statistics**

estimates of the value of these services gives a household's final income. In 1994-95 the average original income for households in the bottom fifth of the distribution was about £38 thousand less than the average for those in the top fifth. After the addition of cash benefits and benefits in kind and the deduction of direct and indirect taxes, the difference was reduced to £21 thousand.

**Decile or quintile group-** The main method of analysing income distribution used in this chapter is to rank units (households, individuals or adults) by a given income measure, and then to divide the ranked units into groups of equal size. Groups comprising 20 per cent of units are known as 'quintile groups' and those comprising 10 per cent of units are known as 'decile groups'. Thus the 'bottom quintile group' is the 20 per cent of units with the lowest incomes.

# 5.17

Taxes and benefits[1]: by income grouping[2], 1994-95

**United Kingdom**

£ thousand per year

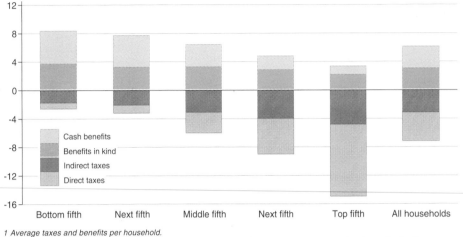

1 Average taxes and benefits per household.
2 Equivalised disposable income has been used for ranking the households into quintile groups. See Appendix, Part 5: Equivalisation scales.

**Source: Office for National Statistics**

**Percentile points** - the term 'percentile point' is used to refer to that income below which a given percentage of the population fall. Thus 10 per cent of units have incomes below the 10th percentile. The 50th percentile is also known as the median.

The average taxes paid and benefits received by households in each quintile group are used in Chart 5.17 to summarise the redistribution of income. Direct taxes and cash benefits are the most effective measures for redistributing income from those on higher incomes to those on lower incomes. Indirect taxes and benefits in kind also have a redistributive effect but to a lesser extent.

Such analyses by the Office for National Statistics (ONS) are based on data from the Family Expenditure Survey (FES) and look at the picture of income redistribution for the latest year. The Department of Social Security (DSS) analyse the FES data (and more recently Family Resources Survey data) focussing on households below average income and changes over time (see Appendix, Part 5: Households Below Average Income). The methodology used differs in several respects from that used by the ONS; in particular it is based on individuals rather than households (see Appendix, Part 5: Difference between Households Below Average Income and Redistribution of Income series). The total equivalised income of a household is used to represent the income level of every individual in that household; all individuals are then ranked according to this level. The equivalisation takes into account the size and composition of the household in order to recognise differing demands on resources. The Institute for Fiscal Studies have extended the DSS analysis, using FES data and the same methodology, to examine longer term trends in the income distribution.

Between 1971 and 1994 average (median) real household disposable income rose by nearly 50 per cent (Chart 5.1). However, the gap between those with high and low incomes has grown over time, particularly during the 1980s. Between 1980 and 1990 incomes grew by 47 per cent at the ninetieth percentile compared with only 6 per cent at the tenth percentile. In the early 1990s the gap has stabilised. This has occurred at the same time as a slowing in the growth in household disposable income (see Chart 5.2) and Gross Domestic Product per head

# 5.18

Percentage of people whose income is below various fractions of average income[1]

**United Kingdom**

Percentages

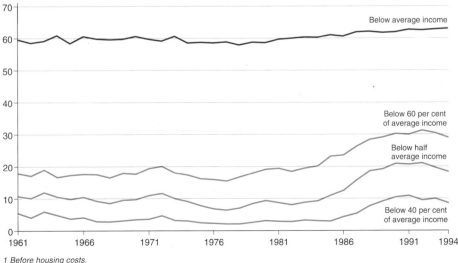

1 Before housing costs.

**Source: Institute for Fiscal Studies**

(see Chart 5.28). In 1994 real incomes grew at each of the percentiles shown in Chart 5.1 but, in contrast to the pattern of the mid-1980s, the gap between incomes at the ninetieth and tenth percentiles decreased.

The income distribution can also be analysed by examining the number of individuals whose income lies below various fractions of average income. The proportion of individuals below average income has generally increased slowly since the late 1970s, reaching 63 per cent in 1994 (Chart 5.18). In contrast, the proportion of people below either 40, 50 or 60 per cent of the average increased rapidly in the 1980s. In recent years these proportions have levelled off and all three were falling by 1994. These trends are features of the widening of the income distribution in the 1980s followed by more stability in the 1990s, as demonstrated in Chart 5.1.

The effects that changes in the income distribution have on society can be better understood if we know what types of household can be found at various levels of income. In 1993-1995 two in five people in the bottom fifth were from families composed of couples with dependent children - the same proportion as in the population as a whole (Table 5.19). People from lone parent families were the most over represented in the bottom fifth where the concentration was twice as high as in the population as a whole. In contrast, couples without children were under represented. Pensioners were less likely to be in the bottom fifth in 1993-1995 than in 1981, whereas single people without children were more likely.

Generally ethnic minority groups are also over represented among low income households in Great Britain (Table 5.20). Nearly two thirds of people in households

with a Pakistani or Bangladeshi head were in the bottom quintile in 1994-95, while only 8 per cent were in the top two quintiles. People in households headed by a person from either the Black or Indian groups were also over represented in the bottom fifth but to a lesser extent. These patterns are a result of differences between ethnic groups in areas such as employment rates, types of employment, female participation in the labour market and family sizes. For example, among the Pakistani/Bangladeshi group, only half the men of working age were in employment in Spring 1995 and three quarters of women of working age were not participating in the labour market - twice the rate for females in the Black and Indian ethnic groups. In contrast, some ethnic groups have relatively few old people (see Table 1.8 in the Population chapter) which will affect their position in the income distribution as there is a high proportion of retired households in the bottom quintile.

# 5.19

Individuals in the bottom income quintile[1]: by family type

| United Kingdom | | | | Percentages |
|---|---|---|---|---|
| | 1981 | | 1993-1995[2] | |
| | Bottom fifth | All individuals | Bottom fifth | All individuals |
| Single pensioner | 12 | 8 | 10 | 8 |
| Pensioner couple[3] | 16 | 9 | 11 | 9 |
| Single person without children[4] | 10 | 16 | 15 | 16 |
| Single person with children[4] | 10 | 5 | 16 | 7 |
| Couple without children[4] | 6 | 18 | 10 | 21 |
| Couple with children[4] | 46 | 45 | 38 | 38 |
| All individuals (=100%)(millions) | 10.9 | 54.7 | 11.5 | 57.3 |

1 Equivalised household disposable income, before housing costs, has been used for ranking the individuals. See Appendix, Part 5: Equivalisation scales.
2 Combined years: 1993-94 and 1994-95.
3 Couples where the husband is above state pension age.
4 Dependent children.
**Source: Department of Social Security**

# 5.20

Distribution of disposable income[1]: by ethnic group[2], 1994-95

| Great Britain | | Percentages |
|---|---|---|
| | Quintile group of individuals | |
| | Bottom fifth | Top four fifths |
| White | 19 | 81 |
| Black | 27 | 73 |
| Indian | 27 | 73 |
| Pakistani/Bangladeshi | 64 | 36 |
| Other ethnic minorities | 36 | 64 |
| All ethnic groups | 20 | 80 |

1 Equivalised household disposable income, before housing costs, has been used for ranking the individuals. See Appendix, Part 5: Equivalisation scales.
2 Ethnic group of head of household.
**Source: Department of Social Security**

# 5.21

Adults moving within the income distribution[1] between 1991 and 1994

**Great Britain**                                           Percentages

| | Income fell 4 or more deciles | Income fell 2-3 deciles | Income stable[2] | Income rose 2-3 deciles | Income rose 4 or more deciles |
|---|---|---|---|---|---|
| **1991 income grouping** | | | | | |
| Lowest decile | . | . | 60 | 22 | 19 |
| 2nd decile | . | . | 75 | 16 | 9 |
| 3rd decile | . | 12 | 61 | 17 | 9 |
| 4th decile | . | 12 | 61 | 16 | 11 |
| 5th decile | 5 | 18 | 49 | 22 | 6 |
| 6th decile | 9 | 14 | 60 | 16 | 2 |
| 7th decile | 11 | 18 | 59 | 13 | . |
| 8th decile | 14 | 12 | 65 | 9 | . |
| 9th decile | 16 | 16 | 68 | . | . |
| Highest decile | 10 | 14 | 76 | . | . |
| All adults | 7 | 12 | 64 | 13 | 5 |

1 Equivalised household gross income has been used for ranking the adults. See Appendix, Part 5: Equivalisation scales.
2 Did not change income group, or fell by one decile or rose by one decile.

**Source: British Household Panel Survey, ESRC Research Centre on Micro-social Change**

# 5.22

Adults moving within the income distribution[1] between consecutive years: by type of household change, 1991 to 1994[2]

**Great Britain**                                           Percentages

| | Income fell 2 or more deciles | Income stable[3] | Income rose 2 or more deciles |
|---|---|---|---|
| No change | 12 | 76 | 13 |
| Birth only | 23 | 68 | 9 |
| Adult child departs only | 19 | 64 | 17 |
| Death of partner only | 10 | 60 | 30 |
| Child leaving parental home[4] | 50 | 32 | 18 |
| Join with partner[5]: | | | |
|   Males | 23 | 50 | 26 |
|   Females | 17 | 49 | 33 |
| Separate from partner[6]: | | | |
|   Males | 20 | 52 | 27 |
|   Females | 44 | 42 | 14 |
| Other changes | 19 | 57 | 25 |
| All adults | 14 | 73 | 14 |

1 Equivalised household gross income has been used to rank the adults. See Appendix, Part 5: Equivalisation scales.
2 Changes in income and household composition for the periods 1991 to 1992, 1992 to 1993 and 1993 to 1994 have been analysed separately and then combined in this table.
3 Did not change income group, or fell by one decile or rose by one decile.
4 Change in income group experienced by the departing child. Includes all children leaving their parental home except those who join with a partner in the same year.
5 Includes all those joining a partner regardless of other changes in the same year.
6 Includes all those who separate from a partner except those who had joined a partner in the same year.

**Source: British Household Panel Survey, ESRC Research Centre on Micro-social Change**

## Income dynamics

Whereas the previous section explored the characteristics of the income distribution at particular points in time, this section analyses the changes that individuals experience over time. In fact people are changing positions in the income distribution all the time. It is important to explore the extent of this mobility, since there is a big difference between the extreme cases of a society where one fifth of the people are in the bottom quintile all the time and a society where everyone is the bottom quintile once every five years. The British Household Panel Survey has been re-interviewing the same sample of people annually since 1991 and can be used to analyse how individuals move between income groupings.

In Table 5.21 the adults have been divided into ten decile groups according to 1991 income; a similar analysis was carried out using 1994 data and movements of adults between income groups were tracked. This shows that around two thirds of adults in Great Britain were in roughly the same position in the income distribution in 1994 compared with 1991. The opportunities for substantial change depend somewhat on the starting point: those in the lowest two decile groups cannot fall further, though they may of course experience a drop in living standards. Those in the lowest decile were more likely to have moved upwards by 1994 than those in the top decile were to have moved downwards. While 33 per cent of all adults were in the lowest two deciles (the bottom quintile) during at least one of the survey periods between 1991 and 1994, only 7 per cent of adults were there during all four survey periods. The overall proportion of people that had changed their position in the income distribution between 1991 and 1994 was greater than the

# 5.23

proportion changing over shorter periods. However, the proportion who had moved between 1991 and 1994, at 36 per cent, was only slightly higher than the 34 per cent that had moved between 1991 and 1993. This is due partly to people returning to their 1991 position between 1993 and 1994, and partly to those who had not moved in the first two years being much less likely to move in subsequent years.

Income mobility is often associated with changes in the composition of the household. Such changes will affect equivalised income due to the changing demands on the resources of the household (see Appendix, Part 5: Equivalisation scales) and may affect the number of people in the household available for work. Whereas Table 5.21 looked at income mobility between 1991 and 1994, Table 5.22 shows year-on-year changes in income and household composition combined over the four year period. Between 1991 and 1994, on average, 17 per cent of households experienced some form of change in household structure each year.

The birth of a child is more likely to result in a fall in equivalised income than a rise: increases in household size cause a decrease in equivalised income, while in some households the mother may have left employment, at least temporarily. Children leaving the parental home were the most likely to experience a fall in household income: the income of their new household was two or more deciles lower in half the cases. A high proportion of women separating from their partners experienced a substantial drop in income, while men were more likely to experience a rise than a fall. This is a result of men being the main earner in the majority of partnerships, even where both partners work full time (see Table 5.10).

**Adults leaving or remaining in the bottom income quintile[1] between consecutive years: by change in employment status, 1991-1994[2]**

Great Britain                                                                    Percentages

|  | Remain in bottom fifth | Leave bottom fifth | Start in bottom fifth |
|---|---|---|---|
| **No change in employment status** | | | |
| Employed[3] | 40 | 60 | 100 |
| Unemployed | 81 | 19 | 100 |
| Retired | 68 | 32 | 100 |
| Other inactive | 71 | 29 | 100 |
| | | | |
| All with no change in employment status | 67 | 33 | 100 |
| **Any change in employment status** | | | |
| Enter employment | 24 | 76 | 100 |
| Leave employment | 68 | 32 | 100 |
| Other change[3] | 67 | 33 | 100 |
| | | | |
| All with a change in employment status | 54 | 46 | 100 |
| **All adults starting in the bottom quintile** | 64 | 36 | 100 |

1 Equivalised household gross income has been used to rank the adults. See Appendix, Part 5: Equivalisation scales.
2 Changes in income and employment status for the periods 1991 to 1992, 1992 to 1993 and 1993 to 1994 have been analysed separately and then combined in this table.
3 Adults changing between the different employment categories of full time, part time and self employed are included in the 'other change' category.
**Source: British Household Panel Survey, ESRC Research Centre on Micro-social Change**

The number of earners in a household is affected not only by changes in household composition, but also by changes in the employment status of existing household members. Table 5.23 summarises the effects on an adult's position in the income distribution of a change in employment status during any one year, concentrating on those who are initially in the bottom quintile group. Three quarters of adults who entered employment between 1991 and 1994 left the bottom quintile group. However, nearly one in three people who left employment also left the bottom quintile group, due to other changes, for example in the composition of their household or in the income of other household members. In particular, it should be noted that an adult's household income can increase due to another member of the household changing employment status.

# 5.24

Composition of the net wealth[1] of the personal sector

**United Kingdom**      Percentages

|  | 1971 | 1981 | 1991 | 1995 |
|---|---|---|---|---|
| Life assurance and pension funds | 15 | 17 | 26 | 34 |
| Dwellings (net of mortgage debt) | 26 | 36 | 36 | 26 |
| Stocks, shares and unit trusts | 23 | 8 | 11 | 15 |
| National Savings, notes and coins and bank deposits | 13 | 10 | 9 | 10 |
| Shares and deposits with building societies | 7 | 8 | 8 | 7 |
| Non-marketable tenancy rights | 12 | 12 | 8 | 5 |
| Other fixed assets | 10 | 11 | 5 | 5 |
| Other financial assets net of liabilities | -6 | -2 | -3 | -2 |
| Total net wealth (=100%)(£ billion at 1995 prices[2]) | 1,207 | 1,459 | 2,658 | 2,830 |

1 See Appendix, Part 5: Net wealth of the personal sector.
2 Adjusted to 1995 prices using the consumers' expenditure deflator.
**Source: Office for National Statistics**

# 5.25

Distribution of wealth[1]

**United Kingdom**      Percentages

|  | 1976 | 1981 | 1986 | 1991 | 1993 |
|---|---|---|---|---|---|
| **Marketable wealth** | | | | | |
| Percentage of wealth owned by[2]: | | | | | |
| Most wealthy 1% | 21 | 18 | 18 | 17 | 17 |
| Most wealthy 5% | 38 | 36 | 36 | 35 | 36 |
| Most wealthy 10% | 50 | 50 | 50 | 47 | 48 |
| Most wealthy 25% | 71 | 73 | 73 | 71 | 72 |
| Most wealthy 50% | 92 | 92 | 90 | 92 | 93 |
| Total marketable wealth (£ billion) | 280 | 565 | 955 | 1,711 | 1,746 |
| **Marketable wealth less value of dwellings** | | | | | |
| Percentage of wealth owned by[2] | | | | | |
| Most wealthy 1% | 29 | 26 | 25 | 29 | 26 |
| Most wealthy 5% | 47 | 45 | 46 | 51 | 51 |
| Most wealthy 10% | 57 | 56 | 58 | 64 | 63 |
| Most wealthy 25% | 73 | 74 | 75 | 80 | 80 |
| Most wealthy 50% | 88 | 87 | 89 | 93 | 93 |

1 Estimates are based on the estates of people dying in those years.
2 Applies to people aged 18 and over.
**Source: Inland Revenue**

## Wealth

Some individuals may maintain a standard of living at a higher level than their current income would suggest by relying on wealth accumulated in previous years. The value of wealth held by the personal sector in the United Kingdom was £2,830 billion in 1995, more than twice as high in real terms as in 1971 (Table 5.24). The personal sector consists mainly of individuals living in households and institutions, but also includes unincorporated private businesses, life assurance and pension funds. The percentage of net wealth held in dwellings (net of mortgage debt) has declined since 1988 as house prices have fallen. The fall in the percentage held in stocks, shares and unit trusts in the 1970s was due to a large fall in share prices in the early part of the decade and a change in the pattern of investment, from direct investment in securities and equities, to indirect investment through life assurance and pension funds. The amount of wealth held in life assurance and pension funds has continued to grow and since 1993 has replaced dwellings as the largest component of wealth.

Wealth is much more unequally distributed than income and this has not changed much over the years. Marketable wealth consists of assets that can be sold or cashed in, such as shares or dwellings. In 1993 half of the adult population of the United Kingdom owned 93 per cent of marketable wealth (Table 5.25). Residential property forms a large part of personal wealth (Table 5.24), but those whose wealth is greater than £500 thousand hold more of their wealth in shares than any other form. Hence the distribution of marketable wealth is more unequal if the value of dwellings is excluded, with over half of wealth owned by 5 per cent of adults. The inclusion of occupational and state pension

## 5.26

rights leads to a slightly more equal distribution: the share of the wealthiest half in 1993 falls to 82 per cent. Wealth in Table 5.25 differs from the net wealth of the personal sector shown in Table 5.24 (see Appendix, Part 5: Distribution of personal wealth).

Membership of certain types of pension scheme varies by earnings and gender (Table 5.26). In 1995-96 membership rates for occupational pensions among full-time employees in Great Britain increased with earnings for both men and women. For each band of earnings shown, women were more likely to have an occupational pension than men. However, men have the higher overall membership rate since there is a much larger proportion of men than women in the top earnings band where membership rates are highest. Men are also more likely to have a personal pension, but there is no clear pattern with earnings. People working part time are less likely to have an occupational or personal pension partly due to their lower weekly earnings, but their membership rates are lower even than for full-time employees in the lowest earnings band, probably due to lower availability of employers' pension schemes. Nearly one in four women working part time had an occupational pension, compared with one in ten men; rates for personal pensions were one in ten for both men and women.

Most adults hold some wealth in the form of a bank or building society account, stocks and shares or a similar investment (Table 5.27). Three quarters of all adults in Great Britain held a current account and nearly half had an ordinary building society account in 1994-95. The forms in which people prefer to hold their wealth vary by age. A higher proportion of 55 to 74 year olds held premium bonds, stocks and shares, unit trusts and tax exempt special

**Membership of a current pension scheme[1]: by gender and earnings, 1995-96**

Great Britain                                                                    Percentages

| | Usual gross earnings (£ per week)[2] | | | | | All earners[3] |
| --- | --- | --- | --- | --- | --- | --- |
| | 0-150 | 150-200 | 200-250 | 250-300 | over 300 | |
| **Males** | | | | | | |
| Occupational pension[4] | 26 | 32 | 44 | 59 | 75 | 58 |
| Personal pension | 22 | 28 | 30 | 32 | 28 | 28 |
| **Females** | | | | | | |
| Occupational pension[4] | 27 | 41 | 59 | 64 | 79 | 55 |
| Personal pension | 20 | 20 | 26 | 16 | 23 | 22 |

1 Percentage of full-time employees in each band of earnings who were members of each type of pension scheme.
2 Bands of earnings include upper limit but exclude lower limit shown.
3 Includes those who did not specify earnings.
4 Including a small number who were not sure if they were in a scheme but thought it possible.
*Source: General Household Survey, Office for National Statistics*

savings accounts (TESSAs) than any other age group. People aged 75 and over were the most likely to hold Post Office accounts and National Savings bonds.

## 5.27

**Adults[1] holding selected forms of wealth: by age, 1994-95**

Great Britain                                                                    Percentages

| | 16-34[2] | 35-54 | 55-74 | 75 and over | All adults[2] |
| --- | --- | --- | --- | --- | --- |
| Current account | 76 | 82 | 71 | 57 | 75 |
| Building society account[3] | 43 | 52 | 52 | 45 | 49 |
| Premium bonds | 13 | 24 | 28 | 24 | 22 |
| Stocks and shares | 8 | 17 | 23 | 15 | 16 |
| Other bank account[3] | 12 | 14 | 15 | 18 | 14 |
| TESSA[4] | 3 | 9 | 14 | 6 | 8 |
| Post Office account | 6 | 6 | 8 | 13 | 7 |
| Unit trusts | 2 | 6 | 9 | 4 | 6 |
| National Savings bonds | 1 | 2 | 10 | 12 | 5 |
| Other account[5] | 2 | 2 | 2 | 1 | 2 |
| Gilts | - | 1 | 2 | 3 | 1 |
| Save as you earn | 1 | 2 | 1 | - | 1 |
| Any | 87 | 90 | 88 | 85 | 88 |

1 Percentage in each age group holding each form of wealth.
2 Excluding 16 to 19 year olds in non-advanced full-time education.
3 Excluding current accounts and TESSAs.
4 Tax exempt special savings account.
5 Any account yielding interest not included in another category.
*Source: Family Resources Survey, Department of Social Security*

# 5.28

### Gross domestic product[1]

**United Kingdom**

Volume index (1990=100)

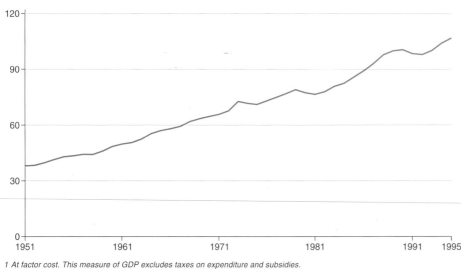

1 At factor cost. This measure of GDP excludes taxes on expenditure and subsidies.

**Source: Office for National Statistics**

# 5.29

### Financing of general government expenditure: by source

**United Kingdom**                                                          Percentages

|  | 1981 | 1986 | 1991 | 1994 | 1995 |
|---|---|---|---|---|---|
| Taxes on expenditure[1] | 36 | 39 | 37 | 34 | 34 |
| Taxes on income, | 31 | 32 | 33 | 28 | 30 |
|   of which: personal sector less tax credits | 24 | 23 | 25 | 22 | 22 |
|           companies[2] | 7 | 9 | 8 | 6 | 8 |
| Social security contributions, | 14 | 16 | 16 | 15 | 15 |
|   of which: employers | 8 | 8 | 9 | 8 | 8 |
|          employees | 6 | 7 | 6 | 6 | 6 |
|          self-employed and non-employed | | | | | |
|           persons | - | - | 1 | 1 | 1 |
| Community charge/council tax | . | . | 4 | 3 | 3 |
| Other current receipts[3] | 10 | 8 | 6 | 5 | 5 |
| Capital receipts | 1 | 2 | 2 | 1 | 1 |
| Total current and capital receipts | 92 | 97 | 98 | 86 | 88 |
| Financial transactions | 8 | 3 | 2 | 14 | 12 |
| Total general government expenditure | | | | | |
|   (=100%)(£ million) | 117,101 | 162,339 | 228,339 | 284,848 | 303,877 |
| Total as a percentage of GDP[4] | 47 | 43 | 40 | 43 | 43 |

1 Includes domestic rates collected in the United Kingdom in 1981 and 1986, and in Northern Ireland in 1991, 1994 and 1995.
2 Includes public corporations and non-residents.
3 Includes rent and royalties such as licence fees on oil and gas production; gross trading surplus; imputed charge for consumption of non-trading capital and miscellaneous current transfers.
4 Gross Domestic Product at market prices (ie including taxes on expenditure and subsidies) adjusted for the abolition of domestic rates.

**Source: Office for National Statistics**

## Income of the nation

The income of the nation as a whole comprises the income of individuals and the income of organisations (for example profits), generated through economic activity. The standard measure of economic activity in the United Kingdom is Gross Domestic Product (GDP) usually expressed at constant prices and factor cost, where the effects of taxes, subsidies and changes in prices over time have been removed. In Chart 5.28 it is presented as an index using 1990 as the base year. Over the period 1951 to 1995 GDP grew at an average rate of about 2.4 per cent per annum although there have been three significant deviations from the trend. These are mostly explained by the oil price rises in the mid-1970s, and the two recessions of the early 1980s (also characterised by a sharp increase in oil prices) and early 1990s. GDP has been growing again since 1992.

The income raised in order to finance expenditure by general government (central government plus local authorities) accounted for over two fifths of GDP in 1995 (Table 5.29). This expenditure (which is analysed by function in Table 6.21 of the Expenditure chapter) is financed mainly through taxes on expenditure, taxes on income and social security contributions. The main changes since 1981 have been the abolition of domestic rates, in Scotland in April 1989 and in England and Wales in April 1990, to be replaced by the community charge; rates are still used in Northern Ireland. The community charge was in turn replaced by council tax in April 1993. It should be noted that in Table 5.29 domestic rates are included under taxes on expenditure, which are therefore not strictly comparable over time. The largest difference between 1981 and 1995 was in the proportion of total expenditure funded by

# 5.30

financial transactions, primarily the general government borrowing requirement, which account for the shortfall between current and capital receipts and general government expenditure.

In **Table 5.30** GDP is presented for the constituent regions of the United Kingdom. GDP for the continental shelf, for example that associated with oil production in the North Sea, has been excluded from this analysis because it cannot be attributed to a particular region. The GDP per head for each region is expressed as an index based on the UK average for that year. In 1994 Northern Ireland and Wales had the lowest GDP per head while the South East had the highest, with both Greater London and the rest of the South East considerably higher than the UK average. East Anglia has experienced the fastest growth since 1981 while the regions with slowest growth were the North and North West.

The United Kingdom's GDP per head in 1995 is compared with that of other countries of the European Union (EU) in **Chart 5.31**. These data, although shown in sterling, have been calculated using purchasing power parities. These provide a better basis for making international comparisons than exchange rates because they adjust for the differences in the price levels between countries. For example, if a particular commodity, such as bread, is more expensive in one country than another, incomes would need to be higher in that country to reach the same standard of living. The country with highest GDP per head in 1995 was Luxembourg (which has a small public debt and almost full employment) - more than two and a half times that of Greece which had the lowest. The United Kingdom had the ninth highest at just below the EU average.

**Gross domestic product at current factor cost[1]: by region**

Index per head (UK=100)

| | 1971 | 1981 | 1986 | 1991 | 1994 |
|---|---|---|---|---|---|
| United Kingdom[2] | 100 | 100 | 100 | 100 | 100 |
| North | 87 | 94 | 90 | 89 | 89 |
| Yorkshire & Humberside | 93 | 92 | 95 | 92 | 89 |
| East Midlands | 97 | 97 | 98 | 98 | 96 |
| East Anglia | 95 | 97 | 102 | 101 | 102 |
| | | | | | |
| South East | 112 | 117 | 116 | 117 | 117 |
| Greater London | 124 | 128 | 124 | 124 | 126 |
| Rest of the South East | 105 | 109 | 110 | 112 | 111 |
| South West | 95 | 93 | 94 | 95 | 96 |
| West Midlands | 103 | 91 | 91 | 93 | 93 |
| North West | 96 | 95 | 94 | 90 | 90 |
| | | | | | |
| England | 102 | 102 | 102 | 102 | 102 |
| Wales | 87 | 84 | 85 | 85 | 84 |
| Scotland | 94 | 97 | 95 | 97 | 100 |
| Northern Ireland | 78 | 79 | 79 | 82 | 82 |

1 This measure of GDP excludes taxes on expenditure and subsidies.
2 United Kingdom less continental shelf.
**Source: Office for National Statistics**

# 5.31

**Gross domestic product[1] per head: EU comparison, 1995**

£ thousand[2]

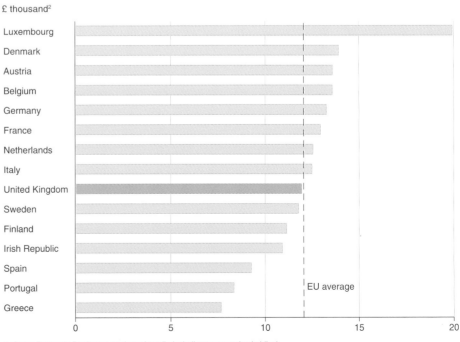

1 Gross Domestic Product at market prices (ie including taxes and subsidies).
2 Purchasing Power Standards (PPS) have been used to convert national currencies into pounds sterling.
**Source: Eurostat**

## References and further reading

The following list contains selected publications relevant to **Chapter 5: Income and Wealth**. Those published by The Stationery Office are available from the addresses shown on the inside back cover of *Social Trends*.

*Changing Households: The British Household Panel Survey*, ESRC Research Centre on Micro-social Change

*Economic Trends*, The Stationery Office

Labour Market Trends (incorporating Employment Gazette), Harrington Kilbride

*Family Resources Survey*, The Stationery Office

*Family Spending*, The Stationery Office

*Fiscal Studies*, Institute for Fiscal Studies

*For Richer, For Poorer*, Institute for Fiscal Studies

*General Household Survey*, The Stationery Office

*Households Below Average Income, A Statistical Analysis*, The Stationery Office

*Inland Revenue Statistics*, The Stationery Office

*Inquiry into Income and Wealth*, Joseph Rowntree Foundation

*New Earnings Survey*, The Stationery Office

*Regional Trends*, The Stationery Office

*Social Security, Departmental Report*, The Stationery Office

*Social Security Statistics*, The Stationery Office

*Tax/Benefit Model Tables*, Department of Social Security

*The Distribution of Wealth in the UK*, Institute for Fiscal Studies

*United Kingdom National Accounts (The ONS Blue Book)*, The Stationery Office

## Contacts

Telephone contact points for further information relating to
**Chapter 5: Income and Wealth**

| | |
|---|---|
| **Office for National Statistics** | |
| Chapter author | 0171 533 5773 |
| Effects of taxes and benefits | 0171 533 5770 |
| General government expenditure | 0171 533 5990 |
| General Household Survey | 0171 533 5444 |
| Labour Force Survey | 0171 533 6180 |
| National accounts | 0171 533 6003 |
| New Earnings Survey | 01928 792614 |
| Regional accounts | 0171 533 5793 |
| **Department of Economic Development, Northern Ireland** | 01232 529383 |
| **Department of Social Security** | |
| Family Resources Survey | 0171 962 8092 |
| Households Below Average Income | 0171 962 8232 |
| **ESRC Research Centre on Micro-social Change** | 01206 872957 |
| **Eurostat** | 00 352 4335 2251 |
| **Inland Revenue** | 0171 438 7370 |
| **Institute for Fiscal Studies** | 0171 636 3784 |

# Chapter 6 Expenditure

**Household and personal expenditure**

Food as a proportion of all household expenditure has fallen by a third since 1971, to 12 per cent in 1995. (Table 6.2)

People in the top quintile income group spent over a third of their income on leisure and travel compared with only a quarter for those in the bottom quintile group. (Table 6.7)

Since 1972 the proportion of households with a telephone has more than doubled to around nine in ten in 1995-96. (Table 6.10)

**Prices**

Over time the purchasing power of the pound has shrunk in value; to purchase what £1 could buy in 1961 you would now have to spend over £11. (Chart 6.14)

The purchasing power of the pound in the European Union shows that in 1994 Portugal, Greece, Spain, Italy and the Irish Republic would have seemed cheaper to a UK resident, and all the other member states would have seemed more expensive, particularly Denmark and Sweden. (Chart 6.15)

**Consumer credit and household saving**

There were 29.6 million credit cards and 28.4 million debit cards in issue in the United Kingdom at the end of 1995; since 1989 debit card use has been growing at a faster rate than credit card use. (Page 117)

**Public expenditure**

Social security accounted for more than a third of general government expenditure in 1995. (Table 6.21)

In 1995 two thirds of people supported increasing spending on education compared with a half in 1983. (Table 6.22)

## 6.1

**Retail prices index**[1]

**United Kingdom**

Percentage change over 12 months

1 See Appendix, Part 6: Retail prices.

**Source: Office for National Statistics**

How people choose to use their income and how government chooses to use the country's wealth can impact in a major way on the economy and on society.

## Household and personal expenditure

Total household expenditure in the United Kingdom increased by 77 per cent in real terms between 1971 and 1995, that is after allowing for inflation (Table 6.2). The pattern of spending changed considerably over this period, reflecting both changes in quantities purchased and in the relative prices of the different categories of goods and services shown in the table. The proportion spent on food has fallen by a third since 1971, to 12 per cent in 1995; that spent on alcohol fell by a quarter to 6 per cent. The largest proportionate decrease has been on tobacco which accounted for only 2 per cent of household expenditure in 1995 compared

with 6 per cent in 1971, reflecting the fall in the number of people smoking which is shown in Chart 7.19 in the Health chapter.

In contrast, the proportion spent on recreation, entertainment and education rose by nearly two thirds over the same period. Among the types of expenditure included in this category are: radio, television and other durable goods, video hire, sports goods and betting and gaming. All of these types of expenditure rose in varying proportions between 1971 and 1995 except for expenditure on newspapers and magazines which fell by 20 per cent. Betting and gaming declined slightly between 1971 and 1994 but rose again in 1995; probably a consequence of the introduction of the National Lottery in November 1994. By far the largest increase within the category, however, is accounted for by radio, television and other durable goods; there was a fourteenfold increase in expenditure on these items between 1971 and 1995.

Transport and communication accounted for the highest proportion of spending having risen by just over a fifth since 1971 to 18 per cent in 1995, the same proportion as food accounted for in 1971. Further information on travel costs is given in Table 12.23 in the Transport chapter. One explanation for the decrease in the proportion spent on food is the increase in the amount spent on eating-out. Catering, which includes meals and accommodation, accounted for 8 per cent of all household expenditure in 1995. Catering expenditure is included in the Other goods and services category shown in Table 6.2.

Chart 6.3 shows the rate of increase in household expenditure on selected items between 1971 and 1995 after allowing for inflation. Although households are spending more on essentials such as food and housing than they did 20 or so years ago,

# 6.2

### Household expenditure[1]

| United Kingdom | | | | | | | Percentages |
|---|---|---|---|---|---|---|---|
| | 1971 | 1976 | 1981 | 1986 | 1990 | 1991 | 1995 |
| Transport and communication | 14.9 | 15.2 | 16.3 | 17.8 | 18.3 | 17.5 | 18.1 |
| Housing | 16.4 | 16.1 | 16.1 | 15.4 | 14.2 | 14.5 | 14.2 |
| Food | 18.0 | 16.5 | 15.5 | 13.7 | 12.3 | 12.6 | 12.2 |
| Recreation, entertainment and education | 6.9 | 8.1 | 8.7 | 9.2 | 10.0 | 10.0 | 11.2 |
| Clothing and footwear | 5.3 | 5.4 | 5.7 | 6.6 | 6.1 | 6.3 | 6.9 |
| Household goods and services | 6.5 | 6.6 | 6.2 | 6.5 | 6.5 | 6.5 | 6.9 |
| Alcohol | 7.7 | 8.7 | 8.1 | 7.2 | 6.3 | 6.2 | 5.7 |
| Fuel, light and power | 5.2 | 4.9 | 4.7 | 4.3 | 3.6 | 4.0 | 3.6 |
| Tobacco | 5.9 | 5.5 | 4.3 | 3.0 | 2.5 | 2.5 | 2.0 |
| Other goods and services | 14.2 | 13.5 | 14.6 | 16.3 | 20.1 | 19.9 | 19.2 |
| All household expenditure (=100%) (£ billion at 1990 prices)[1] | 202 | 223 | 244 | 290 | 340 | 333 | 357 |

1 See Appendix, Part 6: Household expenditure.
**Source: Office for National Statistics**

# 6.3

the increase has been relatively moderate compared with expenditure on some services such as transport and communication. The category which experienced the fastest growth, nearly tripling over the period, was recreation, entertainment and education.

There are regional variations in the spending patterns of households. Table 6.4 shows expenditure per head by region in 1994 using data from the regional accounts. Household expenditure is more narrowly defined here than consumers' expenditure used in Table 6.2 and Chart 6.3, in that it excludes expenditure by private non profit making bodies. Household expenditure per person was highest in the South East in 1994; at £158 this was almost two fifths more than the amount spent in Northern Ireland which had the lowest expenditure. People in Wales and Northern Ireland spent

**Household expenditure[1] on selected items**

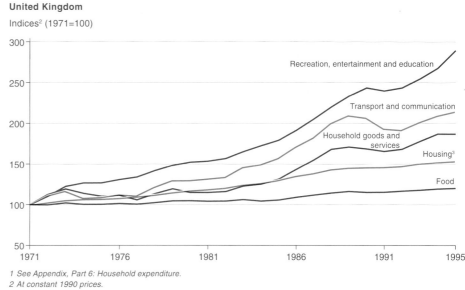

United Kingdom

Indices[2] (1971=100)

1 See Appendix, Part 6: Household expenditure.
2 At constant 1990 prices.
3 Includes domestic rates, but excludes community charge and council tax.
*Source: Office for National Statistics*

# 6.4

## Household expenditure per head: by region, 1994

Percentages

| | Food | Alcohol and tobacco | Clothing and footwear | Housing | Fuel, light and power | Household goods and services | Transport and comm-unicication | Recreation entertain-ment and education | Other goods and services | Average expenditure (=100%) (£ per week) |
|---|---|---|---|---|---|---|---|---|---|---|
| United Kingdom | 11 | 9 | 6 | 16 | 4 | 6 | 18 | 10 | 20 | 138.43 |
| North | 12 | 11 | 6 | 15 | 4 | 7 | 17 | 10 | 18 | 123.00 |
| Yorkshire & Humberside | 11 | 10 | 6 | 14 | 4 | 7 | 17 | 10 | 21 | 129.31 |
| East Midlands | 12 | 10 | 5 | 16 | 4 | 6 | 18 | 10 | 20 | 130.04 |
| East Anglia | 12 | 7 | 5 | 16 | 3 | 7 | 17 | 11 | 22 | 135.36 |
| South East | 11 | 8 | 6 | 17 | 3 | 6 | 18 | 10 | 21 | 158.47 |
| South West | 11 | 8 | 5 | 17 | 3 | 6 | 17 | 11 | 21 | 135.10 |
| West Midlands | 12 | 8 | 5 | 17 | 4 | 6 | 19 | 10 | 20 | 129.57 |
| North West | 11 | 10 | 6 | 15 | 4 | 7 | 17 | 10 | 20 | 133.18 |
| England | 11 | 9 | 6 | 16 | 3 | 7 | 18 | 10 | 21 | 141.04 |
| Wales | 13 | 9 | 6 | 16 | 4 | 6 | 18 | 10 | 18 | 119.85 |
| Scotland | 12 | 10 | 7 | 13 | 4 | 6 | 18 | 11 | 20 | 131.48 |
| Northern Ireland | 13 | 9 | 7 | 15 | 4 | 7 | 18 | 9 | 18 | 115.87 |

*Source: Office for National Statistics*

# 6.5

### Household expenditure, EU comparison, 1994

Percentages

| | Food | Alcohol and tobacco | Clothing and footwear | Household furniture/ equipment | Transport and commun- ication | Gross rent and water charges | Fuel and Power | Recreation, entertain- ment and education | Medical care and health | Other | All household expend- iture |
|---|---|---|---|---|---|---|---|---|---|---|---|
| Austria | 15 | 4 | 8 | 8 | 16 | 15 | 4 | 8 | 7 | 16 | 100 |
| Belgium | 14 | 3 | 7 | 10 | 13 | 14 | 4 | 6 | 12 | 16 | 100 |
| Denmark | 15 | 5 | 5 | 6 | 18 | 22 | 6 | 10 | 2 | 11 | 100 |
| Finland | 16 | 6 | 5 | 6 | 15 | 20 | 5 | 10 | 5 | 12 | 100 |
| France | 15 | 3 | 6 | 7 | 16 | 18 | 4 | 7 | 10 | 16 | 100 |
| Germany | 11 | 4 | 7 | 8 | 15 | 17 | 3 | 9 | 16 | 10 | 100 |
| Greece[1] | 30 | 7 | 8 | 7 | 15 | 11 | 2 | 5 | 4 | 11 | 100 |
| Irish Republic | 19 | 16 | 7 | 6 | 14 | 8 | 4 | 12 | 4 | 11 | 100 |
| Italy | 17 | 3 | 9 | 9 | 12 | 14 | 4 | 9 | 7 | 17 | 100 |
| Netherlands | 12 | 3 | 6 | 7 | 13 | 17 | 3 | 10 | 13 | 17 | 100 |
| Sweden[1] | 15 | 5 | 6 | 7 | 16 | 28 | 5 | 9 | 2 | 7 | 100 |
| United Kingdom | 11 | 9 | 6 | 7 | 17 | 16 | 4 | 10 | 2 | 18 | 100 |

1 Data are for 1993.

**Source: Eurostat**

# 6.6

### Household expenditure[1]: by economic activity status of head of household, 1995-96

**United Kingdom** £ per week

| | Employees | | Self- employed | Unem- ployed | Retired | All house- holds[2] |
|---|---|---|---|---|---|---|
| | Full time | Part time | | | | |
| Food | 65 | 47 | 72 | 40 | 35 | 53 |
| Housing | 70 | 41 | 67 | 25 | 23 | 48 |
| Leisure goods and services | 62 | 41 | 64 | 23 | 26 | 46 |
| Motoring and fares | 59 | 41 | 62 | 27 | 21 | 43 |
| Household goods and services | 51 | 34 | 47 | 25 | 24 | 39 |
| Clothing and footwear | 24 | 16 | 26 | 12 | 7 | 17 |
| Fuel, light and power | 14 | 13 | 15 | 12 | 11 | 13 |
| Alcohol | 16 | 9 | 17 | 8 | 5 | 11 |
| Tobacco | 6 | 5 | 7 | 8 | 3 | 6 |
| Other goods and services | 4 | 2 | 3 | 2 | - | 2 |
| Average household expenditure | 385 | 260 | 396 | 189 | 165 | 290 |

1 See Appendix, Part 6: Household expenditure.
2 Includes households where head of household is unoccupied.

**Source: Family Expenditure Survey, Office for National Statistics**

a higher proportion on food than any of the English regions or Scotland, while the proportion spent on alcohol and tobacco was highest in the North of England. The proportion of spending on housing was lowest in Scotland, partly because of the relatively high proportion of households in social housing as shown in Table 10.6 in the Housing chapter.

How do the spending patterns of UK households compare with our European neighbours? Based on national accounts estimates on households' final consumption, Table 6.5 shows the proportion spent on various commodities in a number of European Union (EU) member states. For many of the countries shown in the table, gross rent and water charges took the largest single share of household expenditure in 1994; in the United Kingdom this represented 16 per cent of the total, a slightly smaller proportion than that spent on transport and communication. By contrast, in Greece, the Irish Republic and Italy the largest single share was taken by food, including non alcoholic drinks. Alcohol and tobacco took the smallest share in several countries but for the Irish Republic they took the second largest share after food. These differences may result from either differences in prices between countries or differences in quantities purchased. They are also influenced by the availability of some goods and services which are free at the point of use. For example, the smallest share of household expenditure in the United Kingdom was spent on medical care and health expenses (2 per cent) which was the same proportion as in Denmark and Sweden.

Different types of households have different spending patterns. Using data from the Family Expenditure Survey (FES), an analysis by economic activity status of head of household shows that UK households headed by someone who was self-employed in 1995-96 spent the most, at an average of £396 a week, while those headed by someone who was retired spent the least, at £165 a week (Table 6.6). All the groups shown in the table spent more on food than any other type of expenditure except for those households headed by someone who was a full-time employee; they spent the most on housing. Not surprisingly, those households headed by someone who was unemployed spent the smallest proportion on leisure goods and services; at an average of £23 a week this was about a third of that for the self-employed and full-time employees. However, unemployed households spent the most on tobacco.

Expenditure also varies according to the income of those spending. Table 6.7 compares the spending patterns of people in different income groups in 1994-95. Not surprisingly, people in the bottom quintile group spent a higher proportion of their household income on necessities such as food, fuel, light and power which accounted

for almost a third of their spending. In contrast, the top quintile group spent only a sixth of their income on these items - over a third of their spending went on leisure and travel compared with only a quarter of that of the bottom quintile group. For more information on quintile groups see the Income distribution section in the Income and Wealth chapter.

Spending by retired households in the United Kingdom varies according to whether or not their main income is derived from state pensions and benefits. Table 6.8 shows that pensioner households mainly dependent on state pensions and benefits, spent on average £98 a week in 1995-96 compared with £215 spent by other retired households. Those mainly dependent on state pension spent over a quarter of their expenditure on food while the other retired spent less than a tenth on food. These households spent a larger proportion on

# 6.7

**Household expenditure[1]: by income grouping, 1994-95**

| United Kingdom | | | | | | Percentages |
|---|---|---|---|---|---|---|
| | Quintile group of households[2] | | | | | All house- holds |
| | Bottom fifth | Next fifth | Middle fifth | Next fifth | Top fifth | |
| Food | 24 | 22 | 19 | 17 | 14 | 18 |
| Leisure goods and services | 12 | 13 | 15 | 16 | 19 | 16 |
| Housing | 15 | 16 | 16 | 16 | 17 | 16 |
| Motoring and fares | 12 | 13 | 14 | 17 | 16 | 15 |
| Household goods and services | 13 | 13 | 13 | 13 | 14 | 13 |
| Clothing and footwear | 6 | 6 | 6 | 6 | 6 | 6 |
| Fuel, light and power | 8 | 7 | 5 | 4 | 3 | 5 |
| Alcohol | 4 | 4 | 5 | 5 | 4 | 4 |
| Tobacco | 4 | 3 | 2 | 2 | 1 | 2 |
| Other goods and services | 4 | 4 | 5 | 5 | 5 | 5 |
| All household expenditure | 100 | 100 | 100 | 100 | 100 | 100 |

1 See Appendix, Part 6: Household expenditure.
2 Equivalised disposable income has been used for ranking the households into quintile groups. See Appendix, Part 5: Equivalisation scales.
**Source: Office for National Statistics**

# 6.8

**Expenditure of pensioner households[1]: by whether or not mainly dependent on state pension, 1995-96**

| United Kingdom | | Percentages |
|---|---|---|
| | Mainly dependent on state pension[2] | Other retired |
| Food | 26 | 19 |
| Leisure goods and services | 13 | 17 |
| Motoring and fares | 7 | 15 |
| Household goods and services | 16 | 14 |
| Housing | 14 | 14 |
| Fuel, light and power | 10 | 6 |
| Alcohol and tobacco | 6 | 5 |
| Clothing and footwear | 4 | 5 |
| Other goods and services | 4 | 6 |
| All household expenditure (=100%) (£ per week) | 98 | 215 |

1 Households where the head of household is over retirement age and is in receipt of a state pension.
2 At least three quarters of the total household income is derived from state pensions and other benefits.
**Source: Family Expenditure Survey, Office for National Statistics**

# 6.9

Household expenditure on charitable donations: by social class of head of household, 1995-96

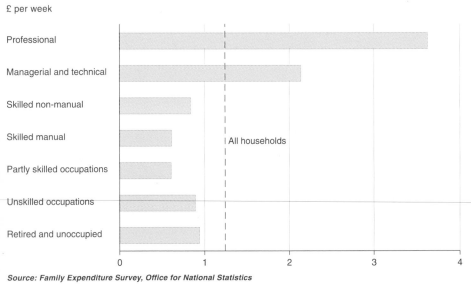

**United Kingdom**
£ per week

Professional
Managerial and technical
Skilled non-manual
Skilled manual
All households
Partly skilled occupations
Unskilled occupations
Retired and unoccupied

0    1    2    3    4

*Source: Family Expenditure Survey, Office for National Statistics*

leisure goods and services than those mainly dependent on state pension and double the proportion on motoring and fares.

The amounts given in charitable donations vary between the different social classes. The average weekly giving in 1995-96 by all households in the United Kingdom was £1.20 (Chart 6.9). Only households headed

by those in the professional and the managerial and technical groups exceeded this average, with giving of £3.60 and £2.20 a week respectively. Households headed by a skilled manual worker or someone in a partly skilled occupation gave the least at only 60 pence a week. These figures come from the FES and cover all charitable donations and subscriptions, which in 1995-96 included buying the Big Issue and giving to carol singers. Charitable donations have approximately doubled in cash terms over the ten years since 1986, compared with a 52 per cent increase in prices as measured by the retail prices index.

Since 1971 there has been an increase in ownership of consumer durables such as domestic appliances (Table 6.10). The proportion of households in the United Kingdom with a television in 1995-96 was virtually at saturation point and has increased by only 2 percentage points since 1981. However, there has been a switch from black and white to colour; back in 1981 nearly a quarter of households had a black and white television only, compared with only 2 per cent in 1995-96. Between 1991-92 and 1995-96 there was a large increase in CD player ownership, with the proportion of households owning one almost doubling while the ownership of home computers also rose, particularly in households with children. The majority of households already had a washing machine in 1972 and nine in ten had one in 1995-96, but there has been very rapid growth in ownership of the more recently available appliances such as microwave ovens.

Information from the International Passenger Survey shows that when UK residents went abroad in 1995 they spent an average of £375 per visit, about £34 a day (Chart 6.11). This amount per visit is £10 less in real terms, than the average spent per visit in

# 6.10

Households with consumer durables

| Great Britain | | 1972 | | 1981 | 1991-92 | 1994-95 | 1995-96 Percentages |
|---|---|---|---|---|---|---|---|
| Colour television | } | 93 | { | 74 | 95 | 97 | 97 |
| Black & white television only | | | | 23 | 4 | 2 | 2 |
| Telephone | | 42 | | 75 | 88 | 91 | 93 |
| Washing machine | | 66 | | 78 | 87 | 89 | 90 |
| Deep freezer | | .. | | 49 | 83 | 88 | 89 |
| Video recorder | | .. | | .. | 68 | 77 | 79 |
| Microwave | | .. | | .. | 55 | 67 | 70 |
| Compact disc player | | .. | | .. | 27 | 47 | 52 |
| Tumble drier | | .. | | 23 | 48 | 50 | 51 |
| Home Computer | | .. | | .. | 21 | 24 | 25 |
| Dishwasher | | .. | | 4 | 14 | 19 | 20 |

*Source: General Household Survey, Office for National Statistics*

1981 and nearly £59 less than the peak of £433 recorded in 1988. It covers accommodation costs and other spending but excludes travel costs to and from the United Kingdom. In contrast, overseas residents visiting the United Kingdom in 1995 spent on average £504 per visit, about £53 a day. This is £134 less than the average spent per visit in 1981 and £192 less than the peak of £696 per visit recorded in 1985. The decrease in the amounts spent by overseas residents visiting the United Kingdom can be explained by the fact that there has been a growth in shorter visits.

## Prices

The rate of growth in retail prices in the United Kingdom, often referred to as the rate of inflation, is measured by the retail prices index (RPI). The index monitors the change from month to month in the cost of a representative 'shopping basket' of goods and services of the sort bought by a typical household. The change in the RPI over the previous 12 months is shown in Chart 6.1 at the beginning of this chapter. Since 1971 this has ranged from a rise of 26.9 per cent in August 1975 to one of only 1.2 per cent in June 1993. There were no falls in the 12 month rate of change in the Index over this period. Since October 1992 the Government has had an explicit inflation objective to keep the measure of the RPI, which excludes mortgage interest payments (sometimes called underlying inflation), in the range of 1 to 4 per cent; in October 1996 it was 3.3 per cent.

Annual changes in the prices of the various categories of goods and services in the United Kingdom can be seen in Table 6.12. Between 1994 and 1995 the all items RPI increased by 3.5 per cent, but within this the cost of tobacco and the cost of housing each

**6.11**

### Real expenditure by overseas residents in the United Kingdom and by UK residents overseas

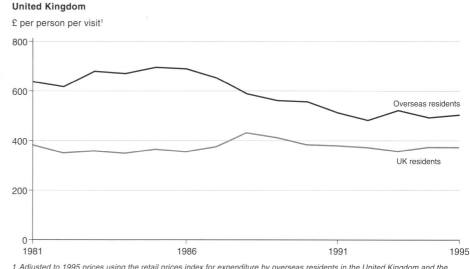

**United Kingdom**

£ per person per visit[1]

1 Adjusted to 1995 prices using the retail prices index for expenditure by overseas residents in the United Kingdom and the consumers' prices index for that by UK residents overseas.

**Source: International Passenger Survey, Office for National Statistics**

**6.12**

### Index of retail prices: rates of change[1]

| United Kingdom | | | | | | | Percentages |
|---|---|---|---|---|---|---|---|
| | 1990 | 1991 | 1992 | 1993 | 1994 | 1995 | 1995 (weights) |
| Housing | 21.0 | -1.8 | -0.7 | -5.4 | 3.3 | 6.7 | 187 |
| Food | 8.1 | 5.2 | 2.1 | 1.8 | 1.0 | 3.9 | 139 |
| Motoring expenditure | 6.1 | 7.4 | 6.8 | 4.3 | 3.5 | 1.8 | 125 |
| Alcohol | 9.7 | 12.4 | 6.4 | 4.5 | 2.5 | 3.8 | 77 |
| Household goods | 4.8 | 6.2 | 3.3 | 1.2 | 0.3 | 3.7 | 77 |
| Leisure services | 8.2 | 11.5 | 8.1 | 4.5 | 3.7 | 3.2 | 66 |
| Clothing and footwear | 4.6 | 3.0 | 0.3 | 0.8 | 0.5 | 0.2 | 54 |
| | | | | | | | |
| Household services | 6.3 | 8.3 | 5.8 | 3.6 | 0.1 | -0.3 | 47 |
| Leisure goods | 4.7 | 4.7 | 2.6 | 1.4 | -0.6 | -0.1 | 46 |
| Catering | 8.5 | 10.0 | 6.3 | 5.2 | 4.2 | 4.3 | 45 |
| Fuel and light | 8.0 | 7.9 | 2.2 | -1.3 | 4.4 | 2.1 | 45 |
| Personal goods and services | 7.5 | 8.7 | 6.6 | 4.0 | 3.7 | 3.2 | 39 |
| Tobacco | 6.8 | 14.3 | 11.0 | 8.5 | 7.5 | 6.7 | 34 |
| Fares and other travel | 7.1 | 9.8 | 6.2 | 5.2 | 2.6 | 2.5 | 19 |
| | | | | | | | |
| All items | 9.5 | 5.9 | 3.7 | 1.6 | 2.4 | 3.5 | 1,000 |
| All items except housing | 6.9 | 7.6 | 4.7 | 3.1 | 2.3 | 2.7 | 813 |
| All items except mortgage interest payments | 8.1 | 6.7 | 4.7 | 3.0 | 2.3 | 2.9 | 958 |

1 Percentage changes on the previous year. See Appendix, Part 6: Retail prices.
**Source: Office for National Statistics**

# 6.13

Length of time necessary to work to pay for selected commodities and services[1], 1971 and 1996

**Great Britain**                                                                                                  Hours and minutes

| | Married couple with husband only working[2] | | Single female parent with child | |
| --- | --- | --- | --- | --- |
| | 1971 | 1996 | 1971 | 1996 |
| 800g white sliced wrapped bread | 0:09 | 0:04 | 0:14 | 0:05 |
| 1 pint milk | 0:05 | 0:03 | 0:08 | 0:03 |
| Dozen eggs, first quality, size 2 | 0:24 | 0:13 | 0:36 | 0:15 |
| 1kg cheddar cheese | 0:49 | 0:36 | 1:13 | 0:43 |
| 1kg of cod fillets | 0:55 | 0:37 | 1:21 | 0:44 |
| 1kg rump steak | 2:24 | 1:00 | 3:32 | 1:12 |
| 1 pint of beer (draught bitter) | 0:15 | 0:13 | 0:22 | 0:15 |
| 20 cigarettes (king size filter) | 0:26 | 0:22 | 0:39 | 0:26 |
| Road fund tax | 40:19 | 18:46 | 59:31 | 22:19 |
| 1 kwh of electricity | 0:01 | 0:06 | 0:02 | 0:07 |
| 1 therm of gas | 0:12 | 0:04 | 0:17 | 0:04 |
| Copy of *Social Trends* | 5:15 | 4:49 | 7:44 | 5:44 |

1 Length of time necessary for a person on average hourly adult earnings for all industries and services to work so that his/her net income pays for the various goods. The earnings figures are based on full-time employees on adult rates whose pay was not affected for the survey period by absence.
2 Married man with non-earning wife and two children under 11.

**Source: Office for National Statistics; Inland Revenue**

# 6.14

Purchasing power of a pound since 1961

**United Kingdom**

Pence

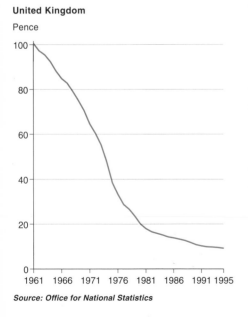

**Source: Office for National Statistics**

rose by nearly twice as much. Motoring expenditure has been increasing year on year since 1990 but the rate of change has been gradually decreasing; it rose by 1.8 per cent between 1994 and 1995 compared with 7.4 per cent between 1990 and 1991.

In the United Kingdom the 'basket' which the RPI represents is composed of more than 600 separate goods and services for which the changes in prices are measured in about 180 towns and cities around the country, leading to around 150 thousand price quotations each month. The composition of the 'basket', that is the relative importance or weight attached to each of the various goods and services it contains, is revised every year to reflect the changes in household expenditure patterns using the Family Expenditure Survey. For example, out of a total weight of 1,000, food accounted for 250 in 1971 but only 139 in

1995, in line with the fall in the proportion of expenditure accounted for by food seen in Table 6.2.

As well as the weights changing each year, some items are taken out of the index and others are added to reflect the changing spending habits of society. For example, in the 1970s, mushrooms, wine, yoghurt, mortgage interest payments and continental quilts were included for the first time; in 1987 CDs and CD players were added; and in 1994 the shampoo and set was replaced by highlights. Items added for 1996 include a cigarette lighter, Doctor Marten style boots and charges for aerobics and exercise classes.

An alternative way to analyse price levels and changes over time is to relate them to earnings by calculating how long someone would have to work to pay for certain goods and services. This is done for Great Britain in **Table 6.13** which compares the net income of a married man, with two children whose wife was not earning, with a lone mother. In general the length of time necessary to work to pay for the items shown in the table fell between 1971 and 1996 indicating that the increase in prices was lower than the increase in the families' incomes. However, there is also greater income parity between the two family types in 1996 than in 1971. For example, the lone mother would have had to have worked 3 hours 32 minutes in 1971 to buy the equivalent of 1 kilogramme rump steak, half as long again as the married man, whereas in 1996 she would only have needed to work for 1 hour 12 minutes, a fifth as long again as the married man.

The RPI is also a measure of purchasing power: as prices increase so the amount of goods and services which can be purchased

# 6.15

with a given sum of money decreases. **Chart 6.14** illustrates the erosion of the purchasing power of the pound since 1961: over time the £1 has shrunk in value so that it was only worth the equivalent of 9 pence in 1995. In other words to purchase what £1 could buy in 1961 you would now have to spend over £11. The effect of the high inflation rates in the mid-1970s seen in Chart 6.1, is marked by a particularly steep gradient in Chart 6.14 over that period. However as incomes have increased at a faster rate, actual purchasing power has also increased.

Chart 6.15 shows how the purchasing power of the pound fared in the EU in 1994. The purchasing power parity between the United Kingdom and another country is the amount of that country's currency needed to buy the equivalent quantity of goods and services costing £1 in the United Kingdom. If this is greater than the official exchange rate that country would seem more expensive to a UK resident, while if it is smaller, it would seem cheaper. In 1994, Portugal, Greece, Spain, Italy and the Irish Republic would have seemed cheaper to a UK resident, and all the other EU member states would have seemed more expensive, particularly Denmark and Sweden.

## Consumer credit and household saving

It is possible to spread payments for purchases over a period of time using one of the many forms of credit available. The amount of consumer credit outstanding in the United Kingdom in real terms increased rapidly between 1987 and 1989, and then fell slightly up to 1993 before rising again. The definition of credit used in **Table 6.16** excludes mortgage borrowing. Bank loans,

**Relative price levels[1]: EU comparison, 1994**

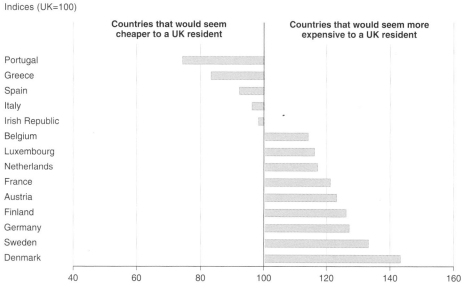

1 Price level indices for private consumption - the ratio of purchasing power parities to the official exchange rates.
**Source: Eurostat**

# 6.16

## Composition of consumer credit

| **United Kingdom** | | | | Percentages |
|---|---|---|---|---|
| | 1987 | 1991 | 1993 | 1995 |
| Bank loans[1] | 63 | 63 | 59 | 56 |
| Bank credit card lending | 16 | 18 | 20 | 21 |
| Other specialist lenders[2] | 12 | 11 | 13 | 16 |
| Retailers | 6 | 5 | 5 | 4 |
| Insurance companies | 3 | 2 | 3 | 2 |
| Building society loans[3] | - | 1 | 1 | 1 |
| Credit outstanding at end of year (=100%)(£ billion at 1995 prices)[4] | 53.6 | 60.9 | 56.5 | 65.0 |

1 Banks and all other institutions authorised to take deposits under the Banking Act 1987.
2 Finance houses and other credit companies (excluding institutions authorised to take deposits under the Banking Act 1987).
3 Building Society unsecured loans to individuals or companies (ie Class 3 loans as defined in the Building Societies Act 1986).
4 Adjusted to 1995 prices using the retail prices index.
**Source: Office for National Statistics**

# 6.17

## Net lending to consumers[1]

**United Kingdom**
£ billion

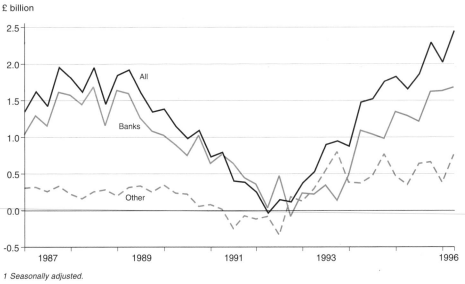

1 *Seasonally adjusted.*
**Source: Bank of England**

# 6.18

## Household saving[1] as a percentage of household disposable income

**United Kingdom**
Percentages

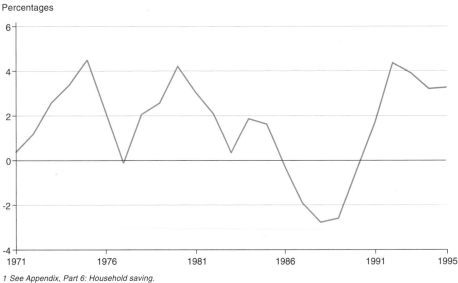

1 *See Appendix, Part 6: Household saving.*
**Source: Office for National Statistics**

although still the largest source of consumer credit, continued to decline in importance to form 56 per cent of total consumer credit in 1995. Bank credit card lending continued to rise from nearly 12 per cent of consumer credit in 1981 to 21 per cent in 1995.

Whereas Table 6.16 covers the total indebtedness of consumers, the amount of new lending to consumers, net of repayments in the United Kingdom, each quarter is illustrated in Chart 6.17; this provides the best measure of the current growth in consumer credit in this country. Its movements clearly mirror the effects of the economic cycle. Net lending to consumers fell from nearly £2 billion in the last quarter of 1987 to a small net repayment in the second quarter of 1992 reflecting the fall-off in consumers' expenditure during the last recession, high interest rates and unemployment. Since then it has recovered again - to £3.1 billion in the third quarter of 1996.

Chart 6.18 shows household saving as a percentage of household disposable income, a measure often known as the saving ratio. From 1986 to 1990, a period of growing inflation, the saving ratio was negative indicating that total household expenditure exceeded disposable income. From 1991, the saving ratio became positive reaching 4.4 per cent in 1992 but falling to just under 4 per cent in 1993. In the latest period, between 1994 and 1995, the ratio rose slightly from 3.2 per cent to 3.3 per cent, implying that household income was increasing at a slightly faster rate than household spending. However, household saving is not measured directly in the UK national accounts but is derived as a residual from two much larger figures which means that the estimates may be subject to a wide margin of error. Information on the composition of savings is given in the Wealth section of the Income and Wealth chapter.

A growing number of people use credit, debit or charge cards to pay for goods and services. There were 29.6 million credit cards and 28.4 million debit cards in issue at the end of 1995. Data compiled by the Credit Card Research Group show that both debit and credit card use continues to grow, suggesting that they are replacing cheques, in particular, as a means of payment. Though the growth rate in credit card use remains high in real terms, debit card use has been growing at a faster rate since 1989 than credit card use. In 1989 credit card spending represented 93 per cent of total credit and debit card expenditure, whereas its share had fallen to 59 per cent by 1995 when the value of all credit card expenditure was £41 billion compared with £28 billion for debit card spending (Table 6.19). Some goods and services such as motoring and travel, are more likely to be purchased with a credit card than the other types of purchases shown in the table. Spending in food and drink retailers dominated debit card use during 1995 totalling £12.6 billion. Much of this so-called spending reflects 'cashback' in supermarkets, which can account for up to half of debit card

supermarket traffic. 'Cashback' enables customer to draw money from their bank account when using a debit card; a facility which is offered in most supermarkets and a growing number of other retail outlets. The value of the average debit card transaction in 1995 was lower than that for credit cards £28 compared with £46 in 1995.

## Public expenditure

So far this chapter has focused on spending by individuals or households. This final section examines government expenditure, both within this country and in the EU.

Like individuals, government spends money on goods, services and interest payments but it also makes transfer payments, such as social security benefits, grants and loans. The measure which includes all these payments is known as General Government Expenditure (GGE) and is used to analyse overall trends in public spending. Growth in GGE can be compared to growth in the economy as a whole by expressing it as a percentage of Gross Domestic Product (GDP) - this is known as the GGE ratio. One of the Government's objectives is to reduce this ratio over time. Chart 6.20 shows that between 1971 to 1995, minor peaks occurred in the ratio in 1975 and 1982. It then fell steadily to reach its lowest level for 22 years in 1988, before rising again until 1993. It fell slightly in 1994 but rose again in 1995 to 43.4 per cent, just above the level in 1993.

Credit and debit card[1] spending: by type of purchase, 1995

| United Kingdom | | | £ billion |
|---|---|---|---|
| | Type of card | | |
| | Credit | Debit | All |
| Food and drink | 5.3 | 12.6 | 17.8 |
| Household | 4.1 | 1.9 | 5.9 |
| Mixed | 3.0 | 2.3 | 5.3 |
| Clothing | 2.7 | 1.8 | 4.5 |
| Other retailers | 5.6 | 2.6 | 8.2 |
| Motoring | 5.7 | 3.7 | 9.5 |
| Travel | 5.8 | 1.2 | 7.0 |
| Entertainment | 2.9 | 0.9 | 3.7 |
| Hotels | 2.3 | 0.2 | 2.5 |
| Other services | 3.7 | 1.1 | 4.8 |
| All credit and debit card expenditure | 41.2 | 28.2 | 69.4 |

1 Mastercard and Visa credit cards and Visa Delta and Switch debit cards.

*Source: Credit Card Research Group*

General government expenditure as a percentage of GDP[1]

**United Kingdom**

Percentages

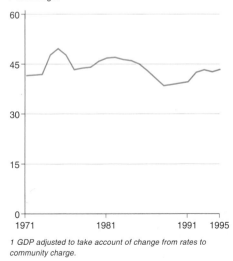

1 GDP adjusted to take account of change from rates to community charge.

*Source: Office for National Statistics*

# 6.21

## General government expenditure: by function

| United Kingdom | | | | | £ billion at 1995 prices[1] |
| --- | --- | --- | --- | --- | --- |
| | 1981 | 1986 | 1991 | 1994 | 1995 |
| Social security | 87 | 92 | 90 | 103 | 102 |
| Health | 37 | 35 | 38 | 41 | 41 |
| Education | 40 | 36 | 36 | 38 | 38 |
| Defence | 35 | 35 | 28 | 25 | 23 |
| Public order and safety | 12 | 13 | 16 | 16 | 15 |
| General public services | 13 | 12 | 14 | 13 | 14 |
| Housing and community amenities | 20 | 15 | 11 | 11 | 10 |
| Transport and communication | 12 | 7 | 8 | 7 | 9 |
| Recreational and cultural affairs | 4 | 5 | 5 | 5 | 4 |
| Agriculture, forestry and fishing | 5 | 4 | 4 | 3 | 3 |
| Other expenditure | 62 | 47 | 29 | 37 | 43 |
| All general government expenditure | 327 | 301 | 278 | 299 | 304 |

1 Adjusted to 1995 prices using the GDP market prices deflator adjusted for the abolition of domestic rates.
**Source: Office for National Statistics**

Total GGE has been falling in real terms for the last decade or so (Table 6.21). At 1995 prices total GGE fell by £28 billion, from £327 billion in 1981 to £299 billion in 1994, but then rose by £5 billion to £304 billion in 1995. Since 1981 expenditure on some functions has continued to increase such as social security and health. Other programmes such as defence, transport and communication and housing and community amenities have fallen, the latter by half to £10 billion in 1995. Just over a third of all GGE went on social security in 1995; health and education took the next largest shares. Information on the recipients of social security benefits can be found in Table 8.4 in the Social Protection chapter.

However the Government spends its resources, some people are likely to think that the money could have been better spent in other ways. When asked, in the British Social Attitudes Survey, on what they would like the government to spend more money, people's order of priorities has changed little over the last decade. Health has always been the area most frequently singled out for extra spending with education and housing usually next on the list (Table 6.22). Support for more spending on education has increased, from around half of all respondents giving this area first or second priority in 1983, to two thirds in 1995. In contrast, the priority given to help for industry has dropped considerably. People tend to be less likely to advocate increases in public spending when the tax consequences are pointed out to them, though even so the majority (three fifths) supported increases in spending on health, education and social security benefits.

Since people differ in how much they benefit personally from different types of public spending, one might expect attitudes towards priorities to differ by age and income as well as other individual and household characteristics. Those giving high priority to health spending are in fact fairly evenly spread amongst all respondents, whereas those giving priority to education, not surprisingly, tend to be those with children of school age.

# 6.22

## People's top priorities for extra government expenditure[1]

| Great Britain | | | | Percentages |
| --- | --- | --- | --- | --- |
| | 1983 | 1986 | 1990 | 1995 |
| Health | 74 | 81 | 70 | 77 |
| Education | 49 | 57 | 60 | 66 |
| Housing | 20 | 21 | 20 | 14 |
| Social security benefits | 12 | 12 | 13 | 11 |
| Help for industry | 29 | 16 | 6 | 9 |
| Police and prisons | 8 | 8 | 4 | 9 |

1 Percentage who gave the spending area first or second priority, when asked: 'Here are some items of government spending. Which of them, if any, would be your highest priority for extra spending? And which next?'
**Source: British Social Attitudes Survey, Social & Community Planning Research**

# 6.23

Taking an even broader picture of expenditure, the EU also has its own budget of which just over half is spent on supporting agriculture. In 1996 total EU expenditure amounted to £69 billion; £35 billion was spent on the European Agricultural Guidance and Guarantee Fund and nearly a third, £22 billion was spent on structural operations. Contributions to the EU budget to support its spending are made by all member states. Some members, however, including the United Kingdom, contribute more that they receive, Germany being by far the largest net contributor. In the case of the United Kingdom this is because we have a comparatively small agricultural sector and hence receive little support in this area and, being one of the more prosperous members, we receive a comparatively small proportion of the available Structural Funds.

The Structural Funds aim to promote a better economic and social balance across the EU and to reduce regional disparities, by co-financing with member states development actions. From 1994 to 1999 the United Kingdom will have received nearly £8 billion from the Structural Funds. In order to lessen disparities, five areas of particular concern, called Objectives, receive financial support from the Structural Funds. Three of these are regionally focused Objectives, and more than 40 per cent of the UK population lives in an area eligible under one of these.

The three regional Objectives are: Objective 1, which assists regions lagging behind in development; Objective 2, which helps with adaptation of declining industrial areas; and Objective 5b, which assists in developing and adjusting the structure of vulnerable rural areas. The whole of Northern Ireland, Merseyside and the Highlands and Islands of Scotland are eligible under Objective 1,

which is the most important in terms of the amount of funds allocated. The areas eligible for Objectives 2 and 5b are spread throughout Great Britain, and are not always entire regions or counties - some are based on Travel to Work Areas, while others may be parts of counties or districts, or groups of wards.

Table 6.23 shows contributions to and receipts from the EU budget in 1991 and 1994 for member states at current prices, that is not adjusted for inflation. This means that it is not possible to make direct comparisons over the two years. However, in proportionate terms comparisons are possible between the years shown. In 1991 the United Kingdom contributed 9 per cent of the total and received 8 per cent of total receipts while in 1994 both contributions and receipts amounted to around 10 per cent.

**Contributions to and receipts from the EU budget[1], 1991 and 1994**

£ billion[2]

|  | 1991 | | | 1994 | | |
|---|---|---|---|---|---|---|
|  | Contri-butions | Receipts | Net receipts | Contri-butions | Receipts | Net receipts |
| Germany | 10.8 | 4.6 | -6.2 | 16.5 | 6.0 | -10.6 |
| France | 7.4 | 5.7 | -1.7 | 9.7 | 7.7 | -2.0 |
| Italy | 6.1 | 5.1 | -1.0 | 6.0 | 4.0 | -2.0 |
| United Kingdom | 3.3 | 2.8 | -0.5 | 5.0 | 4.1 | -0.9 |
| Spain | 3.2 | 4.8 | 1.6 | 3.7 | 6.1 | 2.4 |
| Netherlands | 2.5 | 2.1 | 0.4 | 3.3 | 1.9 | -1.4 |
| Belgium | 1.6 | 1.8 | 0.3 | 2.2 | 1.9 | -0.2 |
| Denmark | 0.7 | 1.0 | 0.2 | 1.0 | 1.2 | 0.2 |
| Portugal | 0.5 | 1.6 | 1.1 | 0.9 | 2.4 | 1.4 |
| Greece | 0.5 | 2.6 | 2.0 | 0.8 | 3.7 | 3.0 |
| Irish Republic | 0.3 | 2.0 | 1.7 | 0.5 | 1.9 | 1.4 |
| Luxembourg | 0.1 | 0.2 | 0.1 | 0.1 | 0.3 | 0.2 |

1 See Appendix, Part 6: Contributions to and receipts from the EU budget.
2 At current prices.
**Source: HM Treasury**

## References and further reading ───────────────

The following list contains selected publications relevant to **Chapter 6: Expenditure**. Those published by The Stationery Office are available from the addresses shown on the inside back cover of Social Trends.

*British Social Attitudes*, Dartmouth Publishing

*Business Monitor MM23 (Retail Prices Index)*, The Stationery Office

*Consumers Trends*, The Stationery Office

*Economic Trends*, The Stationery Office

*Family Spending*, The Stationery Office

*Financial Statement and Budget Report*, The Stationery Office

*General Household Survey*, The Stationery Office

*Monthly Digest of Statistics*, The Stationery Office

*Retail Prices 1914-1990*, The Stationery Office

*Regional Trends*, The Stationery Office

*Social Focus on Women*, The Stationery Office

*Student Income and Expenditure Survey*, Research Services Limited

*The Community Budget: The facts in figures*, European Commission

*Travel Trends*, The Stationery Office

*United Kingdom National Accounts (The ONS Blue Book)*, The Stationery Office

## Contacts ───────────────

Telephone contact points for further information relating to
**Chapter 6: Expenditure**

**Office for National Statistics**

| | |
|---|---|
| Chapter author | 0171 533 5776 |
| Consumer credit | 01633 812782 |
| Consumer's expenditure | 0171 533 5998 |
| Family Expenditure Survey | 0171 533 5754 |
| General government expenditure | 0171 533 5990 |
| General Household Survey | 0171 533 5444 |
| Household saving | 0171 533 6003 |
| Income distribution | 0171 533 5772 |
| International Passenger Survey | 0171 533 5765 |
| Regional accounts | 0171 533 5793 |
| Retail prices | 0171 533 5874 |
| **HM Treasury** | 0171 270 4433 |
| **Inland Revenue** | 0171 438 7370 |
| **Bank of England** | 0171 601 3742 |
| **Credit Card Research Group** | 0171 436 9937 |
| **Eurostat** | 00 352 4335 2251 |
| **Social & Community Planning Research** | 0171 250 1866 extn 369 |

# Chapter 7 Health

**The nation's health**

According to projected mortality rates for 1997, a baby boy can expect to live until 74 years while a baby girl can expect to live to nearly 80. (Chart 7.1)

Almost three fifths of men and just under a half of women aged 16 and over in England were classed as overweight or obese in 1994. (Chart 7.8)

Lung cancer is the most frequently reported cancer in men; in 1991 men in England and Wales were almost three times as likely to suffer from lung cancer as women. (Chart 7.11)

**Health and lifestyles**

Over four fifths of men and women in England in 1994 said that they had participated in at least one period of either moderate or vigorous physical activity in the previous four weeks. (Table 7.18)

Among smokers, men in Great Britain had about 16 cigarettes a day on average in 1994-95, while women had about 14 cigarettes a day. (Page 131)

In 1992-1993 over a third of young adults aged 14 to 25 in England and Wales reported using controlled drugs at some time in their lives and about a fifth had used them in the last year. (Table 7.21)

**Causes of death**

Death rates from heart disease fell by almost half between 1972 and 1995 for men aged under 65 in the United Kingdom. (Chart 7.23)

The rate of accidental deaths in the United Kingdom fell by over 40 per cent between 1971 and 1995. (Table 7.25)

**7.1**

**Expectation of life[1] at birth: by gender**

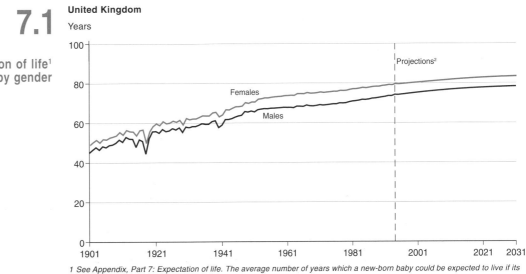

**United Kingdom**

Years

1 See Appendix, Part 7: Expectation of life. The average number of years which a new-born baby could be expected to live if its rates of mortality at each age were those experienced in that calendar year.
2 1994-based projections.

**Source: Government Actuary's Department**

# 7.2

## Infant mortality[1]: by social class[2]

| United Kingdom | Rates per 1,000 live births[3] | | |
|---|---|---|---|
| | 1981 | 1991 | 1994 |
| Professional | 7.8 | 5.0 | 4.5 |
| Managerial and technical | 8.2 | 5.3 | 4.5 |
| Skilled non-manual | 9.0 | 6.3 | 5.1 |
| Skilled manual | 10.5 | 6.3 | 5.5 |
| Semi-skilled | 12.7 | 7.1 | 6.4 |
| Unskilled | 15.7 | 8.2 | 6.8 |
| Other | 15.7 | 12.4 | 8.8 |
| All social classes | 10.4 | 6.4 | 5.4 |

1 Deaths within one year of birth.
2 Based on occupation of father.
3 Inside marriage.

*Source: Office for National Statistics; General Register Office (Scotland); General Register Office (Northern Ireland)*

# 7.3

## Notifications of selected infectious diseases

**United Kingdom**

Thousands

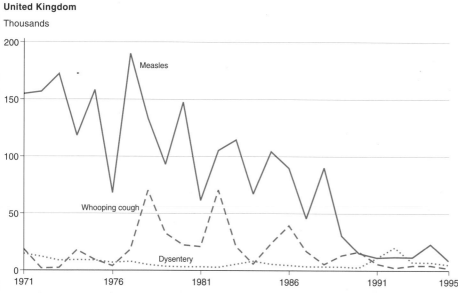

*Source: Office for National Statistics; National Health Service in Scotland; Department of Health and Social Services, Northern Ireland*

Good physical and mental health is an important factor in our overall quality of life.

## The nation's health

A useful overall indicator of the nation's health is life expectancy. There has been a fairly steady increase in the expectation of life at birth throughout the twentieth century so that in 1994 it was over 74 for males and over 79 for females (Chart 7.1). This represents an increase of over 60 per cent compared with the beginning of the century. However, progress was slower between 1950 and 1965, and until 1950 epidemics and severe winters caused higher death rates in some years resulting in falls in life expectancy for those years. Life expectancy has recently been increasing by around two years every decade. It is projected to increase over the next few decades, but at a slower rate as time goes on.

About half the increase in life expectancy this century can be attributed to the reduction in infant and child mortality. Infant and child death rates have continued to fall since 1950 and are now at such low levels that further reductions will have little effect on the expectation of life at birth. Consequently this has become closer to being a measure of normal life span. Indeed, the rate of infant mortality in 1994 in the United Kingdom, was just 5.4 deaths per thousand live births inside marriage which was just over half the rate in 1981 (Table 7.2).

Despite these improvements, differences in infant mortality still exist between the social classes. In 1994 deaths within one year of birth were least common for babies whose fathers were in the two highest social classes and were more frequent among babies whose fathers were in the lowest.

Different patterns also emerge when comparing neonatal mortality, deaths in the first 28 days of life, with post-neonatal mortality, deaths occurring between 28 days and one year of life. Neonatal mortality has steadily decreased over the last 20 years to around four deaths per thousand live births. The post-neonatal mortality rate however was relatively constant at around four deaths per thousand live births through the 1980s up until 1988, after which it decreased rapidly to around two per thousand live births in 1994. Much of this decline has been attributed to the decrease in the incidence of Sudden Infant Death Syndrome (SIDS), which is the medical term for infant deaths which occur without any warning and are more commonly known as cot deaths. It is thought that the reduction in the prevalence of deaths due to SIDS has resulted from changes in parental behaviour towards infant sleeping arrangements following research and publicity.

Much progress has also been made since 1940 in the control of infectious diseases, dramatically reducing the number of early adult deaths. Immunisation (see Table 7.14), antibiotics and improved living conditions have all played a part. However, large year to year fluctuations in the number of notifications of many communicable diseases continues, but at a much reduced level than earlier in the century. In 1995 there were 9 thousand notified cases of measles in the United Kingdom, less than half the number in 1994 (Chart 7.3). Notified cases of dysentery fell by 80 per cent from 15 thousand in 1971 to 3 thousand in 1990, but then experienced a dramatic increase and over 20 thousand cases were recorded in 1992. In the following years the numbers reduced and the number of notified cases in 1995, at between 5 and 6 thousand, was more in line with the numbers recorded during the 1980s. The number of notifications of whooping cough have also fluctuated considerably since 1971. In 1995 just over 2 thousand cases were recorded. This was as low a number as in any other year and just 3 per cent of the peak level in the period covered by the chart of over 70 thousand cases in 1982.

Yet, despite these improvements, the percentage of people who reported chronic sickness (ie a long-standing illness,

**Chronic sickness[1]: by age, 1974 and 1995-96**

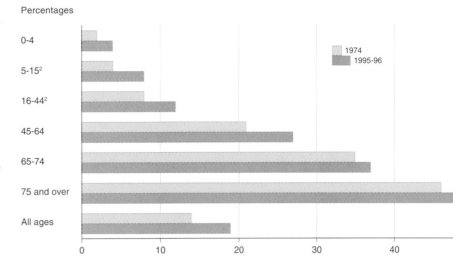

**Great Britain**
Percentages

1 Self-reported limiting long-standing illness.
2 Aged 5 to 14 and 15 to 44 in 1974.
*Source: General Household Survey, Office for National Statistics*

disability or infirmity) has risen over the last 20 years. The likelihood of suffering from chronic sickness naturally increases with age. However, Chart 7.4 shows that a higher proportion of people in all age groups in Great Britain reported chronic sickness in 1995-96 than did in 1974. Overall, 19 per cent of people reported chronic sickness in 1995-96 compared to 14 per cent in 1974. However, it should be noted that this measure of sickness, derived from the General Household Survey (GHS), is based on people's subjective assessments of their health. Therefore changes over time may reflect changes in people's expectations of their health as well as in the prevalence or duration of sickness. Nevertheless, the increase in the numbers reporting chronic sickness is important not least because perceptions of health are likely to affect directly the demand for health services.

# 7.5

Life expectancy[1] and healthy life expectancy at birth: by gender

| England & Wales | | | | | Years |
|---|---|---|---|---|---|
| | 1976 | 1981 | 1985 | 1991 | 1992 |
| **Males** | | | | | |
| Life expectancy | 70.0 | 71.1 | 71.9 | 73.2 | 73.7 |
| Healthy life expectancy | 58.3 | 58.7 | 58.8 | 59.9 | 59.7 |
| **Females** | | | | | |
| Life expectancy | 76.1 | 77.1 | 77.7 | 78.7 | 79.2 |
| Healthy life expectancy | 62.0 | 61.0 | 61.9 | 63.0 | 61.9 |

1 See Appendix, Part 7: Expectation of life.
**Source: Office for National Statistics**

# 7.6

Hospital in-patient cases[1]: by gender and main diagnosis, 1994-95

| United Kingdom | | Percentages |
|---|---|---|
| | Males | Females |
| Digestive system | 13 | 12 |
| Circulatory system | 13 | 10 |
| Neoplasms | 10 | 11 |
| Signs and symptoms | 10 | 11 |
| Injury and poisoning | 10 | 8 |
| Respiratory system | 9 | 7 |
| Genito-urinary system | 8 | 12 |
| Nervous system and sense organs | 6 | 7 |
| Musculoskeletal and connective tissue | 6 | 7 |
| Mental disorders | 4 | 4 |
| Skin | 3 | 2 |
| Endocrine, nutritional, metabolic and immunity | 2 | 2 |
| Perinatal conditions | 2 | 2 |
| Infectious and parasitic diseases | 2 | 1 |
| Congenital anomalies | 2 | 1 |
| Blood | 1 | 2 |
| All diagnoses (excluding pregnancy)(=100%)(thousands) | 4,806 | 5,053 |
| Complications of pregnancy (thousands) | . | 1,005 |
| Other reasons for contact with health services (thousands) | 336 | 443 |
| All in-patient cases[1] (thousands) | 5,142 | 6,501 |

1 Excludes normal deliveries and healthy liveborn infants.
**Source: Department of Health; Welsh Office; National Health Service in Scotland; Department of Health and Social Services, Northern Ireland**

One of the questions raised by decreasing mortality, evidenced by the increase in life expectancy, the reduction in infant mortality and the increased control of infectious diseases, is whether this has led to people living longer but spending an increased number of years in ill-health. Using information on the prevalence of limiting long-standing illness from the GHS, it is possible to calculate an indicator known as healthy life expectancy. The results indicated that, between 1976 and 1992, healthy life expectancy in England and Wales has remained almost stable, fluctuating around 59 years of age for men and 62 for women (Table 7.5). This compares with steady increases in total life expectancy from 70 for men and 76 for women in 1976 to 74 and 79 respectively in 1992. This suggests that the extra years of life gained by elderly people are extra years with a disability, not extra years of healthy life.

One way of finding out what sort of illnesses people suffer from is to look at the reasons why people stay in NHS hospitals. Table 7.6 shows that, of the 4.8 million main diagnoses of male in-patient cases in the United Kingdom in 1994-95, 13 per cent were diagnosed as having digestive system complaints and a similar proportion had circulatory system complaints. A further 10 per cent each were there as a result of neoplasms (cancers) and because of injury and poisoning. There were 5.1 million female diagnoses (excluding those associated with pregnancy); of these, diseases of the genito-urinary system and digestive system complaints each accounted for 12 per cent of cases, and neoplasms and signs for a further 11 per cent. An additional 1 million females were in-patients because of pregnancy complications.

According to the 1994 Health Survey for England, around a quarter of both men and women reported having had at least one cardiovascular disease (CVD) condition at some time in their life. High blood pressure was the most commonly reported CVD condition and 8 per cent of men and 11 per cent of women reported suffering from this at the time of interview (Table 7.7). The prevalence of high blood pressure, like all CVDs, generally increases with age. In 1994 just over half of men and women aged 75 and over reported having had a CVD at some point in their life.

A number of conditions, including high blood pressure and other CVDs, can be related to weight problems. In particular, being overweight increases the risk of younger men and women having a CVD, and for middle aged women being either underweight or obese increases their likelihood. Almost three fifths of men and just under half of women aged 16 and over in England were classed as overweight or obese in 1994 (Chart 7.8). However, a higher proportion of women than men were considered obese; 17 per cent compared with 14 per cent. There is a Health of the Nation target to reduce the prevalence of obesity in those aged 16 to 64 by 2005 from the 1986-87 proportions of 7 per cent of men and 12 per cent of women to no more than 6 and 8 per cent respectively. These proportions have in fact been increasing; the Health Survey for England estimated that 13 per cent of men and 16 per cent of women aged 16 to 64 were obese in 1994.

Psychological factors have also been implicated in the development of CVD. Stress, in its many forms, such as work-related stress or stress due to lack of social

**Percentage of adults who had a cardiovascular disease[1]: by gender, age and type of disease, 1994**

England — Percentages

| | 16-24 | 25-34 | 35-44 | 45-54 | 55-64 | 65-74 | 75 and over | All aged 16 and over |
|---|---|---|---|---|---|---|---|---|
| **Males** | | | | | | | | |
| High blood pressure | 0.5 | 1.2 | 3.4 | 5.7 | 16.9 | 22.5 | 18.6 | 8.0 |
| Angina | - | - | 0.2 | 1.5 | 5.8 | 9.8 | 12.5 | 3.1 |
| Diabetes | 0.8 | 0.8 | 1.0 | 2.5 | 6.4 | 5.8 | 7.5 | 2.9 |
| Abnormal heart rhythm | 0.4 | 0.6 | 0.8 | 2.0 | 3.3 | 3.8 | 5.4 | 1.9 |
| Heart murmur | 0.2 | 0.3 | 0.4 | 0.4 | 1.8 | 1.6 | 1.6 | 0.8 |
| Heart attack | - | - | 0.1 | 0.2 | 1.1 | 2.4 | 3.2 | 0.7 |
| Stroke | - | - | - | - | 0.5 | 2.2 | 2.7 | 0.5 |
| Other heart trouble | - | 0.1 | 0.2 | 0.5 | 0.5 | 0.3 | 1.4 | 0.3 |
| **Females** | | | | | | | | |
| High blood pressure | 0.7 | 1.6 | 3.8 | 7.8 | 20.5 | 27.9 | 26.9 | 10.9 |
| Angina | - | - | 0.2 | 1.3 | 3.1 | 6.2 | 9.0 | 2.3 |
| Abnormal heart rhythm | 0.4 | 1.0 | 1.5 | 2.3 | 2.9 | 3.2 | 4.2 | 2.0 |
| Diabetes | 0.6 | 0.3 | 0.9 | 1.5 | 2.5 | 4.8 | 5.2 | 1.9 |
| Heart murmur | 0.8 | 1.0 | 0.9 | 1.2 | 1.4 | 1.8 | 2.2 | 1.3 |
| Heart attack | - | - | 0.1 | 0.3 | 0.6 | 0.7 | 1.8 | 0.4 |
| Stroke | - | 0.1 | - | 0.1 | 0.3 | 0.4 | 1.8 | 0.3 |
| Other heart trouble | - | 0.1 | 0.1 | 0.2 | 0.7 | 0.9 | 0.8 | 0.3 |

1 At the time of interview for blood pressure; within a year of interview for all other conditions.

*Source: Health Survey for England, Department of Health*

**Body mass[1]: by gender, 1994**

**England**

Percentages

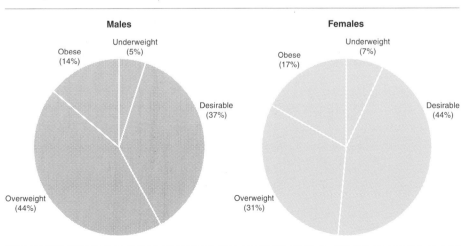

1 People aged 16 and over. Body mass index. See Appendix, Part 7: Body mass index.

*Source: Health Survey for England, Department of Health*

# 7.9

**Experience of stress[1]: by gender and age, 1994**

England                                                                                                      Percentages

| | 16-24 | 25-34 | 35-54 | 55-64 | 65 and over | All aged 16 and over |
|---|---|---|---|---|---|---|
| **Males** | | | | | | |
| None | 21 | 16 | 16 | 37 | 53 | 26 |
| A little | 48 | 43 | 42 | 39 | 37 | 41 |
| A good bit | 18 | 23 | 22 | 13 | 6 | 18 |
| Quite a lot/a great deal | 13 | 18 | 21 | 11 | 4 | 15 |
| **Females** | | | | | | |
| None | 17 | 14 | 15 | 30 | 44 | 24 |
| A little | 49 | 46 | 45 | 43 | 38 | 44 |
| A good bit | 19 | 21 | 20 | 15 | 9 | 17 |
| Quite a lot/a great deal | 15 | 19 | 20 | 12 | 9 | 16 |

1 Respondents were asked: 'In general, how much stress or pressure have you experienced in your daily living in the last four weeks?'.

*Source: Health Survey for England, Department of Health*

# 7.10

**People with raised cholesterol levels[1]: by gender and age, 1994**

England                                    Percentages

| | Males | Females |
|---|---|---|
| 16-24 | 4 | 4 |
| 25-34 | 15 | 10 |
| 35-44 | 31 | 13 |
| 45-54 | 39 | 32 |
| 55-64 | 41 | 58 |
| 65-74 | 38 | 68 |
| 75 and over | 30 | 57 |
| All aged 16 and over | 28 | 32 |

1 Either moderately or severely raised. See Appendix, Part 7: Serum total cholesterol.

*Source: Health Survey for England, Department of Health*

contact, has been identified as one of the most important of these. **Table 7.9** shows that in 1994 men and women reported experiencing very similar levels of stress: 15 per cent of men and 16 per cent of women said that they had experienced quite a lot or a great deal of stress in their daily lives in the four weeks before interview. About a quarter said that they had experienced no stress and about two fifths only a little. Reported stress levels decreased rapidly with age in the older age groups: only 4 per cent of men aged 65 and over and 9 per cent of women in this age group reported high levels of stress.

Respondents were also asked to what extent they felt that stress or pressure experienced in their lives had affected their health: 12 per cent of men and 14 per cent of women said that it had affected their

health either quite a lot or extremely. The proportion was highest for those aged 55 to 64 and was lowest, as might be expected, for those aged 16 to 24.

Another important risk factor in the development of CVD is a person's total cholesterol level. This is partly dependent on dietary saturated fat intake, and reduction of dietary fat intake could yield substantial reduction in deaths from CVD. In 1994 around 30 per cent of adults in England had raised cholesterol levels **(Table 7.10)**, that is levels classified as moderately or severely raised and usually considered to require medical intervention. However, a further 40 per cent of adults were found to have mildly raised levels. The remaining 30 per cent had levels within the desirable range.

The proportions with raised levels increased with age, peaking in the 55 to 64 age group for men and the 65 to 74 age group for women before declining. Mean cholesterol was higher in men than in women for those aged 25 to 54 years after which mean cholesterol was higher in women. The increase in the prevalence of raised cholesterol in women in middle life is consistent with the reported increase in cholesterol in women after menopause.

About one person in three develops a cancer sometime in their life, and cancer now causes about one in four deaths. The incidence of the main types of cancer are, however, very different for men and women. Lung cancer was the most frequently reported cancer in men in England and Wales in 1991. However, the incidence rates of lung cancer for men have fallen by around 20 per cent over the period 1979 to 1991. In contrast, the incidence of lung cancer among women increased by over 20 per cent over the same period. Despite this men were still almost three times as likely to suffer from lung cancer as women in 1991 (Chart 7.11).

The most frequently reported cancer in women was breast cancer which women were about three times as likely to suffer from as the next most common form of cancer. In 1991 the standardised incidence rate of breast cancer in women in England and Wales was 104 per 100 thousand population, which was about 40 per cent higher than in 1979. This increase is partly the result of better detection through the NHS breast screening programme which began in the late 1980s.

Colorectal cancer was the second most frequently reported cancer in men and women, but was almost one and a half times more likely to affect men than women in 1991. Its incidence though, for both men and women, has remained relatively stable between 1979 and 1991. The incidence of stomach cancer was much less common but decreased by a quarter for men and a third for women over the same period.

Prostate cancer is the third most common cancer in men. Its incidence has increased steadily in recent years, with the rate per 100 thousand population increasing by about a half between 1981 and 1991 in England and Wales (Table 7.12). This rise is difficult to interpret, partly because men are

**Standardised incidence rates[1] of selected cancers: by gender**

**England & Wales**

Rates per 100,000 population

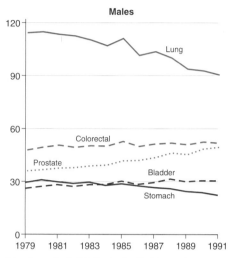

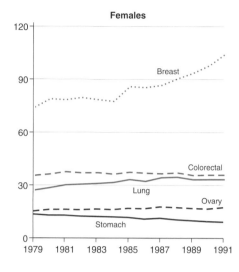

1 See Appendix, Part 7: Standardised incidence rates.
*Source: Office for National Statistics*

more aware of the disease and also because of better diagnostic techniques. However, the consensus is that the rising incidence and mortality rates seen in the United Kingdom and throughout Europe are due to a real increase in the disease, and environmental and dietary factors have been quoted as possible explanations. The incidence of prostate cancer is extremely rare in men under the age of 50 but increases rapidly as they get older, more so than any other form of cancer. There were about 14 thousand cases of prostate cancer diagnosed in England and Wales in 1991.

The incidence of AIDS (Acquired Immune Deficiency Syndrome) has also increased over the last 10 years. The Public Health Laboratory Service (PHLS) estimates that there were 1,780 cases of AIDS in England

**7.12**

**Prostate cancer: by age, 1981 and 1991**

| England & Wales | Rates per 100,000 population | |
| --- | --- | --- |
|  | 1981 | 1991 |
| 0-14 | - | - |
| 15-34 | - | - |
| 35-44 | - | - |
| 45-54 | 5 | 6 |
| 55-64 | 42 | 57 |
| 65-74 | 179 | 238 |
| 75 and over | 455 | 612 |
| All ages | 38 | 56 |

*Source: Office for National Statistics*

# 7.13

AIDS cases per year[1]: by exposure category

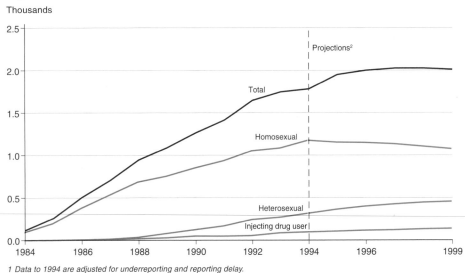

**England & Wales**
Thousands

1 Data to 1994 are adjusted for underreporting and reporting delay.
2 1994-based projections.
**Source: PHLS Communicable Disease Surveillance Centre**

# 7.14

Immunisation of children[1]

| United Kingdom | | | Percentages |
|---|---|---|---|
| | 1981 | 1991-92[2] | 1994-95[2] |
| Diphtheria | 82 | 94 | 95 |
| Poliomyelitis | 82 | 94 | 95 |
| Whooping cough | 46 | 88 | 95 |
| Tetanus | 82 | 94 | 93 |
| Measles, mumps, rubella[3] | 54 | 91 | 91 |

1 See Appendix, Part 7: Immunisation.
2 Scotish data are for 1992 and 1995.
3 Includes measles only vaccine. Combined vaccine was not available prior to 1988.
**Source: Department of Health; Welsh Office; National Health Service in Scotland; Department of Health and Social Services, Northern Ireland**

and Wales in 1994 compared with only 115 in 1984 (Chart 7.13). It is anticipated that the number of new cases will level out over the next few years at around 2 thousand per year. In 1994 there were 1,570 deaths from AIDS in England and Wales. Women accounted for only 11 per cent of reported cases. It is expected that the total number of deaths from AIDS will rise in future years and that almost a quarter more will occur in 1999 than in 1994. Around two thirds of the cases recorded in 1994 were acquired as a result of sexual intercourse between men. This is expected to continue to be the main exposure category, although it is thought that the proportion of cases resulting from sex between men and women will increase in the future.

By the end of 1994, almost 21 thousand cases of diagnosed HIV (Human Immunodeficiency Virus) infections had been reported to PHLS and just over 8 thousand of these had died from AIDS. However, because many people with the HIV infection have yet to be diagnosed, the

difference between the two figures is an underestimate of the actual number of people with HIV in England and Wales. Using data from the Unlinked Anonymous Programme and the National Survey of Sexual Attitudes and Lifestyles, this number was estimated at about 22 thousand at the beginning of 1994.

## Prevention

Some aspects of health can, at least in part, be controlled by taking preventative steps. Over the years there have been a number of campaigns to encourage parents to have their children immunised against major infectious diseases. Nearly all children in the United Kingdom were immunised against diphtheria, whooping cough and poliomyelitis in 1994-95 and over nine in ten were immunised against tetanus, measles, mumps and rubella (Table 7.14). The proportion immunised against whooping cough in 1994-95 was more than double the proportion in 1981, although the number then was particularly low because of fears over vaccine safety. Chart 7.3 shows the success of these programmes in reducing the prevalence of infectious diseases.

National screening programmes are in place for breast and cervical cancer. Cervical cancer is commonly preceded by a long pre-cancerous stage which can be treated. In 1994-95 around 85 per cent of women aged 25 to 64 in England and Wales had undergone a cervical smear test in the previous five years (Table 7.15). This is a considerable improvement on the figure of just over 60 per cent recorded five years earlier (although it should be noted that this figure relates to women aged 20 to 64 less those no longer eligible for screening because of clinical or other reasons).

## 7.15

In 1994-95 the highest cervical screening rate in England and Wales, of over 90 per cent of the target population, was achieved in the Trent Regional Health Authority (RHA). The other RHAs, all achieved rates of over 80 per cent with the exception of North West Thames and North East Thames.

Figures for Northern Ireland included in the table are compiled on a slightly different basis. In 1994-95, 77 per cent of women aged 20 to 64 had been screened in the previous five years, a large increase on the rate of 26 per cent in 1989-90.

## Health and lifestyles

Awareness has been increasing in recent years of how lifestyle and social habits can affect our health. Diet is an important factor in our health and the noticeable changes in what we ate in 1995 compared with what we ate in 1971 suggests that we may be increasingly taking note of 'healthy eating messages'. The consumption of red meats has fallen over the period while that of poultry has risen (Chart 7.16). Average consumption of poultry was 237 grams a week in 1995; about three quarters more than in 1971. Over the same period, the average amount of mutton and lamb consumed decreased by two thirds to 54 grams a week in 1995.

The increase in the consumption of low and reduced fat spreads in preference to butter is also evident. The amount of butter consumed per person in 1995 was less than a quarter of the amount in 1971. In contrast, the average amount of low and reduced fat spreads eaten increased sixfold between 1984 and 1995.

**Percentage of target population[1] screened for cervical cancer in the previous five and a half years: by region**

Percentages

|  | 1989-90 | 1991-92 | 1994-95[2] |
|---|---|---|---|
| Northern | 64 | 83 | 88 |
| Yorkshire | 65 | 85 | 88 |
| Trent | 72 | 87 | 91 |
| East Anglia | 68 | 86 | 89 |
| North West Thames | 42 | 65 | 76 |
| North East Thames | 34 | 64 | 78 |
| South East Thames | .. | 70 | 84 |
| South West Thames | 46 | 78 | 85 |
| Wessex | 75 | 88 | 88 |
| Oxford | 79 | 85 | 88 |
| South Western | 78 | 86 | 88 |
| West Midlands | 71 | 84 | 88 |
| Mersey | 72 | 82 | 85 |
| North Western | 61 | 84 | 86 |
| England | 62 | 80 | 86 |
| Wales | 62 | 85 | 85 |
| Northern Ireland[3] | 26 | 62 | 77 |

1 Women aged 20 to 64 less those no longer eligible because of clinical or other reasons.
2 In England, women aged 25 to 64 screened in the previous five years.
3 Women aged 20 to 64 screened in the previous five years.
**Source: Department of Health; Welsh Office; Department of Health and Social Services, Northern Ireland**

## 7.16

**Changing patterns in consumption of foods at home**

**Great Britain**

Grams per person per week

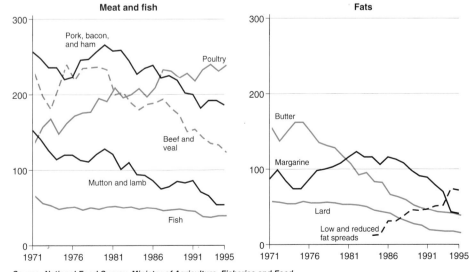

**Source: National Food Survey, Ministry of Agriculture, Fisheries and Food**

# 7.17

Eating habits of young children[1]: by social class of head of household, 1992-1993[2]

**Great Britain**                                                                    Grams per week

|                                               | Manual | Non-manual | All social classes[3] |
|-----------------------------------------------|--------|------------|-----------------------|
| White bread                                   | 245    | 199        | 226                   |
| Potato chips                                  | 217    | 176        | 200                   |
| Meat pies and pastries                        | 162    | 127        | 149                   |
| Chicken and turkey dishes                     | 79     | 99         | 89                    |
| Sugar confectionery                           | 125    | 103        | 115                   |
| Chocolate confectionery                       | 109    | 91         | 101                   |
| Savoury snacks                                | 91     | 77         | 85                    |
| Sugar                                         | 40     | 24         | 33                    |
| Bananas                                       | 228    | 239        | 234                   |
| Apples and pears                              | 207    | 229        | 219                   |
| Wholegrain and high fibre breakfast cereals   | 121    | 127        | 125                   |
| Other breakfast cereals                       | 97     | 85         | 92                    |

1 Mean total quantity of food item consumed by children aged between one and a half and four and a half years as estimated for seven days.
2 July 1992 to June 1993.
3 Includes those households where social class was unknown.
**Source: National Diet and Nutrition Survey, Office for National Statistics**

# 7.18

Physical activity[1]: by gender and age, 1994

**England**                                                                          Percentages

|            | 16-24 | 25-34 | 35-54 | 55-64 | 65-74 | 75 and over | All aged 16 and over |
|------------|-------|-------|-------|-------|-------|-------------|----------------------|
| **Males**  |       |       |       |       |       |             |                      |
| Vigorous   | 69    | 50    | 33    | 14    | 6     | 3           | 33                   |
| Moderate   | 25    | 44    | 56    | 64    | 67    | 46          | 51                   |
| Light      | 4     | 5     | 9     | 14    | 15    | 25          | 10                   |
| Inactive   | 2     | 2     | 3     | 9     | 13    | 26          | 6                    |
| All males  | 100   | 100   | 100   | 100   | 100   | 100         | 100                  |
| **Females**|       |       |       |       |       |             |                      |
| Vigorous   | 43    | 37    | 25    | 13    | 5     | 1           | 23                   |
| Moderate   | 47    | 56    | 65    | 70    | 64    | 38          | 59                   |
| Light      | 6     | 5     | 6     | 9     | 14    | 17          | 8                    |
| Inactive   | 4     | 3     | 4     | 8     | 17    | 44          | 10                   |
| All females| 100   | 100   | 100   | 100   | 100   | 100         | 100                  |

1 Maximum activity level in the four weeks before interview. See Appendix, Part 7: Physical activity levels.
**Source: Health Survey for England, Department of Health**

Dietary patterns vary considerably between people from different social classes. The National Diet and Nutrition Survey of children aged between one and a half and four and a half showed clear patterns and differences in the types of foods consumed by children from manual and non-manual backgrounds. Children from a manual background have a diet with less emphasis on fruit and whole grain cereals (Table 7.17). They ate greater amounts of meat pies and pastries, whereas children from a non-manual background ate more chicken and turkey. Children from the manual group consumed two thirds more sugar than those from the non-manual group and were more likely to have eaten confectionery.

The benefits of a physically active lifestyle have been recognised for some time. Undertaking moderate levels of physical activity can help prevent a number of health conditions, including CVD. Indeed, there is evidence that low levels of physical activity are associated with other risk factors of heart disease such as high blood pressure and obesity. Current guidelines accepted in the United Kingdom suggest that moderate or vigorous exercise, lasting 30 minutes or more, should be taken on at least five occasions a week. Physical activity does not just take place through sport and exercise; it can also involve occupational activity, walking, and home activities such as housework and gardening.

Table 7.18, taken from the 1994 Health Survey for England, shows the maximum level of physical activity undertaken by respondents in the four weeks prior to interview. In 1994 over four fifths of men and women in England said that they had participated in at least one period of either moderate or vigorous physical activity. A greater proportion of men than women however were involved in physical activity at a vigorous level: around a third of men compared with around a quarter of women. Just 6 per cent of men and 10 per cent of women said that they had not taken any physical activity during the period.

Not surprisingly, the maximum level of physical activity undertaken was strongly related to a person's age. Among women, for example, over two fifths in the 16 to 24 age group reported that they had undertaken vigorous physical activity, whereas a quarter in the 35 to 54 age group and only one in a hundred of those aged 75 and over reported doing so. Similarly, just 2 per cent of men and 4 per cent of women in the 16 to 24 age group reported having not taken any physical activity compared with 26 per cent and 44 per cent respectively of those aged 75 and over.

Smoking is a recognised health risk and can lead to diseases such as lung cancer, respiratory disease and heart disease. A Health of the Nation target has been set in England to reduce the percentage of adults who smoke cigarettes to no more than 20 per cent by the year 2000. There is also a target for Wales to reduce the proportion of men who smoke to 20 per cent and women who smoke to 17 per cent by 2002. Chart 7.19 illustrates how the proportion of both men and women in Great Britain who smoked cigarettes has fallen. In 1972-73, 52 per cent of men and 41 per cent of women smoked cigarettes, but by 1994-95 this had fallen to 28 per cent and 26 per cent respectively. However, if the Health of the Nation target is to be achieved, the rate of decline needs to be slightly greater than it has been in recent years.

Although similar proportions of men and women smoked cigarettes in 1994-95, men smoked more cigarettes on average than women: male smokers had about 16

cigarettes a day while female smokers had about 14 cigarettes a day. Around one in ten adults was classed as a heavy smoker in 1994-95 (that is smoked 20 or more cigarettes a day). Smoking is also much more common in the manual social groups than in the non-manual groups. In 1994-95 men in the unskilled manual group were two and a half times more likely to smoke than those in the professional group. People in the 20 to 24 age group were the most likely to smoke cigarettes: around two-fifths smoked cigarettes compared with less than a fifth aged 60 and over.

Smoking among children is of particular concern, and a Health of the Nation target for England was set to reduce the percentage of 11 to 15 year olds smoking regularly from about 8 per cent in 1988 to less than 6 per cent in 1994. Table 7.20 shows that this was not achieved and that cigarette smoking among children has in fact become slightly more prevalent. In 1994, 10 per cent of boys and 13 per cent of girls

## 7.19

Adult cigarette smoking[1]: by gender

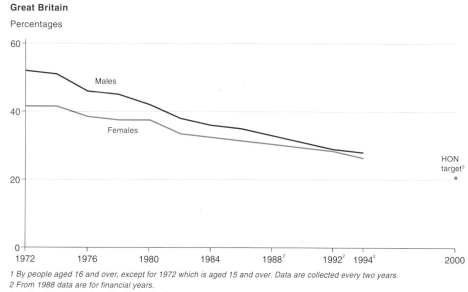

**Great Britain**
Percentages

1 By people aged 16 and over, except for 1972 which is aged 15 and over. Data are collected every two years.
2 From 1988 data are for financial years.
3 Health of the Nation target for England only.
*Source: General Household Survey, Office for National Statistics*

## 7.20

Cigarette smoking among children[1]: by gender

| England | | | Percentages |
|---|---|---|---|
| | 1982 | 1986 | 1994 |
| **Boys** | | | |
| Regular smoker | 11 | 7 | 10 |
| Occasional smoker | 7 | 5 | 9 |
| Used to smoke | 11 | 10 | 7 |
| Tried smoking | 26 | 23 | 21 |
| Never smoked | 45 | 55 | 53 |
| | | | |
| All boys | 100 | 100 | 100 |
| | | | |
| **Girls** | | | |
| Regular smoker | 11 | 12 | 13 |
| Occasional smoker | 9 | 5 | 10 |
| Used to smoke | 10 | 10 | 8 |
| Tried smoking | 22 | 19 | 17 |
| Never smoked | 49 | 53 | 52 |
| | | | |
| All girls | 100 | 100 | 100 |

1 Aged 11 to 15 years.
*Source: Smoking Among Secondary School Children Survey, Office for National Statistics*

# 7.21

## Young people ever using drugs[1]: by gender, 1992-1993[2]

| England & Wales | | | Percentages |
|---|---|---|---|
| | Males | Females | All young people |
| Cannabis | 41 | 25 | 33 |
| Acid/LSD | 11 | 7 | 9 |
| Amphetamines | 13 | 6 | 9 |
| Magic mushrooms | 12 | 4 | 8 |
| Ecstasy | 9 | 5 | 7 |
| Glue/gas | 5 | 3 | 4 |
| Any drug[3] | 45 | 26 | 36 |

1 People aged 14 to 25 who said they had ever used drugs.
2 November 1992 to January 1993.
3 Includes other drugs not mentioned.
**Source: Youth Lifestyles Survey, Home Office**

# 7.22

## Consumption[1] of alcohol: by gender, 1984 and 1994-95

| Great Britain | | Percentages |
|---|---|---|
| | 1984 | 1994-95 |
| **Males** | | |
| High | 25 | 27 |
| Moderate | 21 | 22 |
| Low | 37 | 35 |
| Very low | 10 | 9 |
| Non-drinker | 7 | 7 |
| All males aged 18 and over | 100 | 100 |
| **Females** | | |
| High | 9 | 13 |
| Moderate | 14 | 15 |
| Low | 41 | 37 |
| Very low | 24 | 21 |
| Non-drinker | 13 | 14 |
| All females aged 18 and over | 100 | 100 |

1 See Appendix, Part 7: Alcohol consumption.
**Source: General Household Survey, Office for National Statistics**

were regular smokers in England compared with 7 per cent and 12 per cent respectively in 1986. However, although girls were slightly more likely to smoke than boys, those who did smoke, smoked less than boys. It was estimated that over 350 thousand children aged 11 to 15 were regular smokers in 1994.

The use of drugs is also widespread among young people. The Youth Lifestyles Survey carried out by the Home Office in 1992-1993 in England and Wales indicated that over a third of young adults aged 14 to 25 had, at some time, used controlled drugs (Table 7.21). About a fifth of respondents also reported using them in the last year. Males in this age group were much more likely to have ever used drugs than females: nearly a half of males admitted to having ever used drugs whilst just over a quarter of females did so.

Cannabis was the most commonly used drug by young males and females, whether in the last year or at any time in the past. Acid/LSD and amphetamines were the next most common, with 9 per cent admitting to have ever used each of these drugs. Only a small minority of young adults had ever tried cocaine, crack or heroin: just 2 per cent said that they had ever used cocaine and 1 per cent each said that they had used crack or heroin.

Alcohol consumption above sensible levels is associated with increased likelihood of various health problems such as raised blood pressure and various cancers. The recommended maximum sensible amounts for adults were 21 units per week for men and 14 units per week for women. However, following the publication of the report 'Sensible Drinking' in December 1995, these guidelines are being reconsidered. Consequently, the Health of the Nation

target for England to reduce the proportion of men drinking more than 21 units a week from 28 per cent in 1990 to 18 per cent by 2005 and the proportion of women drinking more than 14 units a week from 11 per cent to 7 per cent over the same period, although still being monitored, is also being reviewed. The target in Wales also uses the previously recognised maximum sensible drinking amounts and aims to reduce the proportion of men drinking more than 21 units a week to 12 per cent and the proportion of women drinking more than 14 units to 5 per cent by 2002. In 1994-95, 27 per cent of men and 13 per cent of women aged 18 and over in Great Britain drank more than the then recognised sensible maximum amounts, which are both an increase on the respective percentages of 25 per cent and 9 per cent reported in 1984 (Table 7.22).

## Causes of death

As mentioned earlier, there have been considerable reductions in the numbers of early adult deaths. Chart 7.23 illustrates the most common causes of death for men and women aged under 65 in the United Kingdom. For men of this age, the three most common causes of death have all fallen since the early 1970s. In particular the death rate from heart disease has fallen by almost half - from 148 deaths per 100 thousand population in 1972 to 76 deaths per 100 thousand in 1995. Despite this fall, the 18 thousand deaths among men aged under 65 caused by heart disease accounted for just over a quarter of all deaths of men in this group in 1995. Deaths from lung cancer and stroke were much less common; together they caused one in eight deaths. The rates of male deaths from both these causes in 1995 were less than half of what they were in the early 1970s.

The death rate among women under 65 from heart disease, at 22 per 100 thousand population, was only 29 per cent of the rate for men in 1995, even though it is one of the major causes of death for women in this age group. In 1994 and 1995 breast cancer caused slightly more female deaths than heart disease. However, the rates of female deaths from both breast cancer and heart disease are continuing to fall gradually.

Causes of mortality vary considerably according to age as well as gender. Table 7.24 analyses the prevalence of selected causes of mortality for different age groups in 1995. The number of deaths due to infectious diseases has been reduced over the years; in 1995 they caused less than 1 per cent of all deaths. However, the few that do occur are usually to younger people. This

**Death rates[1] for selected causes for people aged under 65: by gender**

**United Kingdom**
Rates per 100,000 population

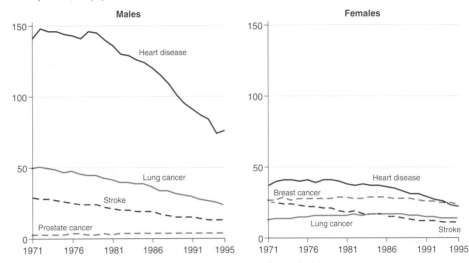

1 Age-standardised to the 1971 population level. See Appendix, Part 7: Standardised death rates.
**Source: Office for National Statistics; General Register Office (Scotland); General Register Office (Northern Ireland)**

# 7.24

**Selected causes of death: by gender and age, 1995**

**United Kingdom**                                                                                                           Percentages

|  | Under 1[1] | 1-14 | 15-24 | 25-34 | 35-54 | 55-64 | 65-74 | 75 and over | All ages |
|---|---|---|---|---|---|---|---|---|---|
| **Males** | | | | | | | | | |
| Circulatory diseases[2] | 1 | 6 | 5 | 9 | 34 | 43 | 46 | 45 | 43 |
| Cancer | - | 17 | 7 | 1 | 28 | 36 | 33 | 22 | 26 |
| Respiratory diseases | 3 | 6 | 3 | 5 | 6 | 7 | 12 | 20 | 15 |
| Injury and poisoning | 2 | 32 | 64 | 51 | 15 | 3 | 1 | 1 | 4 |
| Infectious diseases | 3 | 7 | 2 | 6 | 3 | 1 | - | - | 1 |
| All other causes | 91 | 32 | 19 | 19 | 15 | 9 | 8 | 11 | 11 |
| | | | | | | | | | |
| All males(=100%)(thousands) | 3 | 1 | 3 | 5 | 22 | 36 | 85 | 154 | 309 |
| **Females** | | | | | | | | | |
| Circulatory diseases[2] | 1 | 6 | 8 | 12 | 18 | 29 | 40 | 48 | 43 |
| Cancer | - | 16 | 14 | 29 | 52 | 48 | 35 | 15 | 23 |
| Respiratory diseases | 3 | 8 | 4 | 6 | 5 | 9 | 13 | 19 | 16 |
| Injury and poisoning | 2 | 23 | 44 | 24 | 8 | 2 | 1 | 1 | 2 |
| Infectious diseases | 3 | 7 | 4 | 4 | 1 | 1 | - | - | 1 |
| All other causes | 91 | 40 | 25 | 24 | 16 | 11 | 11 | 16 | 15 |
| | | | | | | | | | |
| All females(=100%)(thousands) | 2 | 1 | 1 | 2 | 15 | 22 | 61 | 230 | 333 |

1 Figures exclude deaths at ages under 28 days.
2 Includes heart attacks and strokes.

**Source: Office for National Statistics; General Register Office (Scotland); General Register Office (Northern Ireland)**

# 7.25

## Accidental deaths: by age

| United Kingdom | | Rates per 100,000 population | | |
|---|---|---|---|---|
| | 1971 | 1981 | 1991 | 1995 |
| 0-14[1] | 18 | 10 | 7 | 5 |
| 15-24 | 33 | 29 | 24 | 19 |
| 25-34 | 21 | 17 | 15 | 14 |
| 35-44 | 19 | 15 | 14 | 12 |
| 45-54 | 22 | 18 | 15 | 13 |
| 55-64 | 31 | 24 | 17 | 15 |
| 65-74 | 54 | 39 | 29 | 25 |
| 75 and over | 231 | 165 | 113 | 114 |
| All ages | 36 | 29 | 23 | 21 |

*1 Figures for 1991 and 1995 exclude deaths at ages under 28 days.*

*Source: Office for National Statistics; General Register Office (Scotland); General Register Office (Northern Ireland)*

Standard mortality ratios (SMRs) are calculated by comparing the observed number of deaths in a group (numerator) against an expected number of deaths (denominator), usually that of the relevant wider population, known as the standard population. This ratio, normally expressed as a percentage, is the SMR. Values over 100 indicate raised mortality compared to the standard; values under 100 indicate relatively lower mortality.

# 7.26

## Death rates[1] from diseases of the circulatory system: EU comparison, 1992

Rates per 100,000 population

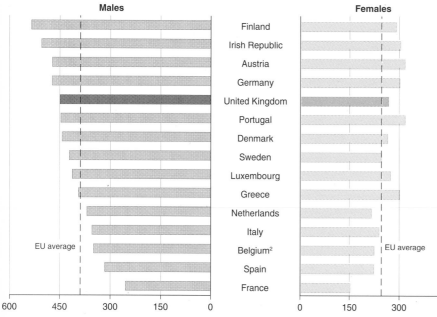

*1 Age standardised using the European Standard population.*
*2 Data are for 1991.*

*Source: World Health Organisation*

is because as children grow up they become more exposed to infection and build up resistance either naturally, as a result of exposure to the diseases, or artificially as a result of immunisation (see Table 7.14).

Among 15 to 24 year olds, injury and poisoning was the most common cause of death; 64 per cent of male deaths and 44 per cent of female deaths were the result of injury and poisoning in the United Kingdom in 1995. However, for both males and females these proportions declined to just over 1 per cent for people aged 65 and over.

Conversely, the proportion of male deaths due to circulatory diseases in the 75 and over age group was about nine times larger than for 15 to 24 year olds, while for females it was about six times larger.

The prevalence of accidental death also varies considerably with age and is particularly high for the elderly. In 1995 there were 114 deaths per 100 thousand population aged 75 and over compared with around 5 per 100 thousand population aged under 15 in the United Kingdom (Table 7.25). However, there has been a considerable reduction in the rates of accidental deaths in the last 25 years, particularly among the population aged under 15, for whom the rate in 1995 was about a quarter of that in 1971. There is a Health of the Nation target for England to reduce the death rate for accidents among children aged under 15, and young people aged 15 to 24, to no more than 4.5 and 17.3 per 100 thousand population respectively in 2005. The progress that has been made in recent years shows that these targets are close to being reached. Overall, the rate of 21 accidental deaths per 100 thousand population in 1995 in the United Kingdom represented a fall of over 40 per cent compared with the rate of 36 deaths per 100 thousand in 1971.

Death rates from diseases of the circulatory system vary considerably between the countries of the European Union (EU). Chart 7.26 shows that France had by far the lowest rates. In 1992 the death rates for both males and females in France were about half those in the Irish Republic, whose rates were among the highest in the EU. The death

# 7.27

rates in the United Kingdom in 1992 were above the EU average for both males and females. Death rates from diseases of the circulatory system were lower in 1992 than those reported in 1970 in all countries except Greece. In Greece, the death rate from circulatory diseases in 1971 was 314 per 100 thousand population compared with 344 per 100 thousand population in 1992.

There is also some evidence to suggest that mortality differences exist between ethnic groups in the United Kingdom. Country of birth is collected on all death certificates and at population censuses and is the best proxy available for ethnic group, though it is becoming less so as the British-born ethnic minority population grows in importance. Table 7.27 provides the all-cause standardised mortality ratios (SMRs - see definitional box) for men and women aged 20 to 69 by country of birth for deaths between 1988 and 1992, with 100 representing the SMR of each gender born in England and Wales. Both men and women born in Scotland and Ireland (Northern Ireland and the Irish Republic combined) had considerably higher mortality rates than their counterparts born in England and Wales (the standard population for the purposes of this table). However, while men born in Scotland had a lower proportion than men born in Ireland, the reverse was true for women.

Men and women born in the Indian subcontinent and the African Commonwealth had similar SMRs over the period 1988 to 1992 to men and women born in England

and Wales. However, the SMRs for both men and women born in the EU, the Old Commonwealth and the Caribbean Commonwealth were all lower than 100. Both men and women born in the Mediterranean Commonwealth had the lowest SMRs of all those shown in the table.

It has also been suggested that there is a relationship between economic activity and health, and more specifically unemployment and ill health. Table 7.28 shows the likelihood of death among men and women of working age between 1981 and 1992 by their economic activity status at the 1981 Census. The standard population in this analysis represents all men and women in the Longitudinal Study.

The results of the study indicated that both men and women in employment have lower mortality than the working age population as a whole, with SMRs of 84 and 80 respectively. In contrast, both men and women in every other category had higher than average mortality with the exception of other inactive males. However, it is not surprising that other inactive males had a SMR below 100 as the majority of this category were students whose average age was younger than the working age population as a whole. Both men and women seeking work, with SMRs of 132 and 133 respectively, had higher than average mortality and considerably higher mortality than their employed counterparts. One explanation put forward for this is that the workforce has a tendency to retain the healthiest people.

## Mortality[1]: by country of birth and gender, 1988-1992

| Great Britain | | SMR[2] |
|---|---|---|
| | Males | Females |
| All Ireland | 140 | 119 |
| Scotland | 129 | 132 |
| Indian subcontinent | 103 | 96 |
| African[3] | 102 | 99 |
| EU countries | 93 | 81 |
| Old Commonwealth | 89 | 83 |
| Caribbean[3] | 83 | 96 |
| Mediterranean[3] | 81 | 78 |

1 People aged 20 to 69.
2 See definitional box.
3 Commonwealth countries.
*Source: National Institute for Ethnic Studies in Health and Social Policy*

# 7.28

## Mortality[1]: by economic activity status and gender at 1981 Census, 1981-1992

| England & Wales | | SMR[2] |
|---|---|---|
| | Males | Females |
| Employed | 84 | 80 |
| Seeking work | 132 | 133 |
| Temporarily sick | 269 | 282 |
| Permanently sick/disabled | 338 | 587 |
| Retired | 160 | - |
| Looking after home/family | - | 108 |
| Other inactive | 94 | 114 |
| All | 100 | 100 |

1 Males aged 16 to 64, females aged 16 to 59.
2 See definitional box.
*Source: Longitudinal Study, Office for National Statistics*

## References and further reading

The following list contains selected publications relevant to **Chapter 7: Health**. Those published by The Stationery Office are available from the addresses shown on the inside back cover of *Social Trends*.

*Cancer Statistics Registrations* (Series MB1), The Stationery Office

*Communicable Disease Statistics (Series MB2)*, The Stationery Office

*General Household Survey*, The Stationery Office

*Health expectancy and its uses*, Bone et al, The Stationery Office

*Health Survey for England*, The Stationery Office

*Hospital Episode Statistics*, Department of Health

*Mortality Statistics for England and Wales*, The Stationery Office

*National Diet and Nutrition Survey: children aged 1° to 4°*, The Stationery Office

*National Food Survey*, The Stationery Office

*On the State of the Public Health*, The Stationery Office

*Population Trends*, The Stationery Office

*Scotland's Health, A challenge to us all*, The Stationery Office

*Scottish Health Statistics*, National Health Service in Scotland

*Sexual Attitudes and Lifestyles*, Johnson et al, Blackwell Scientific Publications

*Smoking among Secondary School Children*, The Stationery Office

*Unlinked Anonymous HIV Survey*, Department of Health, PHLS, Institute of Child Health (London)

*World Health Statistics*, World Health Organisation

*Young people and crime*, Home Office

## Contacts

Telephone contact points for further information relating to
**Chapter 7: Health**

**Office for National Statistics**

| | |
|---|---|
| Chapter author | 0171 533 5781 |
| Cancer statistics | 0171 533 5266 |
| General Household Survey | 0171 533 5444 |
| Longitudinal Study | 0171 533 5184 |
| Mortality statistics | 0171 533 5251 |

**Department of Health**

| | |
|---|---|
| Health Survey for England | 0171 972 5582 |
| Smoking, misuse of alcohol | 0171 972 5551 |
| **Department of Health and Social Services, NI** | 01232 522800 |
| **General Register Office for Scotland** | 0131 314 4243 |
| **General Register Office (Northern Ireland)** | 01232 252031 |
| **Government Actuary's Department** | 0171 211 2667 |
| **Home Office** | 0171 273 3960 |
| **Ministry of Agriculture, Fisheries and Food** | 0171 270 8376 |
| **National Health Service in Scotland** | 0131 551 8899 |
| **Public Health Laboratory Service** | 0181 200 6868 |
| **Welsh Office** | 01222 825080 |
| **World Health Organisation** | 00 4539 17 14 82 |

# Chapter 8 Social Protection

**8.1**

**Real[1] growth in social security benefit and National Health Service expenditure**

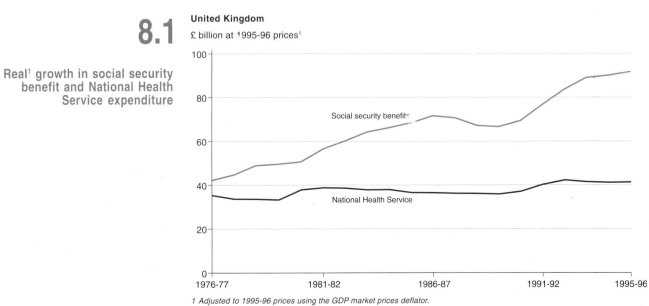

**United Kingdom**

£ billion at [1]1995-96 prices[1]

*1 Adjusted to 1995-96 prices using the GDP market prices deflator.*

**Source: Department of Health; Department of Social Security; Department of Health and Social Services, Northern Ireland**

# 8.2

## Expenditure on social protection benefits: by function, 1993-94

**United Kingdom**
£ billion

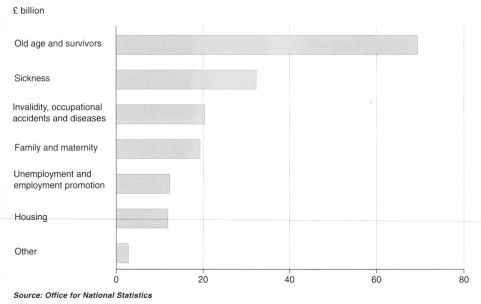

*Source: Office for National Statistics*

# 8.3

## Expenditure[1] on social protection benefits per head: EU comparison, 1994

£ thousand

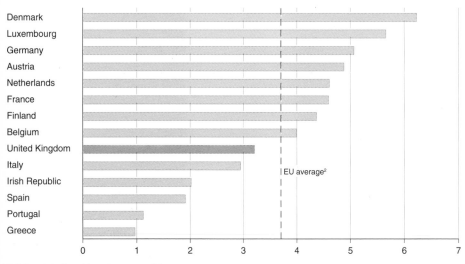

1 Before deduction of tax, where appropriate.
2 Excludes Austria and Finland.

*Source: Eurostat*

This chapter describes the various ways in which central government, local authorities and the private and voluntary sectors act to help people in need. Need may arise through ill health, infirmity, inadequate income or through other sorts of misfortune. Generally people who are in need of help are identified in other chapters of *Social Trends*. This chapter focuses on the response given to those people in need.

## Overview

Some government expenditure programmes are designed specifically to protect people against common sources of hardship such as old age, sickness, unemployment and disability. These programmes can collectively be described as expenditure on social protection, and are those from which households can readily perceive a direct benefit, whether in cash or in kind. Eurostat (the Statistical Office of the European Communities) has designed a framework for the presentation of information on such current expenditure and this has been adopted by member states as the European System of Integrated Social Protection Statistics (ESSPROS).

The sources of hardship or need at which expenditure programmes are directed are called 'functions' and data for 1993-94 for the United Kingdom are illustrated in **Chart 8.2**. The majority of social protection expenditure comes from government programmes. Arrangements made by individuals, such as private medical insurance or a private pension scheme, are not included in this definition of social protection, although cash payment of non-government benefits such as compulsory occupational pensions are included. Around two fifths of expenditure on social protection was spent on the combined function of old

**8.4**

age and survivors, for example widows, in 1993-94. This includes both cash payments and the provision of services such as day care facilities and home helps. Private sector contributions are also aimed principally at this function, mainly in the form of occupational pension schemes.

Expenditure on social protection benefits in the member states of the European Union (EU) are shown in Chart 8.3. In 1994 Denmark spent more on social protection per head of population than any other country in the EU; at £6.2 thousand this was around six times as much as Greece, the country which spent the least. The United Kingdom spent around £3 thousand per head of population, an eighth lower than the EU average. However, it would be wrong to make assumptions about the well-being of individuals in each country based solely on these data. For example, some benefits in some countries are subject to tax.

In Great Britain one of the major forms that social protection expenditure takes is social security benefit payments. In Table 8.4 benefit expenditure is classified according to the main reason a benefit is paid so that, for example, a disability benefit paid to an elderly person is allocated to the long-term sick and disabled rather than to the elderly. By far the largest benefit recipient group in 1995-96 was the elderly; they accounted for over two fifths of all benefit expenditure. However, expenditure on the long-term sick and disabled increased the most between 1981-82 and 1995-96. While overall expenditure on families rose by about three quarters, expenditure on lone parent families increased at a faster rate, more than quadrupling in real terms over the same period. This reflects the increase in the number of lone parent families (see Chart 2.9 in the Households and Families chapter).

Benefit expenditure: by recipient group[1]

| Great Britain | | | | £ million at 1995-96 prices[2] |
| --- | --- | --- | --- | --- |
| | 1981-82 | 1986-87 | 1991-92 | 1995-96 |
| Elderly | 28,408 | 33,570 | 35,616 | 38,785 |
| Long-term sick and disabled | 5,941 | 9,264 | 13,698 | 21,208 |
| Short-term sick | 1,439 | 1,644 | 1,484 | 843 |
| Family, | 9,677 | 11,991 | 13,012 | 17,029 |
| of which: lone parents | 2,135 | 4,113 | 6,423 | 9,510 |
| Unemployed | 7,458 | 11,094 | 8,496 | 9,029 |
| Widows and others | 1,883 | 1,915 | 2,119 | 1,893 |
| All benefit expenditure | 54,806 | 69,478 | 74,425 | 88,787 |

1 See Appendix, Part 8: Benefits to groups of recipients.
2 Adjusted to 1995-96 prices using the GDP market prices deflator.
**Source: Department of Social Security**

Around three in every four families in Great Britain received some sort of social security benefit in 1994-95. Nearly three in five benefit units receiving a retirement pension were single pensioners (Table 8.5). Around two thirds of pensioner couples received income from both the state retirement

**8.5**

Receipt of selected benefits: by family type, 1994-95

| Great Britain | | | | | | | Percentages |
| --- | --- | --- | --- | --- | --- | --- | --- |
| | Housing benefit | Council tax benefit | Income support | Retire-ment pension | Unemp-loyment benefit | Child benefit | All benefit units |
| **Pensioners** | | | | | | | |
| Pensioner couple | 8 | 11 | 4 | 36 | 0 | - | 10 |
| Single pensioner | 31 | 33 | 22 | 58 | 0 | - | 16 |
| **Couples** | | | | | | | |
| Couple with dependent[1] children | 12 | 12 | 12 | - | 31 | 76 | 20 |
| Couple without dependent[1] children | 6 | 8 | 7 | 6 | 24 | - | 19 |
| **Single person** | | | | | | | |
| Single person with dependent[1] children | 23 | 20 | 26 | 0 | 1 | 24 | 6 |
| Single person without dependent[1] children | 20 | 17 | 30 | - | 43 | - | 28 |
| **All family types** | 100 | 100 | 100 | 100 | 100 | 100 | 100 |

1 All those aged under 16 or an unmarried 16 to 18 year old in full-time non-advanced education.
**Source: Family Resources Survey, Department of Social Security**

## 8.6

Health and personal social services staff[1]

**Page 140:** please note that the text in the second paragraph referring to government expenditure on the National Health Service is also incorrect.

| Great Britain | | | | | Thousands |
|---|---|---|---|---|---|
| | 1981 | 1986 | 1991 | 1994 | 1995[2] |
| **Directly employed National Health** | | | | | |
| **Service staff** | | | | | |
| Nursing and midwifery[3] | 457 | 472 | 470 | 426 | 421 |
| Administration and clerical[3] | 129 | 133 | 152 | 161 | 165 |
| Professional and technical | 78 | 91 | 103 | 111 | 115 |
| Ancillary and maintenance | 238 | 184 | 128 | 108 | 100 |
| Medical and dental | 48 | 51 | 56 | 60 | 63 |
| General/senior managers | . | .. | 16 | 26 | 26 |
| Ambulance staff | 21 | 22 | 21 | 22 | 22 |
| Other | 7 | 6 | 9 | 4 | 7 |
| All health service staff | 978 | 959 | 955 | 918 | 917 |
| **General medical practitioners** | 27 | 29 | 31 | 32 | 32 |
| **General dental practitioners** | 15 | 17 | 18 | 19 | 19 |
| **Personal social services[4]** | 240 | 270 | 289 | 294 | 289 |

1 Whole-time equivalents except general medical and dental practitioners in Wales, which are headcounts, and Scotland which are headcounts for 1981 and 1986.
2 Data for non-medical health service staff are based on payscale estimates. See Appendix, Part 8: Health and personal social services staff.
3 See Appendix, Part 8: Health and personal social services staff.
4 Data for Wales for 1995 are not available, 1994 data have been used.
**Source: Department of Health; Welsh Office; National Health Service in Scotland**

## 8.7

Average number of patients of dentists[1] and doctors[2]

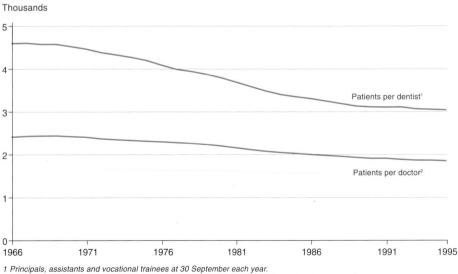

**Great Britain**
Thousands

1 Principals, assistants and vocational trainees at 30 September each year.
2 Unrestricted principals only at 1 October each year. See Appendix Part 8: Unrestricted principals.
**Source: Department of Health**

pension and an occupational pension. In contrast, only 31 per cent of single pensioners received both types of pension. Around three quarters of child benefit recipients were couples with dependent children; the remaining quarter were single with dependent children. Information on household income from cash benefits is shown in Table 5.4.

**Chart 8.1**, at the beginning of this chapter, illustrates government expenditure in real terms on social security benefits and the National Health Service (NHS) since 1976-77. Around a third of general government expenditure in the United Kingdom was spent on the social security programme in 1995 (see Table 6.21 in the Expenditure chapter). In 1995-96 expenditure on social security benefits amounted to nearly £92 billion, more than double in real terms the amount in 1976-77. Over the same period government expenditure on the NHS grew at a slower rate, by only one sixth in real terms, to reach £42 billion in 1995-96. In addition to funding from government, the *Health Service Act, 1980* gave health authorities the power to raise money directly from the public and in the latter half of the 1980s a fund-raising explosion began. According to information from the Charities Aid Foundation, NHS charitable funds in England raised around three fifths of their total income in 1993-94, around £150 million, through charitable donations and fund-raising.

Central and local government employees in the health and social services covered in **Table 8.6** accounted for around 5 per cent of people in employment in Great Britain in 1995. Around 917 thousand people were directly employed by the NHS on a whole-time equivalents basis in 1995. This figure has fallen by around 4 per cent since 1986. The reduction of the working week for

# 8.8

nurses distorts comparisons with earlier years. The composition of the NHS workforce by group has changed since 1986. The proportion of ancillary and maintenance staff fell from 15 to 11 per cent over the period, mainly as a result of competitive tendering exercises.

Generally the number of doctors in general practice (GPs) in Great Britain has increased over the past 35 years. However, there was a reduction in the number GPs, of about 590, between 1963 and 1967 and a small loss in 1990. Overall, since 1961 numbers have increased by two fifths from around 23 thousand to reach just under 32 thousand in 1995. The average number of patients per doctor has fallen from 2.4 thousand in 1969 to 1.8 thousand in 1995 (Chart 8.7). In 1990 more flexible working arrangements for GPs were introduced as part of the new GP contract and, as a result, the proportion of GPs in England working part time more than doubled between 1990 and 1995 from 5.5 per cent to 11.2 per cent. This has resulted in a more flexible workforce so, for example, most women can now register with a woman GP if they wish to. The number of dentists in practice, which includes principals, assistants and vocational trainees, increased by around three fifths between 1961 and 1995, when there were about 19 thousand dentists in practice. The average number of patients per dentist has remained at around 3 thousand since the late 1980s.

An important measure of the services delivered by the NHS is people's perception of them. Between 1987 and 1991, around two in three people said that quality of medical treatment in hospitals was either very good or satisfactory, but this fell to around three in five people in 1995 (Table 8.8) The proportion of people who were satisfied with waiting lists for non-

## Satisfaction with hospital and community health services[1]

| Great Britain | | | Percentages |
|---|---|---|---|
| | 1987 | 1991 | 1995 |
| **Hospital services** | | | |
| Quality of medical treatment | 67 | 65 | 61 |
| General condition of buildings | 44 | 40 | 47 |
| Time spent waiting in out-patient departments | .. | 17 | 27 |
| Waiting lists for non-emergency operations | 10 | 13 | 19 |
| **GP services** | | | |
| Quality of medical treatment by GPs | 72 | 73 | 72 |
| Being able to choose which GP to see | 70 | 72 | 67 |
| Amount of time GP gives to each patient | 66 | 65 | 67 |
| GPs' appointment systems | 51 | 54 | 55 |

1 Percentage of respondents who said that each service was satisfactory or very good when asked: 'From what you know or have heard, say whether you think the NHS in your area is, on the whole, satisfactory or in need of improvement'.
*Source: British Social Attitudes Survey, Social & Community Planning Research*

emergency operations has increased from one in ten in 1987 to one in five in 1995, although this is still one of the areas of least satisfaction with hospital services. Another area which people perceived as needing improvement was the time spent waiting in out-patient departments; about 70 per cent of respondents said this was in need of either some or a lot of improvement.

Some people have needs which can best be provided for in residential care homes; for example some elderly people, some people with a physical or sensory disability and people with learning difficulties. Elderly people are by far the largest client group in residential care homes: in March 1995 this group accounted for nearly eight in ten people in residential care in England and Wales (Table 8.9) However, people with mental illness formed the client group which showed the largest proportional increase between 1991 and 1995, growing by a quarter over this period. It should be noted that information on client groups is based on the primary purpose of the home rather than on the individual; for example, the number of residents in homes primarily for elderly

# 8.9

## Residents in staffed residential care homes: by client group, 1991[1] and 1995[1]

| England & Wales | | Thousands |
|---|---|---|
| | 1991 | 1995 |
| Elderly people | 248.8 | 238.0 |
| People with learning disabilities | 28.4 | 34.7 |
| People with mental illness | 9.6 | 12.0 |
| Elderly mentally infirm[2] | 7.2 | 8.8 |
| Physically/sensorily disabled | 7.8 | 7.6 |
| Other adults[3] | 1.9 | 2.2 |
| All client groups | 303.7 | 303.3 |

1 Data are at 31 March for each year.
2 Data are for England only.
3 Includes people in homes for alcohol and drug abuse.
*Source: Department of Health; Welsh Office*

# 8.10

### Citizens Advice Bureaux enquiries: by type of problem, 1995-96

| England, Wales & Northern Ireland | Percentages |
|---|---|
| Social security | 29 |
| Consumer | 17 |
| Housing | 11 |
| Employment | 10 |
| Legal | 10 |
| Relationships | 8 |
| Taxation | 4 |
| Health and community | 3 |
| Other problems | 9 |
| | |
| All problems (=100%)(millions) | 6.5 |

*Source: National Association of Citizens Advice Bureaux*

people is collected rather than the number of elderly people in homes. In Scotland, there were 22 thousand people in residential care homes in 1995, of which around 70 per cent were elderly people and 18 per cent were people with learning disabilities.

Residential homes are not just run by local authorities but also by the private and voluntary sectors. In March 1995 homes run by the private sector accommodated around three fifths of residents in homes for elderly people in England. In contrast, the voluntary sector accounted for more than seven in ten residents in homes for adults with a physical or sensory disability.

There are many different voluntary organisations that provide advice and counselling to people in need. The National Association of Citizens Advice Bureaux is one of the largest of these organisations. Around 6.5 million problems were dealt with by the Citizens Advice Bureaux in England, Wales and Northern Ireland in 1995-96 (Table 8.10). Social security problems accounted for three in ten problems dealt with during the year. Another organisation

which helps people in need is the Samaritans. Samaritan volunteers provide a 24 hour service, primarily by telephone, to befriend people who are experiencing personal crises and are in imminent danger of taking their lives. In 1995 the Samaritans received nearly 3.9 million calls, an increase of 23 per cent since 1985.

Other voluntary organisations raise money to assist those in suffering or need. Attitudes towards the sources of charitable expenditure differ depending on the cause of hardship. In 1995 over three quarters of people thought that money for housing homeless people in Great Britain should come mainly or entirely from the government (Table 8.11). In contrast over half the respondents believed that money for protecting rare animals throughout the world should come mainly or entirely from charities. In 1993-94 the Charities Aid Foundation estimated that total central government funding to the voluntary sector was nearly £3.6 billion, of which 83 per cent went to housing associations. However, central government support for housing associations fell by 14 per cent from 1992-93 whereas support for other areas in the voluntary sector increased over the period. Local authorities in the United Kingdom provided an estimated £1.3 billion in support of the voluntary sector in 1994-95 for areas such as social services, education and recreation.

## Sick and disabled people

Whereas the Health chapter discusses the nature of health and ill-health amongst the population, this section focuses on the response provided to support the sick and people with disabilities.

# 8.11

### Attitudes towards sources of charitable expenditure[1], 1995

| Great Britain | | | | Percentages |
|---|---|---|---|---|
| | Entirely or mainly from government | Shared equally | Entirely or mainly from charities | Can't choose / not answered |
| Housing for homeless people in Britain | 78 | 14 | 3 | 5 |
| Helping British children in need | 65 | 27 | 5 | 3 |
| Helping British AIDS sufferers | 38 | 31 | 20 | 11 |
| Helping AIDS sufferers worldwide | 19 | 32 | 34 | 15 |
| Giving food aid to starving people in poor countries | 18 | 36 | 37 | 8 |
| Helping children in need throughout the world | 18 | 41 | 34 | 6 |
| Helping prevent cruelty to animals in Britain | 11 | 34 | 46 | 8 |
| Protecting rare animals throughout the world | 9 | 27 | 52 | 12 |

*1 Respondents were asked to indicate where they thought the money should come from for each cause.*

*Source: British Social Attitudes Survey, Social & Community Planning Research*

# 8.12

NHS activity for sick and disabled in-patients is shown in **Table 8.12**. Care should be taken when using this table as, due to changes in the administrative system, hospital in-patient cases are a combination of finished consultant episodes (FCEs) and deaths and discharges as follows: data for England are FCEs throughout; for Wales they are FCEs in later years (1991-92 and 1994-95) and deaths and discharges in earlier years; for Northern Ireland they are also FCEs in these later years, but only for acute patients; for Scotland they are deaths and discharges for all years (see Appendix, Part 8: In-patient activity).

In the United Kingdom the number of hospital in-patient cases in the acute sector rose by over a fifth between 1981 and 1994-95. The number of in-patient episodes for people with learning disabilities also increased over this period, mainly due to an increasing number of episodes of care lasting less than a week. The average time spent in hospital by acute patients fell to 5 days in 1994-95 compared with 254 days for in-patients with learning disabilities.

There have also been increases in the number of people being treated as an accident and emergency patient, or on an out-patient or day case basis. The number of day case admissions in the acute sector was nearly four times as high in 1994-95 than in 1981 **(Table 8.13)**. Since NHS trusts were introduced in 1990-91 the number of self-governing trusts carrying out in-patient or day case activity has increased from 52 to 399. In England the proportion of FCEs treated in NHS trust hospitals rose from around 68 per cent in 1993-94 to almost 100 per cent in 1995-96.

## National Health Service activity for sick and disabled people: in-patients

**United Kingdom**

|  | 1981 | 1986 | 1991-92 | 1994-95 |
|---|---|---|---|---|
| **Acute[1]** | | | | |
| Finished consultant episodes[2] (thousands) | 6,178 | 6,763 | 7,285 | 7,566 |
| In-patient episodes per available bed (numbers) | 33.7 | 40.1 | 49.8 | 55.1 |
| Mean duration of stay (days) | 7.7 | 6.5 | 5.8 | 5.4 |
| **Mentally ill** | | | | |
| Finished consultant episodes[2] (thousands) | 256 | 279 | 293 | 316 |
| In-patient episodes per available bed (numbers) | 2.3 | 2.9 | 4.2 | 5.4 |
| Mean duration of stay (days) | .. | .. | 109.9 | 49.6 |
| **People with learning disabilities[3]** | | | | |
| Finished consultant episodes[2] (thousands) | 34 | 58 | 62 | 59 |
| In-patient episodes per available bed (numbers) | 0.6 | 1.2 | 2.2 | 3.2 |
| Mean duration of stay (days) | .. | .. | 553.5 | 254.4 |

1 Wards for general patients, excluding elderly, maternity and neonate cots in maternity units.
2 All data for Scotland and Wales and data for Northern Ireland except acute after 1986 are for deaths and discharges. See Appendix, Part 8: In-patient activity.
3 Excluding mental handicap community units.
**Source: Department of Health; Welsh Office; National Health Service in Scotland; Department of Health and Social Services, Northern Ireland**

# 8.13

## National Health Service activity for sick and disabled people: accident and emergency, out-patients and day cases

**United Kingdom[1]**                                                                                    Thousands

|  | 1981 | 1986 | 1991-92 | 1994-95 |
|---|---|---|---|---|
| **Accident and emergency services** | | | | |
| New attendances | 11,321 | 12,663 | 13,397 | 14,482 |
| Total attendances | 15,957 | 16,606 | 16,289 | 16,880 |
| **Out-patient services** | | | | |
| Mentally ill | | | | |
| New attendances | 230 | 247 | 280 | 342 |
| Total attendances | 2,021 | 2,146 | 2,120 | 2,520 |
| People with learning disabilities[2] | | | | |
| New attendances | 3 | 4 | 4 | 6 |
| Total attendances | 23 | 35 | 46 | 71 |
| **Day case admissions** | | | | |
| Acute | 817 | 1,207 | 1,894 | 3,049 |
| Mentally ill | 12 | 13 | 1 | 2 |
| People with learning disabilities[2] | 1 | 4 | 1 | 2 |

1 Data for 1981 and 1986 for out-patient services and day case admissions exclude Northern Ireland.
2 Excluding mental handicap community units.
**Source: Department of Health; Welsh Office; National Health Service in Scotland; Department of Health and Social Services, Northern Ireland**

# 8.14

Patients waiting over 12 months[1]: by specialty

| England, Scotland & Northern Ireland | | | | | | Percentages |
|---|---|---|---|---|---|---|
| | 1991 | 1992 | 1993 | 1994 | 1995 | 1996 |
| Plastic surgery | 48 | 27 | 17 | 16 | 7 | 2 |
| Oral surgery | 21 | 10 | 6 | 6 | 4 | 1 |
| Trauma and orthopaedics | 20 | 10 | 8 | 7 | 4 | 1 |
| Urology | 20 | 10 | 6 | 6 | 4 | 1 |
| General surgery | 18 | 9 | 6 | 6 | 3 | 1 |
| Ophthalmology | 14 | 9 | 6 | 6 | 2 | - |
| Ear, nose and throat | 14 | 8 | 5 | 5 | 2 | 1 |
| Obstetrics and gynaecology | 10 | 6 | 4 | 4 | 2 | - |
| Other specialties | 11 | 7 | 5 | 4 | 2 | 1 |
| All specialties | 18 | 9 | 6 | 6 | 3 | 1 |

1 Ordinary (in-patient) and day cases combined. Excludes repeat and deferred waiting lists. Data for Northern Ireland include self-deferrals. At March each year.

**Source: Department of Health; National Health Service in Scotland; Department of Health and Social Services, Northern Ireland**

Information on the time patients had to wait between referral by their GP and being seen in an out-patient clinic was first published in 1994-95. In the three months ending 30th March 1996 around 97 per cent of patients referred in England were seen within 26 weeks and 83 per cent seen within 13 weeks.

# 8.15

Site of NHS GP consultation

| Great Britain | | | | | Percentages[1] |
|---|---|---|---|---|---|
| | 1971 | 1981 | 1991-92 | 1994-95 | 1995-96 |
| Surgery[2] | 73 | 79 | 81 | 83 | 84 |
| Home | 22 | 14 | 11 | 10 | 9 |
| Telephone | 4 | 7 | 8 | 8 | 7 |
| All consultations | 100 | 100 | 100 | 100 | 100 |

1 Percentage of consultations at each site in the 14 days prior to interview.
2 Includes consultations with a GP at a health centre and those who answered 'elsewhere'.

**Source: General Household Survey, Office for National Statistics**

During the early 1990s there were notable reductions in England, Northern Ireland and Scotland in the proportion of patients waiting over 12 months for hospital treatment, either as an ordinary admission or as a day case. In March 1991, 18 per cent had been waiting over 12 months but by 1993 this had fallen to only 6 per cent (Table 8.14). Overall there were around 1.2 million people on waiting lists in 1996, a fifth of which were waiting for general surgery. Waiting times for hospital treatment generally depend on the type of treatment sought, the urgency of the treatment and the area of the country. Generally, people waiting for plastic surgery are more likely to wait for more than a year than those waiting for other specialties. From April 1995, under the Patient's Charter, the aim is that no one will have to wait over 18 months for admission. Data for Wales are not comparable with the other countries prior to 1996. However, most specialties have shown reductions in the proportion waiting over 12 months in recent years.

The proportion of GP consultations which take place at the patient's home has more than halved since 1971 to reach 9 per cent in Great Britain in 1995-96 (Table 8.15) Consultations at home are most likely among children and the elderly. However, for those aged 75 and over the proportion of GP consultations taking place at home fell from 61 per cent to around 35 per cent between 1971 and 1995-96. The proportion of consultations by telephone has almost doubled since 1971, although they still accounted for only 7 per cent of all consultations in 1995-96. In Northern Ireland

**8.16**

a higher proportion of consultations take place by telephone - around 12 per cent of all consultations in 1995-96.

The majority of health care services are provided by the state but some people also look to the private sector to deliver services. Over 5.7 million people in the United Kingdom were covered by private medical insurance in 1995 (Chart 8.16). However this number has fallen by 14 per cent since 1990, the peak year, when it reached 6.7 million. Care should be taken when interpreting the chart as figures prior to 1984 are not directly comparable with those for later years. Also figures for 1984 to 1994 have been revised to exclude individuals covered by the Post Office and Civil Service Sanitorium Society as the cover provided was much more limited.

The number of prescriptions dispensed in Great Britain has been gradually increasing; in 1995, 520 million prescriptions were dispensed - two fifths more than in 1981. The number of prescriptions per head of population increased from about seven to nine over the same period (Chart 8.17). Many people, such as children and elderly people, are exempt from prescription charges and people on low incomes qualify for charge remission; in addition, certain items are free. There were around 360 million prescriptions dispensed by community pharmacists and appliance contractors in England in 1995, where the patient did not pay a charge, about 84 per cent of the total. In 1981, the figure was 68 per cent.

**People insured by private medical insurance[1]**

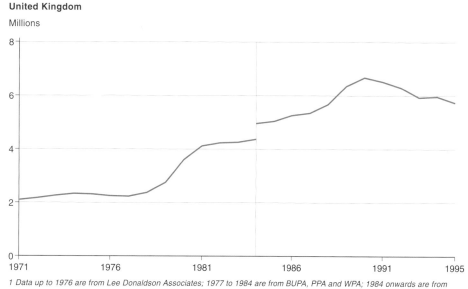

1 Data up to 1976 are from Lee Donaldson Associates; 1977 to 1984 are from BUPA, PPA and WPA; 1984 onwards are from Department of Health.

*Source: Lee Donaldson Associates; BUPA; PPP; WPA; Department of Health*

**8.17**

**Average number of prescriptions[1] per person**

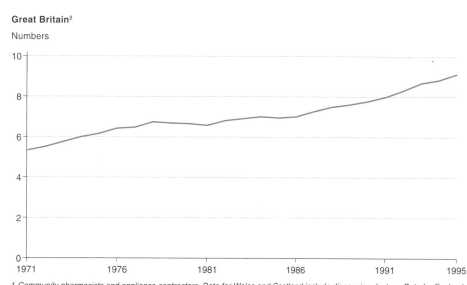

1 Community pharmacists and appliance contractors. Data for Wales and Scotland include dispensing doctors. Data for England are fee-based prior to 1991 and item based from 1991 onwards; data for Scotland are item-based; data for Wales are fee-based.
2 Data for 1971 and 1972 exclude Wales.

*Source: Department of Health; Welsh Office; National Health Service in Scotland*

# 8.18

Sight tests: by source of funding and socio-economic group, 1994-95

| United Kingdom | | | | | Percentages[1] |
|---|---|---|---|---|---|
| | NHS | Provided free by optician | Paid for by the individual | Paid for by employer or insurance company | All sources of funding |
| Professional | 12 | 9 | 71 | 8 | 100 |
| Employers and managers | 12 | 6 | 73 | 9 | 100 |
| Intermediate non-manual | 14 | 8 | 68 | 10 | 100 |
| Junior non-manual | 19 | 6 | 64 | 11 | 100 |
| Skilled manual | 24 | 9 | 60 | 7 | 100 |
| Semi-skilled manual | 35 | 10 | 52 | 4 | 100 |
| Unskilled manual | 37 | 12 | 48 | 3 | 100 |
| All socio-economic groups[2] | 24 | 9 | 60 | 7 | 100 |

1 Percentage of sight tests funded by each source in each socio-economic group.
2 Includes full-time students, armed forces and those whose socio-economic group was not known.

**Source: General Household Survey, Office for National Statistics; Continuous Household Survey, Northern Ireland Statistics and Research Agency**

# 8.19

Recipients of benefits for sick and disabled people

| Great Britain | | | | Thousands |
|---|---|---|---|---|
| | 1981-82 | 1986-87 | 1991-92 | 1994-95 |
| **Long-term sick and people with disabilities** | | | | |
| Invalidity benefit/severe disablement allowance | 826 | 1,228 | 1,741 | 2,115 |
| One of the above benefits plus income support | 103 | 136 | 240 | 335 |
| Income support only | . | . | 229 | 425 |
| **Short-term sick** | | | | |
| Sickness benefit only | 393 | 110 | 138 | 127 |
| Sickness benefit and income support | 24 | 16 | 28 | 40 |
| Income support only | . | . | 79 | 87 |
| **Disability living allowance or attendance allowance**[1] | 582 | 1,113 | 1,758 | 2,562 |

1 Attendance allowance and mobility allowance before April 1992.

**Source: Department of Social Security**

Certain groups of people in the United Kingdom, such as children and adults receiving income support or family credit, are also exempt from charges for NHS sight tests. Adults in the unskilled manual socio-economic group are the most likely to have their sight test paid for by the NHS (Table 8.18). The General Household Survey found that overall, around a quarter of all sight tests were funded by the NHS in 1994-95. However, care should be taken when interpreting the data as people are not always aware of the distinction between NHS sight tests and those provided free by opticians.

Some cash benefits provided by the social security system are for people who are sick or have disabilities. In 1994-95 over 2 million people were in receipt of invalidity benefit or severe disablement allowance (Table 8.19). This represents over two and a half times the number in 1981-82. The rise in the number of those receiving invalidity benefit is partly due to an increase in the duration of claims rather than an increase in new claims. Regional variations in the number of households receiving sickness, invalidity or disability related benefits are highlighted by the Family Resources Survey: 19 per cent of all households in the North received at least one of these benefits in 1994-95 compared with 9 per cent of households in the South East. Of the constituent countries of Great Britain, Wales had the largest proportion of households receiving these benefits - around 19 per cent, compared with 16 per cent in Scotland and 12 per cent in England. In April 1995 sickness benefit and invalidity benefit were

# 8.20

replaced by incapacity benefit which is paid at three rates depending on the duration of incapacity.

## Elderly people

Information on the increase in the number of elderly people, together with projections for the future, are contained in the Population chapter (Chart 1.1) .This section focuses on services and other forms of help provided to elderly people.

Generally, the use of the various personal social services by elderly people in the United Kingdom increases with age. While about 9 per cent of people aged 65 to 69 received help from a local authority home help or home care worker in 1994-95, the proportion is much higher for people aged 85 and over, at around 30 per cent (Table 8.20). The proportion of people aged 65 and over using a private home help in Great Britain increased from 4 per cent in 1991-92 to 7 per cent in 1994-95. One voluntary organisation which provides a range of services for the elderly is Age Concern whose network consists of over 14 hundred local organisations throughout the United Kingdom. Age Concern are involved in the community care services, enabling many older people to remain in their own homes. Much of the work is done by volunteers, the majority of whom are retired.

Services provided by local authorities include the provision of meals and funding of day centres for the elderly. During a week

in September 1995 there were around 34 people per thousand aged 65 and over receiving meals in England (Table 8.21). The total number of meals provided amounted to over 800 thousand. The independent sector provided about two fifths of the meals to people's homes and three fifths of the meals in luncheon clubs; this was mainly voluntary sector activity. In Northern Ireland, around 3.2 thousand people received meals in their own home. Local authorities provided 67 per cent of all day centre places for elderly people aged 65 and over in England in 1995. Hospitals also provide services for elderly people; in 1994-95 there were over 2.5 million elderly in-patient episodes.

**Use of selected personal social services[1]: by age, 1994-95**

United Kingdom                                           Percentages

|  | 65-69 | 70-74 | 75-79 | 80-84 | 85 and over | All aged 65 and over |
|---|---|---|---|---|---|---|
| Meals-on-wheels | 3 | 17 | 11 | 28 | 40 | 100 |
| Local authority home help | 9 | 15 | 20 | 25 | 30 | 100 |
| District nurse/health visitor | 10 | 17 | 19 | 27 | 28 | 100 |
| Voluntary organisation | 8 | 15 | 27 | 27 | 23 | 100 |
| Private home help | 14 | 20 | 25 | 20 | 20 | 100 |
| Lunch club | 16 | 17 | 19 | 30 | 19 | 100 |
| Day centre | 16 | 24 | 21 | 26 | 13 | 100 |

1 Percentage of the services provided to each age group in the month before interview.

*Source: General Household Survey, Office for National Statistics; Continuous Household Survey, Northern Ireland Statistics and Research Agency*

# 8.21

**Health and personal social services for elderly people[1], 1994-95**

England                           Rates per 1,000 people[1]

|  | 1994-95 |
|---|---|
| Hospital in-patients | 328 |
| Residents in private nursing and residential care homes for the elderly[2] | 45 |
| People receiving meals[2] | 34 |
| Day centre attendances paid for by local authorities | 18 |

1 Aged 65 and over.
2 During survey week in September 1995.
*Source: Department of Health*

# 8.22

Hospital and local authority expenditure on elderly people[1]

| England | | | | | £ million at 1994-95 prices[1] |
| --- | --- | --- | --- | --- | --- |
| | 1986-87 | 1991-92 | 1992-93 | 1993-94 | 1994-95 |
| **Hospitals[2]** | 7,435 | 8,527 | 8,932 | 9,099 | 9,192 |
| **Local authorities[3]** | | | | | |
| Residential | 1,091 | 1,333 | 1,422 | 1,588 | 1,369 |
| Non-residential | 1,108 | 1,184 | 1,096 | 1,346 | 1,899 |
| Purchasing[3] | .. | .. | .. | .. | 299 |

1 Adjusted to 1994-95 prices using the GDP market prices deflator.
2 Includes community health services. Data for 1991-92 onwards are not comparable with earlier years due to changes in accounting practices.
3 Data for 1994-95 are on a different basis to earlier years following changes in accounting guidelines introduced by CIPFA in 1994.

**Source: Department of Health**

Local authority expenditure on elderly people in England rose by 62 per cent between 1986-87 and 1994-95 (Table 8.22). However, expenditure increased at a faster rate for those who were not in residential care homes. In England, hospital and community health expenditure on elderly people increased by around 8 per cent in real terms between 1991-92 and 1994-95. Figures for hospital expenditure for 1986-87 are not comparable with those for 1991-92 onwards due to changes in accounting practices. Since 1993, local authorities have been responsible for funding placements for

new residents who cannot afford the fees themselves in both residential and nursing homes. In Scotland local authority expenditure on elderly people amounted to £400 million, of which two fifths was spent on those in residential care homes.

The social security benefit system provides financial assistance for elderly people to complement the health and social services provided by the NHS and local authorities. These benefits include retirement pensions and income support. Around 9.5 million people in Great Britain were in receipt of a retirement pension in 1994-95, an overall increase of 8 per cent since 1981-82 (Table 8.23). The number of overseas recipients has increased at a faster rate than that for those living in Great Britain; in 1994-95 683 thousand pensions were payable overseas compared with 252 thousand in 1981-82. The age at which men and women receive state pension is to be equalised to 65; this will be phased in over 10 years starting in April 2010. Women born before 6 April 1950 will be unaffected, while the pensionable age for those born between 6 April 1950 and 5 March 1955 will gradually increase. All women born on or after 6 March 1955 will become eligible to receive state pension at age 65.

# 8.23

Recipients of selected benefits[1] for elderly people[2]

| Great Britain | | | | Thousands |
| --- | --- | --- | --- | --- |
| | 1981-82 | 1986-87 | 1991-92 | 1994-95 |
| Retirement pension only | 7,205 | 7,657 | 8,147 | 8,064 |
| Retirement pension with income support[3] | 1,624 | 1,592 | 1,307 | 1,428 |
| UK pensions payable overseas | 252 | 372 | 594 | 683 |
| Pensioners with income support only[3] | 113 | 124 | 146 | 173 |

1 Retirement pension data are at 31 March except 1981 which is at 30 June. Income support/supplementary benefit data are from annual and quarterly enquiries.
2 Aged 60 and over.
3 Income support replaced supplementary benefit in April 1988.

**Source: Department of Social Security**

## Children and families

In 1995 there were 732 thousand live births in the United Kingdom, the majority of which took place in hospital. In common with other hospital services, the number of maternity in-patient cases has been increasing while the number of beds available has fallen and the average duration spent in hospital for childbirth has declined (Table 8.24). Between 1981-82 and 1994-95 it fell by more than

# 8.24

## Maternity services

**United Kingdom**

|  | 1981-82[1] | 1986-87[2] | 1991-92 | 1994-95 |
|---|---|---|---|---|
| **In-patient services** | | | | |
| Finished consultant episodes[3] | | | | |
| (thousands) | 1,032 | 1,105 | 1,209 | 1,245 |
| In-patient episodes per available | | | | |
| bed (numbers) | 45 | 55 | 69 | 84 |
| Mean duration of stay (days) | 5.3 | 4.3 | 3.4 | 2.5 |
| | | | | |
| **Out-patient services** | | | | |
| New attendances (thousands) | 796 | 828 | 828 | 715 |
| Average attendances per new | | | | |
| patient (numbers) | 5.6 | 5.0 | 4.3 | 4.0 |
| | | | | |
| **Contacts with midwives and health** | | | | |
| **visitors (thousands)[4]** | | | | |
| Ante-natal | .. | .. | 3,521 | 4,313 |
| Post-natal | .. | .. | 6,422 | 5,896 |

1 Data for Wales and Northern Ireland are for 1981.
2 Data for Northern Ireland are for 1986.
3 Data for Scotland, Wales and Northern Ireland are for deaths and discharges. See Appendix, Part 8: In-patient activity.
4 Data are England and Scotland only.

*Source: Department of Health; Welsh Office; National Health Service in Scotland; Department of Health and Social Services, Northern Ireland*

# 8.25

## Recipients of benefits for families

**Great Britain**          Thousands

|  | 1981-82 | 1986-87 | 1991-92 | 1994-95 |
|---|---|---|---|---|
| **Child benefit** | | | | |
| Number of children | 13,079 | 12,217 | 12,405 | 12,730 |
| Number of families | 7,174 | 6,816 | 6,854 | 7,000 |
| | | | | |
| **Lone parent families** | | | | |
| One parent benefit only | 469 | 606 | 475 | 576 |
| One parent benefit and income | | | | |
| support | 146 | 250 | 361 | 373 |
| Income support only | 222 | 360 | 584 | 676 |
| | | | | |
| **Other benefits** | | | | |
| Maternity allowance | 115 | 110 | 18 | .. |
| Statutory maternity pay | . | . | 85 | .. |
| Family credit | 120 | 215 | 356 | 602 |

*Source: Department of Social Security*

---

half from 5.3 days to 2.5 days. Ante-natal contacts with midwives and health visitors in England and Scotland increased by over a fifth between 1991-92 and 1994-95, while post-natal contacts declined. This is a result of changes in the provision of maternity services. Women can now make more informed choices about their treatment, which has led to an increase in ante-natal contacts. A more flexible service and changes in the frequency of contacts by midwives, based on the needs of mothers and babies, has led to a decrease in post-natal contacts.

Families with dependent children are offered support by the social security benefit system: around a fifth of all benefit expenditure in 1995-96 was received by these families (see Table 8.5). The most significant non income-related benefit for families in 1994-95, in terms of both recipients and expenditure, was child benefit; this was received by 7 million families in Great Britain (Table 8.25). Benefits are not the sole means of financial assistance to families. *The Child Support Act 1991* introduced a new system intended to remove discretion from the assessment of child maintenance after marriage break-up and ensure that both parents meet their responsibilities towards the support of their children. In April 1993 the Child Support Agency (CSA) was set up to replace the role of the courts in assessing, collecting and enforcing child maintenance. During 1995-96 the CSA dealt with 327 thousand cases, over two fifths fewer than in 1994-95. This fall was due to a larger amount of resources being concentrated on managing the maintenance accounts for existing clients, and this is reflected in the fact that the amount of maintenance collected was more than double that of the previous year.

# 8.26

### Children looked after by local authorities[1]: by type of accommodation

**England, Wales & Northern Ireland**                                                               Percentages

|  | 1981 | 1993 | 1994 |
|---|---|---|---|
| With foster parents | 39 | 60 | 62 |
| In local authority homes | 28 | 12 | 12 |
| Placement with parent regulations[2] | 19 | 10 | 10 |
| Voluntary homes and hostels | 4 | 2 | 1 |
| Schools for children with special educational needs[3] | 3 | 1 | 1 |
| Other accommodation[4] | 7 | 13 | 12 |
| All children in care (=100%)(thousands) | 99 | 57 | 55 |
| All children in care per 1,000 population aged under 18 | 7.6 | 4.7 | 4.5 |

*1 At 31 March. Data for Northern Ireland and data for 1981 for England and Wales relate to children in care.*
*2 Data for Northern Ireland and data for 1981 for England and Wales relate to children under the charge and control of a parent, guardian, relative or friend.*
*3 Data are for England and Wales only.*
*4 Includes those placed for adoption and 16 and 17 year olds in lodgings as a preparation for leaving care and living independently.*

**Source: Department of Health; Welsh Office; Department of Health and Social Services, Northern Ireland**

# 8.27

### Children[1] on child protection registers: by area, 1995[2]

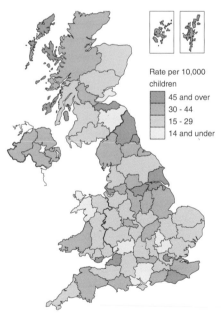

Rate per 10,000 children
- 45 and over
- 30 - 44
- 15 - 29
- 14 and under

*1 Aged under 18.*
*2 At 31 March.*

**Source: Department of Health; Welsh Office; The Scottish Office, Social Work Services Group; Department of Health and Social Services, Northern Ireland**

Local authorities are obliged to provide accommodation for children who need it. Reasons for such a need include children having no parent or guardian, abandonment or because the parents are unable to provide for them. Local authorities also have the power to accommodate children, if they consider that to do so would promote their welfare, and to apply to a court for a care order. The number of children looked after by, or in the care of, local authorities in England, Wales and Northern Ireland fell by 44 per cent between 1981 and 1994 (Table 8.26). The proportion of these children with foster-parents increased from about two fifths to over three fifths over the same period. This reflects the fact that the overall number of children in care or looked after by local authorities has been steadily decreasing, while the actual number of children in foster placements has remained fairly stable. Scotland has a different definition of children in care which means the data are not comparable with the rest of

the United Kingdom. In Scotland, children who are under a non-residential supervision requirement from a Children's Hearing are considered to be in care whereas in England those under a supervision order are not. In 1994 there were 12 thousand children in care in Scotland.

Personal social services also exist to help children who are considered to be at risk of abuse. All local authority social services departments hold a central register of such children. Registration takes place following a case conference in which decisions are made about the level of risk to the child. Subsequently, the child's name may be placed on the register and a plan set out in order to protect the child. The registers are not records of child abuse: some children will not have been the victim of abuse but were considered to be at risk, whilst some who have been victims of abuse will not have been placed on the register if there was no need for a protection plan. A child may be on the register of more than one local authority at a time. This may occur, for example, where a child is looked after by one authority but placed with foster-parents in another authority.

There are wide variations between different local authorities in the rates of children under 18 on child protection registers (Chart 8.27). However, this may be due to differing policy or management practices as well as different local circumstances. For example, some authorities may feel that children at risk of physical neglect can be helped without initiating child protection procedures. Areas with particularly high rates in 1995 were the London boroughs of Islington and Lambeth with over 80 per 10 thousand children under 18 on child protection

# 8.28

registers. Overall, there were 17 local authorities with rates in excess of 50 per 10 thousand children under 18. In contrast Fife had a rate of 7 per 10 thousand, one of the lowest rates in the United Kingdom.

The voluntary sector also provides for children in danger or distress. In 1986, ChildLine was introduced to provide a free, national, confidential phone counselling service for any child with any problem, 24 hours a day. In 1995-96 ChildLine counselled around 90 thousand children, nearly four times as many as in 1986-87

(Table 8.28). Although the overall proportion of contacts about physical abuse fell from 18 per cent in the first year of ChildLine to 10 per cent in 1995-96, the number of calls more than doubled over the period, from 4.2 to 8.9 thousand. The number of calls about bullying increased by over 14 times over this period, mainly due to a high profile campaign about this issue. About a quarter of the calls in 1995-96 fell into the 'other' category, which includes adoption, domestic violence, suicide and concern for others. The ratio of girls to boys calling was around 4 to 1.

**ChildLine enquiries[1]: by type of problem**

| United Kingdom | | Percentages |
|---|---|---|
| | 1986-87[2] | 1995-96 |
| Family relationship | 20 | 15 |
| Bullying | 3 | 11 |
| Physical abuse | 18 | 10 |
| Sexual abuse | 27 | 9 |
| Problem with friends | 4 | 9 |
| Pregnancy | 6 | 8 |
| Runaway | 2 | 3 |
| | | |
| School | 2 | 2 |
| Substance abuse | 2 | 2 |
| Health | 1 | 2 |
| Risk of abuse | 3 | 1 |
| Self abuse | 1 | 1 |
| Bereavement | - | 1 |
| Other problems | 11 | 27 |
| | | |
| All calls and letters (=100%)(thousands) | 23.5 | 89.8 |

1 First time callers and letter writers only.
2 Data relate to year to 31 October 1987, the first year of ChildLine.
***Source: ChildLine***

## References and further reading

The following list contains selected publications relevant to **Chapter 8: Social Protection**. Those published by The Stationery Office are available from the addresses shown on the inside back cover of *Social Trends*.

*British Social Attitudes,* Dartmouth Publishing
*Family Resources Survey,* Department of Social Security
*General Household Survey,* The Stationery Office
*Health and Personal Social Services Statistics for England,* The Stationery Office
*Health and Personal Social Services Statistics for Northern Ireland,* Department of Health and Social Services, Northern Ireland
*Health Statistics Wales, Welsh Health Survey 1995,* Welsh Office

*Hospital Episode Statistics for England,* Department of Health
*Hospital Statistics for Northern Ireland,* Department of Health and Social Services, Northern Ireland
*Dimensions of the Voluntary Sector,* Charities Aid Foundation
*Scottish Health Statistics,* National Health Service in Scotland, Common Services Agency
*Social Protection Expenditure and Receipts,* Eurostat
*Social Security Departmental Report,* The Stationery Office
*Social Security Statistics,* The Stationery Office
*Social Work Services group of the Scottish Office,* Statistical Bulletins
*Statistical Publications on aspects of Health and Personal Social Services activity in England (various),* Department of Health

## Contacts

Telephone contact points for further information relating to

**Chapter 8: Social Protection**

| | |
|---|---|
| **Office for National Statistics** | |
| Chapter author | 0171 533 5779 |
| General Household Survey | 0171 533 5444 |
| **Department of Health** | |
| Adults' services | 0171 972 5582 |
| Children's services | 0171 972 5575 |
| Community and Environmental Health service | 0171 972 5536 |
| Financial data | 0171 972 5593 |
| General dental and community dental service | 0171 972 5536 |
| General medical services manpower | 01532 545909 |
| General ophthalmic services | 0171 972 5507 |
| General pharmacy services | 0171 972 5504 |
| Mental illness/handicap | 0171 972 5546 |
| NHS medical Staff | 01532 545882 |
| NHS non-medical manpower | 01532 545905 |
| Non-psychiatric hospital activity | 0171 972 5525 |
| Personal social services budget data | 0171 210 5699 |
| Prescription analysis | 0171 972 5519 |
| Staffing | 0171 972 5595 |
| Waiting lists | 01532 545549 |
| **Department of Health and Social Services, Northern Ireland** | |
| Health and personal social services activity | 01232 522800 |
| Social security | 01232 522280 |
| Health and personal social services manpower | 01232 522008 |
| **Department of Social Security** | 0171 962 8248 |
| **National Health Service in Scotland** | 0131 551 8899 |
| **Northern Ireland Statistics and Research Agency** | 01232 252653 |
| **The Scottish Office, Social Work Services Group** | 0131 244 5431 |
| **Welsh Office** | 01222 825080 |
| **Charities Aid Foundation** | 01732 520000 |
| **Eurostat** | 00 352 4301 34567 |
| **The Samaritans (General Office)** | 01753 532713 |
| **Social and Community Planning Research** | 0171 250 1866 extn 369 |

# Chapter 9 Crime and Justice

**Offences**
Many crimes are never reported to the police: a little under half in England and Wales, and a similar proportion in Scotland, go unreported. (Page 154)

The amount of recorded crime has fallen slightly since the early 1990s. The number of notifiable offences recorded by the police in England and Wales peaked at 10.5 for every 100 people in 1992 and fell to 9.5 per 100 in 1995. (Chart 9.3)

Almost 23 thousand firearms were handed in to the police in Great Britain during the amnesty period which followed the massacre at Dunblane Primary School in 1996. (Page 156)

**Victims**
Households living in inner city areas were twice as likely to be the victim of a burglary than other households in England and Wales in 1995. (Table 9.8)

**Offenders**
Young adults account for a large proportion of known offenders: almost four in ten offenders in England and Wales in 1995 were aged 14 to 20. (Table 9.12)

Most offenders have already been convicted of a previous offence: seven in ten males who were convicted in England and Wales in 1994 had already been convicted on at least one previous occasion. (Table 9.15)

**Prisons and probation**
The prison population in Great Britain fell in the late 1980s and early 1990s but has been growing since 1993. There were, on average, 57 thousand people in prison in 1995. (Chart 9.1)

**Resources**
There were 35 police service employees for every 10 thousand people in Great Britain in 1995 - a third more than in 1971. (Table 9.29)

## 9.1

**Prison population and accommodation**

**Great Britain**
Thousands

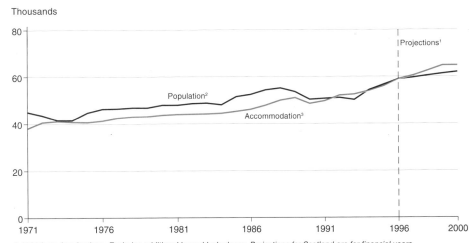

1 1995-based projections. Excludes additional houseblock places. Projections for Scotland are for financial years.
2 Includes those held in police cells in England and Wales from 1980.
3 In use Certified Normal Accommodation at 30 June each year. From 1993 accommodation which is not yet operational is excluded in England and Wales.
**Source: Home Office; The Scottish Office Home Department**

# 9.2

### Crimes committed: by outcome[1]

| England & Wales | | | | Percentages |
| --- | --- | --- | --- | --- |
| | 1981 | 1991 | 1993 | 1995 |
| Reported | 36 | 49 | 47 | 46 |
| Recorded | 22 | 30 | 26 | 23 |

*1 As a percentage of crimes committed.*
**Source: British Crime Survey, Home Office**

# 9.3

### Notifiable offences[1] recorded by the police

Rates per 100 population

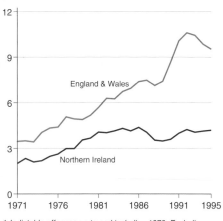

*1 Indictable offences up to and including 1978. Excluding offences of criminal damage of value £20 and under in England and Wales. See Appendix, Part 9: Types of offences in England, Wales and Northern Ireland. Includes possession of controlled drugs in Northern Ireland.*
**Source: Home Office; Royal Ulster Constabulary**

## Offences

Crime and its consequences are a continual problem for government and society. This chapter explores the nature and impact of crime, and the measures used to deal with it.

England and Wales, Scotland and Northern Ireland are often shown separately in this chapter because of their different legal systems.

The true level of crime in this country is difficult to determine. There are two main measures of crime; both of these have different strengths and weaknesses. One measure is the amount of crime recorded by the police. This information is a by-product of the administrative procedure of making out a crime record for offences investigated by the police. However not all offences are reported or recorded. A second measure of crime includes offences which are not recorded by the police. This measure comes from surveys of victims such as the British Crime Survey (BCS) which is now carried out every other year in England and Wales. Although the BCS covers unrecorded crime, it covers a narrower range of offences than police records; only offences against individuals and their property are included. A similar survey is also conducted in Scotland.

The proportions of crime reported to, and recorded by, the police have changed over time. Table 9.2 uses information from the BCS for those offences which can be compared with police figures only. The proportion of these offences which were reported to the police increased during the 1980s but has since fallen slightly so that, in England and Wales in 1995, 46 per cent were reported. In Scotland in 1992, the latest year for which results are available,

half of crimes were reported to the police. The rise in reporting during the 1980s may be linked to the increase in telephone ownership which has made crimes easier to report. Also more victims became insured during this period which may have led to higher reporting rates as reporting to the police may be a necessary step in making a claim. In 1991, 50 per cent of theft or damage incidents in England and Wales were covered by insurance compared with 45 per cent in 1983. The slight fall in reporting since 1991 may also be linked to insurance: the proportion of incidents involving property theft or damage which are covered by insurance has dropped since 1991 and there has been a fall in the number of claims made by insured victims perhaps because households are protecting no-claims bonuses, are fearful of an increase in premiums or because high 'excess' levels mean it is not worth claiming. The proportion of crimes reported also varies between different offences. More than four in five burglaries with loss were reported to the police in 1995 in England and Wales compared with only one in four acts of vehicle vandalism.

Not all crimes which are reported to the police will be recorded by them: in 1995 only half of crimes reported to the police in England and Wales were recorded. Police may choose not to record a reported crime for a number of reasons. For example, they may consider that the report of a crime is mistaken, too trivial or that there is insufficient evidence to say that a crime has been committed. Also the victim may not want the police to proceed.

While the figures for notifiable offences recorded by the police do not give the full picture, they do allow detailed analyses to be carried out. However, due to differences in the legal systems, recording practices and classifications, comparisons between England and Wales, Scotland and Northern Ireland should only be made with care. In Scotland the term 'crimes' is used for the more serious criminal acts (roughly equivalent to indictable offences in England and Wales) while less serious crimes are termed 'offences'; in Northern Ireland the definitions used are broadly comparable with those used in England and Wales.

The number of notifiable offences recorded by the police in England and Wales increased steadily from the early 1950s, when there were less than half a million a year, to a peak of 5.6 million in 1992. Since then the number has decreased so that in 1995 there were 5.1 million. However figures for the 12 months to June 1996 show a small rise in the number of recorded offences of less than half of 1 per cent over the previous 12 months. The rate of notifiable offences per 100 population (excluding offences of criminal damage of value £20 and under) peaked at 10.5 in 1992 and fell to 9.5 in 1995 (Chart 9.3). In Northern Ireland the rate has fluctuated since the peak of 4.4 in 1986 and in 1995 it was 4.2. The trend in Scotland has been similar to that in England and Wales: there was a peak of 11.6 crimes per 100 population in 1991 falling to 9.8 in 1995.

Within these general trends, the changes over time for different categories of offence have varied. The category with the largest number of offences recorded is theft and handling stolen goods (Table 9.4). The number of notifiable offences in England and Wales in this category fell by 14 per cent between 1992 and 1995. However the number of offences of violence against the person, criminal damage, drug trafficking and robbery all increased over this period.

## 9.4

### Notifiable offences[1] recorded by the police: by type of offence

Thousands

| | England & Wales | | Scotland | | Northern Ireland | |
|---|---|---|---|---|---|---|
| | 1981 | 1995 | 1981 | 1995 | 1981 | 1995[2] |
| Theft and handling stolen goods, | 1,603 | 2,452 | 201 | 222 | 25 | 33 |
| of which: theft of vehicles | 333 | 508 | 33 | 38 | 5 | 8 |
| theft from vehicles | 380 | 813 | .. | 71 | 7 | 7 |
| Burglary | 718 | 1,239 | 96 | 74 | 20 | 16 |
| Criminal damage[3] | 387 | 914 | 62 | 87 | 5 | 4 |
| Violence against the person | 100 | 213 | 8 | 16 | 3 | 5 |
| Fraud and forgery | 107 | 133 | 21 | 22 | 3 | 5 |
| Robbery | 20 | 68 | 4 | 5 | 3 | 2 |
| Sexual offences, | 19 | 30 | 2 | 3 | - | 2 |
| of which: rape | 1 | 5 | - | 1 | - | - |
| Drug trafficking | .. | 21 | 2 | 8 | - | - |
| Other notifiable offences[4] | 9 | 29 | 12 | 65 | 3 | 2 |
| All notifiable offences | 2,964 | 5,100 | 408 | 503 | 62 | 69 |

1 See Appendix, Part 9: Types of offences in England, Wales and Northern Ireland and Offences and crimes.
2 No longer includes assault on police and communicating false information regarding a bomb hoax. These offences have been removed from the categories 'Violence against the person' and 'Other notifiable offences'.
3 In Northern Ireland excludes criminal damage valued at £200 or less.
4 In Northern Ireland includes 'possession of controlled drugs' and 'offences against the state'.
**Source: Home Office; The Scottish Office Home Department; Royal Ulster Constabulary**

The number of drug seizures in the United Kingdom has increased dramatically since 1981 (Table 9.5). Most seizures involve cannabis rather than class A drugs such as cocaine and heroin. Between 1981 and

## 9.5

### Seizures[1] of selected drugs: by type of drug

**United Kingdom**                                              Numbers

| | 1981 | 1991 | 1993 | 1994 |
|---|---|---|---|---|
| Cannabis | 17,227 | 59,420 | 69,707 | 88,540 |
| Heroin | 819 | 2,640 | 3,677 | 4,480 |
| MDMA (Ecstasy) | .. | 1,735 | 2,336 | 3,574 |
| Cocaine[2] | 503 | 1,984 | 2,954 | 2,992 |
| LSD | 384 | 1,636 | 2,529 | 2,289 |
| Methadone | 402 | 427 | 613 | 729 |
| Morphine | 243 | 119 | 137 | 135 |
| Opium | 137 | 49 | 65 | 35 |
| Pethidine | 135 | 33 | 18 | 23 |

1 See Appendix, Part 9: Drugs seizures. A seizure can include more than one type of drug.
2 Includes 'crack' from 1991 onwards.
**Source: Home Office**

# 9.6

**Notifiable offences[1] recorded by the police in which firearms were reported to have been used: by type of principal weapon**

**England & Wales**

Thousands

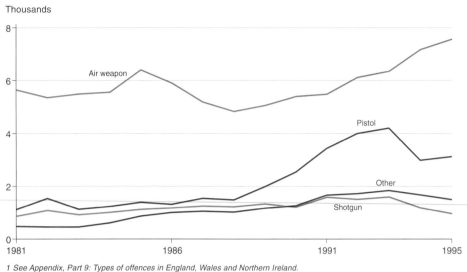

*1 See Appendix, Part 9: Types of offences in England, Wales and Northern Ireland.*
**Source: Home Office**

Firearms are used in only a small proportion of offences. In 1995 there were 13 thousand offences in which firearms were reported to have been used in England and Wales which represents 0.3 per cent of all notifiable offences. In Northern Ireland there were around 0.5 thousand offences involving firearms and in Scotland the figure was 1.7 thousand crimes. However, although small in number, these offences are potentially more serious than many others. In over half of the cases in England and Wales in 1995 the firearm involved was an air weapon. The proportion of firearm offences involving a pistol doubled to 30 per cent between 1983 and 1993 although it has fallen since then **(Chart 9.6)**. In Scotland 12 per cent of the crimes where firearms were reported to have been used involved a pistol, revolver or shot gun while 66 per cent involved an air weapon.

From time to time the police have amnesty periods when people can hand in firearms without the police taking any action. For example, there was a firearms amnesty in 1996 following the massacre at Dunblane Primary School. During this amnesty period almost 23 thousand firearms were handed in throughout Great Britain, although this was less than half the number handed in during the previous amnesty in 1988. One of the reasons for the large number of firearms handed in during 1988 was that there had not been an amnesty for 20 years.

Motoring offences make up a large proportion of summary offences - the less serious category of offence. The police and parking attendants recorded 9 million offences relating to motor vehicles in England and Wales in 1995. Legislation to

# 9.7

**Motoring offences detected by automatic cameras: by type of offence and action taken**

**England & Wales** — Thousands

| | Fixed penalty[1] | Prose-cutions | All offences |
|---|---|---|---|
| **Speeding** | | | |
| 1992 | - | - | - |
| 1993 | 26 | 6 | 32 |
| 1994 | 96 | 21 | 116 |
| 1995 | 170 | 37 | 207 |
| **Traffic lights** | | | |
| 1992 | 6 | 12 | 18 |
| 1993 | 19 | 20 | 39 |
| 1994 | 26 | 14 | 40 |
| 1995 | 33 | 15 | 48 |

*1 Fixed penalty paid and no further action taken.*
**Source: Home Office**

1994 the number of seizures of cannabis increased more than fivefold to almost 90 thousand. The drug which showed the largest percentage increase in the number of seizures during the early 1990s was MDMA (ecstasy): there were 3.6 thousand seizures of this drug in 1994 which was more than double the number in 1991.

In 1995 the British Social Attitudes Survey, carried out by Social and Community Planning Research, included a question about people's attitudes to cannabis. Around three in ten people in Great Britain agreed with the statement that 'Smoking cannabis should be legalised', while more than four in ten disagreed strongly. This shows a change in attitudes since 1983 when only one in eight agreed and more than six in ten strongly disagreed.

# 9.8

facilitate the use of automatic cameras to provide evidence for motoring offences was first introduced in England and Wales on 1 July 1992 and since then the number in use has been increasing. At the start of 1994 there were 84 speed and traffic light cameras in use to service 422 sites in all police forces in England and Wales; in 1996 there were 102 cameras servicing more than 700 sites in ten police force areas which were thought to be broadly representative of the 43 police forces in England and Wales. In 1995, 255 thousand offences were detected by automatic cameras, around 80 per cent of which were for speeding (Table 9.7). A recent study at some of these sites by the Police Research Group has shown that speeds were reduced by an average of 4.2 miles per hour when cameras were introduced. Cameras have also been introduced in parts of Scotland; the first were in Strathclyde in 1993. They are not used in Northern Ireland.

The quality of people's lives can be affected not only by actually being the victim of crime but also by being worried about crime. Overall people in England and Wales were slightly less worried about crime in 1996 than they were in 1994. In general women tended to worry about crime more than men and younger people worry more than older people. Men were more likely to be worried about the theft of their car than the other offences shown in Table 9.9, with almost a quarter of male car owners saying they were very worried about this type of crime in 1996. Rape was the crime for which the largest proportion of women were very worried: almost a third were very worried about this crime. In Scotland, housebreaking was the crime that people were most likely to worry about with a fifth being very worried in 1993.

**Risk of being a victim of crime: by type of area, 1995**

| England & Wales | Indices[1] | |
|---|---|---|
| | Inner city | Non-inner city |
| **Household offences** | | |
| Home vandalism | 110 | 100 |
| Burglary | 180 | 90 |
| Vehicle vandalism[2] | 145 | 95 |
| Vehicle thefts[2] | 150 | 95 |
| Bicycle thefts[3] | 165 | 95 |
| Other household theft | 140 | 95 |
| All household offences | 125 | 95 |
| **Personal offences** | | |
| Assaults | 140 | 95 |
| Robbery/theft from person | 185 | 90 |
| Other personal theft | 105 | 100 |
| All personal offences[4] | 135 | 95 |

1 All areas=100.
2 Indices relate to households with vehicles only.
3 Indices relate to households with bicycles only.
4 Excludes sexual offences.
*Source: British Crime Survey, Home Office*

# Victims

# 9.9

The type of area in which people live can affect the likelihood that they will be the victim of a crime. Generally people living in inner city areas are more likely to be victims than those living elsewhere. This is particularly true for certain types of crime. For example, information for England and Wales from the BCS indicated that in 1995 households located in the inner city were twice as likely to be the victim of a burglary than other households (Table 9.8). Younger people were far more likely to have been the victim of a personal offence, such as an assault, than older adults.

**Fear of crime[1]: by gender and age, 1996**

| England & Wales | | | | | | | | Percentages |
|---|---|---|---|---|---|---|---|---|
| | Males | | | | Females | | | |
| | 16-29 | 30-59 | 60 and over | All aged 16 and over | 16-29 | 30-59 | 60 and over | All aged 16 and over |
| Theft of car[2] | 28 | 23 | 19 | 23 | 30 | 26 | 22 | 26 |
| Theft from car[2] | 26 | 20 | 16 | 20 | 22 | 21 | 16 | 20 |
| Burglary | 18 | 18 | 18 | 18 | 27 | 26 | 25 | 26 |
| Mugging | 12 | 11 | 13 | 12 | 28 | 25 | 26 | 26 |
| Rape | .. | .. | .. | .. | 44 | 31 | 22 | 32 |

1 Percentage of people aged 16 and over who were 'very worried' about each type of crime.
2 Percentage of car owners.
*Source: British Crime Survey, Home Office*

# 9.10

**Fear of burglary[1]: international comparison, 1992**

Percentages

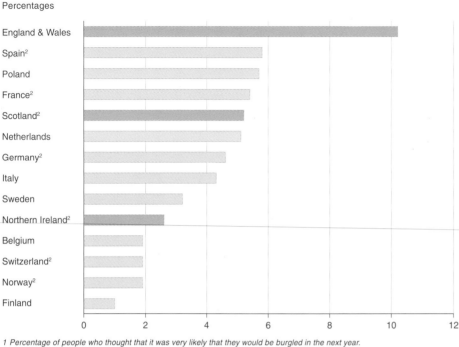

1 Percentage of people who thought that it was very likely that they would be burgled in the next year.
2 Data are for 1989. Data for Germany are for West Germany.

*Source: International Crime Surveys, Home Office*

# 9.11

**Risk of car theft: by selected parking location, 1993[1]**

| England & Wales | Thefts per 100,000 cars per 24 hours |
|---|---|
| | 1993 |
| Work street | 118 |
| Home street | 117 |
| Other street | 327 |
| Public car park | 454 |
| Work car park | 37 |
| Home drive | 40 |
| Home garage | 2 |

1 Data for parking location are from 1993; data for location of thefts are from five sweeps of the British Crime Survey to improve reliability and relate to the period 1981 to 1993.

*Source: British Crime Survey, Home Office*

There are many factors which affect whether people worry about crime. Information from the 1994 BCS showed that worry about mugging was not related to having been a victim of street crime, although those who knew other victims were more anxious. The people most fearful of street crime were those in the lower income groups, those who lived in neighbourhoods with noisy neighbours or with teenagers hanging around and those who were more vulnerable in terms of their physical size and health.

Fear of crime also varies between people in different countries. International crime surveys were carried out using comparable methods in many European countries in 1989 and again in 1992. Chart 9.10 uses information from the 1992 survey, where this is available, and 1989 information where the

country did not take part in the later survey. People in England and Wales were more likely than those in any other country to think they would be burgled: 10 per cent thought it very likely that they would be burgled in the next 12 months compared with only 1 per cent in Finland.

A common type of crime is theft of, or from, a vehicle. In 1995 almost one in five car owners was the victim of this type of crime. However the risk of having a car stolen varies depending on where it is parked. Table 9.11 uses information from the BCS to show the relative risk of having a car stolen from various locations. Not only does it measure the number of cars stolen from each location but it also takes into account the amount of time that a car is parked there. The parking information relates to 1993 whereas the theft information is taken from five surveys to improve accuracy and relates to the period 1981 to 1993 (although the pattern for 1993 was similar to that of the combined surveys). The table shows that for cars parked for the same length of time, a car parked in a public car park was four times more likely to be stolen than a car parked in the street where the owner lives and more than 200 times more likely to be stolen than if it were parked in the owner's garage.

## Offenders

In 1995 almost 480 thousand people were found guilty of, or cautioned for, an indictable offence in England and Wales. This compares with a peak of almost 600 thousand in 1985 which was nearly four times the number in 1951. In Scotland, in 1994, there were 157 thousand people with charges proved for crimes and offences, which compares with around 100 thousand in 1951.

Almost four in ten offenders found guilty of, or cautioned for, an indictable offence in 1995 were aged 14 to 20 years old (Table 9.12). Among males, half of all offenders found guilty or cautioned for burglary and robbery were between these ages. In Scotland 14 to 20 year olds accounted for 23 per cent of males and 14 per cent of females with a charge proved for crimes and offences in 1994.

The Youth Lifestyles Survey (YLS), commissioned by the Home Office, provided information on self-reported offending of young people in England and Wales in 1992-1993. Results from this survey suggest that offending amongst young people is much more widespread than the police figures suggest. For example, one in four males aged 18 to 21 and around one in eight females aged 14 to 17 admitted committing a theft or burglary in the previous year (Table 9.13). As with the police figures, rates of self-reported offending were higher among males than females. Rates for young females declined with increasing age, whereas for males, rates were higher for those in their late teens than for younger teenagers and they remained high for those in their twenties.

The YLS indicated that young people who lived with one parent or in a step-family were more likely to say they had offended than those living with both natural parents. Young people who played truant from school or who had been excluded from school were also more likely to report that they had offended than other young people.

## 9.12

**Offenders found guilty of, or cautioned for, indictable offences[1]: by gender, type of offence and age, 1995**

England & Wales    Percentages

| | 10-13 | 14-17 | 18-20 | 21-34 | 35 and over | All aged 10 and over (=100%) (thousands) |
|---|---|---|---|---|---|---|
| **Males** | | | | | | |
| Theft and handling stolen goods | 8 | 24 | 16 | 37 | 15 | 160.9 |
| Drug offences | - | 13 | 24 | 53 | 10 | 71.9 |
| Burglary | 8 | 30 | 20 | 37 | 5 | 43.9 |
| Violence against the person | 4 | 21 | 14 | 43 | 17 | 41.8 |
| Criminal damage | 10 | 24 | 15 | 39 | 12 | 12.2 |
| Sexual offences | 4 | 14 | 8 | 30 | 45 | 6.8 |
| Robbery | 7 | 36 | 19 | 32 | 6 | 5.3 |
| Other indictable offences | 1 | 8 | 17 | 58 | 17 | 52.4 |
| | | | | | | |
| All indictable offences | 5 | 20 | 18 | 43 | 14 | 395.2 |
| **Females** | | | | | | |
| Theft and handling stolen goods | 12 | 28 | 12 | 32 | 16 | 60.1 |
| Drug offences | - | 10 | 19 | 56 | 16 | 7.9 |
| Burglary | 12 | 43 | 15 | 24 | 4 | 1.9 |
| Violence against the person | 8 | 36 | 11 | 34 | 12 | 7.7 |
| Criminal damage | 8 | 27 | 13 | 35 | 17 | 1.2 |
| Sexual offences | 6 | 13 | 6 | 50 | 24 | 0.1 |
| Robbery | 7 | 55 | 16 | 20 | 2 | 0.5 |
| Other indictable offences | - | 9 | 15 | 59 | 16 | 5.0 |
| | | | | | | |
| All indictable offences | 10 | 26 | 13 | 36 | 15 | 84.4 |

1 See Appendix, Part 9: Types of offences in England, Wales and Northern Ireland.
*Source: Home Office*

## 9.13

**Young people offending in the past year[1]: by gender, age and type of offence, 1992-1993[2]**

England & Wales    Percentages

| | Males | | | Females | | |
|---|---|---|---|---|---|---|
| | 14-17 | 18-21 | 22-25 | 14-17 | 18-21 | 22-25 |
| Theft or burglary | 17 | 25 | 27 | 13 | 9 | 3 |
| Violent offences | 12 | 9 | 4 | 7 | 4 | 1 |
| Vandalism or arson | 8 | 8 | - | 8 | 1 | - |
| | | | | | | |
| Any of the above offences | 24 | 31 | 31 | 19 | 11 | 4 |

1 Percentage of each age group who admitted committing an offence in the past year.
2 November 1992 to January 1993.
*Source: Youth Lifestyles Survey, Home Office*

# 9.14

Known offenders[1] as a percentage of the population: by gender and age, 1995

**England & Wales**

Percentages

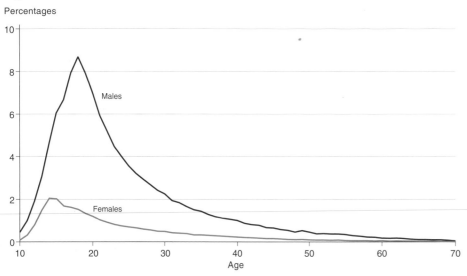

1 People found guilty or cautioned for indictable offences; excludes those whose age was not known.
**Source: Home Office**

# 9.15

People convicted[1]: by gender, age and number of previous convictions, 1994

**England & Wales**                                                                                       Percentages

| | Number of previous convictions | | | | | All |
|---|---|---|---|---|---|---|
| | 0 | 1 | 2 | 3 to 9 | 10 or more | people convicted |
| **Males** | | | | | | |
| 10-17 | 52 | 17 | 11 | 19 | 1 | 100 |
| 18-34 | 26 | 12 | 9 | 34 | 19 | 100 |
| 35-54 | 25 | 11 | 7 | 26 | 31 | 100 |
| 55 and over | 40 | 11 | 6 | 19 | 24 | 100 |
| | | | | | | |
| All males aged 10 and over | 30 | 13 | 8 | 31 | 18 | 100 |
| **Females** | | | | | | |
| 10-17 | 67 | 18 | 7 | 8 | 0 | 100 |
| 18-34 | 44 | 17 | 9 | 24 | 6 | 100 |
| 35-54 | 51 | 15 | 8 | 20 | 6 | 100 |
| 55 and over | 41 | 22 | 4 | 22 | 11 | 100 |
| | | | | | | |
| All females aged 10 and over | 47 | 17 | 8 | 22 | 6 | 100 |

1 People convicted on fifteen particular days of 1994 of standard list offences only. For a definition of standard list offences see
Appendix, Part 9: Types of offences in England, Wales and Northern Ireland.
**Source: Home Office**

According to police figures, the peak age for offending for males in England and Wales was 18 in 1995: almost 9 per cent of 18 year old males were found guilty of, or cautioned for, an indictable offence in that year (Chart 9.14). For females, rates of offending were lower and the peak age was younger at 14: 2 per cent of 14 year old females offended in 1994. These peak ages have changed over time. Before 1972 the peak age of offending for both males and females was 14; this rose to 15 for males following the raising of the school leaving age from 15 to 16 in 1972. By 1988 the peak age for males had risen to 18 while that for females fluctuated between 14 and 15.

A small proportion of offenders are responsible for a large proportion of offences. Information from the YLS showed that about 3 per cent of offenders were responsible for around 25 per cent of all offences. The main source of information on the criminal histories of offenders in England and Wales comes from the Home Office's Offenders Index which holds nearly 6 million criminal histories. Analyses from this source show that seven in ten males aged 10 and over who were convicted in 1994 had already been convicted on a previous occasion and almost half had at least three previous convictions (Table 9.15). Among convicted females aged 10 and over more than half had a previous conviction.

The proportion of those convicted who were first time offenders varies with the type of offence. Only 22 per cent of males convicted of burglary had no previous convictions compared with 45 per cent of males convicted of sexual offences. The chance of receiving an immediate custodial sentence increased in line with the number of previous convictions, particularly for young males.

# 9.16

## Police and courts action

Since 1986 the police in England and Wales have had certain powers to stop and search people and vehicles under the *Police and Criminal Evidence Act 1984*. Since then the number of searches has been growing: in 1995 the police stopped and searched more than 690 thousand people or vehicles - a fifth more than in 1994 and over six times as many as in 1986 (Table 9.16). Seven in ten of these searches in 1995 were to look for stolen property or drugs. The proportion of stops and searches which resulted in an arrest has been falling steadily since these powers were introduced, from 17 per cent in 1986 to 12 per cent in 1995.

In England, Wales and Northern Ireland, following an arrest the police may: release the suspect without further action; caution, either formally or informally; or charge. Offences are said to be cleared-up by primary means when someone is cautioned, charged or summoned to appear in court, or by secondary means when a prisoner admits to further offences.

Combined primary and secondary clear-up rates fell between 1981 and 1995 in England and Wales: two fifths of notifiable offences were cleared-up at the start of this period compared with only a quarter at the end (Table 9.17). In contrast rates in Northern Ireland were higher in 1995 than in 1981. In Scotland, where secondary means for clear-up are not used, primary clear-up rates were also higher at the end of this period than at the beginning.

Clear-up rates vary by type of offence: for violence against the person and sexual offences around three quarters of offences recorded by the police were cleared-up in England and Wales in 1995 compared with

only an eighth of thefts from vehicles. Rates also vary by police force area. Based on primary rates, the Dyfed-Powys force achieved the highest clear-up rate in England and Wales, at 47 per cent, while the West Midlands had the lowest rate at 13 per cent. In Scotland the highest rates were achieved by the Northern constabulary.

In England and Wales, where an offender admits his guilt, there is sufficient evidence for a conviction and it does not seem to be in the public interest to institute criminal proceedings, a formal caution may be given. In 1995, 203 thousand people in England and Wales were cautioned for indictable offences - a fall from the peak of 216

**Stops and searches made by the police: by reason for search**

| England & Wales | | | Percentages |
|---|---|---|---|
| | 1986 | 1991 | 1995 |
| Stolen property | 44 | 37 | 37 |
| Drugs | 30 | 36 | 34 |
| Going equipped[1] | 9 | 17 | 18 |
| Offensive weapons | 6 | 5 | 6 |
| Firearms | 1 | 1 | 1 |
| Other | 10 | 4 | 5 |
| | | | |
| All reasons (=100%) | | | |
| (thousands) | 110 | 304 | 690 |

1 Searches for items which could be used in a theft or burglary.
*Source: Home Office*

# 9.17

**Clear-up rates for notifiable offences[1]: by type of offence, 1981 and 1995**

| | | | | | | Percentages |
|---|---|---|---|---|---|---|
| | England & Wales | | Scotland | | Northern Ireland | |
| | 1981 | 1995 | 1981 | 1995 | 1981 | 1995[2] |
| Drug trafficking | .. | 98 | 99 | 100 | 100 | 86 |
| Violence against the person | 75 | 77 | 83 | 77 | 47 | 67 |
| Sexual offences, | 73 | 76 | 65 | 77 | 71 | 82 |
| of which: rape | 68 | 75 | 74 | 77 | 45 | 82 |
| Fraud and forgery | 70 | 50 | 78 | 80 | 66 | 63 |
| Robbery | 25 | 23 | 26 | 29 | 15 | 19 |
| | | | | | | |
| Theft and handling stolen goods, | 38 | 23 | 28 | 26 | 27 | 31 |
| of which: theft of vehicles | 28 | 19 | 26 | 24 | 14 | 18 |
| theft from vehicles | 23 | 12 | .. | 13 | 12 | 10 |
| Burglary | 30 | 21 | 20 | 17 | 22 | 19 |
| Criminal damage[3] | 27 | 19 | 22 | 21 | 17 | 33 |
| Other notifiable offences[4] | 91 | 94 | 90 | 99 | 33 | 93 |
| | | | | | | |
| All notifiable offences | 38 | 26 | 31 | 39 | 27 | 36 |

1 Excluding offences of criminal damage of value £20 and under in England and Wales. See Appendix, Part 9: Types of offences in England, Wales and Northern Ireland and Offences and crimes.
2 No longer includes assault on police and communicating false information regarding a bomb hoax. These offences have been removed from the categories 'Violence against the person' and 'Other notifiable offences'.
3 In Northern Ireland excludes criminal damage valued at £200 or less.
4 In Northern Ireland includes 'possession of controlled drugs' and 'offences against the state'.
*Source: Home Office; The Scottish Office Home Department; Royal Ulster Constabulary*

# 9.18

### Offenders cautioned for indictable offences[1]: by type of offence

**England & Wales** Percentages

| | 1971[2] | 1981 | 1991 | 1995 |
|---|---|---|---|---|
| Theft and handling stolen goods | 69.2 | 76.2 | 60.3 | 51.8 |
| Drug offences[3] | .. | 0.3 | 11.8 | 23.8 |
| Violence against the person | 3.0 | 5.4 | 10.8 | 10.1 |
| Burglary[4] | 16.0 | 10.8 | 7.4 | 5.2 |
| Fraud and forgery | 1.3 | 1.3 | 3.1 | 3.9 |
| Criminal damage | 4.7 | 2.0 | 2.1 | 1.9 |
| Sexual offences | 5.0 | 2.7 | 1.8 | 1.1 |
| Robbery | 0.3 | 0.1 | 0.3 | 0.3 |
| Other[3] | 0.4 | 1.3 | 2.3 | 2.0 |
| | | | | |
| All offenders cautioned (=100%) | | | | |
| (thousands) | 77.3 | 103.9 | 179.9 | 202.6 |

1 Excludes motoring offences.
2 Adjusted to take account of the Criminal Damage Act 1971.
3 Data for 1971 are included in 'Other'.
4 See Appendix, Part 9: Offenders cautioned for burglary.
**Source: Home Office**

thousand in 1992 (Table 9.18). Prior to this the number had risen steadily since 1979 when only 97 thousand cautions were given. The change in this trend may partly reflect the issuing of Home Office guidance, in draft in 1993 and in its final form in March 1994, which discouraged the use of cautions for serious offences and for offenders who had been cautioned previously.

The number of cautions for drug offences rose sharply in the 1980s and has continued to rise in the 1990s while cautions for theft and handling stolen goods have fallen. There were only a few hundred cautions for drug offences in England and Wales in 1981 but the number had grown to more than 20 thousand in 1991. By 1995 cautions for drug offences had increased to almost 50 thousand - almost a quarter of all cautions for indictable offences.

# 9.19

### Offenders sentenced for indictable offences[1]: by type of offence and type of sentence[2], 1995

**England, Wales & Northern Ireland** Percentages

| | Discharge | Fine | Community sentence | Fully suspended sentence | Immediate custody | Other | All sentenced (=100%) (thousands) |
|---|---|---|---|---|---|---|---|
| Theft and handling stolen goods | 26 | 29 | 30 | 1 | 14 | 1 | 119.2 |
| Burglary | 10 | 7 | 43 | 1 | 38 | 1 | 36.4 |
| Drug offences[3] | 15 | 49 | 17 | 1 | 17 | - | 32.3 |
| Violence against the person | 17 | 15 | 33 | 3 | 28 | 4 | 30.9 |
| Fraud and forgery | 19 | 21 | 36 | 3 | 19 | 2 | 17.8 |
| | | | | | | | |
| Motoring[3] | 6 | 61 | 17 | 1 | 14 | 1 | 11.2 |
| Criminal damage | 28 | 19 | 33 | 2 | 11 | 7 | 10.5 |
| Robbery | 4 | 1 | 26 | 1 | 63 | 5 | 5.4 |
| Sexual offences | 8 | 12 | 24 | 3 | 50 | 3 | 4.9 |
| Other offences | 15 | 50 | 15 | 1 | 14 | 5 | 42.1 |
| | | | | | | | |
| All indictable offences | 19 | 30 | 28 | 1 | 20 | 2 | 310.6 |

1 See Appendix, Part 9: Types of offences in England, Wales and Northern Ireland.
2 See Appendix, Part 9: Sentences and orders.
3 For Northern Ireland motoring offences are Crown Court disposals only.
**Source: Home Office; Northern Ireland Office**

## 9.20

For those offenders who are charged or summonsed and then found guilty, the court will impose a sentence. Sentences can include immediate custody, a community sentence, a fine or, if the court considers that no punishment is necessary, a discharge. In 1995 three in ten offenders sentenced for indictable offences in England, Wales and Northern Ireland received a fine (Table 9.19). A similar proportion received a community sentence where they are required to perform unpaid work such as outdoor conservation projects and decorating houses for elderly or handicapped people. Those sentenced for robbery or for sexual offences were the most likely to receive custodial sentences while offenders sentenced for motoring offences were the most likely to be fined.

In Scotland, of the 51 thousand people with a charge proved for a crime (the more serious type of offence) in 1994, 48 per cent received a fine. Custodial sentences were given in 38 per cent of cases of crimes of violence (excluding sexual crimes).

The changes in the types of sentences given to young offenders aged 14 to 17 in England and Wales since 1981 are shown in Chart 9.20. The types of sentences given during this period have been affected by the various *Criminal Justice Acts* which came into force in the 1980s and 1990s. For example, the *Criminal Justice Act 1991* introduced the principle that the way young people are dealt with should closely reflect their age and development.

Since 1981 there has been an increase in the proportion of offenders aged 14 to 17 sentenced for indictable offences who have received community sentences. This has been a result of the increase in the range of community sentences which are available and the fact that the confidence of those

sentencing has grown in them. In 1981 there were 24 thousand offenders aged 14 to 17 sentenced for all crimes and offences in Scotland, of which 73 per cent were given fines. By 1994 the number of these offenders had fallen to only 9 thousand with 43 per cent receiving fines. Part of the explanation for this is the fall in the population aged 14 to 17 in Scotland over this period.

Custodial sentences will normally be imposed on the most serious, dangerous and persistent offenders. In 1995 the average sentence length imposed on men aged 21 and over in the Crown Court in England and Wales was 22 months; this had risen from a little under 17 months in the early 1980s (Chart 9.21). Men sentenced for robbery tended to get the longest sentences: these averaging 51 months for those in 1995. For women the longest sentences were given to those convicted of drug offences at an average of 33 months.

**Offenders aged 14 to 17 sentenced for indictable offences[1]: by type of sentence[2]**

**England & Wales**

Percentages

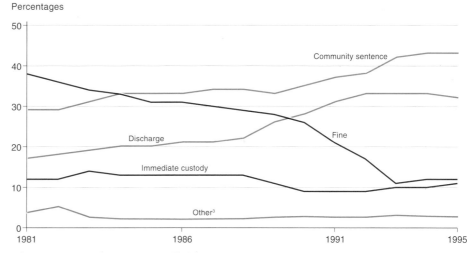

1 See Appendix, Part 9: Types of offences in England, Wales and Northern Ireland.
2 See Appendix, Part 9: Sentences and orders.
3 Includes fully suspended sentences, compensation orders, hospital orders and other minor disposals.
*Source: Home Office*

## 9.21

**Average sentence length for males[1]: by type of court**

**England & Wales**

Months

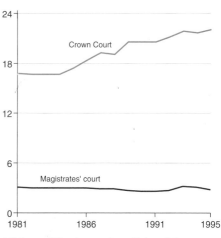

1 Males aged 21 and over sentenced to immediate imprisonment for indictable offences.
*Source: Home Office*

# 9.22

## Successful appeals[1]: by type of court and type of appeal

| England & Wales | | | Percentages | |
|---|---|---|---|---|
| | 1971 | 1981 | 1991 | 1994 |
| **Crown Court** | | | | |
| Against conviction | .. | 27 | 38 | 43 |
| Against sentence | .. | 51 | 49 | 38 |
| **Court of Appeal** | | | | |
| Against conviction | 11 | 10 | 13 | 13 |
| Against sentence | 8 | 20 | 26 | 20 |

1 Percentage of appeals of each type and in each court which were successful.
*Source: Home Office*

Sentence lengths imposed by magistrates' courts are generally much shorter: such sentences must be between five days and six months for one offence and not more than 12 months in total for two or more offences. Average sentence lengths imposed by magistrates' courts have remained at around three months since the early 1980s.

After conviction and sentencing, the defendant can appeal against the sentence, the conviction or both. In England and Wales appeals against decisions made at magistrates' courts are heard at the Crown Court while appeals against decisions of the Crown Court are made at the Court of Appeal. Although only a small proportion of defendants appeal, the numbers have been growing: in 1994 there were 28 thousand appeals against either sentence or conviction heard at the Crown Court compared with 19 thousand in 1991.

In 1981 appeals against sentence in the Crown Court were nearly twice as likely to be successful as those made against conviction. However, in 1994 the proportion which were successful for both types of appeal was around two fifths (Table 9.22). Generally a higher proportion of appeals heard in the Crown Court are successful compared with those heard at the Court of Appeal.

# 9.23

## Population of sentenced male adult prisoners[1]: by ethnic group and type of offence, 1995

| England & Wales | | | | | Percentages |
|---|---|---|---|---|---|
| | White | Black[2] | Indian | Pakistani/ Bangladeshi | Other ethnic minorities |
| Violence against the person | 24 | 20 | 20 | 20 | 25 |
| Burglary | 15 | 12 | 5 | 6 | 10 |
| Robbery | 13 | 24 | 10 | 13 | 14 |
| Drug offences | 9 | 17 | 13 | 19 | 16 |
| Theft and handling | 9 | 6 | 10 | 7 | 9 |
| Rape | 5 | 6 | 3 | 5 | 4 |
| Other sexual offences | 7 | 1 | 2 | 3 | 3 |
| Fraud and forgery | 3 | 2 | 14 | 6 | 6 |
| Other offences | 12 | 7 | 20 | 18 | 10 |
| Offence not recorded | 3 | 4 | 2 | 4 | 4 |
| Fine defaulters | 1 | 1 | 1 | 1 | 1 |
| All sentenced adult male prisoners (=100%)(thousands) | 26.0 | 2.8 | 0.2 | 0.3 | 0.4 |

1 British Nationals.
2 Black Caribbean, Black African and Other Black.
*Source: Home Office*

## Prisons and probation

The prison population in Great Britain fell in the late 1980s, but has been growing since 1993. Chart 9.1, at the beginning of this chapter, shows that there were 57 thousand people in Prison Service establishments in 1995. Projections based on 1995 indicate that the prison population is expected to continue growing to reach 62 thousand in the year 2000. The prison population in Northern Ireland fell throughout most of the 1980s before rising in the early 1990s; it fell again in the two years up to 1995 when it stood at 1.8 thousand.

Black people in England and Wales are over represented in the prison population relative to their numbers in the population as a whole; this is especially true for Black females. However the proportion of ethnic minority prisoners reduces for all ethnic minority groups, particularly Black women, once foreign nationals are excluded although ethnic minorities are still over represented. There are many factors which affect the level of crime in each ethnic group; these include the younger age structures of the ethnic minority population (see Table 1.8) and the higher proportions who are unemployed.

Sentenced male adults in England and Wales from the Black group were more likely than any other ethnic group to be in prison for robbery: 24 per cent were in prison for this offence in 1995 (Table 9.23). A higher proportion of male adult prisoners from all ethnic minority groups were serving sentences for drug offences compared with those from the White group. Among female adult prisoners, 46 per cent of those from the Black group were serving sentences for drug offences compared with only 17 per cent of White female prisoners.

In England, Wales and Northern Ireland, 32 males aged 15 and over were received under sentence for every 10 thousand in the population in 1995 - a rise from 25 per 10 thousand in 1991 (Table 9.24). The highest rate for males was among those aged 18 to 24. The rate for females aged 15 and over was much lower than that for males at 2 per 10 thousand population in 1995. In Scotland the term receptions is not equivalent to persons received. For example, where custodial sentences are imposed on a person by two or more courts in one day, this is counted as two or more receptions.

On this basis, there were 55 direct receptions into prisons in Scotland in 1995 relating to males aged 15 and over for every 10 thousand in the population.

In England and Wales, while custody is the sentence given for the most serious offences, crimes such as burglary are more likely to result in the offender receiving a criminal supervision order. These mostly involve community service or probation. In 1995, 111 thousand people received a criminal supervision order in England and Wales; this was virtually the same as in 1994 but 40 per cent more than in 1981 (Table 9.25). The same person may receive more than one order hence the number of orders issued exceeds the number of people receiving orders.

# 9.24

## Receptions of males under sentence into Prison Service establishments[1]: by age

| England, Wales & Northern Ireland | | | Rates per 10,000 population | |
|---|---|---|---|---|
| | 1981 | 1986 | 1991 | 1995 |
| 15-17 [2] | 73 | 54 | 30 | 46 |
| 18-24 | 100 | 100 | 82 | 107 |
| 25-29 | 48 | 50 | 47 | 65 |
| 30-39 | 27 | 27 | 25 | 35 |
| 40-49 | 16 | 14 | 11 | 14 |
| 50 and over | 3 | 3 | 2 | 3 |
| All aged 15 [2] and over | 33 | 32 | 25 | 32 |

1 Receptions under sentence excluding fine defaulters and prisoners held only in police cells.
2 Includes 14 year olds in England and Wales in 1981, 1986 and 1991.
*Source: Home Office; Northern Ireland Office*

# 9.25

## People commencing criminal supervision orders[1]

| England & Wales | | | | | Thousands |
|---|---|---|---|---|---|
| | 1981 | 1986 | 1991 | 1994 | 1995 |
| Community Service | 28 | 35 | 42 | 50 | 49 |
| Probation | 36 | 40 | 45 | 50 | 47 |
| Combination | . | . | . | 13 | 15 |
| Under the Children and Young Persons Act 1969 | 12 | 6 | 2 | 3 | 3 |
| Other | 8 | 7 | 8 | 6 | 5 |
| All persons commencing supervision orders [2] | 79 | 83 | 91 | 112 | 111 |

1 Supervised by the probation service. See Appendix, Part 9: Sentences and orders.
2 Individual figures do not sum to the total because each person may have more than one type of order.
*Source: Home Office*

# 9.26

**Writs and summonses issued[1]**

**England & Wales**
Millions

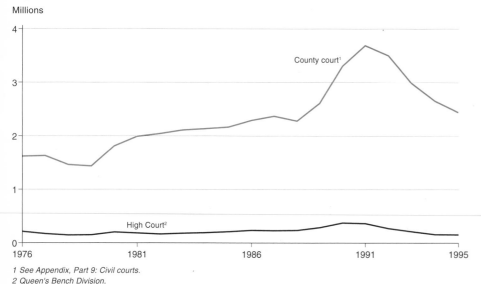

1 See Appendix, Part 9: Civil courts.
2 Queen's Bench Division.
**Source: Court Service**

# 9.27

**Complaints against the police[1]: by outcome**

**England & Wales**
Thousands

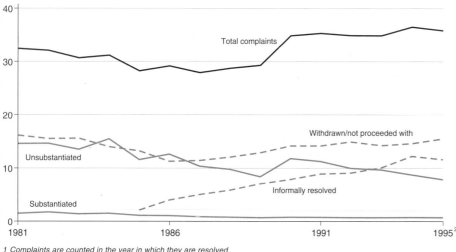

1 Complaints are counted in the year in which they are resolved.
2 Data for 1995 are for the financial year 1995-96.
**Source: Home Office**

## Civil justice

While this chapter has so far looked at cases where a charge has been made on behalf of the Crown, for example by the Crown Prosecution Service in England and Wales, a case may also be brought under civil law by others, including an individual or a company. The majority of these cases are handled by the county courts and High Court in England, Wales and Northern Ireland and by the Sheriff Court and Court of Session in Scotland. The High Court and Court of Session deal with the more substantial and complex cases. Civil cases may include consumer problems, claims for debt, negligence and recovery of land.

Following the issuing of a summons or writ many cases are settled without the need for a court hearing. The total number of writs and summonses issued in England and Wales rose sharply from 1.6 million in 1979 to more than 4 million in 1991 (Chart 9.26). This rise may be explained, in part, by the increase in lending as a consequence of financial deregulation which led to more cases concerned with the recovery and collection of debt. By 1995 the number of writs and summonses issued had fallen to 2.6 million. Part of the reason for the fall was more controlled lending by creditors. In Scotland 150 thousand civil justice cases were initiated at the Sheriff Court or Court of Session in 1994 which was a fall from the peak of almost 200 thousand cases in 1991.

Individuals and organisations may also make a complaint against the police. Between 1985 and 1995-96 the number of complaints dealt with in England and Wales increased by a quarter to almost 36 thousand (Chart 9.27). However the number which are substantiated is small and has decreased over this period: only 750 complaints were substantiated in 1995-96, mostly for failure in duty or oppressive behaviour. In Northern Ireland there were 5 thousand complaints in 1995 and only 73 were substantiated. The police also receive many commendations and letters of thanks: in 1995-96 over 63 thousand commendations and letters of thanks were received by the police in England and Wales.

## Resources

Public expenditure on the criminal justice system in England and Wales has been rising in real terms for more than ten years. Around two thirds of this expenditure was on the police in 1995-96: at £6.6 billion, this was more than a third higher than in 1986-87 after allowing for inflation (Table 9.28). A further £1.7 billion was spent on prisons in 1995-96.

Labour costs form the largest component of police force expenditure. In 1995, 198 thousand people were employed by the police service in Great Britain including 57 thousand civilians (Table 9.29). Overall, this represents 35 police service employees per 10 thousand population which is an increase of a third since 1971. In Northern Ireland 17 thousand people were employed in the police service in 1995 of which 3.5 thousand were civilians.

In addition to paid police service employees, there were 21 thousand Special Constables in England and Wales at the end of 1993. These are part-time volunteers who have full police powers within their force area. They undertake regular officers' routine duties when required which enables regulars to be freed at times of emergency for those tasks which only they can perform.

Other employees in the criminal justice system work in the prison and probation services. The numbers employed in both these services have increased over the past 25 years: in 1995 there were 40 thousand people employed in the prison service in England and Wales which was more than double the number in 1971.

# 9.28

## Public expenditure on the criminal justice system, 1986-87 and 1995-96

| England & Wales | £ million at 1995 prices[1] | |
| --- | --- | --- |
| | 1986-87 | 1995-96 |
| Police | 4,818 | 6,633 |
| Prisons | 1,078 | 1,658 |
| Lord Chancellor's Department[2] | 319 | 744 |
| Probation | 339 | 481 |
| Magistrates' courts | 178 | 416 |
| Crown Prosecution Service[3] | 68 | 297 |

1 Adjusted to November 1995 prices using the GDP market prices deflator.
2 Criminal work only.
3 The Crown Prosecution Service was not fully operational in 1986-87.
*Source: Home Office*

# 9.29

## Employment in the criminal justice system[1]

**Great Britain**

| | Thousands | | | | Rates per 10,000 population | |
| --- | --- | --- | --- | --- | --- | --- |
| | 1971 | 1981 | 1991 | 1995 | 1971 | 1995 |
| **Police service** | | | | | | |
| Police | 109 | 133 | 142 | 141 | 20.0 | 24.8 |
| Civilian staff[2] | 31 | 41 | 51 | 57 | 5.6 | 10.0 |
| All police service | 139 | 174 | 192 | 198 | 25.6 | 34.8 |
| **Prison service[3]** | 17 | 24 | 33 | 40 | 3.5 | 7.8 |
| **Probation service[4]** | .. | 13 | 18 | 18 | .. | 3.5 |

1 At December each year.
2 Data for England and Wales excludes traffic wardens and cadets; data for Scotland includes traffic wardens, clerical and technical staff and excludes cadets.
3 England and Wales only. For 1991 and earlier years excludes headquarters staff and prison officer class trainees.
4 England and Wales only. Full-time plus part-time workers and includes some temporary officers and also some trainees from 1981 onwards. Excludes non-probation officer grade hostel staff.
*Source: Home Office; The Scottish Office Home Department*

## References and further reading

The following list contains selected publications relevant to **Chapter 9: Crime and Justice**. Those published by The Stationery Office are available from the addresses shown on the inside back cover of Social Trends.

*British Crime Survey*, Home Office

*Civil Judicial Statistics, Scotland*, The Stationery Office

*Chief Constables's Annual Report*, Royal Ulster Constabulary

*A Commentary on Northern Ireland Crime Statistics*, The Stationery Office

*Crime and the quality of life: public perceptions and experiences of crime in Scotland*, The Scottish Office

*Criminal proceedings in Scottish Courts*, The Scottish Office

*Criminal Statistics, England and Wales*, The Stationery Office

*Criminal Statistics, Scotland*, The Stationery Office

*Crown Prosecution Service, Annual Report*, The Stationery Office

*Digest 3: Information on the Criminal Justice System in England and Wales*, Home Office

*Digest of Information on the Northern Ireland Criminal Justice System 2*, The Stationery Office

*Home Office Annual Report and Accounts*, The Stationery Office

*Home Office Statistical Bulletins* and *Research Findings Series*, Home Office

*Judicial Statistics, England and Wales*, The Stationery Office

*Northern Ireland Judicial Statistics*, Northern Ireland Court Service

*Police Statistics, England and Wales*, CIPFA

*Prison Service Annual Report and Accounts*, The Stationery Office

*Prison Statistics, England and Wales*, The Stationery Office

*Prisons in Scotland Report*, The Stationery Office

*Probation Statistics, England and Wales*, Home Office

*Race and the Criminal Justice System 1994*, Home Office

*Report of the Parole Board for England and Wales*, The Stationery Office

*Report on the work of the Northern Ireland Prison Service*, The Stationery Office

*Scottish Crime Survey*, The Scottish Office

*The Criminal Justice System in England and Wales 1995*, Home Office

*The Offenders Index*, Home Office

*The Scottish Office Statistical Bulletins Series*, The Scottish Office

*The Work of the Prison Service*, The Stationery Office

*Young people and crime*, Home Office

## Contacts

Telephone contact points for further information relating to
**Chapter 9: Crime and Justice**

**Office for National Statistics**

| | |
|---|---|
| Chapter author | 0171 533 5782 |
| **Court Service** | 0171 210 1773 |
| **Home Office** | 0181 760 8340 |
| **Northern Ireland Office** | 01232 527534/8 |
| **Royal Ulster Constabulary** | 01232 650222 extn 24135 |
| **The Scottish Office Home Department** | 0131 244 2227 |

# Chapter 10 Housing

**Characteristics of different types of tenure**

People's housing tenure varies with age. In 1995-96 those under 25 were much more likely to be renting than buying while over seven in ten of all outright owner-occupiers were over 60. (Table 10.3)

**Types and condition of housing**

Two thirds of owner-occupiers live in detached or semi-detached houses compared with only a quarter of council tenants. (Table 10.7)

**Housebuilding**

The rate of housebuilding per thousand population was lower in the United Kingdom in 1994 than in all other European Union countries apart from Denmark and Sweden. (Chart 10.13)

**Mobility**

People renting furnished accommodation move house most frequently while those owning their home outright do so least frequently. (Table 10.15)

A fifth of moves were prompted by a desire for a better house or flat in 1995-96 and a tenth by a desire for a better neighbourhood. (Table 10.16)

**Local authority housing**

Homeless households took up about a quarter of new tenancies for local authority housing in the United Kingdom in 1994-95. (Table 10.19)

**Housing costs and expenditure**

Owner-occupiers with mortgages pay about three times as much for their housing as social sector tenants. (Tables 10.22 and 10.23)

The proportion of households in arrears with housing costs was about 4 per cent for both mortgagors and private renters in England in 1995-96 and around twice as great for local authority and housing association tenants. (Page 182)

**10.1**

Stock of dwellings[1]:
by tenure

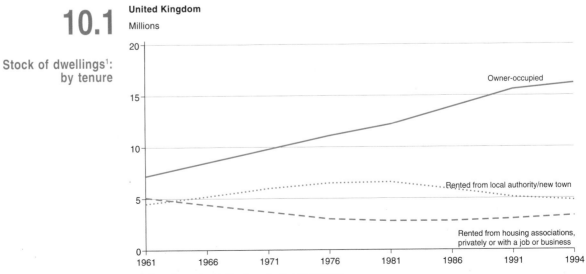

**United Kingdom**

Millions

1 At December each year. See Appendix, Part 10: Dwellings.

*Source: Department of the Environment; Welsh Office; The Scottish Office; Department of the Environment, Northern Ireland*

## 10.2

Owner-occupation[1]: by socio-economic group[2], 1981 and 1995-96

| Great Britain | | Percentages |
|---|---|---|
| | 1981 | 1995-96 |
| Professional | 87 | 87 |
| Employers and managers | 83 | 88 |
| Intermediate non-manual | 75 | 82 |
| Junior non-manual | 62 | 75 |
| Skilled manual | 52 | 76 |
| Semi-skilled manual | 35 | 55 |
| Unskilled manual | 27 | 43 |
| Economically inactive | 42 | 55 |
| All socio-economic groups | 54 | 68 |

1 Percentage in each socio-economic group who were owner-occupiers.
2 Excludes members of the Armed Forces, economically active full-time students and those who were unemployed and had never worked.

**Source: General Household Survey, Office for National Statistics**

For many years the housing market has been polarised between owner-occupation (either outright ownership or buying with mortgage), social renting (from local authorities or housing associations) and private renting (furnished or unfurnished). Chart 10.1 shows that the relative sizes of the three sectors have altered considerably since 1961. In recent years there have also been major changes in the characteristics of households, the different types of tenure, the relationships between these and the direction of government policy.

## Characteristics of different types of tenure

Housing tenure has traditionally been closely related to social class and economic status. In the past, the differences may have owed something to the attitudes and expectations of different groups in society, as well as their ability and opportunity to buy houses, but in the last fifteen years such divisions have become much less pronounced, as Table 10.2 illustrates. In Great Britain owner-occupation increased in almost all socio-economic groups between 1981 and 1995-96 but the increases have been much more marked among the manual groups.

Not all households wish to buy accommodation even if they are able to do so. For example, those whose work is geographically mobile may find renting more convenient. In households whose head is in a professional occupation, the 'saturation level' for owner-occupation appears to be about seven eighths of households: a plateau which professionals had already attained by 1981 and which employers and managers, as a group, have reached since then. Compared with these two groups, owner-occupation is slightly less common for other non-manual households with those at more junior levels having a lower level of owner-occupation, but a faster rate of increase, than the intermediate socio-economic group.

It is among manual groups, however, that the largest proportionate rises in owner-occupation have occurred. The proportion of skilled manual workers in owner-occupation increased from half in 1981 to three quarters in 1995-96, when it roughly equalled that for junior non-manuals. The proportion in the semi-skilled and unskilled manual groups in 1995-96, though still below those of other groups, were well over half as great again as in 1981.

Among owner-occupiers, nearly two fifths of households in the United Kingdom owned their property outright in 1995-96 while the remainder were owners with a mortgage (Table 10.3). Seven in ten of all outright owner-occupiers were over 60 reflecting the fact that they have had time to pay off their mortgage debts.

## 10.3

Tenure: by age of head of household, 1995-96

| United Kingdom | | | | | | | | Percentages |
|---|---|---|---|---|---|---|---|---|
| | Under 25 | 25-29 | 30-44 | 45-59 | 60-64 | 65-79 | 80 and over | All ages |
| **Owner-occupied** | | | | | | | | |
| Owned outright | 1 | 1 | 4 | 23 | 50 | 56 | 52 | 26 |
| Owned with mortgage | 28 | 55 | 67 | 56 | 24 | 7 | 3 | 42 |
| **Rented unfurnished** | | | | | | | | |
| Local authority/new town | 25 | 17 | 15 | 13 | 18 | 26 | 29 | 18 |
| Housing association | 6 | 6 | 4 | 3 | 2 | 5 | 7 | 4 |
| Privately | 15 | 9 | 4 | 3 | 3 | 5 | 9 | 5 |
| **Rented furnished** | 22 | 9 | 3 | 1 | 1 | 1 | - | 3 |
| **Rented with job or business** | 2 | 3 | 3 | 2 | 2 | 1 | 0 | 2 |
| **All tenures[1]** | 100 | 100 | 100 | 100 | 100 | 100 | 100 | 100 |

1 Excludes those living in rent free accommodation in Northern Ireland.

**Source: General Household Survey, Office for National Statistics; Continuous Household Survey, Northern Ireland Statistics and Research Agency**

The life cycle effect – changes in tenure as people get older – is explored in Table 10.3 which analyses tenure in the United Kingdom by the age of the head of household. In 1995-96 those under 25 were much more likely to be renting than buying whereas for heads of household aged 30 and over it was the other way round. A striking feature is the move out of furnished renting as people progress through their twenties. The proportion of households renting from a local authority/new town or housing association declines as people go through their working lives, with corresponding increases in the proportion of owner-occupiers. Between the ages of 30 and 60 there is a gradual shift out of mortgaging and into outright ownership, but after 60 there is an increase in local authority renting which may be due to people moving into retirement accommodation.

Other aspects of the relationship between personal circumstances and housing tenure in the United Kingdom in 1995-96 are shown in Table 10.4, which categorises households by type. Households made up of two or more unrelated adults or a lone parent were much more likely to rent than those with one adult (whether above or below retirement age). The group most likely to own a property outright was one person under pensionable age households followed by married couple without dependent children households and then those consisting of two or more families.

Housing tenure also varies according to the ethnic group of the head of household (Table 10.5). The ethnic minority groups taken together were as likely as the White group to be owner-occupiers with mortgages in 1995-96 in England, but only half as likely to be outright owners. This is, in part, another reflection of the effect of the life cycle -

**Household composition[1]: by tenure, 1995-96**

**United Kingdom** — Percentages

| | Owned outright | Owned with mortgage | Rented[2] | All tenures[3] |
|---|---|---|---|---|
| **One person** | | | | |
| Under pensionable age | 47 | 6 | 47 | 100 |
| Over pensionable age | 13 | 42 | 45 | 100 |
| **Two or more unrelated adults** | 19 | 21 | 60 | 100 |
| **One family** | | | | |
| Married couple | | | | |
| Without dependent children | 38 | 41 | 21 | 100 |
| With dependent children | 11 | 67 | 22 | 100 |
| Lone parent | 13 | 29 | 57 | 100 |
| **Two or more families** | 33 | 47 | 20 | 100 |
| **All households** | 21 | 50 | 29 | 100 |

1 See Appendix, Part 10: Household type.
2 Includes those renting from a housing association or with a job or business.
3 Includes those living in rent free accomodation.
*Source: General Household Survey, Office for National Statistics; Continuous Household Survey, Northern Ireland Statistics and Research Agency*

# 10.5

**Ethnic group of head of household: by tenure, 1995-96**

**England** — Percentages

| | Owned outright | Owned with mortgage | Rented from social sector | Rented privately | All tenures (=100%) (thousands) |
|---|---|---|---|---|---|
| **Ethnic minority group** | | | | | |
| Black | 8 | 29 | 49 | 15 | 412 |
| Indian | 20 | 60 | 12 | 8 | 281 |
| Pakistani | 19 | 41 | 16 | 24 | 104 |
| Bangladeshi | 12 | 37 | 37 | 14 | 25 |
| Other ethnic minorities | 11 | 40 | 29 | 20 | 245 |
| All ethnic minority groups | 13 | 41 | 31 | 15 | 1,067 |
| **White** | 26 | 42 | 22 | 10 | 18,844 |
| **All ethnic groups[1]** | 25 | 42 | 22 | 10 | 19,918 |

1 Includes ethnic group unknown.
*Source: Survey of English Housing, Department of the Environment*

# 10.6

Dwellings: by region and tenure, 1995[1]

|  | | Rented | | | |
|---|---|---|---|---|---|
|  | Owner-occupied | Local authority/ new town | Housing association | Privately | All tenures[2] (=100%) (thousands) |
| North | 61 | 26 | 4 | 9 | 1,317 |
| Yorkshire & Humberside | 65 | 22 | 3 | 10 | 2,087 |
| East Midlands | 71 | 18 | 3 | 9 | 1,709 |
| East Anglia | 69 | 13 | 5 | 13 | 908 |
| South East | | | | | |
| Greater London | 57 | 22 | 7 | 15 | 2,993 |
| Rest of South East | 74 | 12 | 5 | 10 | 4,510 |
| South West | 72 | 12 | 4 | 12 | 2,048 |
| West Midlands | 68 | 21 | 4 | 8 | 2,145 |
| North West | 68 | 20 | 4 | 8 | 2,653 |
| England | 68 | 18 | 4 | 10 | 20,371 |
| Wales | 72 | 17 | 4 | 7 | 1,228 |
| Scotland | 58 | 31 | 4 | 7 | 2,231 |
| Northern Ireland | 65 | 24 | 2 | 3 | 600 |

Percentages

1 At December.
2 Includes vacant dwellings in Northern Ireland.
*Source: Department of the Environment; Department of the Environment, Northern Ireland*

# 10.7

Type of dwelling: by tenure, 1995-96

**United Kingdom**

Percentages

|  | House or bungalow | | | Flat or maisonette | | | |
|---|---|---|---|---|---|---|---|
|  | Detached | Semi-detached | Terraced | Purpose-built | Con-verted | Other dwellings | All dwellings |
| **Owner-occupied** | | | | | | | |
| Owned outright | 34 | 35 | 23 | 7 | 1 | - | 100 |
| Owned with mortgage | 27 | 36 | 29 | 7 | 2 | - | 100 |
| **Rented** | | | | | | | |
| Local authority/new town | - | 27 | 34 | 37 | 1 | - | 100 |
| Housing association | 1 | 15 | 30 | 45 | 9 | - | 100 |
| Other rented | 16 | 19 | 26 | 16 | 20 | 3 | 100 |
| **All tenures** | 22 | 31 | 28 | 15 | 4 | 1 | 100 |

*Source: General Household Survey, Office for National Statistics; Continuous Household Survey, Northern Ireland Statistics and Research Agency*

ethnic minority householders being, on average, younger than their White counterparts. The greatest contrast, however, is between the ethnic minority groups themselves. For example, Indian households were more than twice as likely to be owner-occupiers than those from the Black group. Comparable information for 1984 shows that, broadly speaking, owner-occupation has increased among ethnic minorities, though not as rapidly as White households.

The general rise in the proportion of households who own their own homes is reflected in all ethnic groups except the Pakistani group. For this group, although the actual number of households who owned their own homes rose by over a third between 1984 and 1995-96, the proportion of owner occupiers has fallen due to the substantial growth in the Pakistani population. In 1984 the proportion in the Pakistani group who were owner-occupiers stood at 77 per cent which was 16 percentage points above the proportion of the White group: around ten years later the proportion had fallen to 60 per cent, which was lower than the White group at 68 per cent.

The regional dimension of tenure is shown in Table 10.6. Greater London and Scotland stand out as areas which had lower proportions of owner-occupiers than other regions in December 1995. In the former case this was balanced by a higher proportion of privately rented accommodation and in the latter by a large social renting sector. The South East excluding Greater London, the South West and Wales had the largest proportions of owner-occupiers.

# 10.8

## Types and condition of housing

There are marked regional variations not only in housing tenure but also in the type of dwelling occupied. For example, in Northern Ireland in 1995-96, 36 per cent of all dwellings were terraced houses and only 8 per cent were flats, whereas in Great Britain the proportions were 28 and 19 per cent respectively. Table 10.7 shows, for the United Kingdom as a whole, how dwelling type varies according to tenure. For example, two thirds of owner-occupiers live in detached or semi-detached houses compared with around a quarter of council tenants and barely one in six of those renting from housing associations. Looked at a different way, over 90 per cent of detached houses and over three-quarters of semi-detached ones, but only 30 per cent of flats, are owner-occupied rather than rented.

Table 10.8 relates the type of property to its date of construction, and encapsulates some very long-run changes in housebuilding preferences. Over half of all purpose built flats and maisonettes in Great Britain in 1995-96 have been built since 1965 and the same applies to detached houses. However, for semi-detached houses the proportion less than 30 years old is only a quarter. Over a third of terraced houses date from before 1919, as do four fifths of converted flats and maisonettes (though of course the conversion is likely to have been much more recent).

In itself the age of a property does not necessarily say much about the standard of accommodation it provides. More relevant indicators of this are overcrowding and its opposite, under-occupancy, both normally measured by a bedroom standard which

### Type of dwelling: by construction date, 1995-96

**Great Britain** Percentages

| | Before 1919 | 1919 -1944 | 1945 -1964 | 1965 or later | All years |
|---|---|---|---|---|---|
| House or bungalow | | | | | |
| Detached | 16 | 14 | 17 | 52 | 100 |
| Semi-detached | 10 | 29 | 33 | 27 | 100 |
| Terraced | 35 | 19 | 19 | 27 | 100 |
| Flat or maisonette | | | | | |
| Purpose built | 12 | 13 | 24 | 51 | 100 |
| Converted | 79 | 16 | 3 | 2 | 100 |
| Other dwellings | 73 | 12 | 6 | 10 | 100 |
| | | | | | |
| All dwellings | 21 | 20 | 23 | 35 | 100 |

*Source: General Household Survey, Office for National Statistics*

compares the number of bedrooms available to a household with a calculation of bedroom requirement based on its size and composition. Table 10.9 shows that, in 1995-96 in the United Kingdom, most households

# 10.9

### Under-occupation[1] and overcrowding[2]: by type of household[3], 1995-96

**United Kingdom** Percentages

| | Under-occupation[1] | Overcrowding[2] |
|---|---|---|
| **One person** | | |
| Under pensionable age | 16 | - |
| Over pensionable age | 13 | 0 |
| | | |
| **Two or more unrelated adults** | 1 | 5 |
| | | |
| **One family** | | |
| Married couple | 68 | 59 |
| Without dependent children | 58 | 8 |
| With dependent children | 10 | 51 |
| Lone parent | 2 | 28 |
| | | |
| **Two or more families** | - | 8 |
| | | |
| **All households** | 100 | 100 |

1 Two or more above bedroom standard. See Appendix, Part 10: Bedroom standard.
2 One or more below bedroom standard. See Appendix, Part 10: Bedroom standard.
3 See Appendix, Part 10: Household type.

*Source: General Household Survey, Office for National Statistics; Continuous Household Survey, Northern Ireland Statistics and Research Agency*

## 10.10

Satisfaction with selected aspects of accommodation, 1994-1995[1]

| England | | | | | Percentages |
|---|---|---|---|---|---|
| | Very satisfied | Fairly satisfied | Neither satisfied nor dissatisfied | Slightly or very dissatisfied | All households |
| Heating | 56 | 27 | 3 | 14 | 100 |
| Insulation and draught-proofing | 38 | 33 | 7 | 23 | 100 |
| Number of rooms | 59 | 27 | 4 | 11 | 100 |
| Size of rooms | 53 | 33 | 3 | 11 | 100 |
| Layout of house or flat | 52 | 35 | 5 | 9 | 100 |
| State of repair | 44 | 36 | 5 | 15 | 100 |
| General appearance | 48 | 38 | 5 | 9 | 100 |
| Overall satisfaction | 57 | 33 | 3 | 8 | 100 |

1 Data are for October 1994 to March 1995 except for overall satisfaction which are 1994-95.
*Source: Survey of English Housing, Department of the Environment*

## 10.11

Housebuilding completions: by sector

**Great Britain**
Thousands

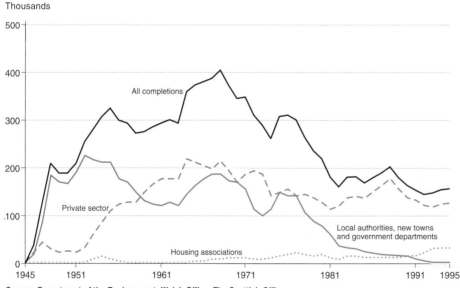

*Source: Department of the Environment; Welsh Office; The Scottish Office*

had, on these criteria, more than enough space. However, over half of households consisting of a married couple with dependent children and three in ten lone parent households were classified as overcrowded. Households without children, and particularly two adult households, were often found in accommodation which was well above the standard: six in ten married couple households without dependent children lived in homes which were considered to be under-occupied.

Though actual overcrowding is rare, there is a progressive relationship between occupation density and people's attitudes to their accommodation. For example, in England in 1994-95, households with less than one and a half rooms per person were almost three times as likely than average to be dissatisfied with the number of rooms. However, as Table 10.10 shows, this was not a major source of discontent. The most common concerns were with insulation and draft-proofing, followed by state of repair (particularly for rented property) and then heating, but in the latter two cases the proportion who were slightly or very dissatisfied was only about 15 per cent. Less than one in ten households were dissatisfied overall, though it needs to be borne in mind that people tend to make positive responses when faced with generalised questions about satisfaction. The types of household showing relatively high levels of dissatisfaction included those whose heads were lone parents or people not working but below retirement age. Flats in general and property built before 1945 also gave rise to some dissatisfaction.

# 10.12

## Housebuilding

Chart 10.11 shows trends in housebuilding in Great Britain back to 1945. In the early post-war years most of the construction was undertaken by local authorities. Private sector housebuilding began to take off in the 1950s and in 1968, when total completions reached an all-time peak, the private and public sectors each completed about 200 thousand dwellings. Since then the public sector's contribution has declined while private sector activity has fluctuated broadly in line with the economic cycle. The bulk of social sector building is now carried out by housing associations.

There are pronounced regional variations in the scale of housebuilding, measured as the number of dwellings completed per thousand population, and in the balance between the private sector and housing associations. In 1995 East Anglia, the East Midlands and Scotland saw most activity in the private sector and Greater London the least (Table 10.12). On the other hand, Scotland and Wales saw most housing association activity in relation to their population. Local authority/new town completions were relatively small by comparison with only 0.2 completions per thousand population in Scotland and fewer elsewhere.

The EU comparison in Chart 10.13 shows that, together with Denmark and Sweden, the United Kingdom had the lowest rate of housebuilding in 1994 at 3.1 per thousand population. Austria, Spain, Portugal, Finland and the Netherlands all had rates well over

### Housebuilding completions: by region and sector, 1995

Rates per 1,000 population

|  | Private sector | Housing association | Local authority/ new town |
|---|---|---|---|
| North | 2.3 | 0.6 | - |
| Yorkshire & Humberside | 2.3 | 0.7 | - |
| East Midlands | 3.4 | 0.6 | 0.1 |
| East Anglia | 3.6 | 0.7 | - |
| South East | 2.4 | 0.7 | - |
|    Greater London | 1.6 | 0.7 | - |
|    Rest of South East | 2.9 | 0.6 | - |
| South West | 2.9 | 0.6 | - |
| West Midlands | 2.4 | 0.5 | - |
| North West | 2.3 | 0.6 | - |
| England | 2.5 | 0.6 | - |
| Wales | 2.3 | 0.8 | 0.1 |
| Scotland | 3.6 | 1.0 | 0.2 |

*Source: Department of the Environment*

# 10.13

### Housebuilding completions: EU comparisons, 1994

Rates per 1,000 population

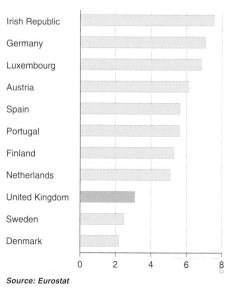

*Source: Eurostat*

# 10.14

Completions of new specialised dwellings for elderly, chronically sick and disabled people

| England & Wales | | | Numbers |
|---|---|---|---|
| | 1981 | 1991 | 1995 |
| **Sheltered housing for elderly people** | | | |
| Private sector | 130 | 1,675 | 408 |
| Housing associations | 1,929 | 1,537 | 785 |
| Local authorities | 5,558 | 1,627 | 90 |
| **Other housing for elderly people** | | | |
| Private sector | 62 | 319 | 37 |
| Housing associations | 261 | 657 | 493 |
| Local authorities | 4,636 | 333 | 82 |
| **Housing for chronically sick and disabled people** | | | |
| Housing associations | 235 | 466 | 670 |
| Local authorities | 4,181 | 352 | 47 |
| **Completions of specialised dwellings as a percentage of all completions** | | | |
| Private sector | 0.2 | 1.4 | 0.3 |
| Housing associations | 14.0 | 15.0 | 5.8 |
| Local authorities | 24.6 | 27.1 | 21.9 |

*Source: Department of the Environment; Welsh Office*

# 10.15

Length of time at current address: by tenure, 1995-96

| Great Britain | | | | | Percentages |
|---|---|---|---|---|---|
| | Under a year | 1-4 years | 5-10 years | Over 10 years | All households |
| **Owner-occupied** | | | | | |
| Owned with mortgage | 7 | 28 | 34 | 31 | 100 |
| Owned outright | 2 | 9 | 15 | 73 | 100 |
| **Rented unfurnished** | | | | | |
| Local authority/new town | 9 | 25 | 23 | 43 | 100 |
| Housing associations | 16 | 38 | 22 | 24 | 100 |
| Privately | 27 | 30 | 11 | 31 | 100 |
| **Rented furnished** | 49 | 41 | 7 | 3 | 100 |
| **Rented with job or business** | 28 | 31 | 20 | 21 | 100 |

*Source: General Household Survey, Office for National Statistics*

half as great again, while those in Luxembourg, Germany and the Irish Republic were more than twice as great as the United Kingdom rate.

Table 10.14 looks at one aspect of housebuilding: that of specialised dwellings for elderly, chronically sick and disabled people. The social sector contribution was proportionately lower in 1995 than 1981 in England and Wales while that of the private sector, having expanded during the 1980s, has since fallen, mirroring the pattern of general housebuilding. However, it should be noted that new housing construction is not the only way of providing suitable accommodation for vulnerable groups. In recent years there has been increasing emphasis on the conversion and adaptation of the existing accommodation of these groups.

## Mobility

Table 10.15 shows that in Great Britain in 1995-96 among outright owner-occupiers, who are predominantly retired people, nearly three quarters had lived in their houses for more than ten years. Other tenure groups were more mobile: owner-occupiers with mortgages and local authority tenants had lived in their accommodation for about seven years and other tenants for about half that. The difference in duration between local authority and housing association lets may reflect not only the types of household provided for but also the fact that the latter sector has been growing at the expense of the former in recent years. Most footloose of all are those renting furnished accommodation, mainly young people, half of whom had been at their

# 10.16

current address for no more than a year, while nine in ten had durations of not more than four years.

Reasons for moving are analysed in Table 10.16 according to the type of tenure to which households had moved. For social sector tenants, family or personal considerations were most likely to have prompted a move, and the desire for a larger or better property was common in all tenure groups. For other tenants, the desire for larger or better accommodation was more likely to have prompted a move than family or personal reasons. Only around one in ten moves were motivated by a desire for a change of neighbourhood. One in twelve of all moves were made because of divorce or separation.

In the 1980s some moves by owner-occupiers may have been prompted by a desire to purchase a property as an investment, in the expectation that further house price increases would create capital gains. Following the house price slump of the late 1980s and early 1990s (examined in more detail in the Housing costs and expenditure section later in this chapter) such returns on investment in housing are now seen as less certain. In the first half of 1996 over half of owner-occupiers surveyed in England thought that house prices would increase in the next twelve months, but by no more than the general rate of inflation, while a further quarter were expecting no increase at all (Table 10.17). However, relatively few anticipated a fall. These perceptions were more optimistic than in 1992, when prices had been falling rapidly for several years (see Chart 10.25) and showed little sign of levelling-off. However, they represented only a marginal

improvement in optimism since such questions were last asked in the period October 1994 to March 1995.

While investment considerations may now loom less large in decisions about the purchase of a main residence, they are still a factor for the relatively small number of

**Main reason for moving[1]: by current tenure, 1995-96**

England — Percentages

| | Owner-occupied | Rented from social sector | Rented privately | All tenures |
|---|---|---|---|---|
| Larger or better house or flat | 28 | 21 | 14 | 22 |
| Family/personal reasons | 10 | 23 | 11 | 14 |
| To move to a better area | 12 | 11 | 10 | 11 |
| Change of job/nearer to job | 10 | 3 | 18 | 11 |
| Wanted smaller or cheaper house or flat | 6 | 9 | 3 | 6 |
| Accommodation no longer available | 1 | 9 | 11 | 6 |
| Divorce or separation | 7 | 8 | 11 | 8 |
| Wanted to buy | 15 | - | - | 6 |
| Marriage or cohabitation | 7 | 3 | 5 | 5 |
| Could not afford mortgage or rent | 1 | 4 | 3 | 2 |
| Other reasons | 4 | 10 | 15 | 9 |
| All households (=100%)(thousands) | 660 | 406 | 565 | 1,631 |

1 Continuing household heads who moved in the year before interview.
*Source: Survey of English Housing, Department of the Environment*

# 10.17

**Owner-occupiers' expectations about changes in house prices compared with inflation over the next year[1]**

England — Percentages

| | 1992 (Feb-May) | 1994-95 (Oct-Mar) | 1996 (Jan-Jun) |
|---|---|---|---|
| Cost will go up faster than inflation | 8 | 13 | 13 |
| Cost will go up the same as inflation | 19 | 24 | 24 |
| Cost will go up less than inflation | 22 | 21 | 28 |
| Cost will stay the same | 30 | 28 | 25 |
| Cost will fall | 10 | 6 | 5 |
| Don't know | 11 | 8 | 6 |
| All owner-occupiers | 100 | 100 | 100 |

1 Respondents were asked:'How do you think that house prices will compare with inflation over the next year?'
*Source: Housing Attitudes Survey and Survey of English Housing, Department of the Environment; Omnibus Survey, Office for National Statistics*

# 10.18

### Reasons for having a second home, 1995-96

| England | Thousands |
|---|---|
| Holiday/retirement/weekend cottage | 65 |
| Investment | 46 |
| Working or living away from home or student | 40 |
| Marital breakdown | 5 |
| Other reasons | 47 |
| All second homes[1] | 185 |

1 Individual figures do not sum to the total because respondents could give more than one reason.

Source: Survey of English Housing, Department of the Environment

# 10.19

### Allocation of local authority housing

United Kingdom

| | 1986-87 | 1990-91 | 1991-92 | 1993-94 | 1994-95 |
|---|---|---|---|---|---|
| **New tenants** (percentages) | | | | | |
| Ordinary waiting list | 65 | 57 | 52 | 57 | 61 |
| Homeless[1] | 22 | 29 | 32 | 30 | 27 |
| Other new towns[2] | 13 | 14 | 17 | 12 | 12 |
| New tenants (=100%)(thousands) | 315.6 | 310.3 | 300.2 | 297.6 | 303.2 |
| **Tenants transferring or exchanging**[3] | | | | | |
| (thousands) | 229.2 | 205.5 | 198.6 | 211.9 | 208.1 |
| **All tenants** (thousands) | 544.9 | 515.7 | 498.8 | 509.6 | 511.2 |

1 See Appendix, Part 10: Homeless households.
2 Data for England include homeless people given new non-secure tenancies.
3 Data for Wales include dwellings let to tenants through the 'tenants exchange scheme'.

Source: Department of the Environment; Welsh Office; The Scottish Office; Department of the Environment, Northern Ireland

households with a second home. It is estimated that there were 185 thousand second homes in England in 1995-96 owned or rented by people whose main residence was also in England – less than 1 per cent of the total housing stock. In a quarter of cases investment was a reason, though not necessarily the only one, for having the property (Table 10.18). Just over a fifth had two homes because they were working or living away from home (including houses and flats occupied by students). However, the most common reason was that the second home was a holiday or retirement home or a weekend cottage.

## Local authority housing

The total number of local authority dwellings allocated each year since 1986-87 in the United Kingdom, at around half a million, is about a tenth of the total local authority stock (Table 10.19). This includes a substantial number of transfers and exchanges: 41 per cent of the total in 1994-95.

A little over a quarter of all new local authority housing tenancies in 1994-95 went to homeless households, which represented a slight reduction from recent years. Local authorities are statutorily obliged to secure suitable accommodation for homeless people who are assessed as being in one or other of various defined categories of 'priority need'. The largest category, making up three fifths of those found accommodation in 1994, consisted of families with young children, while the second largest, with an eighth of the total, was households where one of the members was pregnant. Smaller groups regarded as being in priority need are those households which include people who are vulnerable by virtue of mental illness, age or physical handicap, together accounting for a sixth of the total in 1994.

Local authorities may also, at their discretion, help homeless households not classified as being in priority need. These represent only a small proportion - about one in twenty - of all lettings to homeless households, but they may be assisted in other ways, for example through advice enabling them to find accommodation for themselves.

People become homeless for a variety of reasons. Figures for 1994 relating to England, Wales and Northern Ireland show that about a third of homeless people found accommodation by local authorities were previously living with parents, relatives or friends who became unable or unwilling to go on providing accommodation for them. A further fifth were homeless because a relationship with a partner had broken down and a tenth as a result of court orders following from mortgage default or rent arrears. Other explanations included loss of a privately rented dwelling or a service tenancy.

## 10.20

Within England there were significant regional variations in the distribution of reasons given for homelessness. For example in 1994, leaving parents, relatives or friends accounted for 42 per cent of cases in Greater London but for only 23 per cent in the South West. On the other hand breakdown of a relationship with a partner was responsible for 14 per cent of cases in Greater London but for over 25 per cent in the North, Yorkshire and Humberside and both the East and West Midlands. Mortgage arrears were a common cause in the South East, apart from Greater London, while loss of rented or tied accommodation was a particular problem in the South West.

When a household in difficulties applies to a local authority for housing it must first be assessed as to whether the case is one of homelessness and, if so, whether the applicants are in priority need. If both criteria are satisfied then suitable housing must be found, though not necessarily from the council's own stock: it could be arranged with a housing association or private landlord. Even so local authorities often find it impossible to place homeless people in permanent homes straight away and therefore put them into temporary accommodation of one sort or another including short-term leasing. **Chart 10.20** shows that the use of temporary accommodation in Great Britain increased more than sixfold in the ten years to 1992. However, since 1992 the number of households in temporary accommodation has fallen by a quarter to stand close to 50 thousand at the end of both 1994 and 1995. The use of bed and breakfast accommodation fell particularly steeply between 1991 and 1993.

Since the 'right to buy' legislation was enacted in 1980 the stock of local authority owned dwellings in the United Kingdom has

**Homeless households in temporary accommodation[1]**

**Great Britain**
Thousands

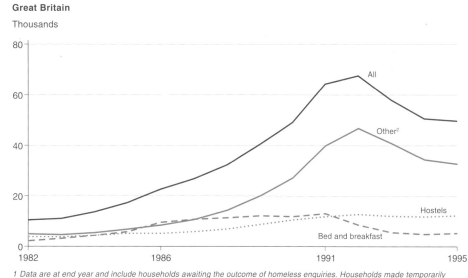

1 Data are at end year and include households awaiting the outcome of homeless enquiries. Households made temporarily homeless through flooding in Wales in 1990 and 1993 are excluded.
2 Includes short-life leasing. Data for Wales from 1987 include those households placed in women's refuges.
*Source: Department of the Environment; Welsh Office; The Scottish Office*

## 10.21

fallen considerably because of sales to sitting tenants and other transfers. Over the 16 year period since then about 2.2 million dwellings have been sold. **Chart 10.21** shows that, after the high level of sales in 1982, there was a further peak in 1989 which, in part, reflected increases in the discounts available. Sales have subsequently been bolstered by a big increase in large scale voluntary transfers whereby, provided tenants vote in favour and the Secretary of State for the Environment (in Scotland, the Secretary of State for Scotland) approves, whole blocks of dwellings can be transferred from local authorities to new landlords, normally non-profit making housing associations. Since 1991 the flow of disposals (sales and block transfers combined) has stabilised at about 100 thousand each year.

**Sales of dwellings owned by local authorities and new towns[1]**

**United Kingdom**
Thousands

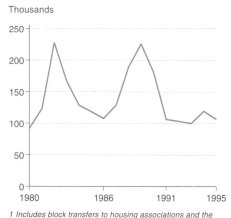

1 Includes block transfers to housing associations and the private sector in Great Britain. Block transfers from new towns to local authorities and from local authorities to housing action trusts are excluded.
*Source: Department of the Environment; Welsh Office; The Scotish Office; Department of the Environment, Northern Ireland*

# 10.22

**Average expenditure on housing[1]: by tenure, 1995-96**

Great Britain           £ per week

| | Owner-occupied | | Rented unfurnished | | | | |
| | Owned outright | Owned with mortgage | Local authority | Housing association | Other | Rented furnished | All tenures[2] |
|---|---|---|---|---|---|---|---|
| Mortgage interest payments | . | 48.14 | . | . | . | . | 20.36 |
| Rent | . | . | 16.19 | 17.94 | 38.40 | 56.78 | 7.97 |
| Council tax | 9.45 | 10.25 | 3.49 | 3.58 | 5.69 | 4.26 | 7.94 |
| Repairs and maintenance | 9.24 | 8.78 | 1.63 | 1.33 | 1.81 | 0.86 | 6.47 |
| Water and sewerage charges | 4.00 | 4.07 | 2.31 | 3.02 | 2.41 | 1.36 | 3.45 |
| Structural insurance | 2.81 | 3.34 | .. | .. | 0.10 | .. | 2.11 |
| Other housing costs | 0.74 | 0.42 | 0.00 | 0.00 | 0.00 | 0.00 | 0.37 |
| All housing expenditure | 26.24 | 75.01 | 23.65 | 25.89 | 48.41 | 63.28 | 48.67 |

1 Net of housing benefit, rebates and allowances received.
2 Includes households living rent free.
*Source: Family Expenditure Survey, Office for National Statistics*

# 10.23

**Expenditure on net rent or mortgage as a percentage of household disposable income: by tenure and income, 1995-96**

Great Britain      Percentages

| | | Rented unfurnished | | | |
| | Owned with mortgage | Local authority | Housing association | Other rented-unfurnished | Rented furnished |
|---|---|---|---|---|---|
| **Disposable income** | | | | | |
| Under £4,000 | .. | 7 | .. | 11 | 29 |
| £4,000 - £7,999 | 25 | 9 | 11 | 16 | 25 |
| £8,000 - £14,999 | 15 | 12 | 14 | 18 | 25 |
| £15,000 - £24,999 | 12 | 10 | 12 | 15 | 20 |
| £25,000 and over | 10 | 7 | 9 | 15 | 16 |
| All income levels | 11 | 10 | 11 | 16 | 20 |

*Source: Family Expenditure Survey, Office for National Statistics*

## Housing costs and expenditure

Households from the different tenure groups face very different levels and structures of housing costs, as Table 10.22 shows for households in Great Britain in 1995-96. Even without counting mortgage interest payments, the average expenditure of owner-occupiers was slightly higher than that of local authority or housing association tenants. They spent more by virtue of higher council tax (reflecting the fact that owner-occupied property is generally more valuable), water and sewerage charges and the inclusion of repairs, maintenance and structural insurance which, in the case of rented property, are generally paid for by the landlord.

When mortgage interest payments are added they increased the average expenditure of those in the process of purchase to about three times that of social sector tenants and outright owners. However, the average mortgage payment is only the central point of a very broad range. Mortgagors who bought their property many years ago are likely to have much smaller payments while for those who have bought

# 10.24

recently, or at the high prices of the late 1980s, the size of the mortgage payment may be much greater. Another noteworthy feature of Table 10.22 is the very high rents of those in furnished properties, which are higher on average than mortgage interest, although tenants of furnished properties have relatively little expenditure on the other elements of housing costs.

The figures in Table 10.22 are net of means-tested benefits, that is housing benefit and income support. The contribution these make towards housing costs is very large. In the case of tenants the average benefit, for those receiving benefit, is around 90 per cent of the average gross rent; rather more for private tenants and rather less for those renting from housing associations. For mortgagors on income support, the average contribution from social security benefits in 1994-95 was about 80 per cent of the average mortgage interest payment (though it should be noted that the eligibility criteria have been tightened since these data were collected). Here and elsewhere all figures for mortgage interest payments are net of tax relief given at source through the MIRAS scheme.

Because of social security benefits the accommodation costs actually paid by low income tenants in Great Britain tend to account for a lower percentage of their household disposable income than they do for those on middle incomes. For higher income households the percentage is lower again because the housing they occupy, though it may be more expensive, is not proportionately so. **Table 10.23** shows this relationship in 1995-96 and also that the pattern is quite different in the cases of owner-occupiers and tenants of furnished accommodation for whom accommodation costs represent a progressively greater burden as income decreases. Taking all

levels of income together the table shows that mortgage holders and social sector tenants each devote about a tenth of their disposable income to accommodation but that the proportion is almost twice as high for those in rented furnished accommodation.

Many changes in the characteristics of mortgages have been seen in recent years in the United Kingdom. These have been accompanied by changes in the market for mortgage finance, some of which are shown in Table 10.24. The main institutional development has been the increasing participation of banks, whose share of total advances increased from 14 per cent in

## Trends in the characteristics of mortgages

**United Kingdom**

| | 1984 | 1989 | 1995 |
|---|---|---|---|
| **Source of mortgages** (percentage of total gross mortgage advances) | | | |
| Building societies | 83 | 70 | 59 |
| Banks[1] | 14 | 27 | 37 |
| **Percentage of first-time buyers** | | | |
| Building societies | 52 | 52 | 53 |
| Banks[1] | 28 | 40 | 40 |
| **Average percentage advance[2]** | | | |
| First time buyers | 85 | 83 | 89 |
| Previous owner-occupiers | 58 | 57 | 65 |
| **Advance to income ratio[2]** | | | |
| First time buyers | 1.93 | 2.16 | 2.23 |
| Previous owner-occupiers | 1.84 | 2.12 | 2.05 |
| **Average mortgage period[2]** (years) | 23 | 24 | 23 |
| **Average age of borrowers[2]** | | | |
| First time buyers (including sitting tenants) | 31 | 34 | 31 |
| Previous owner-occupiers | 36 | 36 | 39 |
| **Basic mortgage interest rate** (annual average rate for largest building societies) | 11.8 | 13.6 | 7.8 |

1 Includes Abbey National from July 1989 and Cheltenham and Gloucester from August 1995.
2 Building societies and Abbey National.
**Source: Department of the Environment**

# 10.25

Average dwelling prices[1]

**United Kingdom**

Index (1990=100)

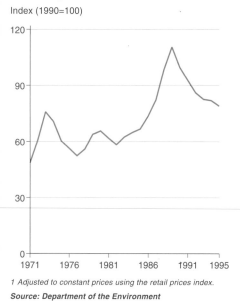

1 Adjusted to constant prices using the retail prices index.

**Source: Department of the Environment**

# 10.26

**Repossession of properties[1]: warrants issued and executed**

**England & Wales**

Thousands

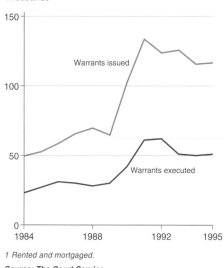

1 Rented and mortgaged.

**Source: The Court Service**

1984 to 37 per cent in 1995, all at the expense of the building societies which have traditionally dominated housing finance. In expanding their business the banks have also broadened their clientele, notably by serving a higher proportion of first-time buyers. The percentage of house price advanced and the ratio of advance to borrower's income have both increased, for first-time borrowers and also for previous owner-occupiers.

The house price slump which started in 1989 is put into its long-term context in Chart 10.25. Averaged over the whole period since 1969 house prices, in the United Kingdom have risen by about 2 percentage points a year faster than the general rate of inflation (10.7 per cent as against 8.6). However, during this period there have been two booms, peaking in 1973 and 1989, when house prices shot up much faster in real terms. The fall-back from the 1989 peak was less steep than after 1973 (25 per cent compared with 31 per cent - both measured over four years) but, unlike the earlier occasion, house prices fell in absolute as well as relative terms. This created the phenomenon of negative equity where houses are worth less than the mortgage debts secured on them. Since 1993 nominal house prices have recovered a little but, until recently, have not kept pace with inflation. As the chart illustrates, house prices have continued to drift downwards between 1993 and 1995.

The fall in house prices after 1989, and emergence of negative equity, prompted a surge in mortgage default causing lenders to seek repossessions of property. In England and Wales this involves an application to the county court by the mortgage lender for a possession order against the borrower. If a possession order is granted, the lender can then ask the court to issue a warrant for

possession which is executed by the bailiff. However, in a typical year less than half of all warrants result in repossession as it often proves possible to agree alternative arrangements between the parties. Chart 10.26 shows that the number of warrants actually executed more than doubled between 1989 and 1991 and, after falling back by 11 thousand in 1993, now appears to have stabilised at about 50 thousand a year. This includes action against tenants as well as owner-occupiers.

Even though the number of repossessions is small in relation to the total stock of dwellings – about 0.2 per cent have been affected each year in the 1990s – the number facing less serious difficulties with their accommodation costs is rather larger. The proportion actually in arrears was about 4 per cent for both mortgagors and private renters in England in the year to March 1996, and around twice as great for local authority and housing association tenants. However, this may be partly because social sector landlords are more tolerant of late payment.

The comparisons between average rent and average mortgage payment shown in Table 10.22 do not indicate the relative costs and benefits of being a tenant as opposed to an owner-occupier. Most obviously this is because, at the end of each year, tenants have nothing to show for their expenditure whereas owner-occupiers are affected by the change which has taken place in the capital value of their property which can either increase or decrease. However, there is more to assessing the net benefits of owner-occupation than just examining house price movements. Interest rates are also relevant, not only for that part of the house purchase financed by borrowing but also for whatever was financed by the owner-occupiers' savings, since interest which

# 10.27

could otherwise have been earned on this capital has been foregone by the owner-occupier. Other factors to be taken into account include the tax treatment of housing finance, the costs of repair, maintenance and buildings insurance (which are faced by the owner-occupier but not usually by the tenant) and the provision for physical depreciation of the property. Taking all these elements into account produces what is known as a 'user cost'. This can be regarded as the owner-occupier's equivalent of rent, but including notional or 'imputed' costs as well as cash outlays. It can be set against what the owner-occupier would actually have to pay for renting similar accommodation. The difference, expressed as a percentage of the property's value, gives a consistent measure of the net benefit each year from being in owner-occupation.

Though the theory of user cost is well established, the estimation of some of its elements is difficult and uncertain so any results should be interpreted with caution. However, **Chart 10.27** shows clearly the general pattern of change over time in the net benefit of owner-occupation. Strictly speaking the figures relate to those owner-occupiers who were first-time buyers in the years shown. During 1972, 1973, 1979 and 1988 those who were first-time buyers enjoyed hugely positive net benefits at these times whereas in some other years, especially 1974, 1981, 1982, 1991 and 1992, these turned into net dis-benefits. Those who held on to their property throughout the last two decades can perhaps regard all this as 'swings and roundabouts' but those who have bought since about 1990 have seen only negative effects, brought about primarily by falling house prices but also by a tax regime progressively less favourable to owner-occupiers.

**Net benefits of owner-occupation[1]**

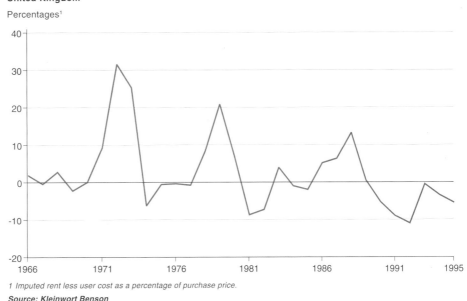

**United Kingdom**
Percentages[1]

1 *Imputed rent less user cost as a percentage of purchase price.*
*Source: Kleinwort Benson*

## References and further reading

The following list contains selected publications relevant to **Chapter 10: Housing**. Those published by The Stationery Office are available from the address shown on the inside back cover of *Social Trends*.

*Changing Households: The British Household Panel Survey*, ESRC Research Centre on Micro-social Change

*Department of the Environment Annual Report*, The Stationery Office

*English House Condition Survey*, The Stationery Office

*Family Spending*, The Stationery Office

Family Resources Survey, The Stationery Office

*Living in Britain*, The Stationery Office

*Housing and Construction Statistics, Great Britain, annual and quarterly*, The Stationery Office

*Housing Finance*, Council of Mortgage Lenders

*Housing in England*, The Stationery Office

*Local Housing Statistics*, The Stationery Office

*Northern Ireland House Condition Survey*, Northern Ireland Housing Executive

*Northern Ireland Housing Statistics*, CSRB

*Our Future Homes*, The Stationery Office

*Private Renting in England*, The Stationery Office

*Private Renting in Five Localities*, The Stationery Office

*Projections of Households in England to 2016*, The Stationery Office

*Regional Trends*, The Stationery Office

*Rent Officer Statistics*, Department of the Environment Statistical Bulletin

*Shared Accommodation in Five Localities*, The Stationery Office

*Social Focus on Women*, The Stationery Office

*Statistical Bulletins on Housing*, The Scottish Office

*Statistics on Housing in the European Community*, Commission of the European Communities

*Welsh House Condition Survey*, Welsh Office

*Welsh Housing Statistics*, Welsh Office

## Contacts

Telephone contact points for further information relating to
**Chapter 10:Housing**

**Office for National Statistics**

| | |
|---|---|
| Chapter author | 0171 533 5776 |
| Family Expenditure Survey | 0171 533 5754 |
| General Household Survey | 0171 533 5444 |
| Omnibus Survey | 0171 533 5310 |
| **Court Service** | 0171 210 1773 |
| **Department of the Environment** | 0171 890 3303 |
| **Department of the Environment, Northern Ireland** | 01232 540808 |
| **Northern Ireland Statistics and Research Agency** | 01232 252 653 |
| **The Scottish Office** | 0131 244 7234 |
| **Welsh Office** | 01222 825087 |
| **Eurostat** | 00352 4335 2251 |

# Chapter 11 Environment

**Environmental concern and conservation**

Around 10 per cent of adults in Great Britain belonged to an environmental organisation or charity in 1996. (Table 11.2)

The number of bottle bank sites in Great Britain has increased rapidly from 17 in 1977 to nearly 13 thousand in 1994. (Chart 11.5)

**Global atmosphere and climate**

Globally, nine out of ten of the hottest years on record have occurred since 1983. (Chart 11.1)

Carbon dioxide emissions in the United Kingdom have fallen since 1991, reflecting the replacement of coal by gas and nuclear energy. (Table 11.11)

**Air quality**

Over the period 1990 to 1994, the South East of England had the highest number of days with 8-hour periods which exceeded World Health Organisation guidelines on ground level ozone concentrations. (Chart 11.14)

**Radioactivity**

Generally, around 5 per cent of the 39 thousand deaths from lung cancer in the United Kingdom each year are attributable to radon gas. (Page 192)

**Water quality**

In 1995 over 90 per cent of the total length of rivers and canals in England and Wales was of 'good' or 'fair' quality. (Table 11.16)

**Natural Resources**

There was an overall decline in reservoir stocks in England and Wales in late 1995, owing to a long period of hot weather and the driest five-month period in over 200 years. (Chart 11.19)

## 11.1

**Global temperature variations[1]**

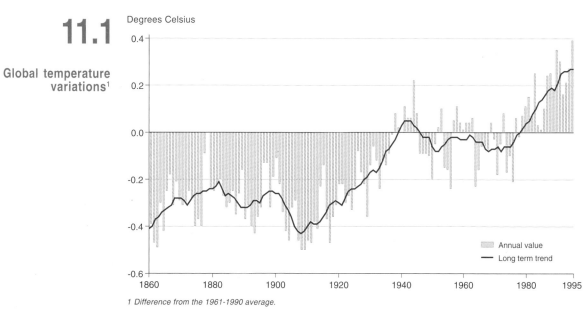

1 Difference from the 1961-1990 average.

**Source: Hadley Centre for Climate Prediction and Research; University of East Anglia**

# 11.2

## Environmental action[1]

**Great Britain**                         Percentages

| | 1988 | 1991 | 1993 | 1996 |
|---|---|---|---|---|
| Given money to or raised money for environmental issues[2] | 28 | 57 | 54 | 51 |
| Used unleaded petrol in car | .. | 35 | 42 | 51 |
| Selected one product over another because of its environmentally friendly packaging, formulation or advertising | 19 | 49 | 44 | 36 |
| Requested information from an organisation dealing with environmental issues[3] | 7 | 15 | 13 | 16 |
| Subscribed to a magazine concerned with environmental issues[3] | 8 | 15 | 13 | 14 |
| Been a member of an environmental group or charity (even if joined more than two years ago) | 6 | 13 | 12 | 10 |

1 Respondents were asked: 'Which, if any, of the following things have you done in the last year or two?'.
2 Wildlife, conservation or Third World charities.
3 Wildlife, conservation, natural resources or Third World.
**Source: Business & the Environment Survey, MORI**

# 11.3

## Public perceptions of future environmental problems[1], 1995

**Great Britain**                         Percentages

| | Definitely true | Probably true | Probably not true | Definitely not true | Can't choose/ not answered |
|---|---|---|---|---|---|
| Traffic congestion | 42 | 45 | 8 | 1 | 5 |
| Traffic noise | 20 | 43 | 27 | 4 | 6 |
| Greenhouse effect | 15 | 46 | 23 | 4 | 12 |
| Oil and gas shortages | 12 | 43 | 25 | 5 | 14 |

1 Respondents were asked how true they thought the following statement was for each problem: 'Within the next twenty years or so, this will be one of the most serious problems for Britain'.
**Source: British Social Attitudes Survey, Social & Community Planning Research**

Over recent years the environment has become an area of increasing interest and concern for government, society and the individual. It affects everyone in one way or another and, unlike many other important issues, ordinary people can make a contribution.

## Environmental concern and conservation

One way of measuring people's concern about environmental matters is by looking at the action they take in response to these issues. Surveys conducted by MORI each year since 1988 found that the proportion of people in Great Britain taking a range of environmental actions increased substantially between 1988 and 1991: for example, the proportion of people who gave or raised money for environmental issues doubled over this period (**Table 11.2**). The proportion of people who selected one product over another because of its environmentally friendly packaging, formulation or advertising saw an even sharper increase over the same period, but has since declined. The use of lead-free petrol is the only action, of those shown in the table, to have increased consistently over the period. The 1996 survey also showed that over seven in ten adults had either taken bottles, glass, paper, cans or other materials to be recycled, or left them for others to collect for recycling, in the previous two years.

Perceptions of future environmental problems vary depending on the type of problem. The British Social Attitudes Survey found that, in 1995, nearly nine in ten people believed that traffic congestion would either definitely or probably be one of the most serious problems for Britain over the next 20 years or so. (Table 11.3) Over three in five believed the same about traffic noise. Further information on attitudes towards transport is given in Table 12.7 in the Transport chapter. The greenhouse effect, whereby increased gases around the Earth trap more of the sun's heat, was also perceived as becoming an increasing problem; around three fifths said that it was definitely or probably true that this would be one of the most serious problems in the future.

Individuals can help protect and improve the environment by participating in recycling schemes run by their local authorities or voluntary organisations. Some of these schemes require householders to take their sorted waste to collection points, which are often at civic amenity sites or shopping centres. The use of recycled materials can help industry to reduce air emissions and lower their energy consumption. Many different ratios are used to measure recycling performance. Following the Department of Environment's practice, the recycling rates shown in Chart 11.4 measure the amount of scrap material used as a percentage of consumption in each year. The recycling rate for glass rose from around 8 per cent in the United Kingdom in 1984 to 28 per cent in 1994; the government target is 58 per cent by the year 2000. Aluminium can recycling rates, in particular, have increased since 1990, from one twentieth to around a quarter in 1994. Around 1.5 billion aluminium cans were collected in 1994.

**Recycling levels: by material**

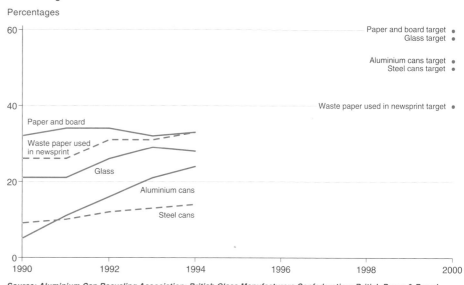

Source: Aluminium Can Recycling Association; British Glass Manufacturers Confederation; British Paper & Board Industry Federation; British Steel; Steel Can Recycling Information Bureau

The number of bottle bank sites in Great Britain has increased rapidly from 17 in 1977 to nearly 13 thousand in 1994 (Chart 11.5). In 1994 over 386 thousand tonnes of glass were collected in bottle banks in local authority, private and voluntary schemes: this accounted for three quarters of all glass collected for recycling during the year. Many charities now raise extra revenue through aluminium can and newspaper recycling. Other charitable organisations, such as Scope and the Salvation Army, also operate textile recycling banks, of which there were about 3 thousand in England and Wales in 1994. In 1995 there were over 100 local authority kerbside collection schemes in operation; this involves the collection of recyclable materials separated by the householder into a dedicated sack or box. By 1997 it is hoped that such schemes will cover half a million homes.

**11.5**

**Sites participating in the bottle bank scheme**

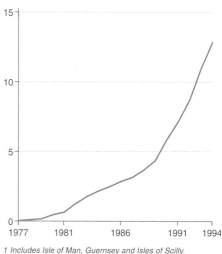

1 Includes Isle of Man, Guernsey and Isles of Scilly.
Source: British Glass Manufacturers Confederation

# 11.6

## Imports of hazardous waste: by country of origin, 1993-94

**England & Wales**
Percentages

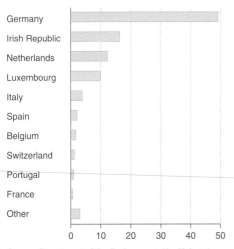

Source: Department of the Environment; Her Majesty's Inspectorate of Pollution

In England and Wales just under 300 kilograms per person of waste was collected in 1991-92. Household waste consists of dustbin collections and waste taken by householders to civic amenity sites; it accounted for around 5 per cent of all waste in 1994 in the United Kingdom. Other types of waste treated and disposed of in the United Kingdom include agricultural waste, sewage sludge, special wastes which contain substances dangerous to life and imported hazardous waste from other countries. Hazardous waste imports into the United Kingdom, under the *Transfrontier Shipment Regulation, 1988* increased by nearly 70 per cent between 1988-89 and 1993-94. Around half of all hazardous waste imported into England and Wales in 1993-94 was from Germany (Chart 11.6), a large part of which was garage wastes such as fuels, oils and greases. Overall, 32 countries exported over 66 thousand tonnes of hazardous waste for disposal in England

and Wales, around three fifths of which were disposed of by incineration. Around 30 per cent of all hazardous waste imported in 1993-94 entered through the port of Dover - twice the amount entering through any other port.

Noise has become a major concern in recent years and around 3.5 thousand complaints per million population about noise from domestic premises were received by Environmental Health officers in England and Wales in 1993-94 (Chart 11.7). This represents over four and a half times the rate in 1981. However, this rise does not necessarily indicate an increase in noise levels but may reflect an increasing tendency for people to complain. Most noise incidents are dealt with informally; just over 1 per cent of confirmed nuisance cases resulted in formal prosecution in 1993-94. People appear more likely to report noise disturbances following the introduction, by some local authorities, of an out-of-hours service to investigate complaints at the time the noise occurs. Recommendations relating to the introduction of a new night noise offence, and the confiscation of noise making equipment, are being taken forward in a Private Member's Bill.

The National Noise Attitude Survey carried out by the Building Research Association in 1991 found that almost three quarters of people who experienced noise from neighbours and other people objected to it. Respondents who objected to noise said that is caused emotional reactions such as annoyance, anger, anxiety and resentment. It was noise from neighbours and children crying, noise from traffic, aircraft and trains which was considered unacceptable by many people.

# 11.7

## Complaints about noise from domestic premises received by Environmental Health Officers

**England & Wales**
Number per thousand population

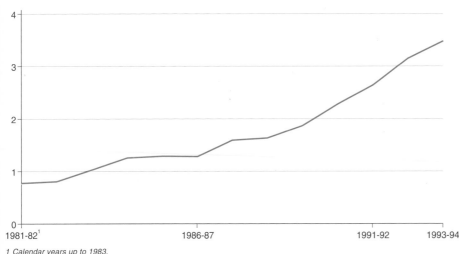

1 Calendar years up to 1983.

Source: Chartered Institute of Environmental Health Officers

## 11.8

Between October 1995 and March 1996 only around a fifth of households in England in considered noise to be a problem in their area (Table 11.8). Of greater concern in the local environment were crime and vandalism or hooliganism. Around a third of respondents said that litter or rubbish caused a problem in their area. However, this proportion varied according to the type of area in which they lived; from over half of those in council estates or low income areas to a fifth of those in affluent suburban and rural areas. In contrast, more than two fifths of households in affluent urban areas experienced a problem with litter or rubbish.

Many people join environmental organisations as a result of concerns about issues such as preservation and protection of land, nature and wildlife. Table 11.2 shows that, in 1996, about 10 per cent of adults in Great Britain belonged to an environmental organisation or charity. Membership of some of these organisations has increased rapidly in recent years. One such organisation, the National Trust, celebrated its centenary year in 1995, when membership was about 2.3 million people and over 11 million people visited its properties in England, Wales and Northern Ireland (Table 11.9). As well as protecting over 200 historic houses, the National Trust works to preserve places of interest and natural beauty. The National Trust has a unique statutory power to prevent land being sold without special parliamentary procedure and owns almost 240 thousand hectares of countryside and about 900 kilometres of coastline. The National Trust for Scotland is a separate charity supported by a membership of over 230 thousand. It is Scotland's leading conservation organisation with 75 thousand hectares of

countryside in its care and over 100 properties visited by around 1.8 million people each year.

Another organisation which has seen a large increase in membership is the Royal Society for the Protection of Birds (RSPB), which works to protect wild birds and their habitats. In 1995 the RSPB managed over 130 nature reserves which helped protect 63 of the 77 most rare or threatened breeding birds in the United Kingdom. Membership of the RSPB increased by about nine times between 1971 and 1995. Around 5 per cent of Britain's lowland wet grassland and inter-tidal areas are managed by the RSPB; these areas provide a refuge for wildfowl and wading birds during winter.

**Local environmental problems[1], 1995-1996[2]**

| England | | | Percentages |
| --- | --- | --- | --- |
| | Serious problem | A problem, but not serious | All problems |
| Crime | 15 | 42 | 57 |
| Vandalism or hooliganism | 8 | 29 | 37 |
| Litter or rubbish | 9 | 26 | 35 |
| Dogs | 9 | 19 | 28 |
| Graffiti | 3 | 15 | 18 |
| Noise | 4 | 14 | 18 |
| Neighbours | 3 | 8 | 11 |
| Racial harassment | 1 | 2 | 3 |

1 Percentage of households which said each problem was a problem in their area.
2 October 1995 to March 1996.

*Source: Survey of English Housing, Department of the Environment*

## 11.9

**Membership of selected voluntary organisations**

| United Kingdom | | | | Thousands |
| --- | --- | --- | --- | --- |
| | 1971 | 1981 | 1991 | 1995 |
| National Trust[1] | 278 | 1,046 | 2,152 | 2,293 |
| Royal Society for the Protection of Birds | 98 | 441 | 852 | 890 |
| Greenpeace | .. | 30 | 408 | 380 |
| Civic Trust[2] | 214 | .. | 222 | 301 |
| Wildlife Trusts[3] | 64 | 142 | 233 | 260 |
| National Trust for Scotland | 37 | 105 | 234 | 230 |
| World Wide Fund for Nature | 12 | 60 | 227 | 219 |
| Woodland Trust | .. | 20 | 150 | 150 |
| Friends of the Earth[1] | 1 | 18 | 111 | 110 |
| Ramblers Association | 22 | 37 | 87 | 109 |
| Council for the Protection of Rural England | 21 | 29 | 45 | 45 |

1 Data are for England, Wales and Northern Ireland only.
2 Members of local amenity societies registered with the Civic Trust at 12 November 1996.
3 Includes The Royal Society for Nature Conservation.

*Source: Organisations concerned*

# 11.10

## Breeding populations of selected birds

**Great Britain**                                                                          Indices (1971=100)

| | Principal breeding season habitat | 1971 | 1981 | 1991 | 1995 | Change between 1971 and 1995 indices |
|---|---|---|---|---|---|---|
| Woodpigeon | Woodland | 100 | 188 | 347 | 379 | +279 |
| Pheasant | Farmland | 100 | 89 | 152 | 187 | +87 |
| Wren | Woodland | 100 | 148 | 105 | 155 | +55 |
| Great tit | Woodland | 100 | 137 | 122 | 137 | +37 |
| Robin | Woodland | 100 | 139 | 100 | 132 | +32 |
| Blue tit | Woodland | 100 | 126 | 132 | 128 | +28 |
| Chaffinch | Woodland | 100 | 125 | 119 | 126 | +26 |
| Blackbird | Woodland | 100 | 93 | 74 | 85 | -15 |
| Starling | Farmland | 100 | 123 | 85 | 71 | -29 |
| Yellowhammer | Farmland | 100 | 113 | 75 | 70 | -30 |
| Dunnock | Woodland | 100 | 95 | 57 | 62 | -38 |
| Song thrush | Woodland | 100 | 76 | 50 | 61 | -39 |
| Skylark | Farmland | 100 | 96 | 51 | 48 | -52 |

*Source: British Trust for Ornithology*

All wild bird species in the United Kingdom are protected by the *Countryside Act 1981*. Breeding populations of some of the most common birds in Great Britain changed between 1971 and 1995. The British Trust for Ornithology's Common Birds Census found that the populations of a number of farmland birds, which include the skylark, yellowhammer and starling, have declined over this period (Table 11.10). Overall, about half of the 46 farmland species have declined in number over the last 20 years or so. Of woodland birds, the woodpigeon saw the largest increase over the same period. Over three fifths of seabird species have also shown an increase in numbers.

## Global atmosphere and climate

Climate change has become an increasingly important issue in recent years. The Intergovernmental Panel on Climate Change, in its 1995 report, stated that 'the balance of evidence now suggests that there is a discernible human influence on global climate'. Globally, nine out of ten of the hottest years on record have occurred since 1983 (Chart 11.1) and studies of this trend show that the increase in temperature is unlikely to be entirely natural in origin. Much of the observed rise in the global sea level over the same period may also be related to the increase in global temperature.

Carbon dioxide is the main greenhouse gas contributing to global warming and, therefore, climate change. In 1994, 149 million tonnes of carbon dioxide were emitted from the United Kingdom, about three fifths of which came from industry and power stations (Table 11.11). Total emissions of carbon dioxide from power stations in the United Kingdom have fallen since 1991, reflecting the replacement of gas and nuclear energy for coal. In contrast, emissions of carbon dioxide from road and other transport increased by more than half between 1980 and 1994. The second most important greenhouse gas, methane, accounted for 3.9 million tonnes of emissions from the United Kingdom in 1994, of which 46 per cent came from landfill sites and 29 per cent from animals. Overall, the United Kingdom contributes about 2 per cent

# 11.11

## Emissions of carbon dioxide: by source

**United Kingdom**                                                            Million tonnes

| | 1971 | 1976 | 1981 | 1986 | 1990 | 1991 | 1994 |
|---|---|---|---|---|---|---|---|
| Industry[1] | 72 | 64 | 52 | 49 | 47 | 47 | 46 |
| Power stations | 56 | 56 | 56 | 54 | 54 | 54 | 44 |
| Transport[2] | 21 | 22 | 23 | 28 | 33 | 32 | 33 |
| Domestic | 25 | 22 | 23 | 25 | 22 | 24 | 23 |
| Other | - | 1 | 3 | 2 | 2 | 2 | 2 |
| All emissions | 173 | 165 | 157 | 157 | 157 | 159 | 149 |

1 Includes commercial and public service, agriculture, refineries and other industry.
2 Includes road and other.

*Source: National Environmental Technology Centre*

# 11.12

towards all global man-made emissions of carbon dioxide and between 1 and 1.5 per cent of total man-made methane emissions.

There is now conclusive evidence that stratospheric ozone depletion is being caused by man-made emissions of substances containing chlorine and bromine. Global production and consumption of ozone depleting substances are controlled through the Montreal Protocol. Timetables for phasing out chlorofluorocarbons, halons and other ozone-depleting substances are being implemented internationally.

## Air quality

There has been concern about the effects of air pollutants on people and ecosystems for many years. For example, it is thought that the increase in the number of people with asthma, particularly young children, may be partly attributable to an increase in vehicle emissions. The Department of Environment funds three national automated networks to monitor air pollution; one urban, one rural and one for hydrocarbons, which give instantaneous measurements of air pollutants at a variety of locations throughout the country. By the end of 1996, the urban network will included almost 90 sites and provided comprehensive coverage on air quality in cities in the United Kingdom. Between 1971 and 1994 emissions of black smoke and sulphur dioxide fell by about half (Chart 11.12). Emissions of sulphur dioxide fell by more than half over the same period, largely as a result of a reduction in the use of coal by power stations. Carbon monoxide emissions peaked in 1989, at 6.5 million tonnes, and then fell by over a quarter between 1989 and 1994. Nitrogen oxide emissions also peaked in 1989 at 2.7 million tonnes and then fell by a fifth between 1989

**Air pollutants: emissions of selected gases**

**United Kingdom**
Million tonnes

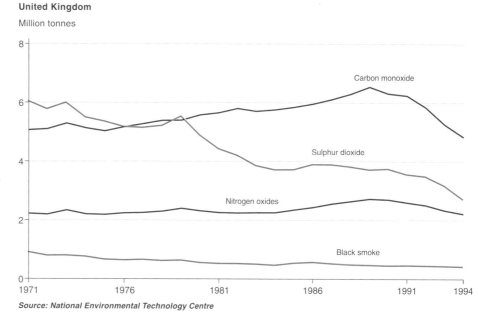

Source: National Environmental Technology Centre

and 1994. The decline in carbon monoxide and nitrogen oxide is due, in part, to more people using diesel cars and the increasing use of catalytic converters in petrol-fuelled cars.

In 1994 road transport accounted for around nine tenths of all carbon monoxide emissions, about three fifths of black smoke and nearly half of nitrogen oxide emissions in the United Kingdom (Table 11.13). Volatile

# 11.13

**Air pollutants: by source, 1994**

**United Kingdom**                                                                                   Percentages

|  | Carbon monoxide | Sulphur dioxide | Nitrogen oxides | Volatile organic compounds | Black smoke |
|---|---|---|---|---|---|
| Road transport | 89 | 2 | 49 | 33 | 58 |
| Electricity supply | - | 65 | 24 | - | 4 |
| Domestic | 6 | 3 | 3 | 2 | 22 |
| Other sources | 5 | 30 | 24 | 65 | 15 |
| All sources (=100%) (million tonnes) | 4.8 | 2.7 | 2.2 | 2.2 | 0.4 |

Source: National Environmental Technology Centre

# 11.14

## Ground level ozone levels, 1990-1994

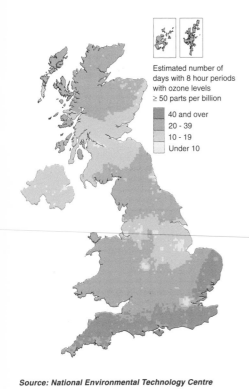

Estimated number of days with 8 hour periods with ozone levels ≥ 50 parts per billion

- 40 and over
- 20 - 39
- 10 - 19
- Under 10

*Source: National Environmental Technology Centre*

# 11.15

## Radon affected areas[1], 1996

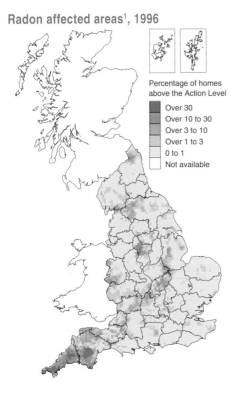

Percentage of homes above the Action Level

- Over 30
- Over 10 to 30
- Over 3 to 10
- Over 1 to 3
- 0 to 1
- Not available

1 Estimated proportion of homes exceeding the Action Level of 200 Bq/m³ in each 5km square.

*Source: National Radiological Protection Board*

organic compounds cover a wide range of chemical compounds, the largest being methane, toluene and butane gas. Apart from methane, most of these originate from petrol combustion or solvent use. As with carbon monoxide, emissions of volatile organic compounds increased during the 1970s and 1980s and then fell during the 1990s with the introduction of catalytic converters in petrol cars and increased use of diesel cars.

One air pollutant which occurs naturally but which can increase as a result of reactions with other pollutants, including nitrogen oxide and volatile organic compounds, is ground level ozone. Concentrations of ground level ozone increase substantially in summer heat waves, when there are long hours of bright sunlight, temperatures above 20 degrees Celsius and little or no wind. Once formed, ground level ozone can persist for several days and may affect people's health and damage plants and crops. In the United Kingdom, the South East had the highest number of days with 8-hour periods in excess of the World Health Organisation guideline of 50 parts per billion between 1990 and 1994 (Chart 11.14). Parts of Kent and East Sussex had more than 50 days above the guideline over this period. In contrast, parts of Greater London, Glasgow and Lincolnshire had less than 10 days exceeding the recommended level.

## Radioactivity

Unlike some forms of air pollution, radiation is mostly undetectable by people. Around 85 per cent of the average total radiation dose to individuals in the United Kingdom comes from natural sources such as radon gas, gamma and cosmic radiation. Radon gas is a naturally occurring radioactive gas which

comes out of the ground, particularly from rocks such as granite, and disperses in the open air. However, concentrations can accumulate in buildings. Generally, around 5 per cent of the 39 thousand deaths from lung cancer each year in the United Kingdom are attributable to radon, the second most important cause of the disease after smoking. Cornwall and Devon are particularly affected by radon, with an estimated 60 thousand dwellings above the Government's recommended Action Level (Chart 11.15). Remedial techniques to reduce radon levels in homes include the installation of an extractor fan under the floor.

Gamma radiation consists of rays emitted from natural radioactive elements within rocks and soil together with a minor amount of radioactive fallout. Overall, gamma accounts for a seventh of all types of exposure to radiation of the United Kingdom population. Radon accounted for about a half.

## Water quality

Water quality can be affected by both climatic conditions and by human activities. Periods of low rainfall, such as the summer of 1995, can lead to a reduction in water quality as there is less water available to dilute waste effluents. However, high rainfall can also adversely affect water quality by causing greater leaching of pollutants from the soil into the water although it can, in turn, have a diluting effect on other sources of pollution.

Since 1990 the chemical quality of rivers and canals has been monitored by a system introduced by the former National Rivers Authority (whose responsibilities have now

# 11.16

passed to the Environment Agency) called the General Quality Assessment scheme. It is estimated that there was an overall improvement of 28 per cent of the total length of rivers and canals in England and Wales between 1990 and 1995. In 1995, over 90 per cent of rivers and canals were of 'good' or 'fair' quality (Table 11.16).

The quality of beaches and bathing waters has been an area of public concern in recent years as these areas can sometimes be affected by discharges from sewerage works, storm sewage overflows and pollutants discharged by ships and boats. The number of bathing waters in the United Kingdom complying with European Union (EU) mandatory coliform standards has increased since 1991, with around nine tenths of bathing waters complying in 1995 compared with three quarters in 1991 (Table 11.17). In 1995 the North West was the only region where less than half of its bathing waters complied with the EU standard. In every other region, more than four fifths of bathing waters complied. In 1987 the Blue Flag award was set up by the Foundation for Environmental Education in Europe in co-operation with the EU. This award is granted to resort bathing beaches that meet the EU Bathing Water Directive and other criteria on facilities, cleanliness and safety. In 1995, all 18 resorts in the United Kingdom which applied for the Blue Flag received this award.

One pollutant that can endanger marine life and damage ecosystems is oil. Oil pollution may be caused by accidental or illegal spillage from ships and offshore installations. The number of oil spills reported in the United Kingdom declined between 1990 and 1994 by around 30 per

## River and canal quality: by region[1], 1995

Percentages

|  | Good | Fair | Poor | Bad |
|---|---|---|---|---|
| Welsh[2] | 91 | 7 | 2 | - |
| South West | 75 | 21 | 3 | - |
| North East | 62 | 24 | 12 | 1 |
| Southern | 56 | 36 | 7 | 1 |
| North West | 54 | 30 | 14 | 2 |
| Thames | 49 | 45 | 6 | - |
| Midlands | 45 | 46 | 8 | 1 |
| Anglian | 39 | 48 | 12 | 1 |
| England & Wales | 60 | 32 | 8 | 1 |

1 National Rivers Authority regions.
2 Regional boundaries are based on river catchment areas.
**Source: The Environment Agency**

# 11.17

## Bathing waters complying with mandatory coliform standards[1]: by coastal region, 1991 and 1995

**United Kingdom**

|  | Identified bathing waters (numbers) | | Percentage complying | |
|---|---|---|---|---|
|  | 1991 | 1995 | 1991 | 1995 |
| United Kingdom | 453 | 464 | 76 | 89 |
| South West | 133 | 134 | 79 | 95 |
| Southern | 67 | 67 | 67 | 93 |
| Welsh | 51 | 56 | 88 | 88 |
| Wessex | 39 | 42 | 92 | 95 |
| Northumbrian | 33 | 34 | 64 | 97 |
| Anglian | 33 | 34 | 88 | 88 |
| North West | 33 | 33 | 30 | 45 |
| Yorkshire | 22 | 22 | 86 | 91 |
| Thames | 3 | 3 | 67 | 100 |
| England & Wales | 414 | 425 | 75 | 89 |
| Scotland | 23 | 23 | 65 | 83 |
| Northern Ireland | 16 | 16 | 100 | 94 |

1 See Appendix, Part 11: Quality of bathing water.
**Source: Department of the Environment; The Scottish Office, Environment Department; Department of the Environment, Northern Ireland**

# 11.18

## Oil spills reported

| United Kingdom | | | | | Numbers |
|---|---|---|---|---|---|
| | 1990 | 1991 | 1992 | 1993 | 1994 |
| Number of incidents | 791 | 705 | 611 | 676 | 540 |
| Spills over 100 gallons[1] | 174 | 143 | 100 | 99 | 99 |
| Spills requiring clean-up | 136 | 169 | 156 | 155 | 123 |
| Costs incurred[2] (£ thousands at 1994 prices)[3] | 1,363 | 317 | 132 | 5,208 | 1,020 |

1 Not directly comparable with 'number of incidents'.
2 1993 includes costs of £4.1 million relating to the 'Braer' tanker incident in the Shetlands.
3 Adjusted to 1994 prices using the retail prices index.
**Source: Advisory Committee on Protection of the Sea**

cent (Table 11.18). Most oil spills are small and do not require a clean-up operation. However two shipping accidents, the Braer in January 1993 and the Sea Empress in February 1996, resulted in oil spillages in excess of 70 thousand tonnes. The clean-up cost of the Braer incident, which occurred in the Shetland Islands, amounted to over £4 million. Oil discharges from offshore oil and gas installations have fallen since the mid 1980s due to reductions in discharges from drill cuttings.

# 11.19

## Reservoir stocks[1]: by month

**England & Wales**

Percentages

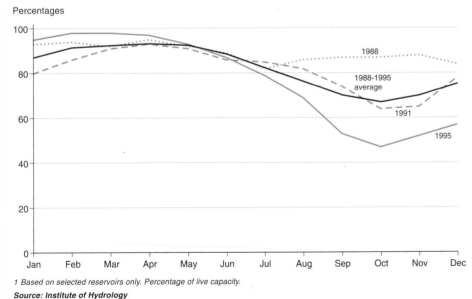

1 Based on selected reservoirs only. Percentage of live capacity.
**Source: Institute of Hydrology**

## Natural resources

Water is one of the most important natural resources at our disposal. One consequence of the unusual climatic conditions over the last decade has been fluctuations in reservoir stocks. Significant stress on water resources occurred in 1989, 1990 and again in 1995 when, following the second wettest winter this century, England and Wales experienced the driest five-month period in over 200 years. This, together with a high demand for water due to the long period of hot weather, resulted in a decline in overall reservoir stocks in 1995, reaching a low of 47 per cent of live capacity in October, despite widespread hosepipe bans (Chart 11.19). Stocks were particularly low in parts of northern England and in West Yorkshire water had to be transported into the region by tanker in order to maintain supplies to some communities.

The levels of fish stocks in the sea are determined by the intensity of fishing and by natural factors such as breeding success and the extent to which species prey on each other. North Sea herring stocks were

## 11.20

seriously affected by over-fishing during the 1970s but closure of the North Sea fishery between 1978 and 1982 meant their stocks recovered. However they have since declined again; the spawning stock biomass (the weight of fish capable of reproducing) of herring in the North Sea fell by a fifth between 1990 and 1994 (Chart 11.20). Most stocks are over-exploited and some are at an historically low level. North Sea cod stocks have been in general decline over the past 25 years and are currently a third of their peak level in the early 1970s. Stocks of Western Atlantic mackerel rose in the 1980s but declined by about 27 per cent between 1991 and 1994.

Since the 1960s two other important products of the waters around the United Kingdom have been oil and gas. By the end of 1995 there were 20 onshore and 78 offshore oil and condensate fields in production with a total output of 130 million tonnes of crude oil and natural gas liquids. There were around 605 million tonnes of proven oil reserves remaining from discovered oilfields in the United Kingdom continental shelf at the end of 1995; these are reserves which have a better than 90 per cent chance of being produced (Table 11.21). By 1995, the total cumulative production from oilfields in the United Kingdom amounted to over 1.9 billion tonnes of oil and nearly 1.1 thousand billion cubic metres of gas. Plans for 16 new oil and 8 new offshore gas fields were approved in 1995.

The production of primary fuels, in oil equivalent terms, has more than doubled over the past 20 years. Around 270 million tonnes of oil equivalent primary fuels were produced in the United Kingdom in 1995 of

North Sea fish stocks and stocks of Western Atlantic mackerel[1]

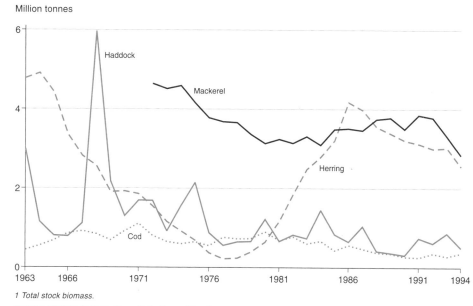

1 Total stock biomass.

Source: Ministry of Agriculture, Fisheries and Food

## 11.21

Oil and gas reserves, 1995

**United Kingdom continental shelf**

| | Oil (million tonnes) | Gas (billion cubic metres) |
|---|---|---|
| Fields already discovered | | |
|    Proven reserves[1] | 605 | 700 |
|    Probable reserves | 765 | 780 |
|    Possible reserves | 520 | 435 |
| Total remaining reserves in present discoveries | 605-1,890 | 700-1,915 |
| Already recovered | 1,916 | 1,052 |
| Estimates of potential future discoveries | 990-4,485 | 395-1,412 |
| Total recoverable reserves | 1,595-6,375 | 1,095-3,327 |
| Potential additional reserves | 130-340 | 140-340 |

1 Excludes volumes of oil and gas already recovered.

Source: Department of Trade and Industry

# 11.22

Production of primary fuels

**United Kingdom**
Million tonnes of oil equivalent

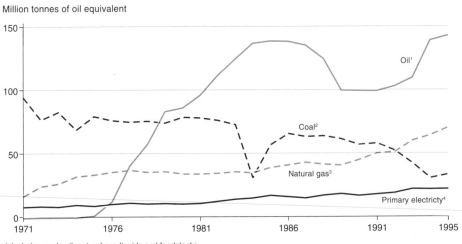

1 Includes crude oil, natural gas liquids and feedstocks.
2 From 1988 includes solid renewables (wood, waste, etc).
3 Includes colliery methane and, from 1988, landfill gas and sewage gas.
4 Nuclear, natural flow hydro-electricity and, from 1988, generation at wind stations.

*Source: Department of Trade and Industry*

# 11.23

Electricity generation: by fuel used, EU comparison, 1994

Percentages

| | Coal and lignite | Nuclear | Hydro, wind and geo-thermal | Natural and der-ived gas | Oil | Biomass and other[1] | All fuels |
|---|---|---|---|---|---|---|---|
| Austria | 7 | 0 | 68 | 16 | 4 | 5 | 100 |
| Belgium | 24 | 56 | 2 | 15 | 2 | 1 | 100 |
| Denmark | 82 | 0 | 3 | 6 | 8 | 2 | 100 |
| France | 4 | 76 | 17 | 1 | 1 | - | 100 |
| Finland | 29 | 30 | 18 | 10 | 3 | 10 | 100 |
| Germany | 55 | 29 | 5 | 9 | 2 | 1 | 100 |
| Greece | 73 | 0 | 7 | - | 20 | 0 | 100 |
| Irish Republic | 50 | 0 | 7 | 26 | 17 | - | 100 |
| Luxembourg | 0 | 0 | 58 | 35 | 1 | 6 | 100 |
| Netherlands | 31 | 5 | - | 58 | 4 | 2 | 100 |
| Italy | 9 | 0 | 22 | 19 | 50 | - | 100 |
| Portugal | 37 | 0 | 34 | - | 26 | 3 | 100 |
| Spain | 38 | 34 | 18 | 3 | 6 | - | 100 |
| Sweden | 2 | 51 | 42 | 1 | 3 | 2 | 100 |
| United Kingdom | 50 | 27 | 2 | 15 | 5 | 1 | 100 |
| EU average | 31 | 35 | 14 | 10 | 9 | 1 | 100 |

1 Wood, wood waste, straw, black liquor, biogas and other organic/non-organic waste fuels.
*Source: Eurostat*

which natural gas production accounted for about a quarter (Chart 11.22). Coal production accounted for 79 per cent of all primary fuel production in 1971; by 1995 it had fallen to 12 per cent. Between 1990 and 1995, industrial fuel prices fell in real terms by around a quarter for gas and coal and about a tenth for electricity. The majority of domestic fuel prices have also fallen in real terms since 1990, although the addition of Value Added Tax (VAT) resulted in increases in 1994 and 1995 for some fuels. Annual average domestic gas prices including VAT were 6 per cent lower in 1995 than in 1990, with electricity 1 per cent higher.

Various sources of energy are used to generate electricity. In 1993, electricity generated using coal contributed to more than a fifth of all greenhouse gas emissions and just under two fifths of acid rain in the United Kingdom. Coal is still the most important fuel for electricity generation in this country; in 1994 it accounted for around half of all electricity generated (Table 11.23).

France generated 76 per cent of its electricity using nuclear power compared with 27 per cent in the United Kingdom. Electricity produced by nuclear power stations results in the emission of far less greenhouse gases, but potential risks such as routine emissions of radioactivity and the problem of waste disposal and radioactive contamination accidents persist. Many EU countries now use environmentally friendly sources of electricity, such as hydro-electricity and wind power; more than two thirds of Austria's electricity was generated by these sources in 1994. Luxembourg imports most of its electricity from power stations in Germany and Belgium.

# 11.24

Agricultural land is a natural resource which may be used for growing different types of crop as well as for grazing purposes. The majority of agricultural land in the United Kingdom is grassland and sole right rough grazing; over 11 million hectares were used for these purposes in 1995 (Table 11.24). In recent years, the amount of agricultural land under crop has declined, mainly as a result of EU Set Aside Schemes established in 1988 to reduce the amount of agricultural land in arable production.

An increasing number of farmers have taken up organic farming methods, which avoid the use of artificial fertilizers and pesticides. By November 1996, there were 906 organic holdings in the United Kingdom with over 49 thousand hectares of registered organic land. However, organic farming accounted for less than 1 per cent of all household food sales in the United Kingdom in 1996. Around two thirds of the organic food market is supplied by imported produce.

### Agricultural land use[1]

| United Kingdom | | | | | Thousand hectares |
|---|---|---|---|---|---|
| | 1961 | 1971 | 1981 | 1991 | 1995 |
| Crop areas | | | | | |
| Wheat | 739 | 1,097 | 1,491 | 1,980 | 1,859 |
| Barley | 1,549 | 2,288 | 2,327 | 1,393 | 1,192 |
| Other cereals (excluding maize) | 768 | 424 | 161 | 127 | 130 |
| Rape grown for oil seed[2] | .. | 5 | 125 | 440 | 354 |
| Sugar beet not for stockfeeding | 173 | 190 | 210 | 196 | 196 |
| Potatoes (early and maincrop) | 285 | 256 | 191 | 176 | 171 |
| Other crops | 761 | 577 | 490 | 644 | 642 |
| All crop areas | 4,276 | 4,838 | 4,995 | 4,956 | 4,544 |
| Bare fallow | 123 | 74 | 76 | 64 | 40 |
| Grasses | 7,999 | 7,240 | 7,013 | 6,846 | 6,696 |
| Sole right rough grazing[3] | 7,359 | 5,550 | 5,021 | 4,685 | 4,516 |
| Woodland | .. | 154 | 277 | 368 | 443 |
| Set-aside[4] | . | . | . | 97 | 633 |
| All other land on agricultural holdings | .. | 131 | 211 | 248 | 286 |
| Common rough grazing | .. | 1,128 | 1,214 | 1,233 | 1,248 |
| All agricultural land[5] | 19,757 | 19,115 | 18,808 | 18,498 | 18,406 |

1 Includes estimates for minor holdings in England, Wales and Northern Ireland for all years and in Scotland prior to 1991.
2 Data are for England and Wales only in 1971 and 1981.
3 Includes common rough grazing in 1961.
4 Data are for England only in 1991.
5 Excludes woodland and all other land on agricultural holdings in 1961.

*Source: Ministry of Agriculture, Fisheries and Food; Welsh Office; The Scottish Office Agriculture and Fisheries Department; Department of Agriculture, Northern Ireland*

## References and further reading

The following list contains selected publications relevant to **Chapter 11:Environment**. Those published by The Stationery Office are available from the addresses shown on the back cover of *Social Trends*.

*Bathing Water Quality in England and Wales 1994*, The Stationery Office

*Biodiversity: The UK Action Plan*, The Stationery Office

*Contaminants Entering the Sea*, The Stationery Office

*Development of the Oil and Gas Resources of the United Kingdom*, Department of Trade & Industry

*Digest of Agricultural Census Statistics*, The Stationery Office

*Digest of Environmental Statistics*, The Stationery Office

*Environmental Digest for Wales*, Welsh Office

*Environment Statistics*, Eurostat (available from The Stationery Office)

*Indicators of Sustainable Development for the United Kingdom*, The Stationery Office

*Making Waste Work*, Department of the Environment

*National Radiological Protection Board Statement on Radon in Homes*, The Stationery Office

*OECD Environmental Data Compendium*, Eurostat

*Organic Farming*, Ministry of Agriculture, Fisheries and Food

*Radon Affected Areas*, The Stationery Office

*Report of the International Council for the Exploration of the Sea's Advisory Committee on Fisheries Management 1995*, ICES

*Scottish Environmental Statistics*, The Scottish Office

*The Energy Report Report, Volume 2: Oil and Gas Resources of the United Kingdom*, The Stationery Office

*The Environment in your Pocket 1996*, Department of the Environment

*The Householder's Guide to Radon*, Department of the Environment

*The UK Environment*, The Stationery Office

*Water Pollution Incidents in England and Wales*, The Stationery Office

*Waterfacts*, Water Services Association

## Contacts

Telephone contact points for further information relating to
**Chapter 11: Environment**

| **Office for National Statistics** | |
|---|---|
| Chapter author | 0171 533 5779 |
| **Department of the Environment** | 0171 276 8422 |
| **Department of Trade and Industry** | 0171 215 5187 |
| **Ministry of Agriculture, Fisheries and Food** | 01904 455100 |
| **Eurostat** | 00 352 4335 2251 |
| **Institute of Hydrology** | 01491 868800 |
| **MORI** | 0171 222 0232 |
| **Social & Community Planning Research** | 0171 250 1866 ext 369 |

# Chapter 12 Transport

## 12.1

### Road traffic[1]

**Great Britain**

Billion vehicle kilometres

1 Excludes two-wheeled traffic.
2 1995-based projections.

*Source: Department of Transport*

# 12.2

## Distance travelled: by mode

| Great Britain | | | | | Billion passenger kilometres |
|---|---|---|---|---|---|
| | 1961 | 1971 | 1981 | 1991 | 1995 |
| **Road** | | | | | |
| Car and van[1] | 157 | 313 | 394 | 584 | 594 |
| Bus and coach | 76 | 60 | 49 | 44 | 43 |
| Pedal cycle | 11 | 4 | 5 | 5 | 5 |
| Motorcycle | 11 | 4 | 10 | 6 | 4 |
| All road | 255 | 381 | 458 | 639 | 646 |
| **Rail[2]** | 39 | 36 | 34 | 38 | 37 |
| **Air[3]** | 1 | 2 | 3 | 5 | 6 |
| **All modes** | 295 | 419 | 495 | 682 | 688 |

1 Includes taxis.
2 Data relate to financial years.
3 Includes Northern Ireland and Channel Islands.
**Source: Department of Transport**

Transport plays a key role in the economy of the country and the lives of its people. During the course of this century there have been some great changes, most notably the growth in car ownership and use, which have had a profound impact on our society and on the environment.

## Overview

The distance people travelled in Great Britain by all modes of transport more than doubled between 1961 and 1990 but since then has fallen slightly to 688 billion passenger kilometres in 1995 (Table 12.2). Almost all of the extra distance covered was by car, van or taxi which accounted for 86 per cent of distance travelled in 1995 compared with only 53 per cent in 1961. While the use of private vehicles has been rising, the use of public transport has been falling. The distance travelled by bus and coach fell by over two fifths between 1961 and 1995. However, the distance travelled

# 12.3

## Journeys[1] per person per year, 1993-1995

| Great Britain | | | | | | | | Percentages |
|---|---|---|---|---|---|---|---|---|
| | Car | Van | Rail[2] | Local bus | Pedal cycle | Walk | Other | All modes (=100%) (numbers) |
| Commuting | 70 | 5 | 6 | 9 | 3 | 4 | 3 | 139 |
| Business | 74 | 17 | 3 | 1 | 1 | 1 | 3 | 34 |
| Education | 41 | 1 | 3 | 26 | 3 | 16 | 11 | 37 |
| Escort education | 85 | 2 | - | 3 | 1 | 9 | 1 | 21 |
| Shopping | 74 | 1 | 1 | 14 | 1 | 7 | 2 | 144 |
| Other personal business | 85 | 2 | 1 | 5 | 1 | 4 | 2 | 138 |
| Social/entertainment | 79 | 2 | 2 | 6 | 1 | 6 | 4 | 185 |
| Holidays/day trips | 79 | 1 | 2 | 3 | 5 | 2 | 7 | 30 |
| Other, including just walk | 10 | - | - | - | - | 88 | 1 | 14 |
| All purposes | 74 | 3 | 2 | 8 | 2 | 7 | 3 | 742 |

1 See Appendix, Part 12: Journey purpose. Excludes journeys under one mile.
2 Includes London Underground.
**Source: National Travel Survey, Department of Transport**

by rail has remained broadly stable while air travel has increased steadily over this period.

Journeys are made for a variety of reasons. Commuting is the most important single purpose for travel, accounting for more mileage travelled than any other journey purpose. It accounted for nearly a fifth of all journeys over one mile made in Great Britain in 1993 to 1995 (Table 12.3). In the last few years commuting journeys have been falling; over this period an average of 139 journeys of over a mile per person each year were to and from work, 15 fewer than in 1989 to 1991. Nearly seven in ten commuters usually travelled by car in 1993-1995, either as a driver or passenger, while only one in ten usually walked to work. Not everyone works of course, though even if the number of journeys over a mile per worker are analysed a similar fall occurs to 316 in 1993-1995 from 328 in 1989-1991. The increased proportion of workers with flexible working arrangements and extra holiday allowances may have contributed to this fall. There was also a fall in the average mileage per person per year on commuting journeys, but this was compensated for by rises in the distances travelled for education, shopping and other personal business and holiday journeys. The increase in escort education mileage was particularly marked, perhaps reflecting concerns for children's safety as well as increased car use.

The average time taken to travel to work in Great Britain has remained stable in recent years at 24 minutes. However, there are wide regional variations in the distance travelled and time taken to get to work. On average, commuters living in Yorkshire and Humberside travelled the shortest distance to work, at just over six miles, while those in the South East, excluding Greater London, commuted the furthest, at just over ten miles

(Table 12.4). However, those in Greater London spent the longest time travelling, at 34 minutes. Those living in the South West, East Anglia and Wales had the shortest commuting time, at 20 minutes. The average for those working in Central London was 56 minutes in 1993-1995, two minutes more than in 1989-1991, while those travelling between London and a workplace in Central London took 48 minutes in 1993-1995.

While greater distances are travelled by car the average distance walked per person each year fell by a fifth between 1975-1976 and 1993-1995, to 321 kilometres a year. This fall was the largest for children aged 5 to 15 where the distance walked per child fell by over a quarter (Chart 12.5). This was heavily influenced by a fall in journeys walked to school for both boys and girls and an increase in car journeys. Although the average distance walked is similar for males and females, at 318 and 324 kilometres a year in 1993-1995 respectively, there are

# 12.4

**Travel[1] to usual place of work: by region of residence, 1993-1995**

|  | Distance travelled (miles) | Time taken (minutes) |
|---|---|---|
| Great Britain | 7.8 | 24 |
| North | 7.1 | 21 |
| Yorkshire & Humberside | 6.1 | 21 |
| East Midlands | 7.0 | 21 |
| East Anglia | 8.9 | 20 |
| South East | 9.2 | 29 |
| Greater London | 7.2 | 34 |
| Rest of South East | 10.4 | 26 |
| South West | 7.6 | 20 |
| West Midlands | 7.6 | 23 |
| North West | 7.0 | 23 |
| England | 8.0 | 24 |
| Wales | 7.1 | 20 |
| Scotland | 7.1 | 22 |

1 Includes journeys under 1 mile.

*Source: National Travel Survey, Department of Transport*

# 12.5

**Average distance walked[1] per person per year: by age, 1975-1976 and 1993-1995**

**Great Britain**
Kilometres per year

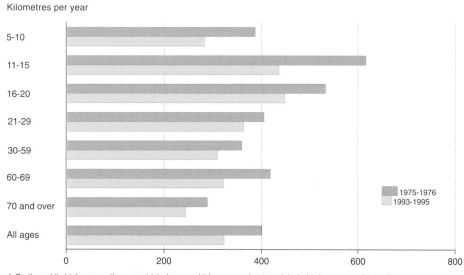

1 On the public highway or other unrestricted areas which are paved or tarred. Includes journeys under 1 mile.
*Source: National Travel Survey, Department of Transport*

# 12.6

Passenger traffic: by mode, EU comparison, 1994

Percentages

| | Car[1] | Bus and coach | Rail[2] | All these modes[2] |
|---|---|---|---|---|
| Great Britain | 88.8 | 6.7 | 4.5 | 100 |
| Belgium | 88.2 | 4.9 | 6.9 | 100 |
| France | 86.5 | 5.7 | 7.8 | 100 |
| Germany | 84.5 | 8.2 | 7.3 | 100 |
| Netherlands | 84.0 | 8.0 | 8.0 | 100 |
| Italy | 82.8 | 10.7 | 6.5 | 100 |
| Sweden | 82.8 | 11.1 | 6.1 | 100 |
| Finland | 82.0 | 13.1 | 4.9 | 100 |
| Portugal | 80.9 | 13.8 | 5.3 | 100 |
| Denmark | 79.7 | 13.5 | 6.8 | 100 |
| Spain | 79.2 | 14.7 | 6.2 | 100 |
| Austria | 74.7 | 15.4 | 9.9 | 100 |

1 Includes taxis.
2 Excludes metro systems.
*Source: Department of Transport*

# 12.7

Attitudes[1] towards transport, 1995

**Great Britain**

Percentages

| | Strongly agree/ agree | Neither agree nor disagree | Disagree/ strongly disagree | Can't choose/ not ans- wered | All respon- dents |
|---|---|---|---|---|---|
| Many more streets in cities and towns should be reserved for pedestrians only | 68 | 16 | 11 | 5 | 100 |
| Cyclists and pedestrians should be given more priority in towns and cities even if this makes things more difficult for other road users | 64 | 16 | 15 | 5 | 100 |
| Buses should be given more priority in towns and cities even if this makes it more difficult for car drivers | 60 | 16 | 18 | 5 | 100 |
| Britain should do more to improve its public transport system even if its road system suffers | 58 | 19 | 16 | 7 | 100 |
| Car drivers still are given too easy a time in Britain's towns and cities | 29 | 26 | 37 | 8 | 100 |
| Local rail services that do not pay for themselves should be closed down | 13 | 17 | 62 | 8 | 100 |
| Local bus services that do not pay for themselves should be closed down | 12 | 16 | 66 | 6 | 100 |

1 Respondents were asked how much they agreed or disagreed with each statement, on a 5-point scale ranging from 'strongly agree' to 'strongly disagree'.
*Source: British Social Attitudes Survey, Social & Community Planning Research*

differences according to age group. Whilst men aged 70 and over and those in the 16 to 20 age group did noticeably more walking than their female counterparts, women aged 21 to 59 did more walking than men. The relatively large number of women who are elderly and generally less active reduced the average for all women considerably. These age and gender differences are also related to car access. Drivers walk fewer miles than non-drivers and, in fact, female drivers walk less than male drivers. Walking continues to dominate short distance journeys of under a mile but despite it being second only to cars for journeys of all lengths, it accounted for only 3 per cent of distance travelled in Great Britain in 1993-1995.

Great Britain had the highest proportion of its passenger traffic travelled by car within the European Union (EU) countries in 1994; Austria had the lowest (Table 12.6). In EU countries the car accounts for the majority, around four fifths, of distance travelled, as is also the case in Switzerland and Norway. By contrast in Japan the car accounted for just over half of distance travelled while rail accounted for over a third. In the United States, where car ownership is very high, passenger traffic by car amounted to 96 per cent of the total distance travelled per person in 1995. Car ownership is also very high in Luxembourg and Italy, at over 500 cars per thousand population compared with Greece which had fewer than 200 cars per thousand population in 1994. However, the largest proportionate increase in the car ownership rate between 1970 and 1994 amongst EU countries was in Greece and Portugal, where the rate rose sevenfold.

With greater car ownership comes heavier car use and, as a consequence, increased traffic pollution. More information about the emissions resulting from road traffic can be found in the Environment chapter. Despite the very high levels of concern about the environmental threats to health raised by traffic pollution, drivers remain attached to their cars to a large extent and few seem to think they can easily find alternative means of getting around. In 1995 the British Social Attitudes Survey asked people in Great Britain about their attitudes towards transport. Nearly three in ten people whose views were sought agreed that 'car drivers still are given too easy a time in Britain's towns and cities' (Table 12.7). However, almost two thirds of people agreed that pedestrians, cyclists, and buses should be given more priority in towns and cities even if it makes things more difficult for other road users.

## Road and rail

Despite the fact that most people would prefer less traffic on our roads, for many the car has become an integral part of life. According to a survey carried out in 1995 by MORI on behalf of Lex Service plc, half of the adult population of Great Britain aged 17 and over said that they drove at least four days a week (Chart 12.8). Nearly seven in ten adults held a driving licence in 1993-1995 compared with five in ten in 1975-1976. Although much of this increase is accounted for by women, men are still more likely than women to hold a licence. The incidence of car licence holding is highest between the ages of 30 and 39 for both genders, but for women it decreases more sharply with age. This is largely because many older women never acquired a licence when younger nor at a later age. Reliance on the car extends to non-drivers. According to the MORI survey non-drivers, particularly those in a household with a car, are reliant on the car for many of their journeys; two thirds of non-drivers travel in a car at least

once a week. Non-drivers and occasional drivers (those who drive less than once a month) were also asked why they did not drive or did not drive more. The predominant reasons given by non-drivers for not driving were never having learnt or because they were driven around by others. Amongst non-drivers ten per cent said they did not drive because of illness or disability.

The proportion of households with regular use of a car increased sharply in the 1960s but has levelled off since the early 1970s (Chart 12.9). However, the proportion of households with regular use of two or more cars continued to rise into the early 1990s, reaching a peak in 1992 when 24 per cent of households in Great Britain had the use of two or more cars. In 1993 this rate fell slightly to 23 per cent and remained at this level in 1994. In Northern Ireland the rate was lower at 20 per cent in 1993-94 and 18

### Frequency of driving a motor vehicle[1], October 1995

**Great Britain**

Percentages

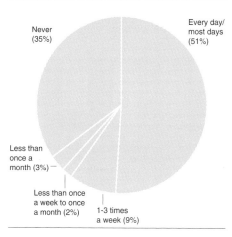

1 By all adults aged 17 and over.
*Source: MORI for Lex Service plc*

12.9

### Households with regular use of a car[1]

**Great Britain**

Percentages

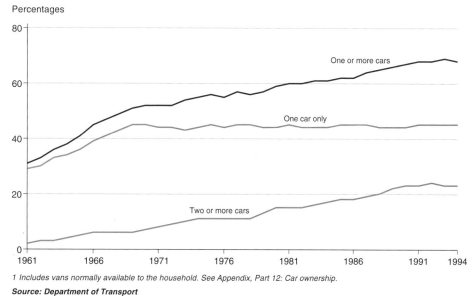

1 Includes vans normally available to the household. See Appendix, Part 12: Car ownership.
*Source: Department of Transport*

# 12.10

### Car occupancy: by journey purpose, 1993-1995

**Great Britain**
Number of people per car

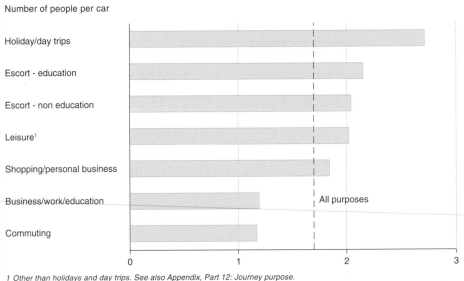

1 Other than holidays and day trips. See also Appendix, Part 12: Journey purpose.
**Source: National Travel Survey, Department of Transport**

# 12.11

### Bus travel[1]

**Great Britain**
Indices (1981=100)

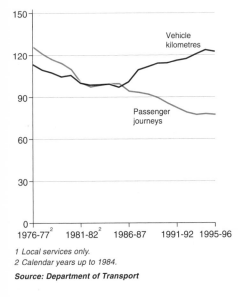

1 Local services only.
2 Calendar years up to 1984.
**Source: Department of Transport**

to 800 billion vehicle kilometres according to upper forecasts. The survey by MORI, mentioned at the beginning of this section, asked people how much of a problem road congestion was in peak times in the area five miles round where they lived. Fifty six per cent of respondents said it was a very bad or a fairly bad problem. The environmental impact of continually rising road traffic levels is high. Road transport accounts for a large share of major pollutants such as carbon monoxide and nitrogen oxides. Measures have been taken to try to reduce vehicle pollutants. The tightening of vehicle emission standards which has taken place since 1992 has been reinforced by stricter limits for in-service testing, introduced in September 1995, and an intensified programme of roadside enforcement to remove the worst offenders from the road. Further information on the source of air pollutants is given in Table 11.12 in the Environment chapter.

per cent in 1994-95. The proportion of households without a car was slightly higher in Northern Ireland at 35 per cent in 1994-95, compared with 32 per cent in Great Britain in 1994.

Road traffic levels have been rising sharply since 1951 and are projected to continue to increase well into the next century as shown in Chart 12.1 at the beginning of this chapter. Levels increased eightfold between 1951 and 1995 to 427 billion vehicle kilometres. The late 80s and early 90s saw a levelling out of road traffic levels probably as a consequence of the economic downturn. By the year 2025 road traffic levels are forecast to rise by 55 per cent to 660 billion vehicle kilometres according to lower forecasts and

Low car occupancy can be viewed as a wasteful use of energy resources. Car occupancy in 1993-1995 averaged 1.70 people per car (Chart 12.10), slightly lower than the figure of 1.75 recorded in 1985-1986. There was a small decline in occupancy rates of all types of journeys, except for holiday and day trips. However, the change in the mix of journey purposes was too small to affect the figures very much. Car commuters had an average occupancy rate of 1.17, while holiday and day-trip journeys averaged 2.71.

After the car, bus travel is the second most common form of road transport. Although the number of passenger journeys made by local bus continues to fall, local bus mileage

# 12.12

increased by 26 per cent between 1985-1986 and 1995-1996 although there was a small decline between 1994-95 and 1995-96 (Chart 12.11). More frequent services using smaller buses may partly explain the increase. Local bus services were deregulated in October 1986 with the aim of promoting competition. Outside London widespread privatisation of public sector bus operations took place from 1986 and the process continued in the 1990s. Within London the operating divisions of London Buses were privatised by the end of 1994. One general effect of the changes was that funding for 'cheap fares' policies pursued in some areas was no longer available, as most services were provided on a purely commercial basis after deregulation.

The average daily flow of vehicles on all types of roads in Great Britain increased by about half between 1981 and 1995 (Table 12.12). Motorways experienced the greatest increase, with flows virtually doubling. Data for Northern Ireland have only been available since 1991. However, between 1991 and 1995 traffic flow on the motorways in Northern Ireland increased by 19 per cent compared with 13 per cent in Great Britain. Motorways continue to carry the highest flows of traffic, with an average daily flow of over 60 thousand vehicles in Great Britain in 1995 and around 28 thousand vehicles in Northern Ireland.

Table 12.13 shows the average traffic speeds recorded at sites where traffic was flowing freely on different classes of road in Great Britain in 1995. Not surprisingly the highest speeds were recorded on motorways, where the vehicles travelling the fastest were cars at an average of 70 miles per hour (mph).

Over half of car drivers exceeded the speed limit on motorways, but only one in ten did so on single carriageway A roads. Buses and coaches, restricted from driving in the outside lane if over seven and a half tonnes, travelled 8 miles an hour slower on average than cars on motorways, averaging 62 mph; just over a tenth exceeded the speed limit. On single carriageway A roads, where the speed limit is ten miles an hour lower for buses and coaches than it is for cars, they travelled on average only four miles an hour slower than cars, averaging 43 mph; over a fifth exceeded the speed limit. According to research carried out by the Transport Research Laboratory speeding accounts for a third of all road accident fatalities.

Lower driving speed is only one contributor to road safety; the condition of road vehicles is another. Although every vehicle over a

**Average daily flow[1] of motor vehicles: by class of road**

| Great Britain | | | Thousands |
|---|---|---|---|
| | 1981 | 1991 | 1995 |
| **Motorways[2]** | 30.6 | 53.9 | 60.9 |
| **Built-up roads** | | | |
| Trunk | 13.6 | 18.5 | 19.2 |
| Principal | 12.3 | 15.2 | 15.0 |
| **Non built-up roads** | | | |
| Trunk | 9.0 | 15.0 | 15.5 |
| Principal | 4.5 | 6.8 | 7.2 |
| **All minor roads** | 1.0 | 1.3 | 1.4 |
| **All roads** | 2.2 | 3.1 | 3.2 |

1 Flow at an average point on each class of road.
2 Includes motorways owned by local authorities.
*Source: Department of Transport*

# 12.13

**Average traffic speeds: by class of road and type of vehicle, 1995**

| Great Britain | | | Miles per hour |
|---|---|---|---|
| | Motorways | Dual carriageways | Single carriageway A roads |
| Cars | 69.6 | 68.4 | 46.7 |
| Buses and coaches | 62.0 | 56.9 | 43.2 |

*Source: Department of Transport*

# 12.14

Reason for failing road vehicle (MOT) tests[1]: by type of vehicle, 1995-96

**Great Britain**                                                                                                 Percentages

|  | Cars | Motor-cycles | Light goods vehicles | Private passenger vehicles[2] |
|---|---|---|---|---|
| Lights | 20 | 12 | 23 | 17 |
| Steering | 17 | 10 | 21 | 16 |
| Brakes | 15 | 9 | 17 | 13 |
| Tyres | 10 | 6 | 9 | 7 |
| Petrol emission | 7 | . | 4 | 5 |
| Diesel emission | 1 | . | 4 | 2 |
| Registration plates and VIN[3] | 2 | - | 2 | 2 |
| Other | 18 | 10 | 20 | 18 |
| Any reason | 37 | 24 | 36 | 33 |

1 The percentage of vehicles in each class failing the test for each of the reasons shown. A vehicle may have more than one fault and consequently the totals of the percentage of separate faults exceed the percentage failed.
2 More than 12 passenger seats.
3 Vehicle identification number.

**Source: Department of Transport**

# 12.15

Goods moved by road and rail[1]

**Great Britain**

Billion tonne kilometres

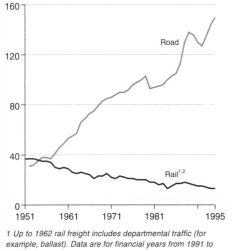

1 Up to 1962 rail freight includes departmental traffic (for example, ballast). Data are for financial years from 1991 to 1994.

**Source: Department of Transport**

certain age has to pass an MOT test each year, many fail. Cars were more likely than any other vehicle to fail their test in 1995-96 (Table 12.14). The reasons for failure vary between types of vehicle, though the highest proportions of all four-wheeled vehicles failed because of the condition of vehicle lights. In an attempt to reduce vehicle pollutants, exhaust emissions testing was introduced to the MOT in November 1991; diesel smoke emissions testing was introduced in January 1993 and re-introduced in February 1994 after being temporarily withdrawn the previous year. The inspection of registration plates and vehicle identification numbers was also added to the MOT test in January 1993. According to a MORI survey carried out in 1996 on behalf of Lex Service plc, 5 per cent of drivers admitted to driving without a valid MOT certificate.

As well as the use of the road system made by private cars and public transport vehicles, it is also used to transport freight. Freight

carried by road in Great Britain has increased fivefold between 1952 and 1995 to 150 billion tonne kilometres (Chart 12.15). The other main methods of moving freight include water, pipeline and rail, though the railway system has declined in importance over the last 40 or so years. In 1954 similar amounts of goods were moved by rail and road. Since then, as road freight has increased, rail freight has decreased to only 9 per cent of the amount of road freight in 1995. There is a considerable difference in average journey length between the two modes of transport. The average journey length by rail was 130 kilometres in Great Britain in 1995-1996 compared with 89 kilometres by road.

The number of passenger journeys by main line rail remained broadly unchanged between 1981-82 and 1995-96 (Table 12.16). Implementation of the government's railway privatisation plans continues. In April 1995 the Special Train Unit of British Rail was sold to Flying Scotsman Railways, who became the first new operator under privatisation. Railtrack - the Government-owned company which owns and manages the railway infrastructure - was sold by stock market flotation in 1996. In addition to main line railways, Great Britain has two underground railway systems - one in London and the other in Glasgow. For much of the time since 1985-86 more journeys have been on the London Underground than on the mainline network although the average distance travelled on the Underground is much shorter than on the mainline system.

Technological changes brought about the switch from steam to diesel and electric traction, and subsequently the construction of the so-called light railway. Tyne & Wear and London Docklands already have such systems. Further developments in light railway technology are evident in the modern trams now operating in Manchester and Sheffield. Although it has proved difficult to identify the precise proportion of Greater Manchester Metrolink passengers who would otherwise be using the car, estimates range from 11 to 22 per cent. A monitoring study commissioned jointly by the Department of Transport and the Greater Manchester Public Transport Executive estimated that, in the morning peak period, the number of trips switched from car to tram amounted to between 4 per cent and 6 per cent of traffic entering Manchester city centre from areas along the Metrolink alignment. However, this makes up less than 2 per cent of all traffic to the city centre in this period.

## 12.16

### Rail journeys[1]: by operator

| Great Britain | | | | | Millions |
|---|---|---|---|---|---|
| | 1981-82 | 1991-92 | 1993-94 | 1994-95 | 1995-96 |
| **Main line/underground** | | | | | |
| London Underground | 541 | 751 | 735 | 764 | 784 |
| British Rail | 719 | 741 | 713 | 702 | 738 |
| Strathclyde PTE[2] | 11 | 14 | 14 | 15 | 14 |
| All main line/underground | 1,270 | 1,505 | 1,463 | 1,481 | 1,536 |
| **Light railways and trams** | | | | | |
| Tyne and Wear PTE[2] | 14 | 41 | 38 | 37 | 36 |
| Docklands Light Railway | . | 8 | 8 | 11 | 14 |
| Greater Manchester Metro | . | . | 11 | 12 | 13 |
| South Yorkshire Supertram | . | . | . | 2 | 5 |
| All light railways and trams | 14 | 49 | 58 | 63 | 68 |
| **All journeys by rail** | 1,284 | 1,554 | 1,520 | 1,543 | 1,605 |

1 Excludes railways operated principally as tourist attractions.
2 Passenger Transport Executive.
**Source: Department of Transport**

## International travel

The number of visits made to the United Kingdom more than doubled between 1981 and 1995 (Table 12.17). An increasing proportion of visitors arrived by air, accounting for 68 per cent of all visits in 1995. Not surprisingly, around six in ten visits to the United Kingdom in 1995 were from elsewhere in the EU, with most visits from France than any other European country. However, the largest number of visits was from North America. Most visits to the United Kingdom are for holidays. However, business was the second most frequent purpose of visits for people from elsewhere in the EU, the rest of Europe and for those visits from other parts of the world. The average length of stay of overseas residents varies for visitors from different countries. Residents of the EU spent on average less time in the United Kingdom than visitors from other parts of the world, at only seven nights per visit in 1995.

## 12.17

### International travel: by mode[1]

| United Kingdom | | | | Millions |
|---|---|---|---|---|
| | 1981 | 1986 | 1991 | 1995 |
| **Visits to the United Kingdom[2]** | | | | |
| Air | 6.9 | 8.9 | 11.6 | 16.2 |
| Sea | 4.6 | 5.0 | 5.5 | 6.0 |
| Channel Tunnel | . | . | . | 1.8 |
| All visits to the United Kingdom | 11.5 | 13.9 | 17.1 | 24.0 |
| **Visits abroad[3]** | | | | |
| Air | 11.4 | 16.4 | 20.4 | 28.6 |
| Sea | 7.7 | 8.6 | 10.4 | 11.3 |
| Channel Tunnel | . | . | . | 1.9 |
| All visits abroad | 19.0 | 24.9 | 30.8 | 41.9 |

1 Mode of travel from, and into, the United Kingdom.
2 By overseas residents.
3 By UK residents.
**Source: International Passenger Survey, Office for National Statistics**

# 12.18

Channel tunnel traffic: by purpose of visit, 1995

| | | Thousands |
|---|---|---|
| | UK residents[1] | Overseas residents[2] |
| Holiday | 1,112 | 995 |
| Business | 409 | 342 |
| Visiting friends and relatives | 186 | 297 |
| Other | 231 | 160 |
| All purposes | 1,937 | 1,794 |

1 UK residents arriving at the United Kingdom.
2 Overseas residents departing from the United Kingdom.
**Source: International Passenger Survey, Office for National Statistics**

# 12.19

Landings and take-offs at airports[1]: by mode

**United Kingdom**
Thousands

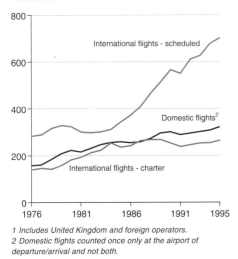

1 Includes United Kingdom and foreign operators.
2 Domestic flights counted once only at the airport of departure/arrival and not both.
**Source: Civil Aviation Authority**

Visits abroad by UK residents also rose over the period 1981 to 1995, and at a faster rate than visits to this country. Much of this increase is due to a rise in the number of holidays. Most people making a holiday visit in 1995 took a package tour when visiting the most popular destinations, namely Spain, Greece, Italy, Portugal, Cyprus and Turkey. Further information on holidays and the most popular destinations is given in Chart 13.26 in the Lifestyles chapter.

In October 1994 a new alternative to air and sea travel began when a limited car carrying service was introduced through the Channel Tunnel. There has been a gradual build up of the services available since then. Scheduled Eurostar services began to Paris and Brussels in November 1994 and Le Shuttle coach operations commenced in June 1995. This was followed by bicycle and full motorcycle services in August and caravan and campervan services in September. In 1995, the first year for which Channel Tunnel traffic data are available from the International Passenger Survey, 1.8 million visits to the United Kingdom were through the Channel Tunnel and so were 1.9 million visits abroad. Table 12.18 shows the number of trips made through the Channel Tunnel in 1995 by destination and purpose of visit. Not surprisingly, almost all UK residents travelling back to the United Kingdom via the Channel Tunnel had been visiting other EU countries; over half had been on holiday and a fifth on business. About three quarters of overseas residents departing from the United Kingdom via the Channel Tunnel were EU residents, but, one in ten was from North America. The

predominant reason for travelling was going on holiday but the second highest reason was business.

In spite of the opening of the Channel Tunnel, the number of international aircraft arrivals and departures at UK airports has continued to increase (Chart 12.19). The number of scheduled international flights has increased every year since 1982 except for 1991 when air transport activity was reduced due to the effects of the conflict in the Gulf. In 1995 scheduled flights accounted for more than half of all landings and take-offs. The number of international charter flights rose by 4 per cent between 1994 and 1995 to reach 265 thousand flights which was still lower than the peak of 268 thousand in 1988 and 1989. Domestic flights increased to 322 thousand in 1995, more than double the number 20 years earlier.

## Transport casualties

The likelihood of being killed or injured while travelling varies according to the type of transport. While road transport generally carries higher risks than other forms of travel, the total number of road accident deaths in Great Britain has fallen from a peak in 1941 although there was a rise in the early 1960s. Fatalities fell by 39 per cent between 1982 and 1995 and the figure of 3.6 thousand road deaths in 1995 was, for the fourth successive year, lower than in any previous year since records began in 1926 (Chart 12.20). Fatalities and serious injuries also fell, by 42 per cent. The total number of casualties, however, has fallen only slightly

**12.20**

in recent years, by 4 per cent between 1981 and 1995, while vehicle kilometres increased by 54 per cent during the same period.

**Chart 12.21** shows that, as would be expected, the number of road accident casualties in the United Kingdom peaks during the weekday morning and evening rush hour periods, though adults and children are affected slightly differently. The morning peak for both adult and child casualties occurs between 8am and 9am. However, in the afternoon, due to the earlier school finishing times, the peak for child casualties occurs slightly earlier than that for adults in winter. In summer however, due to the school holidays, the afternoon peak for child casualties is extended, with the maximum number of casualties between 5pm and 6pm, the same as for adults. At weekends the peak times for both child and adult casualties is between midday and 6pm. Among adult casualties there is also a second lesser peak between 11pm and 1am.

The timing of road accidents is, of course, affected by factors other than simply the number of people on the roads. The consumption of alcohol, for example, increases the risk of being involved in an accident. The numbers failing breath tests begin to rise after 1pm and peak in the evening between 11pm and midnight. Accidents caused by a lack of sleep are also time related. A pilot study by the Sleep Research Laboratory amongst people driving on Midlands' motorways in August 1991 found that sleep related accidents were clustered in three periods of the day:

**Road accident casualties**

**Great Britain**
Indices (1981=100)

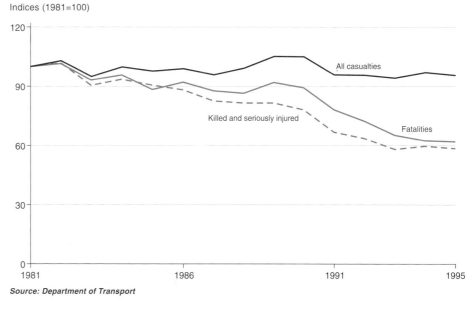

*Source: Department of Transport*

**12.21**

**Road accident casualties on weekdays: by season[1] and hour of day, 1995**

**United Kingdom**
Thousands

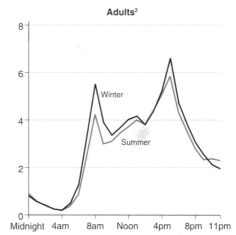

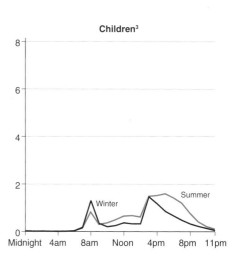

1 See Appendix, Part 12: Road casualties.
2 Aged 16 and over (includes those whose age is unknown).
3 Aged under 16.

*Source: Department of Transport; Royal Ulster Constabulary*

# 12.22

Road deaths[1]: EU comparison, 1971 and 1994

Rate per 100,000 population[2]

| | 1971 | | 1994 | |
|---|---|---|---|---|
| | Adults | Children | Adults | Children |
| Austria | 46.07 | 13.25 | 19.44 | 3.83 |
| Belgium | .. | .. | 19.53 | 3.66 |
| Denmark | 27.71 | 13.87 | 12.12 | 2.70 |
| Finland | 28.82 | 12.52 | 10.74 | 4.02 |
| France | 41.62 | 11.56 | 18.50 | 3.75 |
| Germany | .. | .. | 13.78 | 3.24 |
| Greece[3] | 14.66 | 4.33 | 23.73 | 3.78 |
| Irish Republic | 23.78 | 9.02 | 13.48 | 2.97 |
| Italy | 23.23 | 6.22 | .. | .. |
| Luxembourg | .. | .. | 21.71 | 4.17 |
| Netherlands | 28.46 | 12.57 | 9.62 | 3.30 |
| Portugal[3,4] | 24.43 | 9.95 | 32.45 | 8.84 |
| Spain | .. | .. | 16.23 | 3.55 |
| Sweden | 17.52 | 5.47 | 7.81 | 2.08 |
| United Kingdom | 16.45 | 7.53 | 7.42 | 2.52 |

1 See Appendix, Part 12: Road deaths.
2 Adults aged 15 and over, children aged under 15.
3 Data in 1994 column are for 1993.
4 Data in 1971 column are for 1970.
**Source: Department of Transport**

# 12.23

Household expenditure[1] per head on transport

**United Kingdom** — £ per week at 1990 prices

| | 1971 | 1981 | 1991 | 1995 |
|---|---|---|---|---|
| **Motoring costs** | | | | |
| Motor vehicles and spares | 3.56 | 4.01 | 5.22 | 5.69 |
| Petrol and engine oil | 1.90 | 2.51 | 3.33 | 3.04 |
| Repairs and insurance | 0.99 | 1.45 | 1.88 | 2.26 |
| Vehicle tax | 0.33 | 0.42 | 0.63 | 0.64 |
| Other | 0.38 | 0.71 | 1.91 | 2.05 |
| All motoring expenditure | 7.17 | 9.10 | 12.97 | 13.67 |
| **Fares and other travel costs** | | | | |
| Air | 0.26 | 0.80 | 1.50 | 1.94 |
| Bus and coach fares | 1.36 | 0.95 | 0.78 | 0.73 |
| Rail fares[2] | 0.66 | 0.64 | 0.70 | 0.67 |
| Other | 0.45 | 0.49 | 0.82 | 0.80 |
| All expenditure on transport | 9.89 | 11.98 | 16.77 | 17.81 |

1 See Appendix, Part 6: Household expenditure.
2 Including the Manchester and Sheffield tram systems.
**Source: Office for National Statistics**

midnight to 2am, 4am to 6am (the most likely period) and 2pm to 4pm. According a 1996 survey by MORI, 26 per cent of drivers said they felt themselves dropping off at some time in the last year.

The United Kingdom has one of the lowest road accident death rates per head of population in the EU, a rate of 7.4 per 100 thousand population for adults and a rate of 2.5 for children in 1994 (Table 12.22). The highest rate for road deaths was recorded in Portugal where there were 32.5 deaths per 100 thousand adult population and 8.9 deaths per 100 thousand child population. In fact, between 1971 and 1993-94 road accident death rates fell in all the countries shown in the table, for which data are available, except the rates for adults in Portugal and in Greece, the countries with the largest proportionate increase in the car ownership rate over the period (as discussed in the Overview section of this chapter).

## Resources

Household expenditure per person on transport increased by 80 per cent in real terms between 1971 and 1995, that is after allowing for inflation (Table 12.23). There are marked differences between the various categories of transport expenditure. Expenditure per person on the purchase of motor vehicles (including spares) increased by nearly three fifths over this period and expenditure on air fares increased nearly seven and a half times, while expenditure on bus and coach fares fell by almost half.

Between 1981 and 1996, motoring costs have doubled but this is slightly below the general rate of inflation (Table 12.24). The largest price rises have taken place in

# 12.24

vehicle tax and insurance which trebled between 1981 and 1995 but decreased by 7 per cent in 1996. The fall was mainly due to special offers on motor insurance policies. The component with the largest proportionate price increase between 1995 and 1996 was petrol and oil which rose by 5 per cent. Fares were two and a half times higher in 1996 than in 1981, an increase well above the rate of inflation. This partly reflects the labour-intensive nature of the industries concerned.

Public expenditure on transport in Great Britain in 1995-96 was £9.1 billion (Table 12.25). This represents an increase of 13 per cent in real terms since 1971-72. About a quarter was spent on the national roads system, at around £2.2 billion in 1995-96. This includes construction, reconstruction and re-surfacing of national roads, as well as maintenance of bridges. Expenditure on local roads and car parks (net of car park receipts) fell by 8 per cent in real terms over the same period.

Transport and communication represented 3 per cent of total general government expenditure in 1995 as shown in Table 6.21 in the Expenditure chapter, a decrease since 1981 but an increase compared with 1994. The private sector has been actively encouraged to invest in transport schemes in recent years, on projects such as the Channel Tunnel, the Queen Elizabeth II bridge over the Thames at Dartford, the Skye Bridge and the second Severn Crossing. As part of the Government's Private Finance Initiative, in 1995-96 the Highways Agency awarded eight Design, Build, Finance and Operate projects with a capital value in excess of £500 million, and London Underground negotiated the provision of a new train service on the Northern Line.

## Passenger transport prices[1]

| United Kingdom | | | | | Indices |
|---|---|---|---|---|---|
| | 1981 | 1986 | 1991 | 1995 | 1996 |
| **Motoring costs** | | | | | |
| Vehicle tax and insurance | 100 | 146 | 220 | 320 | 299 |
| Maintenance[2] | 100 | 138 | 195 | 242 | 251 |
| Petrol and oil | 100 | 145 | 156 | 202 | 213 |
| Purchase of vehicles | 100 | 116 | 144 | 161 | 165 |
| All motoring expenditure | 100 | 131 | 163 | 201 | 205 |
| **Fares and other travel costs** | | | | | |
| Rail fares | 100 | 137 | 201 | 246 | 262 |
| Bus and coach fares | 100 | 139 | 198 | 252 | 261 |
| Other[3] | 100 | 107 | 137 | 157 | 156 |
| All fares and other travel costs | 100 | 135 | 186 | 224 | 229 |

1 At January each year based on the retail prices index.
2 Includes spares and accessories and motoring organisation membership fees.
3 Includes licences, car hire and air fares.
*Source: Office for National Statistics*

# 12.25

## Public expenditure on transport in real terms[1]: by type of expenditure

| Great Britain | | | | £ million at 1995-96 prices[1] |
|---|---|---|---|---|
| | 1971-72 | 1981-82 | 1991-92 | 1995-96 |
| **National roads system** | 2,085 | 1,584 | 2,478 | 2,204 |
| **Local transport** | | | | |
| Roads and car parks[2] | 3,835 | 2,941 | 3,410 | 3,510 |
| Public transport[3] | 313 | 1,394 | 567 | 730 |
| Concessionary fares | 46 | 379 | 476 | 480 |
| Ports[4] | . | 31 | 12 | 9 |
| Airports[5] | . | 70 | 7 | 4 |
| All local transport[6] | 4,674 | 5,306 | 4,576 | 4,712 |
| **London Transport** | . | . | 620 | 924 |
| **Railways[7]** | 507 | 2,188 | 1,720 | 524 |
| **Shipping and other ports** | 240 | 211 | 80 | 81 |
| **British Waterways Board** | .. | 54 | 57 | 49 |
| **Aviation** | 233 | 66 | 41 | 43 |
| **Other** | 305 | 279 | 536 | 540 |
| **Total** | 8,044 | 9,689 | 10,109 | 9,080 |

1 Adjusted to 1995-96 prices using the GDP deflator.
2 Net of car park receipts.
3 1971-72 and 1981-82 data include expenditure on London Transport.
4 1971-72 data included in figure for Shipping and other ports.
5 1971-72 data included in figure for Civil Aviation Authority. 1991-92 and 1995-96 data exclude expenditure by public airport companies.
6 1971-72 figure includes administration costs not apportioned in the separate modes. 1991-92 and 1995-96 data include capital receipts and expenditure by public airport companies.
7 Data for 1995-96 not comparable with those for earlier years because of privatisation effects.
*Source: Department of Transport*

## References and further reading

The following list contains selected publications relevant to **Chapter 12: Transport**. Those published by The Stationery Office are available from the addresses shown on the back cover of *Social Trends*.

*British Social Attitudes*, Dartmouth Publishing
*Bus and Coach Statistics, Great Britain*, The Stationery Office
*Consumer Trends*, The Stationery Office
*International Comparisons of Transport Statistics*, The Stationery Office
*International Passenger Transport*, The Stationery Office
*Lex Report on Motoring*, Lex Service plc
*London Area Transport* Survey, London Research Centre; Department of Transport
*National Travel Survey*, The Stationery Office
*New Motor Vehicle Registrations*, Department of Transport
*Quarterly Road Casualties Great Britain*, Department of Transport
*Quarterly Transport Statistics*, Department of Transport
*Road Accidents Great Britain - The Casualty*

*Report*, The Stationery Office
*Road Accidents, Scotland*, Scottish Office
*Road Accidents Statistics English Regions*, The Stationery Office
*Road Accidents: Wales*, Welsh Office
*Road Lengths in Great Britain*, The Stationery Office
*Road Traffic Accident Statistics Annual Report*, The Royal Ulster Constabulary
*Road Traffic Statistics Great Britain*, The Stationery Office
*Scottish Transport Statistics*, Scottish Office
*Traffic in Great Britain - Quarterly Bulletin*, Department of Transport
*Transport of Goods by Road in Great Britain*, The Stationery Office
*Transport Statistics for London*, The Stationery Office
*Transport Statistics Great Britain*, The Stationery Office
*Travel Trends*, The Stationery Office
*UK Airports - Annual Statement of Movements, Passengers and Cargo*, Civil Aviation Authority
*Vehicle Licensing Statistics*, The Stationery Office
*Vehicle Speeds in Great Britain*, Department of Transport
*Welsh Transport Statistics*, Welsh Office

## Contacts

Telephone contact points for further information relating to
**Chapter 12: Transport**

| | |
|---|---|
| **Office for National Statistics** | |
| Chapter author | 0171 533 5776 |
| Consumers' expenditure | 0171 533 5998 |
| Retail prices | 0171 533 5874 |
| **Department of the Environment, Northern Ireland** | 01232 540808 |
| **Department of Transport** | 0171 271 3743 |
| **Royal Ulster Constabulary** | 01232 650222 extn 24135 |
| **Social & Community Planning Research** | 0171 250 1866 extn 369 |

# Chapter 13 Lifestyles

**Time use**
In England and Wales only one in ten males aged 14 to 25 always did the washing up in 1992-1993 compared with three in ten females. (Table 13.3)

**Home-based activities**
People watched an average of over 25 hours of television a week and listened to a little over 16 hours of radio in the United Kingdom in 1995. (Chart 13.6)

Around half of households in the United Kingdom own a pet and in 1995 there were 7.2 million cats and 6.6 million dogs. (Chart 13.14)

**Social and cultural activities**
The most common free-time activity outside the home among adults in Great Britain in 1995-1996 was visiting a public house. (Table 13.15)

Around 70 per cent of UK households had participated in the National Lottery Saturday night draw in the previous two weeks in 1995-1996. (Page 222)

**Sporting activities**
All but 2 per cent of children in England between the ages of 6 and 16 had participated in a sporting activity outside of school lessons in 1994. (Page 223)

**Holidays**
British residents took 59 million holidays of four nights or more in 1995, an increase of 43 per cent on the number taken in 1971. (Chart 13.1)

**Political participation**
Only 4 per cent of adults in Great Britain belonged to a political party in 1995. (Page 227)

## 13.1

**Holidays[1] taken by Great Britain residents: by destination**

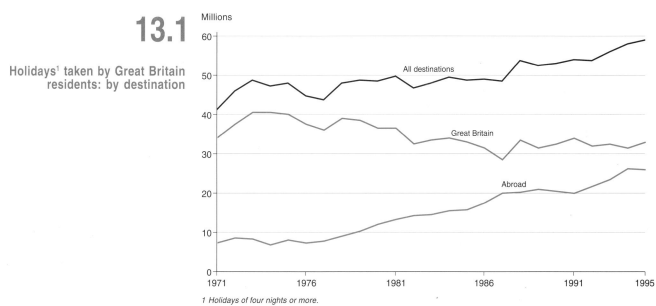

1 Holidays of four nights or more.
*Source: British Tourist Authority*

# 13.2

## Time use: by age, May 1995

| Great Britain | | | | | | Hours |
|---|---|---|---|---|---|---|
| | 15-24 | 25-34 | 35-44 | 45-59 | 60 and over | All aged 15 and over |
| Weekly hours spent on | | | | | | |
| Sleep | 61 | 58 | 60 | 59 | 67 | 62 |
| Free time | 40 | 37 | 33 | 40 | 53 | 42 |
| Paid work[1] | 37 | 30 | 30 | 26 | 4 | 22 |
| Domestic work | 15 | 21 | 24 | 24 | 23 | 22 |
| Personal care | 13 | 19 | 17 | 14 | 16 | 16 |
| Household maintenance | 2 | 3 | 4 | 6 | 6 | 5 |
| Free time per weekday | 5 | 5 | 4 | 5 | 7 | 6 |
| Free time per weekend day | 7 | 7 | 6 | 7 | 8 | 8 |

1 Includes time spent in full-time education.

**Source: ESRC Research Centre on Micro-social Change, from the Omnibus Survey**

# 13.3

## How often young people perform certain household tasks[1]: by gender, 1992-1993[2]

| England & Wales | | | | | | Percentages |
|---|---|---|---|---|---|---|
| | Always | Usually | Some-times | Rarely | Never | Does not apply |
| **Males** | | | | | | |
| Cleaning own room | 42 | 18 | 20 | 10 | 9 | - |
| Making the bed(s) | 34 | 11 | 21 | 15 | 18 | 0 |
| Washing own clothes | 14 | 5 | 14 | 14 | 52 | - |
| Making own meals | 13 | 14 | 44 | 19 | 10 | 0 |
| Household shopping | 11 | 6 | 28 | 20 | 34 | - |
| Washing up | 11 | 15 | 35 | 17 | 21 | - |
| Cleaning rest of house | 8 | 8 | 36 | 22 | 25 | - |
| Looking after younger children | 4 | 8 | 21 | 8 | 32 | 27 |
| Making meals for others in family | 3 | 5 | 26 | 26 | 37 | 3 |
| **Females** | | | | | | |
| Cleaning own room | 64 | 16 | 12 | 5 | 3 | 0 |
| Making the bed(s) | 56 | 13 | 14 | 7 | 9 | 0 |
| Washing own clothes | 38 | 8 | 18 | 10 | 26 | - |
| Making own meals | 30 | 20 | 32 | 11 | 7 | 0 |
| Household shopping | 30 | 11 | 24 | 15 | 20 | - |
| Washing up | 30 | 22 | 30 | 11 | 7 | - |
| Cleaning rest of house | 28 | 16 | 35 | 13 | 8 | - |
| Looking after younger children | 24 | 12 | 19 | 6 | 19 | 20 |
| Making meals for others in family | 22 | 12 | 29 | 20 | 15 | 2 |

1 People aged 14 to 25 were asked how often it was them who did each of the above household tasks.
2 November 1992 to January 1993.

**Source: Youth Lifestyles Survey, Home Office**

This chapter explores some of the many aspects that contribute to people's lifestyles from how long they spend doing certain chores around the home to when they take their holidays.

## Time use

An important indicator of people's lifestyles is the amount of time that they spend on certain activities. Overall, adults spent 22 hours a week in May 1995 in paid work or full-time education in Great Britain and a similar amount on domestic work **(Table 13.2)**. It was those in the 15 to 24 age group who spent the least time doing domestic work, at 15 hours a week. Unsurprisingly, those in the 60 and over age group had the most free time and those in the 35 to 44 group the least.

It appears that the traditional gender roles are filtering down to younger people. The Youth Lifestyle Survey found that while only one in ten young men in England and Wales always did the household shopping, three in ten young women did so **(Table 13.3)**. The same was true for washing up. Also nearly twice as many young women as young men usually, or always, made their own meals. The household tasks most frequently done for both young men and young women were cleaning their own rooms and making the beds; while making meals for others in the family was the task least frequently carried out of those shown in the table.

Women with children spend much more time on average doing household tasks than men. According to the Value of a Mum survey which was carried out for Legal and General in August 1996, mothers spent an average of 62 hours a week doing household chores compared with the 23

# 13.4

hours a week spent on such tasks by fathers (Table 13.4). Many of the household tasks shown in the table are not undertaken in isolation, as parents will often be looking after their children at the same time. Interestingly, whilst the ages of children affects the amount of time that mothers spend on household tasks, it makes little difference to fathers. Mothers with a child aged two spent around 85 hours a week on household tasks. However, for those with 18 year old children mothers only spent around 33 hours a week on such tasks. Mothers who also worked outside the home still spent more time on the household tasks than they spent in their paid place of work, at over 53 hours a week on average.

The survey also asked parents about their attitudes to family life. Over half of parents said that they did not spend as much time together as a family as they would like to; paid employment was given as the main reason for this.

## Home-based activities

Watching television is still the nation's most common home-based leisure activity for both men and women in Great Britain, with virtually everyone watching (Table 13.5). However, for other home-based activities there is quite a difference in participation rates between the genders. For example, while 38 per cent of women in Great Britain participated in dressmaking/needlework/ knitting in the four weeks before interview in 1993-94, only 3 per cent of men did so. Another home-based activity where there is a large difference between men and women is DIY: 57 per cent of men participated compared with 30 per cent of women, although women were more likely to do DIY in 1993-94 than in 1977. Indeed,

participation in most of the activities shown in the table has increased since 1977, with the exception of dressmaking/needlework/ knitting.

Participation in home-based activities varies by age as well as gender. While for some activities such as listening to records and tapes or visiting friends or relations participation decreases with age, participation in others such as gardening, generally increases, although it too falls among those aged 70 and over. In general, participation rates are higher for those in the non-manual occupations than those in manual occupations. While the participation

## Hours spent on household tasks by parents[1]: by gender, August 1996

| United Kingdom | Hours and minutes per week | |
|---|---|---|
| | Fathers | Mothers |
| Cooking/preparing meals | 2:50 | 13:30 |
| Cleaning | 2:00 | 13:15 |
| Washing and ironing clothes | 0:55 | 9:05 |
| Spending time just with the children | 5:05 | 8:45 |
| Shopping | 2:50 | 5:50 |
| Washing up | 2:00 | 3:40 |
| Driving children to school | 1:45 | 2:55 |
| Gardening | 3:00 | 2:00 |
| Sewing/mending clothes | 0:10 | 1:20 |
| Other household tasks | 2:25 | 1:40 |
| All household tasks | 23:00 | 62:00 |

1 Adults with children aged 18 and under.

**Source: Research Services Limited for Legal & General**

# 13.5

## Participation[1] in home-based leisure activities: by gender

| Great Britain | | | | | Percentages |
|---|---|---|---|---|---|
| | 1977 | 1980 | 1986 | 1990-91 | 1993-94 |
| **Males** | | | | | |
| Watching TV | 97 | 97 | 98 | 99 | 99 |
| Visiting/entertaining friends or relations | 89 | 90 | 92 | 95 | 95 |
| Listening to radio | 87 | 88 | 87 | 91 | 91 |
| Listening to records/tapes | 64 | 66 | 69 | 78 | 79 |
| Reading books | 52 | 52 | 52 | 56 | 59 |
| DIY | 51 | 53 | 54 | 58 | 57 |
| Gardening | 49 | 49 | 47 | 52 | 51 |
| Dressmaking/needlework/ knitting | 2 | 2 | 3 | 3 | 3 |
| **Females** | | | | | |
| Watching TV | 97 | 98 | 98 | 99 | 99 |
| Visiting/entertaining friends or relations | 93 | 93 | 95 | 97 | 96 |
| Listening to radio | 87 | 88 | 85 | 87 | 88 |
| Listening to records/tapes | 60 | 62 | 65 | 74 | 75 |
| Reading books | 57 | 61 | 64 | 68 | 71 |
| DIY | 22 | 23 | 27 | 29 | 30 |
| Gardening | 35 | 38 | 39 | 44 | 45 |
| Dressmaking/needlework/ knitting | 51 | 51 | 48 | 41 | 38 |

1 Percentage of those aged 16 and over participating in each activity in the four weeks before interview.

**Source: General Household Survey, Office for National Statistics**

# 13.6

Television viewing and radio listening: by region[1], 1995

Hours per week

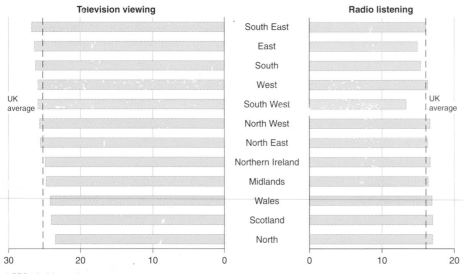

1 BBC television regions.

*Source: Broadcasters' Audience Research Board; British Broadcasting Corporation; AGB Ltd; RSMB Ltd*

# 13.7

Television viewing: by gender and age, 1995

| United Kingdom | Hours and minutes per week | |
| --- | --- | --- |
| | Males | Females |
| 4-15 | 18:51 | 17:14 |
| 16-24 | 18:03 | 20:16 |
| 25-34 | 22:16 | 25:54 |
| 35-44 | 22:51 | 25:10 |
| 45-54 | 24:11 | 26:22 |
| 55-64 | 28:02 | 31:23 |
| 65 and over | 34:29 | 36:42 |
| | | |
| All aged 4 and over | 23:45 | 26:25 |
| | | |
| Reach[1] (percentages) | | |
| Daily | *81* | *83* |
| Weekly | *96* | *96* |

1 Percentage of the population aged 4 and over who viewed TV for at least three consecutive minutes.

*Source: Broadcasters' Audience Research Board; British Broadcasting Corporation; AGB Limited; RSMB Limited*

rates were generally lower for home-based activities in Northern Ireland than Great Britain, the differences in participation between the genders was similar. For example 59 per cent of men and 60 per cent of women listened to records or tapes in the four weeks prior to being interviewed for the Continuous Household Survey in 1993-94, compared with 79 per cent of men and 75 per cent of women in Great Britain.

People watched an average of over 25 hours of television a week and listened to a little over 16 hours of radio in the United Kingdom in 1995, but this varies in different regions. **Chart 13.6** shows that those in the South East BBC television region watched the least at an average of 23.5 hours a week while those in the North watched the most at just under 27 hours. However, those in the

South East and the East listened to the most radio at 17 hours a week while those in Northern Ireland listened to just under 13.5 hours, the least in the United Kingdom. Television viewing and radio listening reach their peak audiences at different times of the day. The largest television audiences are in the evening, between around 6pm and 10.30pm, whilst for radio the largest audience tunes in around breakfast time.

On average females watched more television than males in the United Kingdom in 1995 and this was the case for all age the groups shown in **Table 13.7** except for the youngest (4 to 15 year olds). Those in the older age groups watched the most television. Drama remains the most commonly watched type of programme, accounting for just over a quarter of people's weekly viewing. Light entertainment and films are the next most commonly watched.

In recent years, television viewers' choice of channels has increased with satellite and cable television companies providing many alternatives to the four main terrestrial channels. When asked in the 1995 British Social Attitudes Survey, over one in five people said that they had a satellite dish or were connected to a cable network. A fifth terrestrial television channel should be added in 1997, which will increase the choice of channels for those viewers without satellite or cable.

In 1995-96 nearly eight out of ten households in Great Britain had a video recorder (see Table 6.10 in the Expenditure chapter). This means that these households are able to widen further the choice of what they see on their television screen. In

## 13.8

addition to time shift video recording (where a television programme is recorded to be viewed later) people can watch hired or bought pre-recorded videos. Of those that were bought, feature films were the most commonly purchased in the United Kingdom (Chart 13.8). The most popular bought video in 1995 was The Lion King. Action/adventure was the most common type of feature film purchased, followed by comedy and drama/thrillers. The most popular video rental of 1995 was Forrest Gump.

It is interesting to compare how the rental and retail video markets have displayed different patterns over time. In 1982 the rental sector was worth around £200 million and this rose steadily to a peak of around £570 million in 1989. However, it then went into decline and was worth less than £440 million in 1994, although it has showed signs of improvement in 1995. The retail sector on the other hand has risen from £15 million in 1985 to nearly £790 million ten years later.

Watching a rented video remains a popular social activity with the average audience for a rented video being three people. The watching of hired videos is most common at the weekend: nearly 60 per cent of rented videos were viewed between Friday and Sunday and the most common time for viewing was between 8pm and 10.30pm.

The rise in sales of CDs in recent years showed no sign of slowing down in 1995 when nearly 140 million were sold (Chart 13.9). Sales of singles rose for the third successive year, reaching nearly 71 million, following a steady fall from the late 1970s. LP sales fell still further in 1995,

representing less than 2 per cent of all album sales. The top selling album in 1995 was 'Robson & Jerome' by Robson Green and Jerome Flynn, with Oasis and Celine Dion in second and third places respectively.

Among those aged 16 and over, albums and singles are bought by roughly equal proportions of men and women, but women are likely than men to purchase music videos. Those in social groups AB and C1 bought proportionately more music than the other groups in 1995 - an indication of their greater disposable income.

An area of concern to the music industry is that of piracy. The British Phonographic Industry estimated that in 1995 illegal sales

### Pre-recorded video sales: by type, 1995

**United Kingdom**
Percentages

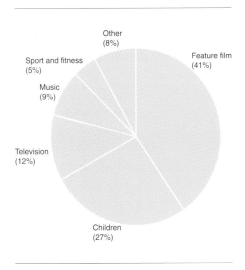

*Source: British Video Association*

## 13.9

### Sales[1] of CDs, LPs, cassettes, and singles[2]

**United Kingdom**
Millions

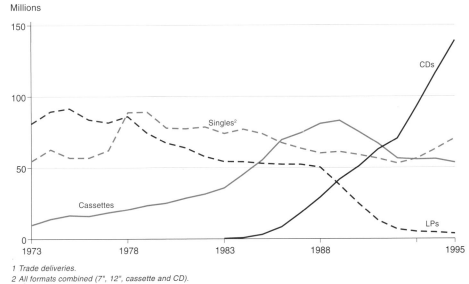

1 Trade deliveries.
2 All formats combined (7", 12", cassette and CD).
*Source: British Phonographic Industry*

# 13.10

### Reading of national daily newspapers: by gender

**Great Britain**                                                                            Percentages

|  | Males | | | | Females | | | |
|---|---|---|---|---|---|---|---|---|
|  | 1971 | 1981 | 1991 | 1995[1] | 1971 | 1981 | 1991 | 1995[1] |
| The Sun | 26 | 31 | 25 | 26 | 15 | 23 | 19 | 19 |
| Daily Mirror | 38 | 27 | 20 | 16 | 29 | 22 | 15 | 13 |
| Daily Mail | 13 | 13 | 10 | 11 | 10 | 11 | 9 | 10 |
| Daily Express | 28 | 16 | 8 | 7 | 20 | 13 | 8 | 6 |
| The Daily Telegraph | 10 | 9 | 6 | 6 | 7 | 7 | 5 | 5 |
| Daily Star | . | 13 | 8 | 6 | . | 8 | 4 | 3 |
| The Times | 3 | 3 | 3 | 4 | 2 | 2 | 2 | 3 |
| The Guardian | 3 | 4 | 3 | 3 | 2 | 2 | 2 | 2 |
| The Independent | . | . | 3 | 2 | . | . | 2 | 1 |
| Financial Times | 3 | 2 | 2 | 2 | 1 | 1 | 1 | 1 |
| Any national daily newspaper[2] | .. | 76 | 66 | 62 | .. | 68 | 57 | 54 |

1 July 1995 to June 1996; earlier years are calendar years.
2 Includes the above newspapers plus the Daily Record, Sporting Life and Racing Post.
*Source: National Readership Surveys Limited*

# 13.11

### Reading of the most popular magazines: by age and gender, 1995-1996[1]

**Great Britain**                                                                            Percentages

|  | 15-24 | 25-44 | 45-64 | 65 and over | Males | Females | All aged 15 and over |
|---|---|---|---|---|---|---|---|
| Reader's Digest | 6 | 10 | 16 | 15 | 12 | 12 | 12 |
| Take a Break | 15 | 13 | 9 | 7 | 5 | 16 | 11 |
| Radio Times | 11 | 9 | 11 | 10 | 10 | 10 | 10 |
| AA Magazine | 4 | 10 | 13 | 8 | 12 | 8 | 10 |
| M & S Magazine | 5 | 10 | 12 | 6 | 5 | 13 | 9 |
| TV Times | 11 | 8 | 9 | 8 | 8 | 9 | 8 |
| Woman's Own | 11 | 9 | 8 | 6 | 2 | 14 | 8 |
| What's on TV | 13 | 10 | 6 | 5 | 7 | 10 | 8 |
| Bella | 7 | 9 | 7 | 6 | 3 | 12 | 8 |
| Viz | 15 | 8 | 1 | - | 8 | 3 | 5 |

1 July 1995 to June 1996.
*Source: National Readership Surveys Limited*

of bootleg, counterfeit and pirate recordings amounted to around £24.5 million. This figure represents a decrease of over a third on the previous year as a result of efforts by the British Phonographic Industry's Anti-Piracy Unit in co-operation with police and trading standards officers.

Well over half of people aged 15 and over read a national daily newspaper in Great Britain in the year to June 1996, though the proportion was lower than the proportion who did so in 1981 (Table 13.10). While The Sun has consistently been the most popular paper in recent years, in 1971 the Daily Mirror was the most popular. The Daily Express has also seen a decline in the proportion of people who read it. In 1971, 28 per cent of males and 20 per cent of females read it while in 1995 only 7 per cent of males and 6 per cent of females did so.

Reading habits differ according to gender and social grade. Over the years, men have been consistently more likely than women to read a national daily newspaper. In addition people in social grade C2 were the most likely to read this type of newspaper, with 62 per cent doing so in 1995-1996. A larger proportion of people read national Sunday newspapers than daily ones, with two thirds doing so in 1995-1996. The News of the World remained the most popular, read by around a quarter of people, with the Sunday Mirror some way behind in second place.

The position of television viewing as the most common home-based leisure activity is reflected in the fact that three out of the top

# 13.12

ten most popular magazines in Great Britain in the year to June 1996 were television-related (Table 13.11). The readership of magazines can be affected by age. For example, while Viz was read by 15 per cent of 15 to 24 year olds, only 1 per cent of 45 to 64 year olds read it. Conversely, Reader's Digest was more commonly read by those in the older age groups than those in the younger groups. There are also differences between the genders in magazine reading. While the Reader's Digest magazine was read by equal proportions of men and women, Take a Break was read by 16 per cent of women compared with 5 per cent of men. On the other hand, the AA Magazine was read by 12 per cent of men and 8 per cent of women. Those in different social grades tended to read different magazines; while the AA Magazine was read by 16 per cent of those in social grades AB, only 4 per cent of those in social grades DE read it. Conversely, 4 per cent of those in social grade AB read Take a Break compared with 14 per cent of those in grades DE.

Over half of people aged 15 and over held a library ticket in the United Kingdom in 1995, although not all ticket holders borrow books regularly. Females were more likely than males to hold a library ticket. A third of females borrowed books at least monthly, compared with only a fifth of males (**Table 13.12**). Of women who held tickets, those aged between 65 and 74 were the most likely to borrow at least monthly, whereas among men those aged between 55 and 64 were the most likely.

**Borrowing of books from libraries[1]: by gender and age, 1995**

Great Britain
Percentages

|  | Borrow at least monthly | | Borrow less than monthly[2] | |
|---|---|---|---|---|
|  | Males | Females | Males | Females |
| 15-24 | 24 | 33 | 35 | 39 |
| 25-34 | 14 | 20 | 24 | 39 |
| 35-44 | 13 | 34 | 36 | 38 |
| 45-54 | 16 | 35 | 28 | 24 |
| 55-64 | 33 | 42 | 22 | 18 |
| 65-74 | 22 | 48 | 27 | 21 |
| 75 and over | 19 | 38 | 16 | 12 |
| All aged 15 and over | 19 | 34 | 28 | 29 |

1 Percentage of all in each group who borrowed.
2 Those who held a library ticket and borrowed less than monthly.
*Source: Book Marketing Limited*

# 13.13

Libraries offer many facilities in addition to the borrowing of books, such as borrowing sound or video recordings, photocopying, obtaining information on careers, business and the community and studying facilities. In 1994 around seven in ten people who borrowed books from public libraries also took advantage of such additional facilities.

In the 12 months ending in June 1995, the author whose books were most commonly borrowed from libraries by adults was Catherine Cookson while Janet and Allan Ahlberg were the most popular among children (**Table 13.13**). The total number of book loans from public libraries in 1994-1995 was just over 550 million, a similar

**Top ten most borrowed adult and childrens authors, 1994-1995[1]**

United Kingdom

| Adult | Children |
|---|---|
| Catherine Cookson | Janet and Allan Ahlberg |
| Danielle Steel | Roald Dahl |
| Dick Francis | Enid Blyton |
| Ruth Rendell | Kate William |
| Agatha Christie | Ann M. Martin |
| Ellis Peters | Goscinny |
| Jack Higgins | John Cunliffe |
| Wilbur Smith | Shirley Hughes |
| Virginia Andrews | Jamie Suzanne |
| Terry Pratchett | Dick King-Smith |

1 July 1994 to June 1995.
*Source: Public Lending Right*

# 13.14

**Number of pets**

**United Kingdom**
Millions

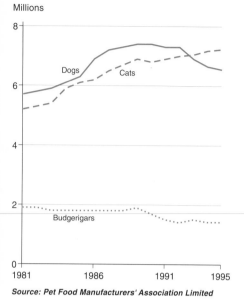

*Source: Pet Food Manufacturers' Association Limited*

number to that in the previous year. This was, however, some 100 million fewer than in 1981-82. The most commonly borrowed types of book in 1994-1995 were general fiction, children's fiction and mystery and detection books.

A common addition to a household is a pet, ranging from cats, dogs and rabbits to more exotic pets such as spiders and snakes. Around half of households in the United Kingdom own a pet. Changes in lifestyle and household structures over the past decade or so have affected the relative population of cats and dogs. Dogs were the most common type of pet until 1993, when cats overtook

them (Chart 13.14). In 1995 there were 7.2 million cats and 6.6 million dogs in the United Kingdom. Many households will own more than one pet. For example, whilst there were over 1.4 million budgerigars in 1995, there were only 0.8 million budgerigar owning-households. Of the 5.2 million households owning a dog, 80 per cent have only one dog. It is more common for a cat owning household to own more than one cat, with only 65 per cent having just one cat. The Pet Food Manufacturer's Association also estimates that there were around 1.4 million rabbits, 600 thousand guinea pigs and 30 million fish.

## Social and cultural activities

The most common free-time activity outside the home among adults in Great Britain in 1995-96 was visiting a public house, with 65 per cent of all adults saying that they had done so in the three months before being interviewed (Table 13.15). Participation in some leisure activities can be affected by age. For example, whereas around seven in ten of those aged between 16 and 24 had gone to a nightclub or disco in the previous three months, only one in ten of those aged 45 to 59 had done so. Fast food was also more commonly eaten by those in the younger age groups.

Some activities are more common among men than women. For example 73 per cent of men claimed to have visited a public house in the previous three months compared with 57 per cent of women. Men were also more likely to attend a spectator sports event, with 30 per cent having done

# 13.15

**Participation[1] in leisure activities away from home: by age, 1995-1996[2]**

**Great Britain**

Percentages

|  | 16-24 | 25-34 | 35-44 | 45-59 | 60 and over | All aged 15 and over |
|---|---|---|---|---|---|---|
| Visit a public house | 78 | 81 | 72 | 62 | 42 | 65 |
| Meal in a restaurant (not fast food) | 57 | 66 | 65 | 65 | 56 | 61 |
| Drive for pleasure | 44 | 51 | 48 | 53 | 45 | 48 |
| Meal in a fast food restaurant | 74 | 61 | 52 | 29 | 12 | 43 |
| Library | 42 | 37 | 42 | 34 | 40 | 39 |
| Cinema | 68 | 49 | 40 | 25 | 9 | 36 |
| Short break holiday | 33 | 32 | 26 | 31 | 28 | 30 |
| Disco or night club | 71 | 44 | 20 | 10 | 3 | 27 |
| Historic building | 23 | 24 | 28 | 27 | 19 | 24 |
| Spectator sports event | 28 | 26 | 27 | 17 | 12 | 21 |
| Theatre | 17 | 19 | 19 | 24 | 19 | 20 |

*1 Percentage aged 16 and over participating in each activity in the 3 months prior to interview.*
*2 December 1995 to September 1996.*
*Source: The Henley Centre*

so compared with just 13 per cent of women. Women were, however, more likely to have visited a library or attended the theatre.

In Great Britain in 1995 three quarters of people aged seven and over said that they ever went to the cinema (Chart 13.16). This was a large increase on ten years previously when less than half of people said that they ever went. Those in the younger age groups were more likely to go than older people, with 96 per cent of those aged 7 to 14 attending. However, in 1995 the total number of admissions decreased slightly when compared with the previous year, although there were still more than in 1993. Nearly one in five adults said that they visited the cinema two to three times a year.

Males were slightly more likely to go to the cinema than females. Attendance also varies by social class, with those in the non-manual social classes being more likely to attend than those in the manual ones. The types of cinema that people go to have been changing over the last ten or so years. In 1985 there was just one multiplex site, with ten screens, but by 1995 there were 83 sites with a total of 732 screens. The most popular film in 1995, according to box-office takings, was Batman Forever, followed by Casper and Goldeneye.

In 1994 there were 5.2 billion leisure day visits from home made in Great Britain. The most common reasons for such a visit were to visit friends or relatives in their home or to eat or drink out (Chart 13.17). The weekend was the most common time for a leisure day visit to occur, with around 40 per cent being on a Saturday or Sunday. The amount of

time spent away from home ranged from under one hour in 12 per cent of visits to over six hours in 10 per cent of visits; around 60 per cent of visits lasted between one and four hours.

The car was the main form of transport used for leisure day visits, although travelling on foot accounted for around three in ten of all visits. Most visits involved total travelling of less than ten miles away from home. A town or city was the most popular destination (71 per cent), followed by the countryside (25 per cent) with the remaining 4 per cent of visits were to seaside resorts or rural coasts. Day visits as defined in the Day Visits Survey may include many short or regular trips, rather than just those that are a form of tourism.

Cinema attendance[1]: by age

**Great Britain**
Percentages

1 Percentage claiming to 'ever go' to the cinema.

*Source: Cinema and Video Industry Audience Research, Cinema Advertising Association Limited*

Day visits from home: by main purpose, 1994

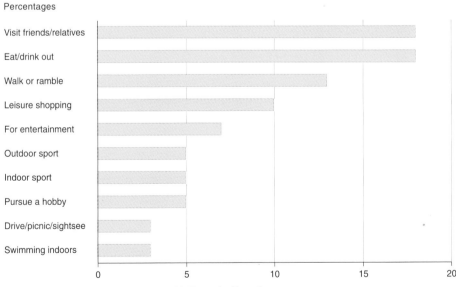

**Great Britain**
Percentages

*Source: UK Day Visits Survey 1994, Countryside Recreation Network*

# 13.18

## Visits to the most popular tourist attractions

**Great Britain**

Millions

| | 1981 | 1991 | 1995 | | 1981 | 1991 | 1995 |
|---|---|---|---|---|---|---|---|
| **Attractions with free admission** | | | | **Attractions charging admission** | | | |
| Blackpool Pleasure Beach | 7.5 | 6.5 | 7.3 | Alton Towers | 1.6 | 2.0 | 2.7 |
| British Museum | 2.6 | 5.1 | 5.7 | Madame Tussaud's | 2.0 | 2.2 | 2.7 |
| National Gallery | 2.7 | 4.3 | 4.5 | Tower of London | 2.1 | 1.9 | 2.5 |
| Strathclyde Country Park | .. | 4.2 | 4.2 | Chessington World of Adventures | 0.5 | 1.4 | 1.8 |
| Palace Pier, Brighton | .. | 3.5 | 3.8 | Science Museum[1] | 3.8 | 1.3 | 1.6 |
| Funland and Laserbowl, London | .. | .. | 2.5 | St Paul's Cathedral[2] | .. | 1.5 | 1.5 |
| Eastbourne Pier | .. | .. | 2.3 | Windsor Castle | 1.2 | | |
| Pleasure Beach, Great Yarmouth | .. | 2.5 | 2.0 | Blackpool Tower | .. | 1.3 | 1.2 |
| Pleasureland, Southport | .. | 1.8 | 2.0 | Thorpe Park | 0.6 | 0.9 | 1.2 |
| Tate Gallery | 0.9 | 1.8 | 1.8 | Natural History Museum[3] | 3.7 | 1.6 | 1.1 |

1 Admission charges were introduced in 1989.
2 Admission charges were introduced in April 1991.
3 Admission charges were introduced in April 1987.

**Source: British Tourist Authority**

# 13.19

## Household expenditure on the National Lottery[1]: by age of head of household, 1995-1996[2]

**United Kingdom**
£ per week

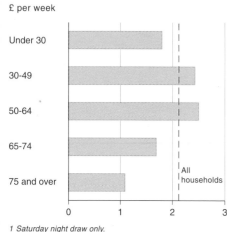

1 Saturday night draw only.
2 October 1995 to March 1996

**Source: Family Expenditure Survey, Office for National Statistics**

Blackpool Pleasure Beach has been Great Britain's most popular tourist attraction for many years and 7.3 million people visited it in 1995 **(Table 13.18)**. The British Museum had 5.7 million visitors in 1995, which was more than double the number it had in 1981, and made it the second most popular attraction. Of those attractions that charged people for admission, Alton Towers and Madame Tussauds were the most popular in 1995, each with 2.7 million visits. While the general trend has been for attractions to receive more visitors, the Science Museum (which introduced admission charges in 1989) and the Natural History Museum (which introduced charges in 1987) both experienced falls in their numbers of visits between 1981 and 1995, though visits to the Science Museum were up on 1991.

Gambling has long been a popular activity in the United Kingdom and with the launch of the National Lottery in November 1994, many households now participate in this particular form of gaming. The Family Expenditure Survey (FES) collects data on people's expenditure on the National Lottery and it found that around 70 per cent of households participated in their two week diary keeping period in 1995-96. The survey also revealed that, on average, households spent £2.12 a week on the National Lottery Saturday night draw between October 1995 and March 1996 **(Chart 13.19)**. Those households where the head was aged between 50 and 65 spent the most on the Saturday night draw, at £2.51, whilst those where the head of household was aged 75 and over spent the least at £1.10. Data from the FES indicate that household expenditure on other forms of gambling has decreased, falling 15 per cent in real terms since 1994-95 to £1.53 per week in 1995-96.

## Sporting activities

Walking a distance of two or more miles has remained the most popular physical activity between 1987 and 1993-94 for both men and women in Great Britain **(Table 13.20)**. Over this period men have been more likely to participate in any activity although the gap has been narrowing. In 1993-94, 72 per cent of men and 57 per cent of women participated in at least one sporting or

# 13.20

physical activity in the four weeks prior to being interviewed for the General Household Survey. However, although men were four times more likely than women to participate in cue sports or golf, women were the more likely to participate in swimming or keep fit/yoga. In general, participation in physical activities decreases with age: 86 per cent of those aged between 16 and 19 had participated in at least one physical activity, only 33 per cent of those aged 70 and over had done so.

Participation also varies by socio-economic group. Among people in the professional group, 82 per cent had taken part in some form of physical activity in the previous four weeks compared with only 48 per cent of those in the unskilled manual group. Participation rates for physical activities were generally lower in Northern Ireland than in Great Britain.

Nearly all children between the ages of six and sixteen had participated in a sporting activity outside school lessons in 1994, according to the Sports Council's Young People and Sport in England Survey; only 2 per cent had done none at all. However, the amount of time spent doing such activities ranged from less than one hour to over 15. On average, children had participated in ten sports at least once out-of-lessons in the 12 months leading up to the survey, but only four sports at least ten times in the year. Boys tended to participate in more sports outside of lessons than girls and they also spent more time on sports than girls. Boys tended to participate in a wider range of sports than girls and were especially likely to take part in team games.

Among secondary school age pupils, cycling/riding a bicycle was the most common activity overall, with 55 per cent of boys and 38 per cent of girls participating at

## Participation[1] in the most popular sports, games and physical activities: by gender

**Great Britain**
Percentages

| | Males | | | Females | | |
|---|---|---|---|---|---|---|
| | 1987 | 1990-91 | 1993-94 | 1987 | 1990-91 | 1993-94 |
| Walking | 41 | 44 | 45 | 35 | 38 | 37 |
| Snooker/pool/billiards | 27 | 24 | 21 | 5 | 5 | 5 |
| Swimming | .. | 14 | 15 | .. | 15 | 16 |
| Cycling | 10 | 12 | 14 | 7 | 7 | 7 |
| Darts | 14 | 11 | 9 | 4 | 4 | 3 |
| Soccer | 10 | 10 | 9 | - | - | - |
| Golf | 7 | 9 | 9 | 1 | 2 | 2 |
| Weightlifting/training | 7 | 8 | 9 | 2 | 2 | 3 |
| Running | 8 | 8 | 7 | 3 | 2 | 2 |
| Keep fit/yoga | 5 | 6 | 6 | 12 | 16 | 17 |
| Tenpin bowls/skittles | 2 | 5 | 5 | 1 | 3 | 3 |
| Badminton | 4 | 4 | 3 | 3 | 3 | 2 |
| At least one activity[2] | 70 | 73 | 72 | 52 | 57 | 57 |

1 Percentage aged 16 and over participating in each activity in the four weeks before interview.
2 This may include those activities not separately listed.
**Source: General Household Survey, Office for National Statistics**

least ten times outside of school lessons in the twelve months leading up to the survey (Chart 13.21). However, for girls, this was the second ranked activity, with 42 per cent

# 13.21

## Sporting activities[1] participated in by secondary school pupils[2] outside of lessons: by gender, 1994

**England**
Percentages

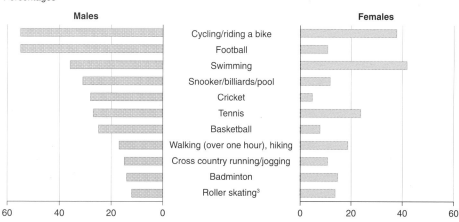

1 Those participating at least ten times in the 12 months leading up to the survey.
2 Secondary school pupils in years 7-11.
3 Includes roller blading and skate boarding.

**Source: Young People and Sport in England, The Sports Council**

# 13.22

Church membership[1] and number of clergy

**United Kingdom**

| | Membership (millions) | | Clergy (numbers) | |
|---|---|---|---|---|
| | 1970 | 1995 | 1970 | 1995 |
| **Trinitarian churches** | | | | |
| Roman Catholic[2] | 2.7 | 2.0 | 9,239 | 7,645 |
| Anglican | 3.0 | 1.7 | 16,915 | 12,059 |
| Presbyterian | 1.8 | 1.1 | 4,082 | 3,015 |
| Methodist | 0.7 | 0.4 | 4,404 | 3,901 |
| Baptist | 0.3 | 0.2 | 2,520 | 3,030 |
| Other free churches | 0.5 | 0.7 | 4,718 | 9,341 |
| Orthodox | 0.2 | 0.3 | 114 | 208 |
| All Trinitarian churches | 9.1 | 6.4 | 41,992 | 39,199 |
| **Non-Trinitarian churches** | | | | |
| Mormons | 0.1 | 0.2 | 110[3] | 400[3] |
| Jehovah's Witnesses | 0.1 | 0.1 | 7,050 | 14,200 |
| Other Non-Trinitarian | 0.1 | 0.3 | 1,482 | 2,265 |
| All Non-Trinitarian churches | 0.3 | 0.6 | 8,642 | 16,865 |
| **Other religions** | | | | |
| Muslims | 0.1 | 0.6 | 900 | 2,900 |
| Sikhs | 0.1 | 0.4 | 80 | 200 |
| Hindus | 0.1 | 0.1 | 80 | 150 |
| Jews | 0.1 | 0.1 | 390 | 450 |
| Others | 0.0 | 0.1 | 289 | 1,792 |
| All other religions | 0.4 | 1.3 | 1,739 | 5,492 |

1 Adult active members.
2 Mass attendance.
3 Bishops.
*Source: Christian Research*

# 13.23

Belief in God[1], 1995

| **Great Britain** | Percentages |
|---|---|
| | 1995 |
| Do not believe in God | 11 |
| Do not know if God exists and cannot find evidence for God's existence | 15 |
| Believe in a higher power of some kind | 12 |
| Believe sometimes | 12 |
| Doubt, but believe | 23 |
| God exists, with no doubts | 21 |
| Can't choose/not answered | 7 |

1 Respondents were asked which statement came closest to their belief about God.
*Source: British Social Attitudes Survey, Social and Community Planning Research*

participating in swimming, their most popular sport. For boys, football was the joint most common activity along with cycling/riding a bicycle. Primary school age pupils had higher participation rates in these most popular activities than secondary school pupils. They spent less time than secondary pupils on sporting activities outside of lessons in term time, but spent more time in the summer holidays. Overall the top three ranked sports outside of lessons were the same for primary pupils as secondary pupils. Information on sports participation by pupils in school lessons is given in Chart 3.12 in the Education and Training chapter.

## Religious activities

Religious activities form an important part of many people's lives. The pattern of membership of the various religions and denominations represented in the United Kingdom has seen contrasting changes over the last quarter of a century. Whilst Trinitarian churches have experienced a fall in membership from 9.1 million adults in 1970 to 6.4 million in 1995, there have been increases in other religions. For example, the Muslim faith experienced a large increase in membership between 1970 and 1995 (Table 13.22). The number of clergy has broadly reflected the changes in the patterns of membership, with increasing numbers of clergy in non-Trinitarian and other religions and decreasing numbers in Trinitarian churches. However, the decline in the number of Trinitarian clergy has not been as rapid as the decline in its membership.

Around 60 per cent of people active in their religion in Great Britain are female. When compared with the size of the population, those aged under 15 and aged over 45 are over-represented while those aged between 15 and 44 are under-represented. Wales had a small average congregation size at just 25 in 1995, compared with 222 for Scotland in 1994. The latest data available for England show that the average congregation size was 128 in 1989.

Despite the overall decrease in church membership most people believe in some form of deity. When asked in the 1995 British Social Attitudes Survey, over one in five people said that they believed in God, with no doubts (Table 13.23). In the same survey, people were asked about their religious affiliation and while two fifths said that they had none, just under a third said they were Church of England/Anglican and a quarter

## 13.24

said that they were affiliated to other Trinitarian religions. One in nine of those with a religious affiliation said that they attended services or meetings connected with their religion at least once a week. However, around half said that they never, or practically never, attended.

## Holidays

The British National Travel Survey found that 59 million holidays of four nights or more were taken by British residents in 1995, an increase of 43 per cent on the number taken in 1971 (Chart 13.1). However, while the overall number of holidays increased, the number taken in Great Britain has been gradually declining over the last quarter century while the number taken abroad has grown strongly. However, there was a small drop in foreign holidays in 1995 compared with the previous year, and a rise in those taken in Great Britain. The United Kingdom Tourism Survey found that one in five holidays taken in the United Kingdom had an activity as their main purpose, with swimming and walking/hiking the most common activities. Nearly 60 per cent of people participated in an activity of some sort while on their holiday. Again, swimming and walking/hiking were common activities but visiting museums and heritage sites was also popular.

The proportion of British adults who take a holiday away from home has fluctuated around 60 per cent for around the last quarter of a century. However, the proportion taking two or more holidays increased by more than half between 1971 and 1995. The likelihood of taking a holiday varies by people's social grade. While only 18 per cent of those in groups AB had no holiday in 1995, 57 per cent of those in groups DE had

no holiday (Table 13.24). Nearly 60 per cent of those in groups AB took holidays abroad in 1995. For those people who stayed in Great Britain for their holidays, the West Country was the most popular destination followed by Scotland and Wales. The preferred mode of transport for holiday journeys was the car and most holidaymakers stayed in self-catering accommodation.

The most common time of year for UK residents to take long holidays (of four nights or more) in this country is in August (Table 13.25). In 1995 almost a quarter of such holidays were taken in this month, with July being the next most popular month. Short holidays are much more evenly spread throughout the year. May is marginally the most common month for short holidays taken in the United Kingdom and March for those taken abroad.

### Holiday taking: by social grade[1], 1995

| Great Britain | | | Percentages[2] |
| --- | --- | --- | --- |
| | Holidays in Britain | Holidays abroad | No holiday |
| AB | 44 | 59 | 18 |
| C1 | 37 | 47 | 31 |
| C2 | 38 | 32 | 38 |
| DE | 28 | 20 | 57 |

1 See Appendix, Part 13: Social grade.
2 Percentage of people in each social grade taking holidays in each location. Percentages do not sum to 100 because some people take holidays in both Britain and abroad.
*Source: British Tourist Authority*

## 13.25

### Holidays taken by UK residents: by month, 1995

Percentages

| | Short holidays[1] | | Long holidays[2] | | All holidays |
| --- | --- | --- | --- | --- | --- |
| | Home | Abroad | Home | Abroad | |
| January | 5 | 6 | 1 | 4 | 3 |
| February | 7 | 5 | 2 | 4 | 4 |
| March | 7 | 12 | 3 | 5 | 5 |
| April | 10 | 11 | 7 | 7 | 8 |
| May | 11 | 10 | 10 | 11 | 11 |
| June | 9 | 6 | 9 | 12 | 10 |
| July | 9 | 8 | 17 | 14 | 13 |
| August | 10 | 8 | 23 | 16 | 16 |
| September | 9 | 9 | 10 | 10 | 10 |
| October | 9 | 10 | 7 | 8 | 11 |
| November | 5 | 11 | 2 | 4 | 3 |
| December | 8 | 5 | 6 | 5 | 4 |
| All months | 100 | 100 | 100 | 100 | 100 |

1 Holidays of one to three nights.
2 Holidays of four nights or more.
*Source: British Tourist Authority*

# 13.26

## Holidays abroad: by destination[1]

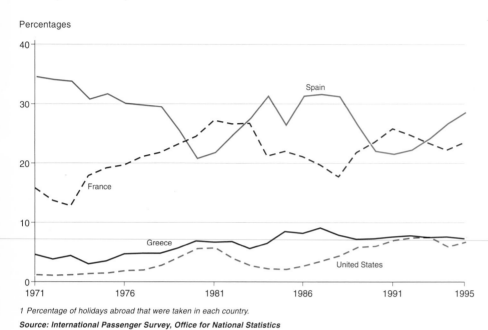

Percentages

1 Percentage of holidays abroad that were taken in each country.

**Source: International Passenger Survey, Office for National Statistics**

Spain was the most common destination for UK holidaymakers going abroad in 1995. Twenty eight per cent of holiday visits were to Spain, with around 24 per cent to France which was the next most popular destination (Chart 13.26). Europe is still much more popular with British holiday makers than other parts of the world although the United States has been growing in popularity and was the fourth most popular destination for holiday visits in 1995. The number of holidays taken in Britain by foreigners has been increasing in recent years with around 6 million holidays of four or more nights being taken in 1995 according to the International Passenger Survey.

# 13.27

## Votes recorded in parliamentary general elections and by-elections: by party

**United Kingdom**

|  | General election 3/5/79 | May 1979 to June 1983 | General election 6/6/83 | June 1983 to June 1987 | General election 11/6/87 | June 1987 to April 1992 | General election 10/4/92 | April 1992 to Sept 1996 |
|---|---|---|---|---|---|---|---|---|
| **Number of by-elections** | . | 20 | . | 31 | . | 24 | . | 16 |
| **Turnout** (percentages)[1] | 76.1 | 61.2 | 72.7 | 62.4 | 75.3 | 57.6 | 76.3 | 52.7 |
| **Votes recorded by party** (percentage of all votes) |  |  |  |  |  |  |  |  |
| Conservative | 43.9 | 23.8 | 42.4 | 16.0 | 42.3 | 23.8 | 41.8 | 18.6 |
| Labour | 36.9 | 25.7 | 27.6 | 14.9 | 30.8 | 38.9 | 35.2 | 39.5 |
| Liberal Democrats[2] | 13.8 | 9.0 | 13.7 | 15.0 | 12.8 | 19.1 | 17.0 | 26.2 |
| Social Democratic Party[2] | . | 14.2 | 11.6 | 5.6 | 9.7 | 3.2 | . | . |
| Plaid Cymru | 0.4 | 0.5 | 0.4 | 0.3 | 0.4 | 2.3 | 0.4 | 0.5 |
| Scottish National Party | 1.6 | 1.7 | 1.1 | . | 1.3 | 4.8 | 1.9 | 5.8 |
| Northern Ireland Parties[2] | 2.2 | 23.3 | 2.5 | 47.4 | 2.2 | 3.7 | 2.1 | 4.7 |
| Green Party[3] | 0.1 | 0.3 | 0.2 | - | 0.3 | 1.8 | 0.6 | 0.1 |
| Other parties | 1.1 | 1.6 | 0.5 | 0.8 | 0.2 | 2.5 | 1.1 | 4.5 |
| All votes (=100%)(thousands) | 31,221 | 715 | 30,671 | 1,979 | 32,530 | 877 | 33,275 | 560 |

1 Estimated by dividing the number of votes cast by the number of people on the electoral registers in force at the time of the elections.
2 See Appendix, Part 13: Parliamentary elections and political parties.
3 Known as the Ecology Party before 1987.

**Source: Home Office**

# 13.28

## Political participation

Over three quarters of those eligible turned out to vote at the UK general election in April 1992 (Table 13.27). Turnouts for by-elections are usually much lower; on average, only just over half of the electorate turned out at by-elections held between April 1992 and September 1996. People also seem more likely to vote for opposition or smaller parties at by-elections than at general elections. The 1995 British Social Attitudes Survey (BSAS) asked people if they belonged to a political party; only 4 per cent of respondents did. In spite of this, nearly two fifths of respondents said that they identified fairly or very strongly with a political party.

Participation in European elections in the United Kingdom is even lower than that in by-elections. At the last election only around a third of the United Kingdom electorate turned out to vote, a similar proportion to the Netherlands and Portugal (Table 13.28). Belgium and Luxembourg had very high turnouts at European elections.

The BSAS asked people in 1995 about what Britain's relationship with the European Union (EU) should be. Nearly 40 per cent of respondents thought that the relationship was about right. Slightly more people thought that Britain should be closer than thought it should be less close - 29 per cent compared with 26 per cent. There does however seem to have been a decline in support for a closer relationship with the EU in recent years. In 1991 nearly four in ten respondents thought that Britain should be closer to the EU and only one in ten thought Britain should be less close.

Among EU countries the proportion of MPs who are women varies considerably. Sweden had the highest proportion after its last general election, with 40 per cent; in both Finland and Denmark 33 per cent of MPs were women in 1995 (Chart 13.29). France and Greece had the lowest proportions, each with 6 per cent. The United Kingdom also has a fairly low proportion of MPs which are women with less than 10 per cent in September 1995. The United States had a similar proportion to the United Kingdom at 11 per cent, while in Canada 18 per cent of its MPs were women.

## Participation in EU elections

| | 1979 | 1984 | 1989 | 1994 |
|---|---|---|---|---|
| | | | | Percentages |
| Belgium | 91.4 | 92.1 | 93.0 | 90.7 |
| Luxembourg | 88.9 | 88.8 | 87.0 | 86.6 |
| Italy | 86.0 | 83.4 | 81.5 | 74.8 |
| Greece | . | 78.4 | 77.7 | 71.2 |
| Germany | 65.7 | 56.8 | 61.5 | 60.1 |
| Spain | . | . | 54.8 | 59.6 |
| | | | | |
| France | 61.2 | 57.4 | 50.4 | 53.7 |
| Denmark | 47.8 | 54.0 | 46.0 | 52.5 |
| Irish Republic | 63.6 | 47.6 | 68.5 | 44.0 |
| United Kingdom | 32.8 | 32.5 | 36.0 | 36.1 |
| Portugal | . | . | 51.2 | 35.6 |
| Netherlands | 58.2 | 50.9 | 47.2 | 35.6 |
| | | | | |
| EU average | 62.5 | 60.1 | 58.5 | 56.8 |

*Source: United Nations Economic Commission for Europe*

# 13.29

### Percentage of MPs[1] who are women: EU comparison, 1995

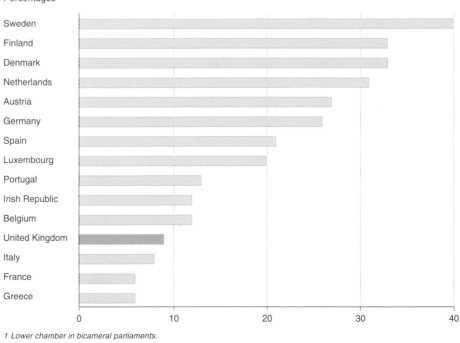

1 Lower chamber in bicameral parliaments.
*Source: United Nations Economic Commission for Europe*

## References and further reading

The following list contains selected publications relevant to **Chapter 13: Lifestyles**. Those published by The Stationery Office are available from the addresses shown on the inside back cover of Social Trends.

*Annual Report of Department of National Heritage*, The Stationery Office

*BBC Handbook*, BBC

*BPI Statistical Handbook*, British Phonographic Industry

*British Social Attitudes*, Dartmouth Publishing

*BVA Yearbook*, British Video Association

*Cinema and Video Industry Audience Research*, CAA

*Cultural Trends*, Policy Studies Institute

*Cultural Trends in Scotland 2*, Policy Studies Institute

*Digest of Tourist Statistics*, British Tourist Authority

*Film and Television Handbook*, British Film Institute

*Leisure Futures*, The Henley Centre

*LISU Annual Library Statistics*, Library and Information Statistics Unit, Loughborough University of Technology

*Living in Britain*, The Stationery Office

*Social Focus on Women*, The Stationery Office

*The UK Tourist*, Tourist Boards of England, Northern Ireland, Scotland and Wales

*Travel Trends*, The Stationery Office

*UK Day Visits Survey*, Countryside Recreation Network, University of Wales Cardiff

*Young People and Sport in England*, The Sports Council

## Contacts

Telephone contact points for further information relating to
**Chapter 13: Lifestyles**

| | |
|---|---|
| **Office for National Statistics** | |
| Chapter author | 0171 533 5778 |
| Family Expenditure Survey | 0171 533 5754 |
| General Household Survey | 0171 533 5444 |
| International Passenger Survey | 0171 533 5765 |
| **Northern Ireland Statistics and Research Agency** | 01232 252653 |
| **British Phonographic Industry** | 0171 287 4422 |
| **British Tourist Authority** | 0181 846 9000 |
| **Christian Research** | 0181 294 1989 |
| **Cinema Advertising Association** | 0171 439 9531 |
| **ESRC Research Centre on Micro-social Change** | 01206 872957 |
| **National Readership Surveys** | 0171 379 0344 |
| **Social & Community Planning Research** | 0171 250 1866 extn 369 |
| **The Henley Centre** | 0171 353 9961 |

# Geographical areas of the United Kingdom used in Social Trends

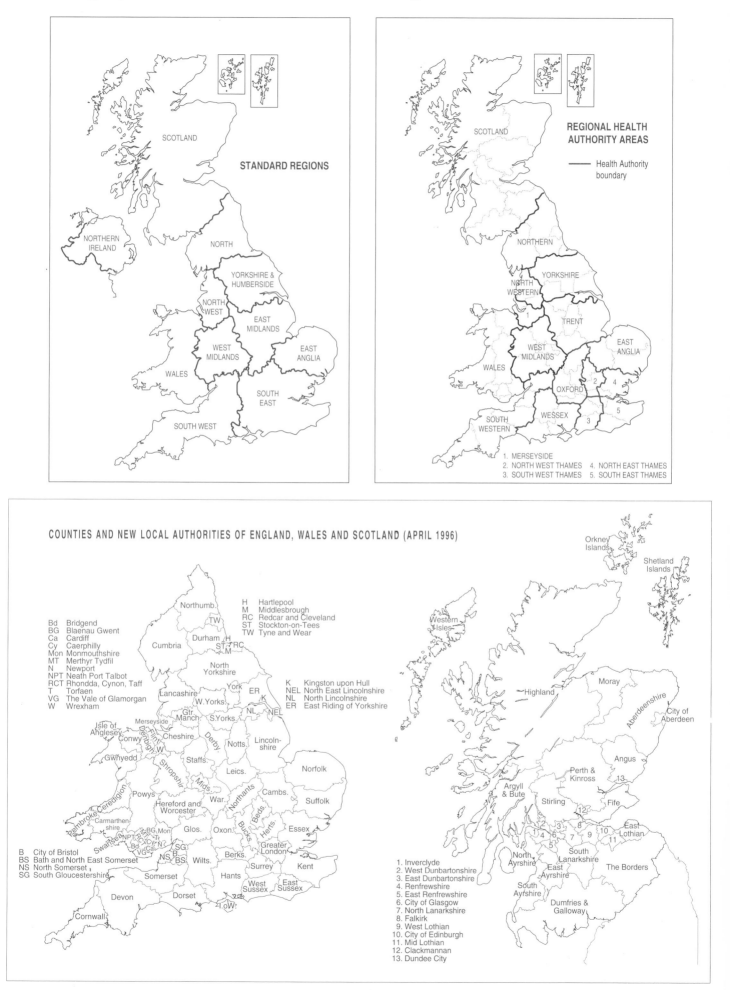

STANDARD REGIONS

SCOTLAND

NORTHERN IRELAND

NORTH

YORKSHIRE & HUMBERSIDE

NORTH WEST

EAST MIDLANDS

WEST MIDLANDS

EAST ANGLIA

WALES

SOUTH EAST

SOUTH WEST

REGIONAL HEALTH AUTHORITY AREAS

— Health Authority boundary

SCOTLAND

NORTHERN

YORKSHIRE

NORTH WESTERN

TRENT

WEST MIDLANDS

EAST ANGLIA

WALES

OXFORD

SOUTH WESTERN

WESSEX

1. MERSEYSIDE
2. NORTH WEST THAMES
3. SOUTH WEST THAMES
4. NORTH EAST THAMES
5. SOUTH EAST THAMES

## COUNTIES AND NEW LOCAL AUTHORITIES OF ENGLAND, WALES AND SCOTLAND (APRIL 1996)

Bd    Bridgend
BG    Blaenau Gwent
Ca    Cardiff
Cy    Caerphilly
Mon   Monmouthshire
MT    Merthyr Tydfil
N     Newport
NPT   Neath Port Talbot
RCT   Rhondda, Cynon, Taff
T     Torfaen
VG    The Vale of Glamorgan
W     Wrexham

H     Hartlepool
M     Middlesbrough
RC    Redcar and Cleveland
ST    Stockton-on-Tees
TW    Tyne and Wear

K     Kingston upon Hull
NEL   North East Lincolnshire
NL    North Lincolnshire
ER    East Riding of Yorkshire

B     City of Bristol
BS    Bath and North East Somerset
NS    North Somerset
SG    South Gloucestershire

Orkney Islands

Shetland Islands

Northumb.

Cumbria

Durham

TW

ST RC
H
M

North Yorkshire

Lancashire

York

ER

K

W.Yorks.

Gtr. Manch.

S.Yorks.

NL

NEL

Merseyside

Cheshire

Derby

Notts.

Lincolnshire

Isle of Anglesey

Conwy

Flint

Denbigh

W

Gwynedd

Shropshire

Staffs.

Leics.

Norfolk

Powys

Mids.

War.

Northants.

Cambs.

Suffolk

Ceredigion

Hereford and Worcester

Oxon

Beds.

Herts.

Essex

Pembroke

Carmarthenshire

Swansea

NPT

BG

Mon

N

Glos.

Bucks.

Greater London

Bd

Cy

T

SG

B

Berks.

NS

BS

Wilts.

Surrey

Kent

VG

Somerset

Hants.

West Sussex

East Sussex

Devon

Dorset

I.o.W.

Cornwall

Western Isles

Highland

Moray

Aberdeenshire

City of Aberdeen

Argyll & Bute

Perth & Kinross

Angus

13

Stirling

Fife

12

North Ayrshire

1 2 3
4
5 6 7 8 9 10 11

East Lothian

South Lanarkshire

The Borders

South Ayrshire

East Ayrshire

Dumfries & Galloway

1. Inverclyde
2. West Dunbartonshire
3. East Dunbartonshire
4. Renfrewshire
5. East Renfrewshire
6. City of Glasgow
7. North Lanarkshire
8. Falkirk
9. West Lothian
10. City of Edinburgh
11. Mid Lothian
12. Clackmannan
13. Dundee City

# Appendix: major surveys

| | Frequency | Sampling frame | Type of respondent | Coverage | Effective sample size[1] (most recent survey included in *Social Trends*) | Response rate (percentages) |
|---|---|---|---|---|---|---|
| British Crime Survey | Biannual | Postcode Address File | Adult in household | EW | 19,808 addresses[2] | 83 |
| British Household Panel Survey | Annual | Postal Addresses | All adults in households | GB | 5,400 households | 95[3] |
| British Social Attitudes Survey | Annual | Postcode Address File | Adult in household | GB | 5,251 addresses | 69 |
| Census of Population | Decennial | Detailed local | Household head | UK | Full count | 98 |
| Continuous Household Survey | Continuous | Valuation and Lands Agency Property Database | All adults in household | NI | 4,107 addresses | 78 |
| Family Expenditure Survey | Continuous | Postcode Address File | Household | UK | 10,150 addresses[2] | 66[4] |
| | | in GB, Rating Lists in NI | | | | |
| Family and Working Lives Survey | One-off | Postcode Address File | Adult aged 16-69 and any partner | GB | 16,987 households[2] | 54 |
| Family Resources Survey | Continuous | Postcode Address File | All adults in household | GB | 39,152 households | 67 |
| General Household Survey | Continuous | Postcode Address File | All adults in household | GB | 11,914 households | 80 |
| Health Survey for England | Annual | Postcode Address File | All adults in household | E | 11,500 addresses | 77[5] |
| International Passenger Survey | Continuous | International passengers at ports and airports | Individual traveller | UK | 248,000 individuals | 86 |
| Labour Force Survey | Continuous | Postcode Address File | All adults in household[6] | UK | 63,000 addresses | 82[7] |
| Longitudinal Study | Continuous | Population | All persons | EW | 1 per cent | [8] |
| National Food Survey | Continuous | Postcode Address File | Person responsible for domestic food arrangements | GB | 12,362 addresses | 66 |
| National Readership Survey | Continuous | Postcode Address File | Individual in home | GB | 62,000 individuals | 62 |
| National Travel Survey | Continuous | Postcode Address File | Household | GB | 4,500-5,000 households per year[2] | 74[9] |
| New Earnings Survey | Annual records | Inland Revenue PAYE | Employee[10] | GB | [10] | [10] |
| Omnibus Survey | Continuous | Postcode Address File | One adult per household | GB | 2,700 individuals[11] | 75[11] |
| Survey of English Housing | Continuous | Postcode Address File | Household | E | 25,000 addresses | 80 |
| Survey of Personal Incomes | Annual | Inland Revenue | Individuals[12] | UK | 80,061 individuals | 96 |
| Youth Lifestyles Survey | One-off | Postcode Address File | Young people aged 14-25 | EW | 3,690 households[13] | 69 |

1 Effective sample size includes non-respondents but excludes ineligible households.
2 Basic sample only.
3 Wave on wave response rate at wave four. This represents 79 per cent of respondents at wave one.
4 Response rate refers to Great Britain.
5 Response rate for fully and partially responding households.
6 Includes some proxy information.
7 Response rate to first wave interviews quoted. Response rate to second to fifth wave interviews 96 per cent of those previously accepting.
8 Linkage rates from Census to Census were 91 per cent for Longitudinal Study members present in both the 1971 and 1981 Censuses and 90 per cent for Longitudinal Study members present for both the 1981 and 1991 Censuses.
9 Response rate for the period January 1993 to January 1996.
10 In the New Earnings Survey employers supply data on a 1 per cent sample of employees who are members of PAYE schemes. For the 1996 sample 216 thousand were selected and there was a 94.2 per cent response but some 38 thousand returned questionnaires did not contain data.
11 The Omnibus Survey changes from month to month. The sample size and response rate are for May 1995.
12 In the Survey of Personal Incomes local tax offices supply data on individuals to a central point in Inland Revenue.
13 Includes a booster sample of ethnic minority young people.

# Appendix: definitions and terms

## PART 1: POPULATION

### Population estimates and projections
The estimated and projected populations of an area include all those usually resident there, whatever their nationality. Members of HM forces stationed outside the United Kingdom are excluded. Students are taken to be resident at their term-time addresses. Figures for the United Kingdom do not include the population of the Channel Islands or the Isle of Man.

The population estimates for mid-1991 were based on results from the 1991 Census of Population and incorporate an allowance for census under-enumeration. Allowances were also made for definitional and timing differences. Estimates for later years allow for subsequent births, deaths and migration. The estimates for 1982-90 have been revised to give a smooth series consistent with both 1981 and 1991 Census results. Due to definitional changes, there are minor discontinuities for Scotland and Northern

Ireland between the figures for 1971 and earlier years. At the United Kingdom level these discontinuities are negligible.

The most recent set of national population projections for the United Kingdom are based on the populations of England, Wales, Scotland and Northern Ireland at mid-1994. Further details of these were published in *National Population Projections: 1994-based Series PP2 No. 20* (The Stationery Office). Subnational projections are also made.

### Social class
Social class is defined by current occupation, or last occupation if the respondent was not working in the reference week but had worked in the last 8 years. Those above working age, in the armed forces, those who did not state their occupation, and those who have not worked in the last 8 years have been excluded from this analysis.

### Asylum
The basis for recognition as a refugee and hence the granting of asylum is the 1951 United Nations Convention relating to the Status of Refugees, extended in its application by the 1967 Protocol relating to the Status of Refugees. The United Kingdom is party to both. The Convention defines a refugee as a person who 'owing to a well-founded fear of being persecuted for reasons of race, religion, nationality, membership of a particular social group or political opinion, is outside the country of his nationality and unable or, owing to such fear, is unwilling to avail himself of the protection of that country'. In addition, the United Kingdom is prepared to grant, to applicants who do not meet the requirements of the Convention, exceptional leave to stay here for an appropriate period, if it would be unreasonable or impracticable, in all the circumstances, to seek to enforce their return to their country of origin.

## PART 2: HOUSEHOLDS AND FAMILIES

### Households
*A household*: is a person living alone or a group of people who have the address as their only or main residence and who either share one meal a day or share the living accommodation. Household projections are based on the definition of a household being people living together who share common housekeeping or a living room.

*Size of household*: is a count of those people who are usually resident in the household irrespective of whether or not they are present on census night. In the General Household Survey the size of the household is the number of people who normally live there.

### Families
*Children*: are never-married people of any age who live with one or both parent(s). They also include stepchildren and adopted children (but not foster children) and also grandchildren (where the parents are absent).

*Dependent children*: in the 1961 Census, were defined as children under 15 years of age, and persons of any age in full-time education. In the 1971 Census, dependent children were defined as never-married children in families who were either under 15 years of age, or aged 15 to 24 and in full-time education. However, for direct comparison with the General Household Survey (GHS) data, the definition of dependent children used for 1971 in Table 2.5 has been changed to include only never-married children in families who were either under 15 years of age, or aged 15 to 18 and in full-time education. In the 1991 Census and the GHS, dependent children are never-married children in families who are aged under 16, or aged 16 to 18 and in full-time education.

*A family*: is a married or cohabiting couple, either with or without their never-married child or children (of any age), including childless couples or a lone parent together with his or her never-married child or children. A family could also consist of grandparent or grandparents with grandchild or grandchildren if there are no apparent parents of the grandchild or grandchildren usually resident in the household.

*A lone parent family* (in the Census) is a father or mother together with his or her never-married child or children.

*A lone parent family* (in the General Household Survey) consists of a lone parent, living with his or her never-married dependent children, provided these children have no children of their own. Married lone mothers whose husbands are not defined as resident in the household are not classified as lone parents because evidence suggests the majority are separated from their husband either because he usually works away from home or for some other reason that does not imply the breakdown of the marriage (see ONS's *GHS Monitor 82/1*).

*A lone parent family* (in the Labour Force Survey) consists of a lone parent, living with his or her never-married children, provided these children have no children of their own living with them.

## PART 3: EDUCATION AND TRAINING

### Qualifications
In England, Wales and Northern Ireland the main examination for school pupils at the minimum school leaving age is the General Certificate of Secondary Education (GCSE) which can be taken in a wide range of subjects. This replaced the GCE O Level and CSE examinations in 1987 (1988 in Northern Ireland). In England, Wales and Northern Ireland the GCSE is awarded in eight grades, A* to G, the highest four (A* to C) being regarded as equivalent to O level grades A to C or CSE grade 1.

GCE A Level is usually taken after a further two years of study in a sixth form or equivalent, passes being graded from A (the highest) to E (the lowest).

In Scotland pupils study for the Scottish Certificate of Education (SCE) S (Standard) Grade, approximately equivalent to GCSE, in their third and fourth years of secondary schooling (roughly ages 14 and 15). Each subject has several elements, some of which are internally assessed in school, and an award is only made (on a scale of 1 to 7) if the whole course has been completed and examined. The SCE H (Higher) Grade requires one further year of study and for the more able candidates the range of subjects

taken may be as wide as at S Grade with as many as five or six subjects spanning both arts and science. Five SCE highers are regarded as being approximately the equivalent of three GCE A levels.

### The National Curriculum: assessments and tests
Under the *Education Reform Act (1988)* a National Curriculum has been progressively introduced into primary and secondary schools in England and Wales. This consists of mathematics, English and science (and Welsh in Welsh speaking schools in Wales) as core subjects with history, geography, information technology and design and technology, music, art, physical education and (in secondary schools) a modern foreign language (and Welsh in non-Welsh speaking schools in Wales) as foundation subjects. For all subjects measurable targets have been defined for four key stages, corresponding to ages 7, 11, 14 and 16. Pupils are assessed formally at the ages of 7, 11 and 14 by their teachers and by national tests in the core subjects of English, mathematics and science (and in Welsh speaking schools in Wales, Welsh). Sixteen year olds are assessed by means of the GCSE examination. Statutory authorities have been set up for England and for Wales to advise government on the National Curriculum and promote curriculum development generally. Northern Ireland has its own common curriculum which is similar but not identical to the National Curriculum in England and Wales. Assessment arrangements in Northern Ireland became statutory from September 1996. In Scotland, though school curricula are the responsibility of education authorities and individual head teachers, in practice almost all 14 to 16 year olds study mathematics, English, science, a modern foreign language, a social subject, physical education, religious and moral education, technology and a creative and aesthetic subject.

### Foundation Targets
Much of further education is vocational in character, ranging from lower-level technical and commercial courses up to those leading to professional qualifications. Courses and examinations are offered by many bodies including the Business and Technology Education Council (BTEC), the City and Guilds of London Institute and the Royal

Society of Arts Examination Board. To provide an integrated framework a National Council for Vocational Qualifications covering England, Wales and Northern Ireland was set up in 1986. The Council does not award qualifications itself but those accredited by it are called National Vocational Qualifications (NVQs). As an extension of these for people seeking a wider range of study General National Vocational Qualifications (GNVQs) have been introduced since 1992 as a vocational counterpart to GCSE and A Level. An intermediate level GNVQ is equivalent to five good GCSEs and an advanced GNVQ to two A Levels. The Scottish Vocational Education Council (SCOTVEC) has similar functions to the National Council but also awards qualifications in its own right.

## Main categories of educational establishments

Educational establishments in the United Kingdom are administered and financed in several ways. Most schools are controlled by local education authorities (LEAs), which are part of the structure of local government, but some are 'assisted', receiving grants direct from central government sources and being controlled by governing bodies which have a substantial degree of autonomy. In recent years under the Local Management of Schools initiative all LEA and assisted schools have been given delegated responsibility for managing their own budgets and staff numbers. Since 1988 it has also been possible for LEA schools in England and Wales to apply for grant maintained status, under which they receive direct funding from the Department for Education and Employment or the Welsh Office. The governing bodies of such schools are responsible for all aspects of their management, including use of funds, employment of staff and provision of most educational support services.

Outside the public sector completely are non-maintained schools run by individuals, companies or charitable institutions.

Higher education courses in higher education establishments are largely publicly funded through block grants from the HE funding councils in England and Wales, the Scottish Office Education and Industry Department and the Northern Ireland Department of Education. HE is also

funded by the HE funding councils and some by FE funding councils. FE colleges in Scotland are funded by The Scottish Office Education and Industry Department.

## Stages of education

Education takes place in several stages: primary, secondary, further and higher, and is compulsory for all children between the ages of 5 (4 in Northern Ireland) and 16. The primary stage covers three age ranges: nursery (under 5), infant (5 to 7 or 8) and junior (up to 11 or 12) but in Scotland and Northern Ireland there is generally no distinction between infant and junior schools. Nursery education can be provided either in separate nursery schools or in nursery classes within primary schools. Most public sector primary schools take both boys and girls in mixed classes. It is usual to transfer straight to secondary school at age 11 (in England, Wales and Northern Ireland) or 12 (in Scotland), but in England some children make the transition via middle schools catering for various age ranges between 8 and 14. Depending on their individual age ranges middle schools are classified as either primary or secondary.

Public provision of secondary education in an area may consist of a combination of different types of school, the pattern reflecting historical circumstance and the policy adopted by the LEA. Comprehensive schools normally admit pupils without reference to ability or aptitude and cater for all the children in a neighbourhood, but in some areas they co-exist with grammar, secondary modern or technical schools. In Northern Ireland, post primary education is provided by secondary and grammar schools.

Special schools (day or boarding) provide education for children who require specialist support to complete their education, for example because they have physical or other difficulties. Many pupils with special educational needs are educated in mainstream schools.

The term further education may be used in a general sense to cover all non-advanced courses taken after the period of compulsory education, but more commonly it excludes those staying on at secondary school and those in higher education, ie courses in universities and colleges leading to

qualifications above GCE A Level, SCE H Grade, BTEC National Diploma or Certificate, and their equivalents.

Higher education is defined as courses that are of a standard that is higher than GCE A level, the Higher Grade of the Scottish Certificate of Education, GNVQ/NVQ level 3 or the BTEC or SCOTVEC National Certificate/Diploma. There are three main levels of HE course: (i) postgraduate courses are those leading to higher degrees, diplomas and certificates (including postgraduate certificates of education and professional qualifications) which usually require a first degree as entry qualification; (ii) first degrees which includes first degrees, first degrees with qualified teacher status, enhanced first degrees, first degrees obtained concurrently with a diploma, and intercalated first degrees; (iii) other undergraduate courses which includes all other higher education courses, for example HNDs and Diplomas in HE.

## Pupil/teacher ratios

The pupil/teacher ratio in a school is the ratio of all pupils on the register to all teachers employed on the day of an annual count. Part-time pupils and teachers are included on a full-time equivalent basis.

## Adult education

This sector spans a wide range of provision, from recreational courses to some at degree level. Until 1992 the main providers were LEAs but since then the Further Education Funding Councils for England and Wales have been responsible for, and funded, those courses which lead to academic or vocational qualifications, prepare students for further or higher education or provide training in basic skills. Advanced courses are funded by the Higher Education Funding Councils. In Northern Ireland all provision is still in the hands of education authorities. In Scotland much adult education provision is made by the education authorities, though further education colleges also make some provision in this area. Throughout the United Kingdom most courses are part-time but a few are full-time and there are some residential courses, both short and long-term, at colleges. Full-time courses at degree level attract mandatory grants but on other courses all students over the age of 19 must pay a fee, though discretionary grants and bursaries may be available.

## Student grants and loans

Students planning to take full-time, certain part-time or sandwich courses of further study after leaving school may be eligible for grants, funded by central government though paid, except in Scotland, by LEAs. Some grants are mandatory, provided the course leads to a degree or designated equivalent qualification and the student satisfies conditions relating to residence and previous education. Other grants are discretionary, each awarding authority deciding its own policy and criteria. Parental contributions are deductible from grants on a sliding scale except for students over 25 who have been self-supporting for at least three years. Usually those receiving grants have their fees paid in full, regardless of parental income. The means-tested maintenance grant is intended to cover the Christmas and Easter vacations as well as term time, but not the summer vacation. Additional allowances are available if, for example, the course requires a period of study abroad. Under legislation enacted in 1990, students receiving mandatory grants are eligible for top-up loans, interest-free but indexed, to be repaid over five to seven years, though this can be deferred if income is low.

## 4: LABOUR MARKET

### Unemployment - ILO definition

The ILO definition of unemployment refers to people without a job who were available to start work within two weeks and had either looked for work in the previous four weeks or were waiting to start a job they had already obtained. Estimates on this basis are not available before 1984, as the Labour Force Survey did not then collect information on job search over a four week period. The former GB/UK Labour Force definition of unemployment, the only one available for estimates up to 1984, counted people not in employment and seeking work in a reference week (or prevented from seeking work by a temporary sickness or holiday, or waiting for the results of a job application, or waiting to start a job they had already obtained), whether or not they were available to start (except students not able to start because they had to complete their education).

### Unemployment - claimant count

People claiming benefit (that is unemployment benefit, income support, or national insurance credits) at Employment Service local offices (formerly Unemployment Benefit Offices) on the day of the monthly count, who on that day state that they are unemployed and that they satisfy the conditions for claiming benefit. (Students claiming benefit during a vacation and who intend to return to full-time education are excluded.)

## Labour disputes

Statistics of stoppages of work caused by labour disputes in the United Kingdom relate to disputes connected with terms and conditions of employment. Small stoppages involving fewer than ten workers or lasting less than one day are excluded from the statistics unless the aggregate number of working days lost in the dispute exceeds 100. Disputes not resulting in a stoppage of work are not included in the statistics.

Workers involved and working days lost relate to persons both directly and indirectly involved (unable to work although not parties to the dispute) at the establishments where the disputes occurred. People laid off and working days lost at establishments not in dispute, due for example to resulting shortages of supplies, are excluded.

There are difficulties in ensuring complete recording of stoppages, in particular near the margins of the definition; for example short disputes lasting only a day or so, or involving only a few workers. Any under-recording would affect the total number of stoppages much more than the number of working days lost.

## Trade Union membership

Includes organisations described as staff associations. Thirty one organisations previously regarded as Trade Unions are excluded from 1975 onwards because they failed to satisfy the statutory definition of a Trade Union in section 1 of the Trade Union and Labour Relations (Consolidation) Act, 1992.

## PART 5: INCOME AND WEALTH

### Household sector

The household sector includes private trusts and individuals living in institutions as well as those living in households. It differs from the personal sector, as defined in the national accounts, in that it excludes unincorporated private businesses, private non-profit-making bodies serving persons, and the funds of life assurance and pension schemes. More information is given in an article in *Economic Trends*, September 1981.

Household disposable income is equal to the total current income of the household sector *less* payments of United Kingdom taxes on income, employees' national insurance contributions, and contributions of employees to occupational pension schemes. It is revalued at constant prices by the consumers' expenditure deflator.

### Standard Occupational Classification

The introduction of the Standard Occupational Classification (SOC) in 1990 meant that some occupations were defined differently to previous years. The change in classification caused a change in average earnings, evaluated at 1990, of less than 5 per cent for the occupations shown in Chart 5.7 with one exception. It caused an eight and a half per cent rise for assemblers/lineworkers. The 'nurse' category in Chart 5.7 was not affected as the data are based on Collective Agreement rather than occupational classification.

### Self-employment income assessable to tax

Self-employment income is taken as profit assessable to tax, less allowable losses and capital allowances. Unused losses made in previous years are allowable in the current year. Capital allowances are allowances made for the depreciation in value of capital assets. If, for any individual, the profits are completely offset by deduction of losses and capital allowances, the amount of self-employment income is shown as nil.

Generally the profits assessable for 1994-95 are those earned in the business accounting period ending in 1993-94. On average, profits assessable for 1994-95 may be regarded as profits arising in the calendar year 1993.

### Equivalisation scales

The Department of Social Security (DSS), the Office for National Statistics (ONS) and the Institute for Fiscal Studies (IFS) all use McClements equivalence scales in their analysis of the income distribution, to take into account variations in the size and composition of households. This reflects the common sense notion that a household of five adults will need a higher income than a single person living alone to enjoy a comparable standard of living. An overall equivalence value is calculated for each household by summing the appropriate scale values for each household member. Equivalised household income is then calculated by dividing household income by the household's equivalence value. The scales conventionally take a married couple as the reference point with an equivalence value of 1; equivalisation therefore tends to increase relatively the incomes of single person households (since their incomes are divided by a value of less than 1) and to reduce relatively incomes of households with three or more persons. For further information see *Households Below Average Income, A Statistical Analysis*, The Stationery Office.

The DSS and IFS use both before and after housing costs scales, whilst the ONS only use before housing costs scales. McClements equivalence scales:

| | Before housing costs | After housing costs |
|---|---|---|
| Household member | | |
| First adult (head) | 0.61 | 0.55 |
| Spouse of head | 0.39 | 0.45 |
| Other second adult | 0.46 | 0.45 |
| Third adult | 0.42 | 0.45 |
| Subsequent adults | 0.36 | 0.40 |
| Each dependent aged: | | |
| 0-1 | 0.09 | 0.07 |
| 2-4 | 0.18 | 0.18 |
| 5-7 | 0.21 | 0.21 |
| 8-10 | 0.23 | 0.23 |
| 11-12 | 0.25 | 0.26 |
| 13-15 | 0.27 | 0.28 |
| 16 or over | 0.36 | 0.38 |

### Redistribution of income (ROI)

Estimates of the incidence of taxes and benefits on household income, based on the Family Expenditure Survey (FES), are published by the ONS in *Economic Trends*. The article covering 1994-95 appeared in the December 1995 issue, and contains details of the definitions and methods used.

### Households Below Average Income (HBAI)

Information on the distribution of income is provided in the DSS publication *Households Below Average Income: 1979 to 1993/94*. This gives a comprehensive statistical analysis of income relating principally to the lower half of the income distribution; and explains the methodology used to derive the figures from the FES.

Two different measures of disposable income are used in HBAI: before and after housing costs are deducted. Housing costs consist of rent, water rates and community water rate charges, mortgage interest, structural insurance and ground rent and service charges.

### Difference between Households Below Average Income and Redistribution of Income series

These are two separate and distinct income series based on the FES, produced by two different government departments. Each series has been developed to serve the specific needs of that department. The DSS series, HBAI, provides estimates of patterns of disposable income in the United Kingdom and of changes over time; as the name suggests, it concentrates on the lower part of the income distribution and shows disposable income before and after housing costs (where disposable income is after deduction of income tax; national insurance contributions; contributions to occupational pension schemes; domestic rates; council tax; repayments of Social Fund loans). The ONS series, ROI, shows how Government intervention through the tax and benefit system affects the income of households; it covers the whole income distribution and includes the effects of indirect taxes like VAT and duty on beer, as well as estimating the cash value of benefits in kind (eg from state spending on education and health care). The ROI results are designed to show the position in a particular year rather than trends in income levels over time, although trends in the distribution of income are given. An important difference between the two series is that HBAI counts individuals and ROI counts households.

### Net wealth of the personal sector

Balance sheet estimates of the net wealth of the personal sector are published in the *United Kingdom National Accounts*, 1996 edition. These figures exclude the stock of consumer durables which are no longer available. Quarterly estimates of net financial wealth (excluding tangible and intangible assets) are published in *Financial Statistics*.

### Distribution of personal wealth

The estimates of the distribution of the marketable wealth of individuals relate to all adults in the United Kingdom. They are produced by combining estimates of the distribution of wealth identified by the estate multiplier method with independent estimates of total personal wealth derived from the Office for National Statistics personal sector balance sheets. The methods used were described in an article in *Economic Trends* (October 1990) entitled 'Estimates of the Distribution of Personal Wealth'. Net wealth of the personal sector differs from marketable wealth for the following reasons:

*Difference in coverage:* the ONS balance sheet of the personal sector includes the wealth of non-profit making bodies and unincorporated businesses, while the Inland Revenue estimates exclude non-profit making bodies and treat the bank deposits and debts of unincorporated businesses differently from ONS;

*Differences in timing:* the ONS balance sheet gives values at the end of the year, whereas Inland Revenue (IR) figures are adjusted to mid-year;

*IR figures:* exclude the wealth of those under 18 and the very wealthy, to avoid producing misleading estimates.

*Funded pensions:* are included in the ONS figures but not in the IR marketable wealth. Also the ONS balance sheet excludes consumer durables and includes non-marketable tenancy rights, whereas the IR figures include consumer durables and exclude non-marketable tenancy rights.

### PART 6: EXPENDITURE

### Retail prices

The general index of retail prices (RPI) measures the changes month by month in the price levels of the commodities and services purchased by all types of households in the United Kingdom, with the exception of certain higher income households and households of retired people mainly dependant on state benefits. These households are:

(a)  the 4 per cent (approximately) where the total household recorded gross income exceeds a certain amount (£991 a week in 1994/95).

(b)  those in which at least three quarters of the total income is derived from state pensions and benefits and which include at least one person over the national insurance retirement age.

The weights which are used to calculate the index are based on the pattern of household expenditure derived from the continuing Family Expenditure Survey. Since 1962 the weights have been revised in February of each year.

Expenditure patterns of one-person and two-person pensioner households differ from those of the households upon which the general index is based. Separate indices

# Appendix

have been compiled for such pensioner households since 1968, and quarterly averages are published in the ONS *Business Monitor MM23 (Retail Prices Index)*. They are chain indices constructed in the same way as the general index of retail prices. It should, however, be noted that the pensioner indices exclude housing costs.

A brief introduction to the RPI is given in the June 1994 issue of ONS *Business Monitor MM23 (Retail Prices Index)*, also available as a booklet from The Stationery Office. Each month's edition of the RPI *Business Monitor* contains further articles of interest, covering topics such as reweighting and indicator items.

## Household expenditure
The national accounts definition of household expenditure, within consumers' expenditure, consists of: personal expenditure on goods (durable and non-durable) and services, including the value of income in kind; imputed rent for owner-occupied dwellings; and the purchase of secondhand goods less the proceeds of sales of used goods. Excluded are: interest and other transfer payments; all business expenditure; and the purchase of land and buildings (and associated costs).

In principle, expenditure is measured at the time of acquisition rather than actual disbursement of cash. The categories of expenditure include that of non-resident as well as resident households and individuals in the United Kingdom.

The methods used for estimating expenditure at constant prices often depend on the methods used for the current price estimates. Where the current price estimate is in value terms only, it is deflated by an appropriate price index. The indices most widely used for this purpose are components of the retail prices index. The index does not, however, cover the whole range of consumers' expenditure, and other indices have to be used or estimated where necessary. If no other appropriate price index is available the general consumer price index implied by the estimates of consumers' expenditure at current and constant prices on all other goods and services is used. Where the estimate at current prices is one of quantity multiplied

by current average value, the estimate at constant prices is in most cases the same quantity multiplied by the average value in the base year. All these revaluations are carried out in as great detail as practicable.

For further details see the article entitled 'Consumers' expenditure' in *Economic Trends*, September 1983.

The Family Expenditure Survey definition of household expenditure represents current expenditure on goods and services. This excludes those recorded payments which are partly savings or investments (for example life assurance premiums). Similarly, income tax payments, national insurance contributions, mortgage capital repayments and other payments for major additions to dwellings are excluded. For purchases financed by hire purchase or loans, the amounts paid under the finance agreement are recorded as expenditure as they occur; the full cost of the item is not recorded at the time of the initial transaction. For further details see *Family Spending*.

The methods used for estimating expenditure at constant prices often depend on the methods used for the current price estimates. Where the current price estimate is in value terms only, it is deflated by an appropriate price index. The indices most widely used for this purpose are components of the retail prices index. The index does not, however, cover the whole range of consumers' expenditure, and other indices have to be used or estimated where necessary. If no other appropriate index is available the general consumer price index implied by the estimates of consumers' expenditure at current and constant prices on all other goods and services is used. Where the estimate at current prices is one of quantity multiplied by current average value, the estimate at constant prices is in most cases the same quantity multiplied by the average value in the base year.

## Household saving
Household saving is the balance of income and expenditure on the current account of households, and is derived from the personal sector account, mainly by subtracting the income and the expenditure (and hence the saving) of the other parts of the personal sector.

*The household saving ratio:* is household saving expressed as a percentage of household disposable income.

*Household income:* comprises
Wages and salaries, and forces' pay
Self-employment income
Rent, dividends and interest
Income in kind
Pensions and benefits paid by life assurance and pension schemes
Social security benefits
Other current transfers

*Household disposable income:* comprises
Household income less
United Kingdom taxes on income
Social security contributions (excluding employers' contributions)
Employees' contributions to occupational pension schemes

*Household expenditure:* comprises
Interest payments
Community charge (until March 1993);
Council tax (from April 1993);
Rates (Northern Ireland)
Expenditure on goods and services
Life assurance premiums etc paid by individuals
Other current transfers

(Note: this definition of household expenditure does not accord with that for national accounts purposes - see above.)

## Contributions to and receipts from the EU budget
The figures in Table 6.23 come from the Court of Auditors Reports and have been converted to sterling at the following exchange rates:

1991 - £1 = 1.4284 ECU
1994 - £1 = 1.2924 ECU

Contribution figures are after account is taken of the United Kingdom's abatement and the bringing to account of surpluses and deficits in respect of member states' contributions in earlier years. The information in the Court of Auditors Reports does not attribute all EU expenditure to the member states. For example, not all administrative expenditure is attributed. The figures shown for the net position in 1991 and 1994 should not, therefore, be regarded as definitive for the member states.

## PART 7: HEALTH

### Expectation of life

The expectation of life, shown in Chart 7.1, is the average total number of years which a person of that age could be expected to live, if the rates of mortality at each age were those experienced in that year. The mortality rates which underlie the expectation of life figures are based, up to 1994, on total deaths occurring in each year and, in the case of subsequent years, on the mortality rates assumed for those years in the Government Actuary's mid-1994 based population projections.

### Body mass index (BMI)

Obesity is linked to ill-health and results in an increased risk of a number of diseases. Body weight is a poor indicator of obesity on its own as it does not take account of skeletal size or body composition. A number of alternative measures of obesity have been developed. Body mass index (BMI) or Quetelet Index, shown in Chart 7.8, is the most widely used index of obesity which standardises weight for height and is calculated as weight (kg)/height(m)$^2$. The index can only be calculated on cases where both height and weight measurements are considered to be valid: 10,361 men and 11,467 women in the Health Survey (1991, 1992 and 1993 combined).

While BMI is the most widely used measure of obesity it is not without faults. BMI does not take account of the relative distribution of fat on different parts of the body nor does it distinguish between body fat and muscle. It is known to give misleading measures of obesity on certain physiques, in particular, individuals with muscular physiques.

For the purposes of analysis, BMI is classified according to the following internationally accepted categories:

| Level of index | Description |
| --- | --- |
| 20 or less | Underweight |
| over 20 to 25 | Desirable |
| over 25 to 30 | Overweight |
| over 30 | Obese |

### Serum total cholesterol

Total cholesterol level is an important determinant of cardiovascular disease (CVD) risk, with the risk of CVD rising with increasing total cholesterol for both sexes. Cholesterol was categorised in the following groups in the Health Survey for England 1994:

| Level of total cholesterol (millimoles per litre) | Description |
| --- | --- |
| Less than 5.2 | desirable |
| 5.2-6.4 | mildly elevated |
| 6.5-7.7 | moderately elevated |
| 7.8 or more | severely elevated |

People with raised cholesterols, as shown in Table 7.10, are those whose cholesterol level was either moderately or severely elevated.

### Standardised incidence rates

Directly standardised cancer incidence rates have been shown in Chart 7.11 to enable comparisons to be made over time which are independent of changes in the age structure of the population. In each year, the crude incidence rates in each five year age group are multiplied by the European standard population for that age group. These are then summed and divided by the total standard population to give an overall standardised rate.

### Immunisation

Data shown in Table 7.14, for 1991-92 and 1994-95 for England, Wales and Northern Ireland relate to children reaching their second birthday during the year and immunised by their second birthday. Data for 1981 in England, Wales and Northern Ireland, and for Scotland in all years, relate to children born two years earlier and immunised by the end of the specified year.

### Physical activity levels

Four main types of physical activity were covered by the questionnaire: activity at work, activity at home (heavy housework, gardening, DIY), walks of 1 mile or more and sports and exercise activities. Activities were classified into four intensity levels, based on an estimate of the energy cost of activities. The levels are:

| Energy cost (kcal/min) | Description |
| --- | --- |
| Less than 2 | inactive |
| 2-4.9 | light |
| 5-7.5 | moderate |
| 7.5 or more | vigorous |

In order to classify activities into the above groupings, information was sought in the questionnaire on the nature of activities. Table 7.18 is an analysis of the maximum intensity level reached based on these classifications in any type of activity during the four weeks prior to interview.

### Alcohol consumption

Table 7.22 categorises alcohol consumption into five classifications according to estimated consumption levels in units of alcohol per week. These are:

| Alcohol consumption level(units per week) | Description |
| --- | --- |
| None | Non-drinker |
| Less than 1 | Very low |
| 1-10 | Low |
| 11-21 | Moderate |
| 22 or more | High |

A unit of alcohol is 8 grams of pure alcohol, approximately equivalent to a half pint of ordinary strength beer, lager or cider, a single measure of pub spirits, one glass of wine, or one small glass of port, sherry or other fortified wine.

### Standardised death rates

To enable comparisons to be made over time, standardised death rates have been calculated by applying a scaling factor to the base year's rates. For Chart 7.23 the scaling factor is the study year's 1971-based standard mortality rates (SMR).

# Appendix

## PART 8: SOCIAL PROTECTION

### Benefits to groups of recipients
*Elderly people*
Retirement pension
Non-contributory retirement pension
Christmas bonus paid with retirement
pension and other non-disability benefits
Principal income-related benefits and social
fund payments to people over 60[1]

*Sick and disabled people*
Invalidity benefit
Attendance allowance
Mobility allowance
Disability living allowance
Disability working allowance
Industrial disablement benefit
Other industrial injuries benefits
Severe disablement allowance
Invalid care allowance
War pensions
Independent living fund
Motability
Christmas bonus paid with disability benefits
Principal income-related benefits and Social
fund payments to disabled people
Statutory sick pay
Sickness benefit

*Unemployed people*
Unemployment benefit
Principal income-related benefits and
payments from the social fund to
unemployed and their families[1]

*Families, widows and others*
Child benefit
One parent benefit
Family credit
Income support
Statutory maternity pay
Maternity allowance
Social fund maternity payments
Principal income-related benefits and social
fund payments to lone-parent families[1]
Housing and council tax benefits paid to
people in work
Widow's benefits
War widow's pensions
Guardian's allowance and child's special
allowance
Industrial death benefit
Social fund funeral payments
Income support paid to people who do not
fall within the other client groups

[1] Principal income-related benefits are
income-support, housing benefit and council
tax benefits.

### Health and personal social services staff
Data for nursing and midwifery staff exclude
Project 2000 students for 1991, 1994 and
1995 (in England there were 10.5 thousand,
32 thousand and 33 thousand respectively).
For Scotland, data excludes nurse teachers,
nurses in training, students in '1992 courses'
in nursing and midwifery, bank and agency
nurses. Some senior nurse managers are
employed on administration and clerical
senior management grades and are not
included in the nursing total.

A new system for classifying NHS non-
medical staff was used for the first time in
1995 which is not directly comparable with
the old systems. To provide comparative
information with earlier years, estimates
based on the old system have been
produced. These estimates only give a
broad indication of 1995 levels of staff and
therefore should be interpreted with caution.

Administrative and clerical figures for 1981,
except England where data are not
available, and 1986 include general/senior
managers. A new management class was
phased in from 1984 following the Griffiths
Report (1983). From 1989 senior
management posts extended below Board
level and to FHSAs and HCHS units. Most
of these posts replaced those formerly
counted within the administrative and
clerical and other staff groups.

### Unrestricted principals
An unrestricted principal is a medical
practitioner who provides the full range of
general medical services and whose list is
not limited to any particular group of
persons. In a few cases (about 20), they
may be relieved of the liability to have
patients assigned to them or to be exempted
from liability and other emergency calls out-
of-hours from patients other than their own.
Doctors may also practise in the general
medical services as restricted principals,
assistants or trainees.

### In-patient activity
In-patient data for England and later years
for Northern Ireland are based on Finished
Consultant Episodes (FCEs). Data for Wales
and Scotland and earlier Northern Ireland
data are based on Deaths and Discharges.
An FCE is a completed period of care of a
patient using a bed, under one consultant, in
a particular District/Special Health Authority.
If a patient is transferred from one
consultant to another within the same
hospital, this counts as an FCE but not a
hospital discharge. Conversely if a patient is
transferred from one hospital to another
within the same district without changing
consultant, this counts as a hospital
discharge but not as an FCE.

## PART 9: CRIME AND JUSTICE

### Types of offences in England, Wales and Northern Ireland
*Notifiable offences:* are broadly the more
serious offences. They include most
indictable offences and triable either way
offences and certain summary offences (for
example, unauthorised taking of a motor
vehicle). Excludes criminal damage of value
£200 or under in Northern Ireland.

*Indictable offences:* are those for which an
adult must be tried at the Crown Court, for
example robbery, arson and rape. Figures
for indictable offences given in this chapter
include those for offences which are triable
either way (see below).

*Triable either way offences:* are offences
triable either on indictment or summarily.
They may be tried in a magistrates' court
unless either the defendant or the
magistrate requests a Crown Court hearing.
Most thefts and less serious violence
against the person fall into this category.

*Summary offences:* are those offences
which are normally tried at a magistrates'
court.

*Standard list offences:* (not applicable to
Northern Ireland) are offences for which the
name of the offender and details of each
sentence have been collected by the Home
Office since 1963. These are linked by
name/criminal record number to enable
research into criminal histories. The
offences include all indictable offences,
triable either way offences and some
summary offences. The full list is given in
Appendices 4 and 5 of *Criminal statistics,
England and Wales 1995.*

### Offences and crimes
There are a number of reasons why figures
for notifiable offences in England, Wales and
Northern Ireland and recorded crime in
Scotland cannot be directly compared:

*Different legal systems*: The legal system operating in Scotland differs from that in England and Wales and Northern Ireland.

*Differences in classification*: There are significant differences in the offences included within the recorded crime categories used in Scotland and the categories of notifiable offences used in England, Wales and Northern Ireland. Scottish figures of 'crime' have therefore been grouped in an attempt to approximate to the classification of notifiable offences in England, Wales and Northern Ireland.

*Counting rules*: In Scotland each individual offence occurring within an incident is recorded whereas in England, Wales and Northern Ireland only the main offence is counted.

*Burglary*: This term is not applicable to Scotland where the term used is 'housebreaking'.

*Theft from vehicles*: In Scotland data have only been separately identified from January 1992. The figures include theft by opening lockfast places from a motor vehicle and other theft from a motor vehicle.

## Drugs seizures

Seizures can involve more than one drug and so figures for individual drugs cannot be added together to produce totals. Seizures of unspecified quantities are not included.

## Offenders cautioned for burglary

In England and Wales offenders cautioned for going equipped for stealing, etc were counted against Burglary offences until 1986 and against Other offences from 1987. Historical data provided in Table 9.18 have been amended to take account of this change. Drug offences were included under Other offences for 1971.

## Sentences and orders

The following are the main sentences and orders which can be imposed upon those persons found guilty in 1993 and subsequently. Some types of sentence or order can only be given to offenders in England and Wales in certain age groups. Under the framework for sentencing contained in the *Criminal Justice Acts 1991* and *1993*, the sentence must reflect the seriousness of the offence. The following

sentences are available for adults (a similar range of sentences is available to juveniles aged 10 to 17):

*Absolute and conditional discharge*: A court may make an order discharging a person absolutely or (except in Scotland) conditionally where it is inexpedient to inflict punishment and, before 1 October 1992, where a probation order was not appropriate. An order for conditional discharge runs for such period of not more than three years as the court specifies, the condition being that the offender does not commit another offence within the period so specified. In Scotland a court may also discharge a person with an admonition.

*Attendance centre order*: Available in England, Wales and Northern Ireland for offenders under the age of 20 and involves deprivation of free time.

*Probation/supervision*: An offender sentenced to a probation order is under the supervision of a probation officer (social worker in Scotland), whose duty it is (in England and Wales only) to advise, assist and befriend him but the court has the power to include any other requirement it considers appropriate. A cardinal feature of the order is that it relies on the co-operation of the offender. Probation orders may be given for any period between six months and three years inclusive.

*Community service*: An offender who is convicted of an offence punishable with imprisonment may be sentenced to perform unpaid work for not more than 240 hours, and not less than 40 hours. In Scotland the *Law Reform (Miscellaneous Provisions) (Scotland) Act 1990* requires that community service can only be ordered where the court would otherwise have imposed imprisonment or detention. Probation and community service may be combined in a single order in Scotland.

*Combination order*: The *Criminal Justice Act 1991* introduced the combination order in England and Wales only, which combines elements of both probation supervision and community service.

*Imprisonment*: is the custodial sentence for adult offenders or, in the case of mentally disordered offenders, hospital orders which

may include a restriction order such that Home Office consent is needed for release or transfer. The *Criminal Justice Act 1991* abolished remission and substantially changed the parole scheme in England and Wales. Those serving sentences of under four years, imposed on or after 1 October 1992, are subject to Automatic Conditional Release and are released, subject to certain criteria, halfway through their sentence. Those serving sentences of four years or longer are considered for Discretionary Conditional Release after having served half their sentence, but are automatically released at the two-thirds point of sentence. All offenders serving a sentence of 12 months or more are supervised in the community until the three quarter point of sentence. A life sentence prisoner may be released on licence subject to supervision and is always liable to recall. In Scotland the *Prisoners and Criminal Proceedings (Scotland) Act 1993* changed the system of remission and parole for prisoners sentenced on or after 1 October 1993. Those serving sentences of less than four years are released unconditionally after having served half of their sentence, unless the court specifically imposes a Supervised Release Order which subjects them to social work supervision after release. Those serving sentences of four years or more are eligible for parole at half sentence. If parole is not granted then they will automatically be released on licence at two thirds of sentence subject to days added for breaches of prison rules. All such prisoners are liable to be 'recalled on conviction' or for breach of conditions of licence ie if between the date of release and the date on which the full sentence ends, a person commits another offence which is punishable by imprisonment or breaches his/her licence conditions, then the offender may be returned to prison for the remainder of that sentence whether or not a sentence of imprisonment is also imposed for the new offence'.

*Fully suspended sentences:* may only be passed in exceptional circumstances. In England, Wales and Northern Ireland, sentences of imprisonment of two years or less may be fully suspended. A court should not pass a suspended sentence unless a sentence of imprisonment would be appropriate in the absence of a power to suspend. The result of suspending a sentence is that it will not take effect unless during the period specified the offender is convicted of another offence punishable with imprisonment. Suspended sentences are not used in Scotland.

*Fines*: The *Criminal Justice Act 1993* introduced new arrangements on 20 September 1993 whereby courts should take account of an offender's means in setting fines. This system replaced the more formal unit fines scheme included in the Criminal justice Act 1991. The Act also introduced the power for courts to arrange deduction of fines from income benefit for those offenders receiving such benefits. The *Law Reform (Miscellaneous Provision) (Scotland) Act 1990* as amended by the *Criminal Procedure (Scotland) Act 1995* provides for the use of supervised attendance orders by selected courts in Scotland. The *Criminal Procedure (Scotland) Act 1995* also makes it easier for courts to impose a supervised attendance order in the event of a default and enables the court to impose a supervised attendance order in the first instance for 16 and 17 year olds.

## Civil courts

*England and Wales:* The main civil courts are the High Court and the county courts. Magistrates' courts also have some civil jurisdiction, mainly in family proceedings. Most appeals in civil cases go to the Court of Appeal (Civil Division) and may go from there to the House of Lords. Since July 1991, county courts have been able to deal with all contract and tort cases and actions for recovery of land, regardless of value. Cases are presided over by a judge who almost always sits without a jury. Jury trials are limited to specified cases, for example, actions for libel.

*Scotland:* The Court of Session is the supreme civil court. Any cause, apart from causes excluded by statute, may be initiated in, and any judgement of an inferior court may be appealed to, the Court of Session. The Sheriff Court is the principal local court of civil jurisdiction in Scotland. It also has jurisdiction in criminal proceedings. Apart from certain actions the jurisdiction of the Sheriff Court is generally similar to that of the Court of Session.

## PART 10: HOUSING

### Dwellings

Estimates of the stock of dwellings are based on data from the Censuses of Population (Great Britain) and Valuation and Lands Agency listings (Northern Ireland), with adjustments for enumeration errors and for definitional changes. The figures include vacant dwellings and temporary dwellings occupied as a normal place of residence. Privately rented dwellings include dwellings rented with farm or business premises and those occupied by virtue of employment.

### Household type

The classification of household type uses the following categories:
*one adult aged 16 to 59.*
*two adults aged 16 to 59.*
*small family*: one or two persons aged 16 or over and one or two persons aged under 16.
*large family*: one or more persons aged 16 and over and three or more persons aged under 16, or three or more persons aged 16 and over and two persons aged under 16.
*large adult household:* three or more persons aged 16 or over with or without one person aged under 16.
*two adults, one or both aged 60 or over.*
*one adult aged 60 or over.*

### Bedroom standard

This concept is used to estimate occupation density by allocating a standard number of bedrooms to each household in accordance with its age/gender/marital status composition and the relationship of the members to one another. A separate bedroom is allocated to each married couple, any other person aged 21 or over, each pair of adolescents aged 10 to 20 of the same sex, and each pair of children under 10. Any unpaired person aged 10 to 20 is paired, if possible with a child under 10 of the same gender: if that is not possible, they are given a separate bedroom, as is any unpaired child under 10. This standard is then compared with the actual number of bedrooms (including bedsitters) available for the sole use of the household, and deficiencies or excesses are tabulated. Bedrooms converted to other uses are not counted as available unless they have been

noted as bedrooms by the informant; bedrooms not actually in use are counted unless uninhabitable.

### Homeless households

*Great Britain*: Households for whom local authorities accepted responsibility to secure accommodation under the *Housing Act 1985* and *Housing (Scotland) Act 1987 Part II.* Data for Wales include some households given advice and assistance only.

*Northern Ireland:* Households for whom Northern Ireland Housing Executive has accepted responsibility to secure permanent accommodation, not necessarily those for whom permanent accommodation has been found.

## PART 11: ENVIRONMENT

### Quality of bathing water

Directive 76/160/EEC concerning the quality of bathing water sets inter alia the following mandatory values for the coliform parameters:

- for total coliforms 10,000 per 100 ml; and
- for faecal coliforms 2,000 per 100 ml.

The Directive requires that at least 95 per cent of samples taken for each of these parameters over the bathing season must meet the mandatory values. In practice this has been interpreted in the following manner: where 20 samples are taken a maximum of only one sample for each parameter may exceed the mandatory values for the water to pass the coliform standards; where less than 20 samples are taken none may exceed the mandatory values for the water to pass the coliform standards.

## PART 12: TRANSPORT

### Journey purpose

The purpose of a journey is normally taken to be the activity at the destination, unless that destination is 'home' in which case the purpose is defined by the origin of the journey. The classification of journeys to 'work' are also dependent on the origin of the journey. The following purposes are distinguished:

*Commuting*: journeys to a usual place of work from home, or from work to home.

*Business*: personal journeys in course of work, including a journey in the course of work back to work. This includes all work journeys by people with no usual place of work (eg site workers) and those who work at or from home.

*Education*: journeys to school or college, etc by full time students, students on day-release and part-time students following vocational courses.

*Escort*: used when the traveller has no purpose of his or her own, other than to escort or accompany another person; for example, taking a child to school. Escort commuting is escorting or accompanying someone from home to work or from work to home.

*Shopping*: all journeys to shops or from shops to home, even if there was no intention to buy.

*Personal business*: visits to services eg hairdressers, launderettes, dry-cleaners, betting shops, solicitors, banks, estate agents, libraries, churches; or for medical consultations or treatment, or for eating and drinking unless the main purpose was entertainment or social. Includes journeys to work other than from home.

*Social or entertainment*: visits to meet friends, relatives, or acquaintances, both at someone's home or at a pub, restaurant, etc; all types of entertainment or sport, clubs, and voluntary work, non-vocational evening classes, political meetings, etc.

*Holidays or day trips*: journeys (within Great Britain) to or from any holiday (including stays of four nights or more with friends or

relatives) or journeys for pleasure (not otherwise classified as social or entertainment) within a single day.

*Just walk*: walking pleasure trips along public highways including taking the dog for a walk and jogging.

### Car ownership
*Car:* the figures for household ownership include four wheeled and three wheeled cars, off-road vehicles, minibuses, motorcaravans and dormobiles.

*Cars and vans*: road motor vehicle other than a motorcycle, intended for the carriage of passengers and designed to seat no more than nine people (including the driver). The term 'passenger car' therefore covers microcars (which need no permit to be driven), taxis and hired passenger cars, provided that they have fewer than ten seats. This category may also include pick-ups.

### Road casualties
The seasons in Chart 12.21 are defined in whole months as follows:

*Winter:* November to February.
*Summer.* May to August.

### Road deaths
The internationally agreed definition of a road accident death is one where death occurs as a result of the accident within 30 days. Most EU countries, including the United Kingdom, collect data to this definition. For those which do not, the national figures have been adjusted to convert them to the 30-day standard.

### PART 13: LIFESTYLES

### Social grade
Social grade categories are based on the occupation of the chief income earner of his or her household as follows:

A: Higher managerial, administrative or professional
B: Intermediate managerial, administrative or professional
C1: Supervisory or clerical and junior managerial, administrative or professional
C2: Skilled manual workers
D: Semi and unskilled manual
E: State pensioners or widows (no other earners), casual or lowest grade workers or long-term unemployed

### Parliamentary elections and political parties
A general election must be held at least every five years, or sooner, if the Prime Minister of the day so decides. The United Kingdom is currently divided into 651 constituencies, each of which returns one member to the House of Commons. To ensure equitable representation, four permanent Boundary Commissions (for England and Wales, Scotland and Northern Ireland) make periodic reviews of constituencies and recommend any change in the number or redistribution of seats that may seem necessary in the light of population movements or for some other reason.

The Social Democratic Party (SDP) was launched on 26 March 1981. In the 1983 and 1987 general elections the Liberals and SDP contested seats as the Liberal-SDP Alliance. In 1988 the Social and Liberal Democrats were formed, after which the Democrats and the SDP contested elections separately. In June 1990 the SDP disbanded.

On 17 December 1985 all 15 Ulster Unionist MPs resigned their seats and sought re-election as a protest against the Anglo-Irish agreement. The 15 by-elections were held on 23 January 1986.

# Articles published in previous editions

**No. 1 1970**
**Some general developments in social statistics** Professor C A Moser, CSO

**Public expenditure on the social services** Professor B Abel-Smith, London School of Economics and Political Science

**The growth of the population to the end of the century** Jean Thompson, OPCS

**A forecast of effective demand for housing in Great Britain in the 1970s** A E Holmans, MHLG

**No. 2 1971**
**Social services manpower** Dr S Rosenbaum, CSO

**Trends in certificated sickness absence** F E Whitehead, DHSS

**Some aspects of model building in the social and environmental fields** B Benjamin, CSC

**Social indicators - health** A J Culyer, R J Lavers and A Williams, University of York

**No. 3 1972**
**Social commentary: change in social conditions** CSO

**Statistics about immigrants: objectives, methods, sources and problems** Professor C A Moser, CSO

**Central manpower planning in Scottish secondary education** A W Brodie, SED

**Social malaise research: a study in Liverpool** M Flynn, P Flynn and N Mellor, Liverpool City Planning Department

**Crimes of violence against the person in England and Wales** S Klein, HO

**No. 4 1973**
**Social commentary: certain aspects of the life cycle** CSO

**The elderly** D C L Wroe, CSO

**Subjective social indicators** M Abrams, SSRC

**Mental illness and the psychiatric services** E R Bransby, DHSS

**Cultural accounting** A Peacock and C Godfrey, University of York

**Road accidents and casualties in Great Britain** J A Rushbrook, DOE

**No. 5 1974**
**Social commentary: men and women** CSO

**Social security: the European experiment** E James and A Laurent, EC Commission

**Time budgets** B M Hedges, SCPR

**Time budgets and models of urban activity patterns** N Bullock, P Dickens, M Shapcott and P Steadman, Cambridge University of Architecture

**Road traffic and the environment** F D Sando and V Batty, DOE

**No. 6 1975**
**Social commentary: social class** CSO

**Areas of urban deprivation in Great Britain: an analysis of 1971 Census data** S Holtermann, DOE

**Note: Subjective social indicators** Mark Abrams, SSRC

**No. 7 1976**
**Social commentary: social change in Britain 1970-1975** CSO

**Crime in England and Wales** Dr C Glennie, HO

**Crime in Scotland** Dr Bruce, SHHD

**Subjective measures of quality of life in Britain: 1971 to 1975** J Hall, SSRC

**No. 8 1977**
**Social commentary: fifteen to twenty-five: a decade of transition** CSO

**The characteristics of low income households** R Van Slooten and A G Coverdale, DHSS

**No. 9 1979**
**Housing tenure in England and Wales: the present situation and recent trends** A E Holmans, DOE

**Social forecasting in Lucas** B R Jones, Lucas Industries

**No. 10 1980**
**Social commentary: changes in living standards since the 1950s** CSO

**Inner cities in England** D Allnutt and A Gelardi, DOE

**Scotland's schools** D Wishart, SED

**No. 14 1984**
**Changes in the Life-styles of the Elderly 1959-1982** M Abrams

**No. 15 1985**
**British Social Attitudes** R Jowell and C Airey, SCPR

**No. 16 1986**
**Income after retirement** G C Fiegehen, DHSS

**No 17 1987**
**Social Trends since World War II** Professor A H Halsey, University of Oxford

**Household Formation and Dissolution and Housing Tenure: a Longitudinal Perspective** A E Holmans and S Nandy, DOE; A C Brown, OPCS

**No. 18 1988**
**Major Epidemics of the 20th Century: from Coronary Thrombosis to AIDS** Sir Richard Doll, University of Oxford

**No. 19 1989**
**Recent Trends in Social Attitudes** L Brook, R Jowell and S Witherspoon, SCPR

**No. 20 1990**
**Social Trends, the next 20 years** T Griffin, CSO

**No. 21 1991**
**The 1991 Census of Great Britain: Plans for Content and Output** B Mahon and D Pearce, OPCS

**No. 22 1992**
**Crime statistics: their use and misuse** C Lewis, HO

**No. 24 1994**
**Characteristics of the bottom 20 per cent of the income distribution** N Adkin, DSS

**No. 26 1996**
**The OPCS Longitudinal Study** J Smith, OPCS

**British Household Panel Survey** J Gershuny, N Buck, O Coker, S Dex, J Ermish, S Jenkins and A McCulloch, ESRC Research Centre on Micro-social Change

# Index

The references in this index refer to table and chart numbers, or entries in the Appendix.

# Index

182951

Printed in the United Kingdom for The Stationery Office
Dd0303211 1/97 10170